Indonesia's Foreign Policy under **Suharto**

The **ISEAS – Yusof Ishak Institute** (formerly Institute of Southeast Asian Studies) is an autonomous organization established in 1968. It is a regional centre dedicated to the study of socio-political, security, and economic trends and developments in Southeast Asia and its wider geostrategic and economic environment. The Institute's research programmes are grouped under Regional Economic Studies (RES), Regional Strategic and Political Studies (RSPS), and Regional Social and Cultural Studies (RSCS). The Institute is also home to the ASEAN Studies Centre (ASC), the Singapore APEC Study Centre and the Temasek History Research Centre (THRC).

ISEAS Publishing, an established academic press, has issued more than 2,000 books and journals. It is the largest scholarly publisher of research about Southeast Asia from within the region. ISEAS Publishing works with many other academic and trade publishers and distributors to disseminate important research and analyses from and about Southeast Asia to the rest of the world.

Indonesia's Foreign Policy under Suharto

Aspiring to International Leadership

SECOND EDITION

LEO SURYADINATA

 YUSOF ISHAK INSTITUTE

First published in Singapore in 2022 by
ISEAS Publishing
30 Heng Mui Keng Terrace
Singapore 119614
E-mail: publish@iseas.edu.sg
Website: http://bookshop.iseas.edu.sg

All rights reserved. No part of this publication may be reproduced, stored in a retrieval system, or transmitted in any form or by any means, electronic, mechanical, photocopying, recording or otherwise, without the prior permission of the ISEAS – Yusof Ishak Institute.

© 2022 ISEAS – Yusof Ishak Institute, Singapore.

The responsibility for facts and opinions in this publication rests exclusively with the author and his interpretations do not necessarily reflect the views or the policy of the publisher or its supporters.

The first edition of the book *Indonesia's Foreign Policy Under Suharto: Aspiring to International Leadership* (ISBN: 9789812100825), by Leo Suryadinata, was published by Times Academic Press in 1996. Copyright of the book reverted to the author in June 2020.

ISEAS Library Cataloguing-in-Publication Data

Name(s): Suryadinata, Leo, author.
Title: Indonesia's foreign policy under Suharto : aspiring to international leadership / Leo Suryadinata.
Description: 2nd edition. | Singapore : ISEAS - Yusof Ishak Institute, 2022. | Includes bibliographical references and index.
Identifiers: ISBN 9789814951616 (soft cover) | ISBN 9789814951623 (pdf) | ISBN 9789814951630 (epub)
Subjects: LCSH: Indonesia—Politics and government—1966-1998. | Indonesia—Foreign relations. | Soeharto—1921-2008.
Classification: LCC DS638 S9 2021

Typeset by International Typesetters Pte Ltd
Printed in Singapore by Mainland Press Pte Ltd

Contents

Preface to the Second Edition		vii
Preface		x
Acknowledgements		xi
INTRODUCTION: Suharto's Foreign Policy		1
1.	Determinants of Indonesia's Foreign Policy: In Search of an Explanation	5
2.	Indonesia's Foreign Policy before the New Order: In Search of a Format	22
3.	Indonesia's Foreign Policy during the "New Order" (I): The Rise of the Military	34
4.	Indonesia's Foreign Policy during the "New Order" (II): The Assertive Role of the President	50
5.	Indonesia's Relations with the ASEAN States: Regional Stability and Leadership Role	66
6.	Indonesia's Relations with Australia and Papua New Guinea: Security and Cultural Issues	91
7.	Indonesia-China Relations: Ideology, Ethnic Chinese and the President	101
8.	Indonesia-Vietnam Relations and the Kampuchean Issue: The Security Factor	122

9. Indonesia-Superpower Relations: Economic and
   Non-Economic Factors   138

10. Indonesia, the Middle East and Bosnia: Islam and
    Foreign Policy   158

11. Indonesia, the Non-Aligned Movement and APEC:
    In Search of a Leadership Role   172

CONCLUSION: To Lead and Not to Be Led   186

POSTSCRIPT: Indonesia's Foreign Policy from the Fall of Suharto
to Joko Widodo: Still Aspiring to International Leadership?   190

Bibliography   219

Appendices   228

Index   235

Preface to the Second Edition

I am delighted that my book *Indonesia's Foreign Policy under Suharto: Aspiring to International Leadership* (Singapore: Times Academic Press, 1996) is now reissued with a postscript.

When the original edition of the book was published, I received feedback from many Indonesian scholars. I was pleasantly surprised. Not long after that Lembaga Penelitian, Pendidikan dan Penerangan Ekonomi dan Sosial (LP3ES), a leading academic publisher in Jakarta, asked for my permission to translate the book into Bahasa Indonesia. I gladly consented. The Indonesian version (*Politik Luar Negeri: Indonesia di Bawah Soeharto*) was to be published in early May 1998, a few weeks before the downfall of President Suharto. Therefore, I included a short postscript for the Indonesian edition, covering the last two to three years of his rule. I was informed that *Politik Luar Negeri* had become a major reference book for the politics and international relations courses at least at the University of Indonesia in Jakarta and Gadjah Mada University in Yogyakarta. I was so pleased that when I met some lecturers and graduates from these universities, they often discussed the book with me. I felt very honoured and encouraged.

In 2019, I received an unexpected request from an editor of the LP3ES in Jakarta that they wanted to reissue the Indonesian version of the book. He told me that there were still demands on the book. Students and scholars are still looking for the book. They asked me to write a new postscript for the book, but I did not have the time to do so as I was busy with my projects. I proposed to write a new preface, explaining briefly why the book, without revision, is still relevant to the present situation. The LP3ES agreed and the book was eventually republished in October 2019.

The reissuing of *Politik Luar Negeri* made me re-read the original version of *Indonesia's Foreign Policy under Suharto*. The book was published when I was still teaching in the Department of Political Science at the National University of Singapore (NUS). It took me several years to complete writing the book. Two chapters had been published in *Asian Survey* before the book was published. I benefited from the discussions with friends and colleagues in writing the manuscript.

The book, which was written about twenty-five years ago, examines Indonesia's foreign policy under Suharto. It not only details his foreign policy behaviour vis-à-vis Indonesia's neighbours and the world's major powers, but also put it in the context of foreign policy analysis. It is worth noting that the book remains as the only full-length study on Indonesia's foreign policy under Suharto. As there was a demand on this book in Indonesia, I feel that the book should be of interest to the younger generation of students and scholars outside Indonesia. I have therefore decided to reissue the English version.

In 2004, the publisher Marshall Cavendish had agreed to reprint some of my earlier studies, including *Indonesia's Foreign Policy under Suharto*. Promotional material, including new book covers, had been released and they can still be found on the Internet today. Six of my books have been reprinted, but *Indonesia's Foreign Policy under Suharto*, which was supposed to be republished in 2007, was suddenly cancelled due to a change in management at Marshall Cavendish. Therefore, the book in your hands now is the actual second edition of the book.

Some friends suggested I do some updating. I agreed, but the text should not be revised. As I had completed the work in 1995, it should remain as it is. I would like the reader to know how I looked at Indonesia's foreign policy then, especially during the Suharto era, and the younger generation of readers can pass their judgement on the arguments that I put forward. I do not wish to revise the book to reflect my current thinking. The updating can be done through the inclusion of a postscript.

The postscript, which I have written and is included after the concluding chapter, is entitled "Indonesia's Foreign Policy from the Fall of Suharto to Joko Widodo: Still Aspiring to International Leadership?". In this postscript, I briefly examine the similarities and differences between the Suharto era and post-Suharto era, in terms of the foreign policy decision-making process and the foreign policy elite. I then follow the structure of the original book and deal with Indonesia's policy towards ASEAN and the ASEAN states, neighbouring Australia, medium power Japan and two superpowers, namely, China and the United States. "Indonesia, the Middle East and Islam" constitute the last section of the postscript as there has been an increase in terms of the role of Islam in Indonesia's foreign policy. Towards the end I have added a brief evaluation on the post-Suharto Indonesia's foreign policy.

Since I rejoined the ISEAS – Yusof Ishak Institute in 2014 as Visiting Senior Fellow, I have been very fortunate to be given the opportunity to do research on Indonesia again. I have also been able to interact with many young and established scholars who came to the institute, which broadened my horizon and deepened my understanding about Indonesian politics and foreign policy. I continue to write about the subjects that I have been writing all my life. This is also the reason why I am still able to write the postscript for this book.

I would like to take this opportunity to thank my colleagues at ISEAS, especially Mr Lye Liang Fook, Mr Daljit Singh and Dr Siwage Dharma Negara, for reading the postscript and made valuable comments and suggestions; Mr Tan Chin Tiong, former Director of ISEAS – Yusof Ishak Institute, for encouraging me to continue to work on Indonesia's foreign policy, and Mr Ng Kok Kiong, Director, Publishing Division, for agreeing to reissue the book. Nevertheless, none of them is responsible for the contents of the book, I am solely responsible.

Leo Suryadinata
21 February 2021
Singapore

Preface

In writing this book, I have benefited greatly from numerous discussions that I have had with many friends and scholars over the last 20 years. I have also profited from various seminars on Indonesia's foreign affairs given by Indonesian officials, diplomats and academics. Many of these seminars and talks were behind closed doors or off the record, and therefore they cannot be cited. Nonetheless, they have had a strong influence on my study.

Many friends in Indonesia have shared their expertise with me, and in doing so have enriched my understanding of both Indonesia's domestic politics and foreign policy. Their names are too many to be mentioned here but I would like to offer all of them my sincere thanks.

A significant portion of the study was conducted between 1988 and 1989 during my sabbatical leave in three institutions: the Institute of Southeast Asian Studies in Singapore (ISEAS), Ohio University and Cornell University. Each possesses an excellent library, and I am grateful to the staff of those libraries for assisting me in my research.

A few friends have read the early version of my manuscript, either in part or in full. I would like in particular to thank Chin Kin Wah, N. Ganesan, Michael Leifer, Jamie Mackie and Nancy Viviani for their useful suggestions. I am also grateful to Triena Ong who has given me editorial advice. Nevertheless, for any mistakes and shortcomings which still exist in this book, I am alone responsible.

Leo Suryadinata
July 1995
Singapore

Acknowledgements

The author wishes to thank the publisher of *Asian Survey* for kind permission to reproduce parts of "Indonesia-China Relations: A Recent Breakthrough", *Asian Survey*, July 1990, pp. 682-696; and "Islam and Suharto's Foreign Policy: Indonesia, the Middle East and Bosnia", *Asian Survey*, (March 1995), pp. 291-303.

The author also wishes to thank the Institute of Southeast Asian Studies, Singapore, for kind permission to reproduce "Indonesia-Vietnam Relations Under Soeharto", taken from *Contemporary Southeast Asia* (March 1991), Vol. 12, No. 4, pp. 331-340.

Introduction

Suharto's Foreign Policy

There are a number of book-length studies on Indonesia's foreign policy, of which very few have been published. Most of the books published can be divided into two broad categories: macro and micro studies. The macro studies (such as works by Franklin Weinstein, Anak Agung Gde Agung and Michael Leifer) deal largely with Indonesia's foreign policy in general,[1] while micro studies (by Jon M. Reinhardt, J.A.C. Mackie, David Mozingo, Dewi Fortuna Anwar and others) focus on specific topics and themes.[2] Of these two types of studies, many cover the Sukarno period or early Suharto era. Particularly lacking are macro studies on Indonesia's foreign policy under Suharto. The existing books which partially or wholly deal with Suharto were either published in the 1970s or early eighties. To my knowledge, there is no up-to-date book that examines comprehensively Indonesia's foreign policy under Suharto.[3] Undoubtedly there is an urgent case for such a book.

It is also worth noting that most of these books do not adopt a specific "theory" or model for examining Indonesia's foreign policy and I have followed the same approach, although I am fully aware of the existence of these "theories" and models.[4] An Indonesian case study such as mine is usually insufficient for generating a useful model. Nevertheless, the information provided in my study may contribute to future model-building on foreign policy behaviour.

Although no model has been used in the study, I have adopted a framework of foreign policy analysis. The framework provides a useful checklist of items required for a study of foreign policy, including the determinants of a country's foreign policy behaviour.[5]

In analysing Indonesia's foreign policy during the Suharto era, however, it appears that the Indonesian military and culture (or political culture) are of crucial importance. The military, together with President Suharto, who was an army general, are initial decision-makers. Their policy tends to be influenced by prevalent political culture in terms of *abangan* (or nominal Muslim-cultural) orientations, and preference for authoritarianism. Nonetheless, it is clear that, in the later period, Suharto became more assertive in foreign policy. He has not always agreed with the military establishment on domestic politics as well as on foreign policy issues as illustrated by his handling of the East Timor issue, especially the recent Dili incident. Due to the crucial role played by Suharto in Indonesia's foreign policy, this study tends to highlight his leadership and whenever possible links him to the New Order foreign policy.

This study will discuss the main factors which have contributed to Indonesia's foreign policy behaviour, including the capability of the state, the perception of major leaders on foreign policy matters, the dominant political culture and the political institutions which impinge upon foreign policy. The personality of the decision-makers will be highlighted as well, especially those of the top political leaders who have been mainly responsible for Indonesia's foreign policy.

The organization of this book deserves explanation. Although the emphasis of this study is Indonesia's foreign policy during the New Order era, a brief examination of the pre-1966 period is included as it is crucial for an in-depth understanding of Suharto's foreign policy. It is followed by an in-depth discussion of the policy during the Suharto era, beginning with the rise of the military as a foreign policy-maker at the expense of other foreign policy-making institutions, and ending with the later emergence of Suharto, who often distanced himself from the military establishment as a foreign policy-maker. It is not easy to document Suharto's role in Indonesia's foreign policy, but in many cases, one can clearly see his guiding hand. The role of Suharto in Indonesia's foreign policy is one of the central themes in this study.

Nonetheless, this study also attempts to identify the patterns and processes of Indonesia's foreign policy through an examination of Indonesia's relations with various countries. In this book, the discussion of these relations has been arranged in accordance with the relative importance of these countries to Indonesia. The order of their importance may, of course, differ from author to author. Again, if economic interactions and volumes of trade are used as indicators, a rather different ranking might emerge.

In terms of Indonesian perceptions of security in a broad sense, the United States and Japan are the most important nations. Nonetheless, if security is defined in military and political terms, geopolitics is a major factor. This does not mean that only a neighbouring country with a strong military capability will pose a threat to Indonesia. Even a small neighbouring state that is occupied or used by a major power hostile to Indonesia may be perceived as a threat. For this reason, the ASEAN states are most important to Indonesia and hence deserve to be discussed first. Of the seven ASEAN members, countries such as Malaysia and Singapore are seen to be more important than others such as Thailand and the Philippines.

After the ASEAN states, Australia is vital to Indonesian interests, especially in relation to the Irian Jaya and East Timor issues. Indonesia has been concerned with developments in Papua New Guinea and Australia's attitude towards its ex-administrative territory because these two factors may affect the situation in Indonesia's Irian Jaya province. Indonesia is also sensitive about Australia's attitude towards East Timor because of possible effects on the ex-Portuguese colony. Any separatist activity in these provinces would in turn affect other minority regions in the republic.

In the north, the People's Republic of China (PRC) has always been viewed by Indonesian leaders as an "expansionist" power and a major competitor for the role of regional leader to which Indonesia aspires. For this reason, Vietnam has been seen as a buffer against the potentially expansionist tendencies of the PRC. Although some military leaders have emphasized the significance of common historical experiences in Indonesian-Vietnamese relations, it was strategic considerations which caused the Indonesian military to recognize the usefulness of Vietnam.

The two superpowers, namely the United States and the former Soviet Union, as well as the economic superpower Japan, were crucial in ensuring the well-being of Suharto's Indonesia. With the disintegration of the Soviet Union, Indonesia's foreign policy focus has turned to the United States and Japan. Indonesia has depended on economic aid and investment from the West led by the United States. Understandably, Indonesia has tolerated an American security presence in Southeast Asia, partly owing to the absence of an alternative. In the long run, however, Indonesia would prefer the United States to be nominally involved in Southeast Asia. One interpretation of this is that the resultant vacuum might be filled by Indonesia.

Indonesia once saw the former Soviet Union as a regional competitor but this is no longer so. Besides, the Commonwealth of Independent States (CIS), the new union which replaces the USSR, is not only weak, but also unimportant economically to Indonesia. On the other hand, Japan is economically essential to Indonesia. This economic giant is not only Indonesia's largest direct investor but also the country's largest trading partner. Almost 60 per cent of Indonesia's crude oil is sold to Japan and the country has also received a significant amount of foreign aid from the "Land of the Rising Sun". Because of Japan's significant role in Southeast Asia, Indonesia is still concerned with its militarization.

The Middle East is another region that is becoming more important to Indonesia because of the resurgence of Islam in the world and also within Indonesia itself. In the past, Indonesia's policy towards the Middle Eastern countries had been responsive rather than proactive. Although this link to the Islamic world has not been significant, increasingly it can no longer be ignored. Nonetheless, recent Indonesia-Middle East relations and Jakarta's policy towards Bosnia have revealed the non-Islamic basis of Indonesia's foreign policy.

As a large and richly-endowed country in Southeast Asia, Indonesia understandably has aspired to become a regional leader and beyond, and desires to be recognized as such. These aspirations have been significant factors in directing Indonesia's foreign policy, as reflected in its involvement in the Non-Aligned Movement, its desire to lead the movement and its prominent role in the APEC Summit. Indonesia's leadership role has often been challenged, however, not only within the region but also outside it. Some of these challenges will be discussed in this study.

Apart from the discussions on Indonesia's relations with the various countries and their concerns, the patterns and processes of Indonesia's foreign policy will also be established. These patterns and processes will serve as a foundation from which future scenarios can be extrapolated.

no t ES

1. Works which fall into this category include Ide Anak Agung Gde Agung, *Twenty Years of Indonesian Foreign Policy 1945–1965* (The Hague: Morton, 1973; reprinted and reissued in 1990 by Duta Wacana University Press in Yogyakarta); Franklin Weinstein, *Indonesian Foreign Policy and the Dilemma of Dependence; From Sukarno to Soeharto* (Ithaca: Cornell University Press, 1976) and Michael Leifer, *Indonesia's Foreign Policy* (London: Allen and Unwin, 1983).
2. Works which fall into this category are larger in number but due to space constraint only four titles are listed: Jon M. Reinhardt, *Foreign Policy and National Integration: The Case of Indonesia,* Monograph Series No. 17 (New Haven: Connecticut, 1971); J.A.C. Mackie, *Konfrontasi: The Indonesia-Malaya Dispute 1963-1966* (Kuala Lumpur: Oxford University Press, 1974); David Mozingo, *China's Policy towards Indonesia 1949-1967* (Ithaca: Cornell University Press, 1981); Dewi Fortuna Anwar, *Indonesia in ASEAN: Foreign Policy and Regionalism* (Singapore: Institute of Southeast Asian Studies, 1994).
3. Even the Ph.D. dissertation of Gordon R. Hein on "Soeharto's Foreign Policy: Second-Generation Nationalism in Indonesia" was submitted to the University of California at Berkeley in 1986.
4. There are five approaches developed by Western (American) scholars regarding foreign policy analysis: the strategic or rational model; the decision-making model; the bureaucratic politics model; the adaptive model; and the incremental decision-making model. For a brief and useful analysis of the various models for explaining foreign policy, see Lloyd Jensen, *Explaining Foreign Policy* Englewood Cliffs: Prentice Hall, 1982, pp. 1-11.
5. For a general framework of foreign policy analysis, See David O. Wilkinson and Lawrence Scheinman, *Comparative Foreign Relations: Framework and Methods* (Belmont, California: Dickinson Publishing Co., 1969). It should be noted that this book is not the first theoretical work on comparative foreign relations. Others dealing with similar topics include Hans J. Morgenthau's classic, *Politics Among Nations* (1954), and Roy C. Macridis (ed.), *Foreign Policy* in *World Politics* (1958, 1st edn.; 1989, 7th edn.). K.J. Hoslti's book entitled *International Politics* (1967) also discusses important aspects of comparative foreign relations. Nonetheless, I am impressed by Wilkinson and Scheinman's systematic attempt to deal with comparative foreign policy. Some books have used the above framework to describe a country's foreign relations, for example, Robert C. North's work on China and Sudershan Chawla's book on India. Due to the difficulty in getting adequate information on Indonesia, especially on the process of foreign policy-making, I have not used Wilkinson and Scheinman's framework rigidly. Rather, I refer to elements of foreign relations discussed in the book where they are relevant. Apart from Wilkinson and Scheinman's work, James N. Rosenau's *Scientific Study of Foreign Policy* (New York: Free Press, 1971) is also useful. I am particularly impressed by his "idiosyncratic" factor (that is, personality factor) in foreign policy, which is crucial for a fundamental understanding of Suharto's foreign policy.

1

Determinants of Indonesia's Foreign Policy
In Search of an Explanation

Introduction

This chapter identifies a number of factors which influence, if not determine, Indonesia's foreign policy. These factors include Indonesian leaders' perceptions of territorial boundaries, Indonesia's role in world affairs, and the constraint on its behaviour posed by the country's available resources. Indonesian political culture and elite perceptions of external threat will also be examined because they may throw light on Indonesia's foreign policy behaviour.

Indonesia's Territory and Role in World Affairs

The perception of Indonesia's territory and role in world affairs by its leaders is important because of its effect on Indonesia's foreign policy behaviour. The difficulty, however, is in determining whose perceptions should be accepted as valid. Should they be those of the foreign policy elite or should they be those of Indonesian leaders in general? It is reasonable to assume that the perceptions of Indonesian leaders responsible for formulating foreign policy are the crucial ones. In the case of Indonesia, however, domestic policy-makers and foreign policy leaders are often the same individuals. This has been reflected in the role of the President, especially during the Guided Democracy and New Order periods.

Indonesia's history and traditions have been mainly responsible for the perceptions of Indonesian leaders concerning the nation's territory and role in world affairs. Indonesia, before August 1945, was known as the Dutch East Indies and the country is still defined today by the former boundaries of the Dutch colony. (Since 1976, Indonesia has also included the former Portuguese East Timor.) Most Indonesian leaders, however, especially the pre-war nationalists and the 1945 generation,[1] consider Indonesia to be a continuation of two ancient empires, Sriwijaya and Majapahit.

Before independence, Indonesian leaders debated the boundaries of an independent Indonesia. One view, represented by Mohammad Yamin, a nationalist poet and statesman, for example, subscribed to the "Great Indonesia" concept (Indonesia Raya).[2] He maintained that the height of the Majapahit Empire was the period of greatest glory in Indonesia's history. Citing the work of Prapanca, a fourteenth century poet of Java, Yamin said that Indonesia, under Majapahit rule, had included the Dutch East Indies, Malaya (Peninsular Malaysia), Borneo, Timor, and Papua (New Guinea). He believed that an independent Indonesia should include the former territory of the Majapahit Empire.

However, Mohammad Hatta, who later became vice-chairman of the sub-committee drafting the constitution for the new nation, was more cautious.[3] He preferred to limit the boundaries of Indonesia to those of the Dutch East Indies. He argued that, to include territory beyond the Dutch colony, would create an impression that Indonesia was imperialistic. Hatta deplored the imperialism of Germany and said that Indonesia should not emulate such behaviour. In the course of debate, however, Hatta conceded on the issue of Malaya. He noted that if the Malayans (Malays) wished to join Indonesia of their own free will, he had no objection. Nonetheless, he insisted that Indonesia must include at least the Dutch East Indies, excluding Papua New Guinea.[4]

Sukarno, who was the chairman of the sub-committee drafting Indonesia's constitution, supported Yamin's view. He stated on 11 July 1945 that Indonesia was not a Dutch legacy and its territory need not be limited to the old Dutch East Indies.[5] In his well-known Pancasila speech which was delivered earlier on 1 June 1945, however, Sukarno referred to the two empires, Sriwijaya and Majapahit, which in his view were "united Indonesian states".[6] But his description of the territory was vague.[7] Thus when Sukarno and Hatta declared independence for Indonesia, the new nation was defined by the boundaries of the Dutch East Indies.

The inspiration drawn from Sriwijaya and Majapahit never faded. This is because Indonesians believe that the Majapahit empire under Gadjah Mada was able to unite the whole Nusantara, or Indonesian archipelago. It is not surprising, therefore, that the first Indonesian university established after independence was Universiteit (Universitas) Gadjah Mada, named after the Prime Minister of Majapahit.[8] Gadjah Mada has also been used for the name of the Indonesian battleship and the Indonesian military police also uses Gadjah Mada as its symbol.[9]

Although the boundaries and the nature of the Majapahit Empire are debatable — some say that Majapahit's influence did not extend beyond Java and that Majapahit was not a united state in a modern sense — many Indonesians, especially political leaders and some scholars, believe in the great achievements of Majapahit. The united country was prosperous and the arts were at their peak.

Sukarno repeatedly referred to Majapahit as an ancient Indonesian nation-state. He did not mention that the Majapahit extended beyond the Dutch East Indies. In a speech made to the American Congress (17 May 1956), Sukarno stated that Indonesia's territory coincided with the Dutch East Indies and that West Irian (now Irian Jaya) was part of it. He also argued that West Irian was part of the Majapahit "nation-state", which was the basis of modern Indonesia.

President Suharto is also obsessed with Majapahit. He named the Indonesian telecommunications satellite, Palapa, after Gadjah Mada's favourite fruit.[10] According to the legend, Gadjah Mada was said to have sworn not to eat the fruit until he had unified the whole Nusantara under the Majapahit Empire.[11] Suharto believes this legend and has stated that Indonesian unity and solidarity have now been achieved.[12]

Although Indonesia's present leaders have repeatedly stated that they have no designs on other territories, there is still a lingering suspicion based on Indonesia's past record, particularly the 1963-1965 Confrontation with Malaysia, on the part of Indonesian neighbours that this may not be true. It appears that they fear that Indonesia may claim irredentism of Sriwijaya or Majapahit lands, especially if irresponsible leaders come to power who might use the historical claim (or myth) to advance their political objectives. This fear has not been clearly stated, however, because of a desire to maintain good relations with Jakarta.

It is worth noting that Indonesia's annexation of East Timor in 1976 was justified in part by the nation's leaders in ethnic and historical terms.[13] Suharto, too, has said that Indonesians were invited to do so by two East Timorese parties who consider Indonesians "their blood brothers" *(saudara mereka)*.[14]

It should be pointed out that Indonesia is still affected by separatist movements, especially in the area which has been recently incorporated into the Republic. Therefore, the preservation of "territorial integrity" has often been a sensitive issue in Indonesia's foreign relations.

If perceptions of Indonesia's territory present a problem in its foreign policy behaviour, the country's role in world affairs is another important factor in determining its foreign policy. Indonesia's size (in terms of population and territory) and natural resources have made its leaders believe that the country is destined to play a major role in international affairs. When Sukarno was in power, he insisted that Indonesia be consulted on any regional matters which were related to its perception of national security. It was reported that he was offended when the formation of Malaysia was announced without giving due respect to Indonesia.[15]

Sukarno considered Indonesia to be not only the major state in Southeast Asia but also a leader among Asian and African states. Not surprisingly, it was through the initiative of the nationalist, Ali Sastroamidjojo, with strong support from Sukarno, that the first Afro-Asian Conference was held in Bandung (in 1955). During the period of Guided Democracy (1959-1965), Sukarno even conceived the concepts of Nefos (Newly Emerging Forces) and Oldefos (Old Established Forces), in which Indonesia was a leader of Nefos.[16] Understandably, after its withdrawal from the United Nations in 1965, Indonesia under Sukarno, with the co-operation of the People's Republic of China (PRC), decided to establish Conefo, or the Conference of New Emerging Forces, with its headquarters in Jakarta. This was supposed to be the United Nations of poor countries. At one time, Sukarno also called Indonesia the "light house" *(Mercu Suar)* of the Third World. In other words, Indonesia perceived itself as a destined leader of the Third World.

Even the leader of the Indonesian Communist Party (PKI), D.N. Aidit, noted the important role played by the Indonesian revolution. He argued that the "victory of the Indonesian revolution will signify a great stride forward in the anti-imperialist struggle, and its rays will shine afar, even beyond the borders of Southeast Asia".[17]

After the fall of Sukarno, however, the new Indonesian leaders did not initially lay great stress on foreign affairs. Attention was paid to domestic/internal development, but later activities indicated that Indonesia's desire to lead on the international front had not faded. The Indonesian effort in establishing ASEAN, the initiative taken in sponsoring the Jakarta Informal Meeting on the Kampuchean issue, the desire to chair the Non-Aligned Movement Conference, the decision to host the thirtieth anniversary of the Afro-Asian Conference in Indonesia, and the official announcement by the new Foreign Minister of Indonesia that Indonesia would play a leading role in international affairs, are good indicators of Indonesia's perception of its role in world affairs. In other words, Suharto's Indonesia also desires to lead.

It is not surprising then that General Sumitro, the former Deputy Chief of Army (1970-1974) and currently a keen observer of Indonesia's foreign policy, has advocated that low profile and inward-looking foreign policy should be replaced with a high profile and outward-looking one.[18] He suggested that Indonesia should begin to lead and discuss controversial issues. Many observers at the Centre for Strategic and International Studies (CSIS, a government think-tank which was established by influential General Ali Murtopo and had links to Minister of Defence, General Benny Murdani), for instance, feel that Indonesia is a major power, or at least a "medium power", and should behave like one. One of them stated bluntly that it is natural for Indonesia to assume an influential, if not leading, position in the region because it is the largest country in Southeast Asia.[19]

Despite this assertion, Indonesia's role in foreign affairs has been restricted by its own limited capabilities.

Capabilities

Two questions can be posed here: "Is Indonesia able to carry out the visions of its leaders?" and "Can Indonesia really lead?". An examination of Indonesia's capabilities in terms of its economic, military and political performance may provide the answers.

First, Indonesia is the world's fifth most populous country. It has 179,300,000 people, of whom 64.9 per cent are below 30 years of age.[20] The country's illiteracy rate is high (15.8 per cent), however, with 30.4 per cent of the population never finishing primary school. Twenty-eight point seven (28.7) per cent receive only primary education while only 1.9 per cent receive tertiary education. Therefore, the quality of manpower is low.[21] Because of this low level of educational attainment, it is very difficult for Indonesia to modernize quickly. Without rapid modernization, the country's capability remains limited.

Second, the economic situation in Indonesia has historically been unstable. The inflation rate in the past was high. When Suharto came to power, his administration was able to slow inflation. Nonetheless, under Suharto, the Indonesian rupiah has been devalued twice. The most recent devaluation in 1986 caused the rupiah's value to drop 30 per cent. The inflation rate in 1986 was 5.9 per cent, and 9.3 per cent in the following year. Foreign debt under the New Order Government is large, with the debt in 1989 reaching $53.11 billion. By early 1994, it had increased to $90 billion.[22] Although the debt problem is not as serious as that of some Latin American countries, it is a cause for concern among many observers.

Indonesia's GDP is large by Southeast Asian standards. In 1990 it was Rp. 197,721.0 billion (US$107.29 billion) and, by 1991, had reached Rp. 227,463.0 billion (US$116.63 billion).[23] Oil has been the most important source of internal revenue for financing development. Oil sales generated approximately 60 per cent of Indonesia's annual foreign exchange earnings — at least before the Pertamina (Indonesian State Oil) debacle of 1975. The decline of oil prices in recent years has forced the Indonesian Government either to defer or abandon some large development projects. Indonesia has also encouraged non-oil exports and this has met with success. This policy is linked to the gradual liberalization of the Indonesian economy. As a result, there has been a rise of a new manufacturing sector. The authoritarian decision-making process remains, however, and this may eventually bring about conflict with the private sector. If this does take place, it will be more likely to happen over the long term rather than in the immediate future.

Nonetheless, oil remains an important export commodity for Indonesia.[24] However, the nation's oil and gas deposits are being depleted. Proven oil reserves may amount to approximately 8.3 billion barrels which will last from 13 to 19 years.[25] In the light of this, the government has decided to develop nuclear energy to cope with the growing demand for power.[26] Although plans to build the first nuclear plant were endorsed by Suharto in 1989, officials have said that the plant is not expected to be operational until 2005.[27]

Indonesia's military strength is also quite limited. The armed forces consist of 283,000 men, of whom 215,000 are in the army, 44,000 in the navy, and 24,000 in the air force.[28] Although it is the largest among the ASEAN states, Indonesia's military is not the most modern. The air force and navy are not very well-equipped. In early 1988, Singapore signed an agreement allowing Indonesian access to its most modern military technology in exchange for the use of training grounds in Indonesia for the Singapore Army.

Apart from the regular armed forces, Indonesia also has 180,000 para military personnel and 300,000 militiamen.[29] It is questionable whether Indonesia would be able to use its military effectively in external ventures in the near future. The Indonesian military has been strong enough to meet challenges from domestic sources however. The two armed rebel groups which continue to be the cause of concern are the Fretilin (Revolutionary Front for an Independent East Timor) in East Timor (about 100 men with small arms) and the Free Papuan Movement (OPM) (a membership of about 500-600 and approximately 100 armed men).[30] There has also been a revival of armed rebellion in Aceh but the scale is small.[31]

In terms of territory, Indonesia consists of at least 13,000 islands, some even without names. It stretches from Sabang (Sumatra) to Marauke (Irian Jaya) and is very rich in natural resources. This makes Indonesia a potential power. The country is still underdeveloped, however, and its resources are under-explored. The nation's present capabilities are very limited indeed and they will remain limited in the near future. In other words, Indonesia does not appear to have the physical capabilities to carry out the high profile foreign policy desired by some of its leaders.

Perception of External Threat and the Archipelago Concept

When studying Indonesia's foreign policy, there are two more factors which should be taken into consideration — the perception of external threat and the archipelago concept — as these affect Indonesia's external behaviour.

First, let us discuss the perception of external threat. Although in recent years most observers have argued that the primary threat to Indonesian political stability has come from *internal* rather than external sources, perception of external threat is still relevant to Indonesia's foreign policy. Before Suharto came to power, the external threat was perceived to have come from Western countries. The counter elite believed that the threat could come from the Communist bloc as well, with the People's Republic of China (PRC) looming large on the horizon.

During the Suharto era, external threat has been seen as coming from the Eastern or Communist states, and, of these, the PRC has been singled out as the most dangerous. The PRC was thought to have been involved in the 1965 coup, and the so-called overseas Chinese in Indonesia were seen as having sympathized with Communists and allowed themselves to be used as Beijing's tools. Evidence has now shown the opposite to be true.[32]

In fact, this Sino-phobia has its origins in Indonesian history. During the colonial period, indigenous Indonesians felt that ethnic Chinese were protected by Dutch authorities at their expense, and during the 1945 revolution, the Chinese were seen as having sided with the Dutch against the Indonesian independence movement. After the establishment of the PRC, however, links between Beijing and the ethnic Chinese were seen as a "security risk" by anti-communist generals.

In order to understand Indonesia's foreign policy, this threat perceived by Indonesian leaders, both civilian and military, should be taken into account. Among the leaders of the New Order, it seems that it is the PRC, rather than other Communist countries, that evoked an emotional reaction. In a foreign policy discussion seminar in 1970, for instance, the participants and speakers concentrated largely on the issue of the PRC and the Chinese.[33] The Soviet Union and other Communist countries did not receive as much attention from the Indonesian political public. Thus, the announcement by Jakarta in February 1989 that the normalization process with Beijing would be started received tremendous attention in the Indonesian press.[34] The security issue again formed the basis of opposition to "early normalization".

In the eyes of Indonesian leaders, the PRC is dangerous in the sense that it is not only Communist but also aggressive. Although there has been no record of military action by the PRC beyond the countries immediately bordering it, Indonesians often cite the invasion of Java by Kublai Khan during the Yuan Dynasty (fourteenth century) as an example of Chinese aggression against Indonesia. The intruders, however, were expelled by the Javanese.[35] In the past, connections between Chinese Communists and the PKI were considered dangerous to Indonesian security. The alleged involvement of the PRC in the

1965 coup — despite inconclusive evidence — has been mentioned consistently by Indonesian leaders as evidence of China's ulterior motives towards the Republic. Both 1945 and 1966 generation leaders[36] remember the coup and continue to harbour ill-feelings against the PRC. It is interesting to note that the 1926 and 1948 Communist rebellions in Indonesia were mainly linked with Moscow rather than Beijing, but this has not concerned Indonesian leaders. It appears that the deeply-rooted prejudice of the Indonesian leaders towards the ethnic Chinese as a group and the perception of a giant red dragon in the north may explain Indonesia's fear of China.[37]

In recent years, China's modernization programme has also caused concern in Indonesia. The Indonesian military is afraid that a militarily-modernized China would pose a challenge to Indonesian security. Perhaps, Indonesians are afraid that China may try to play an active role in Southeast Asia, especially in maritime Southeast Asia, which is Indonesia's sphere of influence. This concern can be seen in Indonesia's eagerness to sponsor various workshops on the South China Sea which has been claimed by China as well as some Southeast Asian states as their territory.

The perception of threat is also linked to Indonesia's position as an island nation. At the time of the campaign to liberate West Irian, Indonesian leaders realized how vulnerable the country's territorial integrity was. Indonesia consists of more than 13,000 islands separated by sea. It is vital for the nation to control its territorial waters. Mochtar Kusumaatmadja, a law professor and former Minister of Foreign Affairs, argued that it was the political and security concern which caused the Indonesian Government to declare the Archipelago Concept or *Konsepsi Nusantara* in December 1957.[38] In fact, the *Konsepsi Nusantara* is often linked to the Indonesian nationalist outlook. *Nusantara* is a term used in the Javanese classics to refer to neighbouring countries of Singasari and, later Majapahit. As stated earlier, Gadjah Mada succeeded in unifying *Nusantara* under the Majapahit Empire.[39] It is not surprising that the term *Nusantara* is preferred.

This Archipelago Concept (also known as the December 1957 Declaration), which was subscribed to by both civilian and military leaders, maintains that "all waters, surrounding between and connecting the Indonesian state, regardless of their extension of breadth, are integral parts of the territory of the Indonesian state and, therefore part of the internal or national waters which are under the exclusive sovereignty of the Indonesian state".[40] In other words, the Indonesian declaration made the high seas Indonesian territorial sea. However, the Declaration notes that "Indonesia will guarantee safe passage for foreign vessels in the Indonesian territorial waters provided that they do not constitute a threat to Indonesian security".[41]

Soon after the promulgation of the December 1957 Declaration, the US, UK and Australia expressed their strong opposition to the *Nusantara* Concept.

Indonesia expected to have the support of the Third World countries during the 1958 Law of Sea Conference but this was not forthcoming. In 1960 when Sukarno was in power, the Declaration of December 1957 was made law. This Indonesian Territorial Waters Law abandoned the Territorial Sea Concept of 1939 during the Dutch colonial period.

The 1960 Law is very significant because it adopted the concept of 12 miles territorial sea (not three miles as stated in the 1939 Territorial Sea Concept). As a result of this new law, Mochtar Kusumaatmadja, who later became Foreign Minister, maintained that the Indonesian territory, which was only 2,027,087 square kilometres (land) was expanded to 5,193,250 square kilometres (including both land and sea), gaining 3,166,163 square kilometres.[42] President Suharto in his autobiography published in 1989 cited the same argument under this new law. He noted that "the Indonesian land area is about 2,000,000 square kilometres, but with the Archipelago Concept, the size of Indonesia became much larger. The water area that would come under the sovereignty of Indonesia would reach 3,000,000 square kilometres plus 800,000 square kilometres of continental shelf and 3,000,000 square kilometres of exclusive economic zone".[43] In fact, Indonesia under Suharto has further consolidated the Archipelago Concept of the Sukarno era and developed it further.

In 1969, Indonesia issued the Continental Shelf Law and eventually succeeded in signing the continental shelf agreements with its neighbours.[44] In 1973 the Indonesian Consultative Assembly passed the Archipelago Outlook *(Wawasan Nusantara)* as a concept and it was incorporated into the General Outline of State Policy.[45] The Outlook maintains that the Indonesians regard land *(darat)* and sea *(laut)* as one entity, as reflected in the Indonesian term *tanah-air* (land and water), which means homeland. Mochtar Kusumaatmadja claimed that the term did not exist in other languages.[46] Mochtar explained the similarity and difference between the two concepts. He argued that the Archipelago Concept is a territorial concept while the Archipelago Outlook is a political one which is based on the territorial concept. This concept that Indonesia is connected by sea rather than separated by it is interesting because this made Indonesian leaders inclined to think of the land and sea as one. The Indonesian Armed Forces later developed its defence doctrine along the lines of *Wawasan Nusantara.*[47]

Under the Archipelago Concept, Indonesia claims jurisdiction over all straits within the Indonesian archipelago. Suharto in his autobiography stated that in 1976 he discussed the question of passage of warships with Mochtar and decided that foreign ships had to inform Indonesia in advance before right of passage would be given.[48] In September 1988, Indonesia temporarily closed the Sunda and Lombok Straits, sparking protest from major powers. If Indonesia continues to apply strictly the Archipelago Concept, it may generate more conflict with major powers in the future.

The Archipelago Concept also reflects Indonesia's concern with the preservation of its national unity. Because Indonesia consists of different ethnic groups occupying different islands, there is always the possibility that some ethnic groups may break away from central control. This is a potential threat to Indonesian territorial integrity. Therefore, the Indonesian perception of threat and the Archipelago Concept/Outlook are two factors that have affected and will affect Indonesia's foreign policy behaviour.

Political Culture and the Foreign Policy Elite

Another important factor which influences Indonesia's foreign policy is, of course, the political culture of the Indonesian elite, especially the foreign policy elite. Indonesian political culture is defined here in terms of the traditions and values which affect Indonesian political behaviour. These include the nominal-Muslim political culture and the authoritarian (some say "feudal") tradition.

The influence of the two main *abangan* and *santri* sub-cultures bears closer examination.[49] These sub-cultures are especially strong among the Javanese who are the most numerous and significant ethnic group in Indonesia. Not surprisingly the Javanese have tended to dominate Indonesia's politics.

The *abangan* Javanese are known as nominal (or liberal) Muslims. It is also called the *Agami Jawi* (the religion of Java), which is a variant of Javanese Islam.[50] Their belief system encompasses a mixture of indigenous beliefs, Hinduism, and Islam. The pre-Islamic elements of their traditions are still very strong. It is not possible to calculate with certainty what portion of the Javanese should be classified as *abangan,* but many observers argue that they form the majority. Many Javanese leaders, including Sukarno and Suharto, can be classified as *abangan.* In fact, numerous bureaucrats and military leaders also originate from this religious-cultural group. Because of their strong pre-Islamic beliefs, *abangan* Javanese have opposed an Islamic state or a Muslim state. They prefer to have a secular Indonesian state where neither Islam nor any other religion forms the basis.

The other group of Javanese is known as the *santri* (rigid or pious Muslim). They are smaller in number and are very active in the economic sector. Unlike their abangan counterparts, the santri are more Islamic with a certain "fundamentalist" disposition. They would like to purify Indonesian (Javanese) Islam at the expense of pre-Islamic culture. Many wish to establish an Islamic state or, at least, to see a state in which Islam plays a major role.

The struggle between the *abangan* and *santri* Javanese in politics is reflected in the conflict between the Pancasila group and political Islam. Before discussing the struggle between the *abangan* and *santri*, it is important to note that Indonesia is a multi-ethnic and multi-religious society. The existence of these two sub-cultures is a result of the uneven penetration of Islam in this vast archipelago. Islam, which came to Indonesians shores in the fourteenth century, never reached the interior areas of Java which were the heart of Javanese culture.[51] The people who live along coastal areas are more Islamic while those from the interior are more indigenous.

In 1945, when Indonesia was about to become an independent state, Sukarno was able to formulate the ideology of Pancasila which is, in fact, the *abangan* concept of a modern state. This concept is included in the 1945 Constitution. The Pancasila ideology, which recognizes religious pluralism in Indonesia, does not give Islam a prominent role in the nation, even though 87 per cent of the Indonesian population are Muslim. The demands of the *santri* to restore the Jakarta Charter, in which there is a clause requiring all Muslims to abide by Shariah Law, were turned down, and the Jakarta Charter was denied inclusion in the 1945 Constitution.[52]

Pancasila (or religious pluralism) has been considered the Indonesian state ideology from the beginning but it has never been rigidly imposed. After Indonesia gained political independence from the Dutch, the *abangan* leadership was very concerned with state ideology. The government had intended to make all Indonesians, especially the political parties, accept Pancasila as the sole Indonesian ideology. It was rejected by two Muslim parties, however. (These were Masyumi and Nahdatul Ulama which are regarded as *santri* parties.) As a result, President Sukarno dissolved the Constituent Assembly and re-adopted the 1945 Constitution.[53]

The struggle between the two traditions (or two political sub-cultures) continued with the *abangan* having the upper hand. It should be noted that the term *abangan* is used here to refer to both Javanese and non-Javanese who are liberal Muslims. They were joined by non-Muslims in their efforts to maintain a secular state in which Islam is not used as its basis. Pancasila is a reflection of their nominal Muslim or non-Muslim culture. This culture was first represented by Sukarno himself, and after his fall, by Suharto and the army. Under the leadership of Suharto, in 1985 Pancasila was eventually pushed through as the sole ideology for all mass organizations in Indonesia. Thus, political Islam as an ideology suffered a further setback. The dominant political sub-culture, the *abangan*/Pancasila culture,[54] was consequently reflected in Indonesia's foreign policy. For instance, Indonesia was eager to become the leader of the Non-Aligned Movement rather than an Islamic Movement. Indonesian support for the Palestine Liberation Organization (PLO) has been based on the principle of national independence rather than religion. This is perhaps one of the major reasons, if not the main reason, for the "non-Islamic" character of Indonesia's foreign policy up to the present.

It is misleading to say that Indonesia's foreign policy has never taken Islam into consideration. It has, in fact, especially in recent years after the international and domestic resurgence of Islam. In contrast to Malaysia where foreign policy towards the Middle East has largely been shaped by Islamic considerations under domestic political pressure, however, Islam has not been a major factor in determining Indonesia's foreign policy.[55]

Apart from the domination of *abangan* or Pancasila culture, the notion of a Javanese kingdom in Suharto's Indonesia is relevant here. Indeed, both of Suharto's books (his book of quotations and his autobiography) reveal his inner world — that of the Javanese rulers.[56] This point will be examined again in Chapter 3 when discussing Suharto as the foreign policy-maker.

Suharto believes that a ruler should follow the Javanese traditions. As a powerful leader, he sees the polity as his court and everyone else as assistants who are supposed to serve him. He is the centre of power and will not tolerate additional centres. Others must carry out his orders.[57] This simplified notion is, of course, a rather distorted one, but his tremendous input into the political system, especially in terms of decision-making cannot be denied. Koentjaraningrat, a leading Indonesian anthropologist, maintains that "Indonesian society is managed from the top down, and from the centre out to the periphery. Policies and decisions from superiors are of course still important determining factors in everyday life".[58]

An understanding of the political culture of the Javanese and the authoritarian nature of the New Order polity is necessary to better appreciate Indonesia's foreign policy decision-making which has, to a large extent, been determined by major input from the President, particularly on matters considered vital by him.

The Javanese notion of Indonesia (especially Java) as the centre of the world is also relevant to foreign policy. Southeast Asian states which have been influenced by Hindu-Buddhist culture have both the concept of divine god-king and the perception of self-centredness.[59] The Javanese who have a long history and civilization also have a similar notion. Mount Semeru is considered the highest mountain in the world. The kings of Java always bore various titles which reflect their world views: The Nail of the Universe (Paku Alam), Holder of the Universe (Mangkubumi) and Controller of the Universe (Hamengkubuwono) are examples. They reflect self-perceived importance.[60] In this light it is understandable if many Indonesian leaders perceive Indonesia to be destined for a leadership role in world affairs.

More must be said about Indonesia's foreign policy elite. Since independence, Indonesia has had only two presidents, Sukarno (1902-1970) and Suharto (1921-). They emerged as the strong men of Indonesia, and consequently Indonesia's foreign policy has unavoidably been imprinted by these two leaders. Their common Javanese *abangan* background and their refusal to consider an "Islamic republic" have already been mentioned. It is also important to note that both were the product of Indonesia's nationalist movement/revolution. Sukarno, however, belonged to the first generation while Suharto belongs to the second generation. Nationalism was important to both of them, and they often identified themselves with anti-colonial struggle. They tended to be suspicious of Western military alliances and bases although Suharto seems to be more tolerant than Sukarno was. This is the major reason that Indonesia has not joined any military alliance sponsored by the west.

By studying the backgrounds of Indonesia's Prime Ministers and Foreign Ministers, it is possible to conclude that *abangan* and secular nationalists tend to be dominant among decision-makers.[61] Of the 11 Prime Ministers who were in office before Sukarno introduced the Guided Democracy system, three stand out: Sutan Sjahrir of the Socialist Party; Mohammad Hatta, also socialist-inclined; and Ali Sastroamidjojo, the leader of the Indonesian Nationalist Party (PNI). Although there were Islamic nationalists such as Mohammad Natsir, Dr Sukiman and Burhanuddin Harahap who served as Prime Minister, their terms of office were too short to have left much mark. Sukiman who wanted to form an alliance with the United States was forced to step down. This shows the strong influence of Indonesian nationalism.

There have been 14 Foreign Ministers since Indonesia proclaimed its independence.[62] Sjahrir and Hatta were among them. Three Foreign Ministers in the early period of the Republic were inclined towards Islam — they were Ahmad Subardjo (lawyer), Haji Agus Salim (ex-journalist) and Moh. Roem (lawyer) — but they did not advocate that foreign policy should be based on Islam because of Indonesia's obsession with nationalism and national unity. The others were closely associated with the PNI or non-Islamic organizations: Mukarto Notowidagdo (PNI), Sunarjo (lawyer, PNI), Anak Agung Gde Agung (lawyer, Democrat), Roeslan Abdulgani (politician, PNI) and Dr Subandrio (physician, PNI). Of these pre-Suharto Foreign Ministers, the longest serving Foreign Minister was Dr Subandrio who was closely associated with Sukarno. He held the position from July 1959 to March 1966.

After Suharto came to power, Adam Malik, a veteran politician who had been a leading journalist and an ex-member of Murba (Indonesian Proletariat Party) was appointed Foreign Minister. He held the position from 1966 to 1978 when he became Vice-President. He was the longest serving Foreign Minister in Indonesia's modern history. His successor, Mochtar Kusumaatmadja, who is a professor of international law, held office for almost ten years (1978-1988). Both were Western-educated "secular nationalists". The current Foreign Minister, Ali (Alex) Alatas, a career diplomat, was appointed in 1988 and also belongs to the same group.

Conclusion

Indonesia's foreign policy has been formulated by the elite rather than the "masses" through a democratic process. This elite, however, has been influenced by its political culture and historical experience when making foreign policy. The *abangan* background and strong sense of nationalism of the elite have been manifested in their foreign policy. This can be seen in Indonesia's policy towards the Middle East and its refusal to have foreign military bases. It is also crucial to note that this elite is conscious of Indonesia's regional entitlement because of Indonesian size and history. Indonesia's limited capabilities, however, have restrained its international behaviour. The "determinants" discussed above have impinged upon Indonesia's foreign policy throughout the years from the revolutionary period to the Suharto era.

NOTES

1. This is the translation of an Indonesian term "Angkatan 1945" which refers to those Indonesians who were involved in the 1945 independence movement.
2. Muh. Yamin (ed.), *Naskah Persiapan Undang-Undang Dasar*, Vol. 1 (Jakarta: Prapantja, 1959), p. 135 (for the full speech, see pp. 125-137). The portions covering discussions held in the meeting of Badan Penjelidik Usaha Persiapan Kemerdekaan Indonesia regarding the territory of Indonesia have been translated into English by the Malaysian Government under the title: *The Territory of the Indonesian State (Background to Indonesia's Policy towards Malaysia)*, (Kuala Lumpur, c. 1963), p. 10. This was published during the Confrontation period as part of Malaysia's propaganda campaign.
3. For the speech of Moh. Hatta, see Yamin, op. cit., pp. 201-202; 212. The English translation of the speech is included in Herbert Feith and Lance Castles (eds.), *Indonesian Political Thinking, 1945-1965* (Ithaca: Cornell University Press, 1970), pp. 441-443.
4. For Sukarno's speech, see Yamin, op. cit., pp. 204-207.
5. Yamin, op. cit., pp. 205-206.
6. For the full text of Pancasila, see Yamin, op. cit., pp. 61-81. It was reprinted by the Ministry of Information, *Lahirnja Pantja Sila* (Departemen Penerangan RI, Penerbitan Chusus 153, n.d.). For the partial English translation of the Sukarno speech, see Feith and Castles, op. cit., pp. 40-49. Sukarno noted that "The national state is only Indonesia in its entirety, which existed in the time of Sriwidjaja and Madjapahit, and which now, too, we must set up together". See Feith and Castles, op. cit., p. 43.
7. "Even a child can tell that the islands of Java, Sumatra, Borneo, Celebes [Sulawesi], Halmahera, the Lesser Sunda Islands, the Moluccas, and the other Islands in between are one unity." See Feith and Castle, op. cit., p. 41.
8. For a short study of Gadjah Mada, see Leo Suryadinata, "Gadjah Mada", *Encyclopaedia Britannica*, 15th edn. (1974), pp. 825-826.
9. See Departemen Pendidikan dan Kebudayaan, *Sejarah Nasional Indonesia Untuk SMA*, Vol. 1 (Jakarta: Balai Pustaka, 1987), p. 139.
10. There are at least two other explanations of the meaning of *palapa*. One has it as spices but the other claims it was Tantrism. See *Sejarah Nasional Indonesia Untuk SMA*, Vol. 1, p. 137, also *Ensiklopedi Indonesia*, Vol. 4 (Jakarta: Ichtiar Baru, 1983), p. 2522.
11. See Soeharto, "Menjelmakan Sumpah Gadjah Mada", in his *Otobiografi: Pikiran, Ucapan dan Tindakan Saya. Seperti dipaparkan kepada G Dwipayana dan Ramadhan K.H.* (Jakarta: Citra Lamtoro Persada, 1989), p. 323. (Hereafter: *Otobiografi Soeharto*.) This is an important source on Suharto.

12 Ibid.
13 Adam Malik stated in his booklet that "Those people who did not agree [with the integration of East Timor into Indonesia], let them study the history of their ancestors who had relations with us. This cannot be denied. It was true!" See Adam Malik, *Sepuluh Tahun Politik Luar Negeri Orde Baru* (Jakarta: Yayasan Idayu, 1976), p. 17.
14 See Soeharto, "Hal Timor Timur", in his *Otobiografi*, p. 317. Ali Murtopo also stressed the ethnic links between Indonesians and East Timorese in his public talks. The author attended one of these talks at the American University in Washington D.C. in 1974.
15 Sukarno complained later that the formation of Malaysia was announced without waiting for the result of the UN mission: "This is the greatest humiliation of Indonesia and the Philippines". See J.A.C. Mackie, *Konfrontasi: The Indonesia-Malaya Dispute 1963-1966* (Kuala Lumpur: Oxford University Press, 1974), p. 201.
16 The concepts of Oldefos and Nefos were first put forward in his speech at the United Nations in September 1960 entitled "Build the World Anew". See George Modelski (ed.), *The New Emerging Forces: Documents on the Ideology of Indonesian Foreign Policy* (Canberra: Australian National University, 1963), pp. 1-31.
17 For an English translation of the Aidit speech, see Feith and Castles, op. cit., pp. 266-270 (especially p. 270).
18 Soemitro, "Memulihkan Postur Politik Luar Negeri Indonesia", *Kompas*, 11 March 1989.
19 J. Soedjati Djiwandono, "Forty Years Indonesian Foreign Policy: Change and Continuity", in *Indonesian Quarterly*, Vol. 13, No. 4 (1985), especially pp. 450-451. Note that Soedjati uses the term "middle power" instead of "medium power".
20 See *Penduduk Indonesia Hasil Sensus Penduduk 1990* (Seri S2) (Jakarta: Biro Pusat Statistik, 1992), p. 3. The figure has been rounded up.
21 Ibid., p. 126; *Statistik Indonesia 1991 (Statistical Yearbook of Indonesia)* (Jakarta: Biro Pusat Statistik, 1992), p. 131.
22 International Institute of Strategic Studies (IISS), *The Military Balance 1992-1993* (London: Brassey's, 1992), p. 148; *Straits Times*, 6 April 1994.
23 Ibid.
24 Between 1975-1990, oil and gas export revenues accounted for 80 per cent of total export earning. In 1990 it stood at 46 per cent. See Purnomo Yusgiantoro, "Impact of the Gulf Crisis on the Oil Industry in ASEAN", Paper presented for the seminar on "In Defence of Oil: The Gulf Crisis and Its Implications for the Asia-Pacific Region", Singapore, 2 October 1990, p. 10.
25 The figure is taken from Yusgiantoro's paper, ibid., p. 10. He also argues that in 1990 Indonesian production was at 1.2 million barrels per day. It was below peak production of 1.7 million barrels per day. If 1.2 million barrels were produced per day, oil reserves will last 19 years; if 1.7 million were produced, reserves will last only 13 years.
26 Mines and Energy Minister Ginanjar Kartasasmita told this to a New Zealand parliamentary delegation in May 1991. See *Straits Times*, 16 May 1991. See also Yusgiantoro, ibid., p. 11.
27 *Straits Times*, 21 August 1992, p. 18. Suharto argued that Indonesia's development needs huge amounts of electricity and "it is time now for us to seriously consider the use of nuclear technology to generate electricity". Ibid.
28 IISS, op. cit., pp. 148-150 .
29 Ibid., p. 149; also IISS, op. cit., p. 161, for the number of militia men.
30 IISS, op. cit., p. 150. On 10 November 1992, Xanana Gusmao, the Fretilin leader was captured. See Atmadji, "Kisah Penangkapan Xanana, Gembong GPK Fretilin", in *Rekaman Peristiwa 1992* (Jakarta: Pustaka Sinar Harapan, 1992), pp. 127-129. This may have weakened the resistance movement in East Timor.
31 There were about 750 armed rebels in Aceh. Ibid., p. 150.
32 See Leo Suryadinata, *China and the ASEAN States: The Ethnic Chinese Dimension* (Singapore: Singapore University Press, 1985), pp. 60-72; 165-195. It should be noted that the Chinese comprise heterogeneous groups with divisive political orientations. No doubt there have been those who supported the PRC but there are also many who are critical of Beijing.

33 Arief Budiman (ed.), *Politik Luar Negeri Indonesia Dewasa Ini* (Jakarta: Jajasan Indonesia, 1972).
34 See Chapter 7 on Indonesia-China relations.
35 See D.G.H. Hall, *A History of Southeast Asia* (London: Macmillan, 1968), pp. 78-79. Indonesian history books also noted the event. See for instance *Sejarah Nasional Indonesia Untuk SMA*, Vol. 1 (Jakarta: Balai Pustaka, published under the auspices of Indonesian Minister of Education and Culture, 1987), pp. 130-131.
36 The 1945 generation refers to the group who participated in the 1945 independence movement, while the 1966 generation refers to the group which participated in the 1966 demonstration against Sukarno.
37 For Indonesian leaders' perceptions of China, see Leo Suryadinata, *Pribumi Indonesians, the Chinese Minority and China: Perceptions and Policies* (Kuala Lumpur and London: Heinemann, 1978), pp. 165-167.
38 Mochtar Kusumaatmadja, *Hukum Laut Internasional* (Jakarta: Binacipta, 1986), p. 188.
39 See *Ensiklopedi Indonesia*, Vol. 4, p. 2415.
40 Cited in Michael Leifer, *Indonesia's Foreign Policy* (London: Allen and Unwin, 1983), p. 38.
41 Kusumaatmadja, *Hukum Laut Internasional*, p. 189.
42 Ibid., p. 195.
43 See *Otobiografi Soeharto*, p. 320.
44 Kusumaatmadja, *Hukum Laut Internasional*, pp. 200-201.
45 Ibid., p. 203.
46 Ibid.
47 Ibid., p. 204; also *Eksiklopedi Indonesia*, Vol. 4, p. 2415.
48 *Otobiografi Soeharto*, p. 322.
49 The concept of *abangan-santri-priyayi* in Java is treated in detail in Clifford Geertz's classic: *The Religion of Java* (New York: Free Press, 1959). The concept has been criticized by a few scholars. For instance, *priyayi* (aristocrats or official class) is a social category but not a religious one. Others maintain that this is an outdated concept as the division has become blurred. Nevertheless, the difference has not disappeared although at the moment some *abangan* have adopted more Islamic rituals.

I am accepting the division of some of the critics that *priyayi* is not a religious criterion but I am of the view that the basic division between *abangan* (nominal Muslim or liberal Muslim) and *santri* (pious Muslim or rigid Muslim) is still extremely useful in explaining the political behaviour of Javanese Muslims up to this point.

It should also be noted that Koentjaraningrat prefers to use the term *agami Jawi* instead of *abangan* in his definitive work, *Javanese Culture* (Singapore: Oxford University Press, 1985), pp. 316-317, and considered *agami Jawi* as "a variant of Javanese Islam". I also accept the argument but prefer the term *abangan* to *agami Jawi* as the former has been widely used without any negative connotation.
50 See Koentjaraningrat, op. cit., pp. 316-445. He explains in detail the nature of this religion and its difference from *agami Islam santri*.
51 Herbert Feith, *The Decline of Constitutional Democracy* (Ithaca: Cornell University Press, 1962), pp. 109-110.
52 On the Jakarta Charter, see H. Endang Saifuddin Anshari, *Piagam Jakarta 22 Juni 1945* (Bandung: Pustaka Perpustakaan Salman ITB, 1981).
53 Ibid., p. 83 ff.
54 I have used *santri* liberally to include non-Javanese pious Muslims as well. As for Pancasila culture, I have used it to refer to the culture of both *abangan* and non-Muslims.
55 Malaysian politics is dominated by Malays who are defined by their religion, Islam. In fact, the two Malay parties, namely UMNO United Malays National Organization) and PAS (Parti Islam Se Malaysia or Pan-Malaysian Islamic Party) competed to champion the interests of Muslims. For a discussion of UMNO and PAS on Islam, see Alias Mohamed, *Malaysia's Islamic Opposition* (Kuala Lumpur: Gateway, 1991). Unfortunately there is no

study on Islam and Malaysia's foreign policy under Mahathir. For Islam and Indonesia's foreign policy, see Chapter 10 of this book.
56 For the full title of Suharto's biography, see note 11 of this chapter. The title of the book of citations is *Butir-Butir Budaya Jawa (Hanggayuh Kasampurnaning Hurip Berbudi Bawaleksana Ngudi Sejatining Becik)* (Jakarta: Yayasan Purna Bhakti Pertiwi, 1990). For a brief discussion on this book, see Leo Suryadinata, *Military Ascendancy and Political Culture: A Study of Indonesia's Golkar* (Athens: Ohio University Press, 1989), p. 130; also *Tempo,* 12 March 1988, pp. 45-48.
57 The concept was first developed by Ben Anderson in his article, "The Idea of Power in Javanese Culture", in Claire Holt et al. (eds.), *Culture and Politics in Indonesia* (Ithaca: Cornell University Press, 1972), pp. 1-69, especially pp. 22, 36-38. This concept was applied by some writers, e.g. Hamish McDonald, *Suharto's Indonesia* (Fontana/Collins, 1980), pp. 112-142; and David Jenkins, *Suharto and his Generals* (Ithaca: Cornell Modern Indonesian Project, 1984), pp. 13-20.
58 See Koentjaraningrat, op. cit., p. 462.
59 For a discussion on these concepts, see Robert Heine-Geldren, *Conceptions of State and Kingship in Southeast Asia,* Southeast Asia Program Data Papers, No. 18 (Ithaca: Cornell University, 1956). The concept of self-centredness reminds me of China, the "central kingdom" and the centre of civilization.
60 Lee Khoon Choy in his interesting book, *Indonesia between Myth and Reality* (Singapore: Federal Publications, 1977), p. 166, has also made this point.
61 For a list of foreign policy elite in Indonesia, see appendix.
62 *Dua Puluh Lima Tahun Departemen Luar Negeri 1945-1970* (Jakarta: Departemen Luar Negeri, 1971), pp. XIV-XV; Mizwar Djamily, *Mengenal Kabinet RI Selama 40 Tahun Indonesia Merdeka* (Jakarta: PT Kreasi Jaya Utama, 1986).

2

Indonesia's Foreign Policy before the New Order
In Search of a Format

Introduction

Using the various "determinants" discussed above as a backdrop, this chapter examines Indonesia's foreign policy before Suharto came to power. What was its nature? What were the major issues? Who made the policies? A brief study of Indonesia's foreign policy before the New Order is important because Suharto's foreign policy, to a certain extent, has shown continuity with that of Sukarno.

Various factors which have been identified in the previous chapter, such as leaders' perceptions of Indonesia's territory and role, the dominant political culture and Indonesia's capabilities, have affected Indonesia's foreign policy throughout the period from the revolution to the Suharto era.

Pre-New Order policy can be divided into at least three periods: the revolutionary period (1945-1949), the Liberal Democracy Period (1950-1958), and the Guided Democracy Period (1959-1965).

The Revolutionary Period (1945-1949)

Before considering Indonesia's foreign policy during the revolutionary period, it is necessary to ask whether there was a foreign policy before December 1949. Some observers argue that, prior to that time, Indonesia was not an independent state because the Dutch had not transferred sovereignty.[1] Accordingly, prior to 1949-1950, Indonesia did not have any foreign policy.

Indonesian nationalists argue that Indonesia was already a sovereign state when independence was declared.[2] A state is defined in terms of independent government (a republic), clear boundaries (those of the Dutch East Indies, although before December 1949 the nationalists were not in full control) and a population (Indonesian peoples who lived in the Dutch East Indies). Moreover, when independence was proclaimed, the Republican Government was the only government because the Japanese had capitulated on 15 August 1945, and Allied troops only arrived a few weeks later. After mid-September, the Allied Forces led by the British intended to restore Dutch rule in Indonesia. Their actions brought them into physical conflict with Indonesians who were then struggling for their independence. Although the republic was initially confined to a limited area and was not recognized by all the major powers, it was recognized by some small states (in the Middle East) and by some major powers (the Soviet Union in 1948, before the Dutch transfer of sovereignty). Since Indonesia was already a state in 1945, its foreign policy also began in that year.

In any case, the fact remains that the Republicans were able to establish a foothold in Java and expand their influence. The Republican Government used diplomacy to secure Indonesia's independence from the Dutch. Thus, foreign policy during this period was used by the Republican Government to serve this purpose. It was during this revolutionary period that the "seeds" of Indonesia's foreign policy were sown.

It should be noted that, in 1943, the Japanese, who had encountered difficulties in gaining international support, began to mobilize the local population and promised independence for Indonesia. This move was aimed at securing Indonesian support for the Japanese war effort. The independence of Indonesia under Japanese sponsorship was scheduled for 18 September 1945. By 15 August 1945 however, Japan had surrendered. Two top Indonesian leaders, Sukarno and Hatta, were forced by the revolutionary groups, composed mostly of youths, to proclaim Indonesia's independence without paying regard to the original schedule. On 17 August 1945, Indonesia's independence was proclaimed.

The government was first established in Jakarta with the Komite Nasional Indonesia Pusat (KNIP) as Indonesia's parliament.[3] Sukarno was appointed President while Mohammad Hatta was made Vice-President. But Sukarno and Hatta were not the only actors in Indonesian politics. There were two other groups, namely the Sjahrir group and the Tan Malaka group, which were also influential in the development of the domestic politics. In fact, the presence of these groups was reflected in Indonesia's foreign relations. These leaders had one thing in common: they were all influenced by left-wing ideology. Sukarno claimed to be a Marxist and developed Marxism into Marhaenism. Hatta was active in socialist-oriented movements (for instance the Perhimpunan Indonesia in the Netherlands), and Sjahrir was similar in his political orientation. Tan Malaka was a communist. It is not surprising that Sukarno, Hatta and Sjahrir achieved some kind of understanding during the revolutionary period and were united in their struggle against the Tan Malaka group.[4]

The two groups also had fundamental differences in their approach for gaining Indonesia's independence. While the Sukarno/Hatta/Sjahrir group was in favour of diplomacy *(diplomasi),* that is, using diplomacy and international pressure to force the Dutch to grant independence to Indonesia, the Tan Malaka group favoured struggle *(perjuangan).* They hoped to mobilize the population to rebel against the colonial power. However, Sukarno's Cabinet, because of his collaborationist record, was initially not acceptable to the Allied Forces and to the Dutch. Only when Sjahrir took over and formed a government did the Dutch agree to negotiate with him because of his anti-Japanese record.

The Tan Malaka group who refused to use *diplomasi* to achieve Indonesia's independence was supported by radical youths and the People's Security Army (Tentara Keamanan Rakyat, or TKR, led by General Sudirman). The Tan Malaka group eventually formed the "United Struggle" *(Persatuan Perjuangan)* and succeeded in forcing Sjahrir to resign. Sukarno then took over the government but later reappointed Sjahrir as Prime Minister so that negotiations could be continued. The "United Struggle" made another attempt to overthrow the government but failed.

In November 1946, under the leadership of Sjahrir, an agreement (the Linggajati Treaty) was reached between the Republic and the Dutch. Under the terms of this agreement, the Dutch acknowledged the existence of the Republic with its territory being Java, Madura and Sumatra. The agreement also stipulated that the Republic and the Dutch would jointly form a new government which was to be federal in nature. The agreement did not unite the Sjahrir Government, however. Sjahrir came into conflict with his Defence Minister, Amir Sjarifuddin, who was supported by many Cabinet Ministers. Sjahrir's Cabinet eventually collapsed. Apparently, Sjahrir's non-Communist stand was opposed by Amir and his radical/Communist sympathizers.

Amir was then appointed Prime Minister by Sukarno, and negotiations with the Dutch continued — this time under the auspices of the United Nations. It is interesting to note that Amir was not able to get more concessions from the Dutch; the Renville Treaty that he finally signed was less favourable than the Linggajati Treaty. Under the Renville Treaty of 1948, the Republic's territory was reduced to part of Java and part of Sumatra. Major political parties in Indonesia opposed the treaty, and Amir was consequently dropped from the Cabinet. Hatta, a moderate, was appointed by Sukarno to replace him.

Hatta continued Sjahrir's diplomacy. During Sjahrir's time, contacts had been made between Indonesia and the international community to gain support for the country's independence. Arabic-speaking Haji Agus Salim was sent to the Middle East and Africa, among other places, to marshall support from Muslim states. In 1947, the Arab League of Nations (including Egypt, Iraq, Syria and others) recognized Indonesia.[5]

The Soviet Union was also eager to support Indonesia's independence. But both Sjahrir and Hatta were suspicious of Soviet intentions. The Soviets were forthcoming with their support, however, and an agreement with them was reached through a Communist Indonesian, Suripno, who was then in Prague.[6] The Soviets wanted the Republic to implement the agreement by exchanging representatives, but Hatta was aware of the Cold War and did not want to create an impression that Indonesia was siding with the Soviet Union. This might not have been in Indonesia's best interest. On 2 September 1948, prior to the Madiun Affair, Hatta made a speech to the working session of the KNIP which later came to be known as the start of Indonesia's "independent and active" *(bebas dan aktif)* foreign policy. In the speech, he asked, "Should the Indonesian people who are fighting for their independence choose between the pro-Soviet and pro-American stand? Can we have any other stand in pursuit of our goal? The Government is of the view that Indonesia should not become an 'object' in the international political struggle. On the contrary, it should become a 'subject' which has the right to make its own choice, that is, to achieve our complete independence ... But this independence should be gained through self-confidence".[7] On 16 September 1948, he further elaborated this policy. Repeating what he said earlier, Hatta added that "Indonesia's [foreign] policy should be decided by its own interests and be implemented in accordance with the situation and reality that we are facing ... Indonesia's policy cannot be determined by another country's policy which is decided by the interest of that country".[8] Hatta's decision not to lean towards the Soviet bloc angered many left-wing Indonesians.

Amir, who was out of power by this time, felt bitter and mobilized the masses to stage a revolutionary movement. The Tan Malaka group, with the support of newly arrived PKI leader, Moeso (Musso), formed another group to agitate for revolutionary change. The Communists were reported to be planning a rebellion in 1949, but an unexpected event in Madiun triggered open conflict between Communists and non-Communists in September 1948. Sukarno and Hatta took a firm stand which led to the collapse of the rebellion. Tan Malaka, Moeso, and Amir were killed. Only D.N. Aidit escaped. He headed the PKI in the 1950s. It was only after the Madiun affair that the United States, in the midst of the Cold War, began to openly support Indonesia's independence.[9] Pressure was put on the Dutch to negotiate with the Republic.

The Dutch wanted a favourable solution for themselves. They staged a military confrontation against the Republic. Yogyakarta fell into their hands, and Sukarno and Hatta were captured. Nonetheless, guerrilla warfare continued because the Indonesian military refused to surrender. Negotiations were resumed in the United Nations, and international support for Indonesia was forthcoming. The United States pressured the Dutch to come to an agreement with the Republic, threatening them with the loss of American aid. A Round Table Conference was eventually held at which an agreement was reached between the Republic and the Dutch-sponsored states which the Dutch had established in Indonesia. A Federal Republic of Indonesia was announced, including the entire Dutch East Indies, except Dutch Papua New Guinea (Irian Jaya), which was to be decided later. Political sovereignty was officially transferred to Indonesian hands in December 1949.

Under the Round Table Conference Agreement of 1949, Indonesia was to become a united states rather than a unitary state. The nationalists still felt that the Dutch were attempting to control Indonesia through their sponsored ethnic states.

The Parliamentary Democracy Period (1950-1958)

Despite any misgivings they may have had, the Republicans signed the Round Table Conference Agreement with the Dutch, which brought the Federal Republic of Indonesia into being. The political situation was still unstable. In this loose federation, the Dutch-sponsored ethnic states tended to be suspicious of the Republican Government. There was a tendency for some states to want their independence. Armed rebellions began to occur. The most serious challenge was from the Moluccans who declared themselves independent in May 1950.[10] This marked the end of the Federal Republic of Indonesia, and signalled the emergence of a unitary state in which power was concentrated in the hands of the Republicans. The Round Table Conference Agreement was abrogated unilaterally by Indonesian nationalists. Indonesia then entered the parliamentary democracy period of its history, where political parties became major actors and also formulators of the nation's foreign policy.

There were at least four major parties: the PNI (basically a Javanese *priyayi* or "official class" party) which received its support from civil servants and some *abangan* Javanese; the PKI (Partai Komunis Indonesia or the Indonesian Communist Party) which drew its support from Java, albeit from the lesser *priyayi* and *abangan* peasants; the NU (Nahdlatul Ulama or Muslim Scholars Association) which garnered support from the Javanese *santri* and traders/businessmen in small towns in central and East Java; and the Masyumi (Modern Islamic Party) which was largely supported by Muslims from the outer islands.[11]

The PKI, which won 16.4 per cent of the vote in the 1955 general elections, was never part of the government. None of the other three parties could gain a majority on its own and they had to form coalition cabinets. The PSI (Partai Sosialis Indonesia, Sjahrir's party) was relegated to a minor role after the 1955 election, signifying the decline of the "Administrators" represented by Sjahrir and Hatta in Indonesia's politics. The "Solidarity Makers", represented by Sukarno, began to play a more important role after the mid-fifties.[12] The PNI,

NU, and Masyumi were suspicious of the PKI. Not surprisingly then, the PKI was excluded from the cabinets and was not directly involved in foreign policy-making.

The first cabinet (December 1949-September 1950) was headed by Mohammad Hatta who is often considered the chief architect of Indonesia's foreign policy. He was anxious to gain the recognition of both Western and Communist states in order to safeguard what he perceived as Indonesia's national interests. He carried out his so-called "independent and active foreign policy" and refused to align with one of the superpowers. As noted above, this policy originated in September 1948 when Hatta was both Prime Minister and Foreign Minister. He believed it was in Indonesian national interest to be friendly with both camps and remained aloof from the Cold War. Accordingly, Indonesia established diplomatic relations with both Communist and non-Communist countries. Jakarta also decided to recognize Beijing instead of Taipei which was acknowledged by the United States as representative of China.

After Hatta, subsequent Indonesian cabinets (Natsir, September 1950-April 1951 and Sukiman, April 1951-April 1952) were dominated by Masyumi. The nation's policy of non-alignment gradually changed, and Indonesia began to lean towards the West. The Masyumi, suspicious of the Communists, believed that the PKI, backed by the People's Republic of China (PRC) and other dissenting elements, was about to overthrow the government. During the Sukiman Government, which was also Masyumi, Indonesia signed a "mutual security" agreement with the United States for the purpose of securing economic, technical and political aid.[13] This was considered by the Indonesian political public as betraying the nation's "active and independent policy". Understandably, the agreement was not ratified by parliament, and such explicit alignment with the West generated strong opposition and led to the fall of the Sukiman Cabinet. This showed that anti-Western sentiment, which was the legacy of the revolution, was strong in Indonesia.

Later, the Sukiman Cabinet was replaced (July 1953-August 1955; March 1956-April 1957) by the PNI-dominated group headed by Ali Sastroamidjojo. Ali, a follower of Sukarno, was known to be a staunch nationalist. He was anti-colonialist and anti-imperialist in his orientation and he enjoyed a close relationship with Sukarno. It was under Ali that Indonesia hosted the historic Afro-Asian conference in 1955 in Bandung and produced the well-known Bandung Principles (Sila Bandung) that advocated non-interference in the domestic affairs of each country and promoted Afro-Asian solidarity. It was under the PNI that Indonesia's foreign policy became more nationalistic in nature.[14] The West Irian (later Irian Jaya) issue was raised again, and the campaign against the Dutch became more intense. A full campaign against the Dutch only took place during the Guided Democracy period when political parties were no longer of major importance in Indonesian politics.[15]

It should be noted that, because of various separatist movements, economic problems and different socio-cultural traditions, the coalition cabinets never lasted long. Major conflict arose between Sukarno, who was a Javanese, and Hatta, who was a Sumatran, over political and economic issues. This resulted in Hatta's resignation as Vice-President in December 1956. The regional armies in Sumatra and Sulawesi were also very active and wanted more independence from the central government in economic and political affairs. Understandably, their relationship with headquarters became tense. With increasing opposition, the Cabinet of Ali Sastroamidjojo (PNI) fell in March 1957, and martial law, which was only lifted in 1963, was proclaimed. Sukarno appointed a non-party cabinet, but it failed to solve political and economic problems. The regional armies wanted Mohammad Hatta to rejoin the Government, but they were disappointed.

By 1957, the PKI was growing stronger. In the mid-year by-election in East Java, the PKI had emerged as the largest party at the expense of the PNI and the NU. Towards the end of 1957, when the United Nations failed to pass a resolution requiring the Dutch to negotiate with Indonesia over the West Irian issue, the PKI and the PNI seized Dutch property. Fearing the PKI's control over the plantation and oil sectors, the army rapidly moved in to take over Dutch enterprises.

The fact that the army and President Sukarno were outside the parliamentary system also made parliamentary democracy less stable. Sukarno, who was influenced by radical ideology (especially Marxism), planned to bring the PKI into the government but the Islamic parties and the army intended to keep the PKI out. The Masyumi and the PSI actively supported regional military officers in Sumatra and demanded a reform in the Cabinet. When their demands were rejected, the army officers openly rebelled against the central government and called for Sukarno to step down. They claimed that they wanted to stop Indonesia from becoming a Communist state. The United States was sympathetic towards the rebels and, at one time, even considered recognizing them as the legitimate government.[16] Some argue that the CIA was, in fact, behind the rebellion because the United States saw the Sukarno-led Government moving further towards the left which would have been detrimental to American interests in Southeast Asia. There is evidence that the United States was actively supporting the rebels: an American pilot was shot down while spying for the rebels, and arms and supplies were sent to the rebels through Malaya and Singapore.[17]

Sukarno refused to give in. General A.H. Nasution, then Minister of Defence, supported Sukarno and decided to crush the rebellions. With the success of his military operation, the strength of the central government army increased. Anti-American and anti-Western feeling grew while Indonesia's domestic politics moved further left. This was also reflected in Indonesia's foreign policy behaviour.

The Guided Democracy Period (1959-1965)

During the Guided Democracy period, Sukarno, the PKI, and the army were the three major actors. Indonesia's foreign policy was then more militantly anti-colonial and anti-Western. At the end of the period, Indonesia was an unofficial ally of the socialist and communist states.

It should be noted that the Guided Democracy period started in 1959 when Sukarno abandoned the provisional constitution and adopted the 1945 constitution which gave greater power to the President. The army needed Sukarno for its legitimacy while Sukarno needed the army for suppressing violent opposition. In order to avoid becoming too dependent on the army, Sukarno cultivated the air force and the PKI. As indicated earlier, his support for the PKI was not merely a tactical move. Ideologically, Sukarno was sympathetic to them. In his 1959 National Day speech, which was later known as Manipol or *Manifesto Politik,* Sukarno identified colonialists and imperialists as Indonesia's major enemies and declared that Indonesia's struggle against Western colonialists and imperialists must continue. But Sukarno failed to solve the country's economic and political problems. To unite the country, he launched a militant foreign policy aimed at liberating West Irian. The army supported this policy because its benefits were apparent. The PKI was able to take advantage of the "revolutionary" situation.

Prior to the Guided Democracy period, Foreign Minister Anak Agung Gde Agung had attempted to negotiate with the Dutch.[18] If the Dutch had given in to Indonesia's demands, it might have helped the moderate group in Indonesia. The Dutch were reluctant to relinquish West Irian and there were indications that they intended to establish a free Papua state.[19] Indonesia's policy towards West Irian became more militant. Drifting further from the West and the United States, Indonesia moved closer to the Eastern bloc, with even the military receiving military aid from Moscow. Under these conditions military confrontation seemed to be inevitable. Indonesia, supported by the Soviet Union, was determined to regain its "lost" territory. The United States, finding that it was not in its interest for Indonesia to turn pro-Soviet, began to pressure the Dutch to "return" West Irian to Indonesia as a face-saving gesture. It was suggested that a referendum be held in West Irian to determine the status of the ex-colony.

After the West Irian issue was settled, Indonesia's foreign policy remained militant. Sukarno classified the world into Nefos (Newly Emerging Forces) and Oldefos (Old Established Forces) with the West as part of the Oldefos.[20] He grouped the Communist states with some of the new states of Asia and Africa in the category of Nefos. He implicitly considered Indonesia a leader, if not the leader, of these new emerging forces. He remained suspicious of the West. In addition, the economic situation in Indonesia had not improved, and there was an eagerness on the part of nation's leaders to look for issues that would divert the people's attention.

Soon after the inclusion of West Irian as part of Indonesia, Sukarno embarked upon a campaign to prevent the formation of the Federation of Malaysia in 1963. This was known as *Konfrontasi*. Sukarno felt that, as leader of a big country, he should have been consulted on the move. He continued to harbour suspicions about the presence of foreign military forces in Southeast Asia. He remembered that Malaya/Singapore had been used by the United States to support Indonesia's rebels in the 1950s. Both the army and the PKI supported Sukarno's confrontation campaign but for different reasons. The army feared the "encirclement" of Indonesia by "Chinese-dominated Malaysia",[21] while the PKI intended to use this as an excuse to create a Fifth Force made up of peasants and workers that would be under the control of the PKI.[22] Sukarno supported the PKI's idea and sent the chief of the air force, Omar Dhani, to negotiate with the PRC for the supply of small arms. The army, however, was strongly against the establishment of the Fifth Force.[23]

The United States was concerned about Indonesia's foreign policy and wanted Sukarno to abandon his aggressive policy in return for continued US aid. But Sukarno rejected American pressure, putting further strain on Jakarta-Washington relations. Indonesia became more oriented towards the Eastern Bloc and even left the United Nations in 1965 in protest against the inclusion of Malaysia in the Security Council as a non-permanent member.

With the improvement in Indonesia-Eastern Bloc relations, Indonesia's international posture became more radical. Once Indonesia left the United Nations, Sukarno proposed the establishment of a Conference of New Emerging Forces (or Conefo) to rival the United Nations. The Conefo idea was strongly supported by Beijing, and the organization's headquarters was to be established in Jakarta with the assistance of the PRC.[24] Other Communist states such as North Korea and North Vietnam were interested in joining the new group. Thus a Peking-Pyongyang-Hanoi-Jakarta axis was formed which was anti-Western in both orientation and action.

Jakarta-Beijing relations during the Guided Democracy period were not always cordial. In the beginning, Jakarta introduced a policy banning aliens (that is, ethnic Chinese) from engaging in retail trade in rural areas. This deprived thousands of "overseas Chinese" of their livelihood. The overseas Chinese, many of whom were PRC nationals, fled to the cities, and some even left Indonesia for China. Beijing attempted to intervene, but this caused Jakarta-Beijing relations to deteriorate. Apparently, there was an anti-PRC group that wanted to make use of the issue to weaken the links between Jakarta and Beijing. This group, led by the army, was able to move closer to the Soviets. When the PRC realized that the overseas Chinese problem only benefited the military group and pushed Indonesia closer to the Soviets, it immediately abandoned its policy of "protecting the overseas Chinese". The PRC decided to tolerate Jakarta's discriminatory measures and regained the government's goodwill.[25] Later, when Sukarno was able to reassert his position, he stemmed the anti-Chinese campaign.

The militant foreign policy of the Guided Democracy era drained Indonesia of its resources (especially its foreign exchange reserves). Inflation was out of control. From December 1962 to December 1963, the inflation rate was about 900 per cent (some say 500 per cent). The economy continued to deteriorate and by 1965, had nearly collapsed. Early in 1961, Sukarno had wanted to introduce the concept of "Nasakom" (nationalism, religion, and communism) in order to unite the various political forces. He insisted that the army should be "Nasakomized", not only in spirit, but also in structure. This was rejected by both General Yani (Minister of Defence) and General Nasution (Army Chief of Staff).[26] The political situation was extremely tense. Sukarno continued to play his balance of power game but favoured the PKI more and more. The balance was eventually upset by the coup in 1965 which marked the end of the Guided Democracy era.

Conclusion

Indonesia's foreign policy prior to the New Order has been characterized by strong nationalism and the prominent role of secular rather than Islamic leaders. The leaders who were perceived to have compromised Indonesian nationalism did not survive, and Indonesia's foreign policy became more militant as time passed. This was partially due to Sukarno's plan to divert attention from domestic problems to external issues. The rise of the PKI and other left-wing groups led Indonesia to adopt a more aggressive foreign policy. Indonesian nationalistic foreign policy became anti-Western and suspicious of Western powers. Sukarno opposed Western military bases in Southeast Asia and this attitude survived his demise. Although the Suharto regime has generally been more sympathetic to the West, opposition to Western military bases is still strong, especially among civilians.

In addition to this anti-Western feeling, Hatta's foreign policy principle, independent and active foreign policy, not only became the stated policy of the Sukarno era but also that of Suharto, although each government tended to give its own interpretation to the principle in accordance with its own purposes.

NOTES

1   The Dutch only transferred political power to Indonesians after signing the Round Table Agreement in December 1949. Many writers consider this to be the beginning of real Indonesian independence. See David Joel Steinberg et al., *In Search of Southeast Asia: A Modern History* (Kuala Lumpur and Singapore: Oxford University Press, 1975), "Chart of

Southeast Asian History Since the Eighteenth Century", bookend pages.
2   This nationalist view is held by many Indonesians. The author is indebted to Drs Tri Cahya Utama of the University of Diponegoro for an elaboration of this view in a lengthy discussion. A Ph.D. thesis submitted to the University of Indonesia defended this point of view. See D. Sidik Suraputra, *Revolusi Indonesia dan Hukum Intemasional* (Jakarta: Penerbit Universitas Indonesia [UI-Press], 1991).
3   Some argue that the KNIP was established during the revolutionary period to function as the People's Representative Assembly, People's Consultative Council and Supreme Deliberative Council. See Ateng Winarmo, *Kamus Singkatan dan Akronim: Baru dan Lama* (Yogyakata, 1991), p. 317.
4   There are many good studies which deal with this period. Two outstanding works by Western scholars are G.T. Kahin's *Nationalism and Revolution in Indonesia* (Ithaca: Cornell, 1962) and Anthony J.S. Reid, *Indonesian National Revolution* (Victoria: Longman, 1974). Most of the information on this period presented here is derived from these books.
5   Kirdi Dipoyudo, "Indonesia's Foreign Policy towards the Middle East and Africa", *The Indonesian Quarterly,* Vol. 13, No. 4, 1985, pp. 474-485 (especially pp. 474-476.)
6   R.Z. Leirissa, *Terwujudnya Suatu Gagasan, Sejarah Masyarakat Indonesia: 1900-1950* (Jakarta: Akademika Pressindo, 1985), p. 102. Leirissa said that the name of the Communist was Suripto. In fact, it should be Suripno.
7   Mohammad Hatta, *Mendayung Antara Dua Karang (Keterangan Pemerintah Diutjapkan oleh Drs Mohammad Hatta dimuka Sidang BP. K.N.P. Di Djokja pada tahun 1948* (Jakarta: Kementerian Penerangan, February 1951), pp. 12-13.
8   Ibid, pp. 40, 42. Note that Hatta later claimed that this argument was presented on 2 September, which was incorrect. See his *Dasar Politik Luar Negeri Republik Indonesia* (Djakarta: Tinta Mas, 1953), pp. 16-17. See also *Dua Puluh Lima Tahun Departemen Luar Negeri 1945-1970* (Jakarta: Deplu, 1971), p. 58, which also contains the same error.
9   On the attitude of the US towards the Hatta government and the Madiun Affair, see Ann Swift, *The Road to Madiun: The Indonesian Communist Uprising of 1948* (Ithaca: Cornell Modern Indonesia Project, Monograph Series, 1989), pp. 81-86.
10 For a study of the Moluccas' rebellion, see Herbert Feith, *Decline of the Constitutional Democracy in Indonesia* (Ithaca: Cornell University Press, 1962), pp. 55-71; also Richard Z. Leirissa, *Maluku Dalam Perjuangan Nasional Indonesia* (Jakarta: Lembaga Sejarah FSUI, 1975), especially pp. 174-201.
11 Daniel Lev, "Political Parties in Indonesia", *Journal of Southeast Asian History,* Vol. 8, No. 1 (March 1967) pp. 52-67.
12 These two categories were created by Feith in his major work, op. cit., p. 113. Feith defines administrators as "leaders with the administrative, technical, legal, and foreign-language skills required to run ... a modern state", solidarity makers were "leaders skilled as mediators between groups at different levels of modernity and political effectiveness, as mass organizers, and manipulators of integrative symbols". It can be argued that Indonesia's foreign policy has been characterized by the leaders in power. When the solidarity makers were in power, more militant/aggressive foreign policy was introduced. For Mohammad Hatta's view, see *Dasar Politik Luar Negeri R.I.* (Jakarta: Tintamas, 1952).
13 Feith, *Decline of Constitutional Democracy,* op. cit., p. 163.
14 Herbert Feith, "Dynamics of Guided Democracy", in Ruth McVey (ed.), *Indonesia* (New Haven: Yale University Press, 1963), pp. 309-409.
15 Ibid.
16 See Brian May, *The Indonesian Tragedy* (Singapore: Graham Brash, 1978), pp.79-80; Also Howard P. Jones, the American ambassador, noted that he told Sukarno that if the rebellion was prolonged he might have to consider the PRRI. See his *Indonesia: The Possible Dream* (Jakarta: Gunung Agung, 1980), p. 116.
17 Ibid.
18 Anak Agung Gde Agung, *Twenty Years of Indonesian Foreign Policy 1945-1965* (The Hague: Mouton, 1973).
19 For a detailed study of the dispute, see Robert C. Bone, *The Dynamics of the* Western *New*

Guinea (Irian Barat) Problem (Ithaca: Cornell Modern Indonesia Project, Interim Reports Series, 1958).

20 For an interesting discussion on the concepts of Nefos and Oldefos, see George Modelski, op. cit., pp. i-viii. In fact, the concept of Nefos was defined by Sukarno as the nations of Afro-Asia, the "socialist countries", more recently, Latin America, and "the progressive elements of capitalist countries", while the Oldefos was not clearly defined. However, Modelski maintains that by "a process of elimination we are led to the conclusion that they must be the 'non-progessive' elements of the capitalist countries of North America, Western Europe and presumably also Australasia" (see p. iii).

21 Hatta, "One Indonesian's View of the Malaysian Issue", *Asian Survey,* Vol. 5, No. 3 (1965), pp. 139-143; J.D. Legge, *Sukarno: A Political Biography* (New York: Praeger, 1972), p. 364.

22 M.C. Ricklefs, A *Short History of Modern Indonesia* (London: Macmillan, 1981), pp. 266-268.

23 Ibid, p. 268.

24 Ganis Harsono, spokesman for the Ministry of Foreign Affairs in 1957 and Deputy Foreign Minister in 1964, noted that Beijing was willing to support Conefo but remained silent on the concept of Nefos. See Ganis Harsono, *Recollections of an Indonesian Diplomat in the Sukarno Era,* C.L.M. Penders and B.B. Hering (eds.), (Brisbane: University of Queensland Press, 1977), pp. 287-289.

25 David Mozingo, "China's Policy Towards Indonesia", in Tang Tsou (ed.), *China in Crisis*, Vol. 2 (Chicago: University of Chicago Press, 1968), p. 336.

26 Ricklefs, *A History of Modern Indonesia,* op. cit., p. 268.

3

Indonesia's Foreign Policy during the New Order (I)
The Rise of the Military

Introduction

This chapter examines Indonesia's foreign policy after the fall of Sukarno and the rise of the military represented by General Suharto. Both eras share many characteristics, but there are also differences. This chapter shows the continuity and change in Indonesia's foreign policy. Special attention will be given to the decision-makers in foreign policy and their institutions, as well as the conflict between the Ministry of Foreign Affairs and the military establishment. The dominant role of the military will also be highlighted.

The Rise of the Military in Foreign Affairs

The political history of Indonesia entered a new phase known as the New Order after the 1965 coup. The army, in assuming power, became the most significant socio-political force in the country.

The involvement of the military in politics did not begin with the 1965 coup. In the 1950s, the military was already very politicized. In 1958, for example, General H.A. Nasution put forward a doctrine known as the "Middle Way". He argued that the military "neither seek to take over the government nor remain politically inactive".[1] The military claimed the right to have representation in the government, legislature, and administration. This concept, defined the role of the military in both security and non-security fields and served as the origin of the dual-function *(dwi fungsi)* concept which is now used as the basis for military involvement in politics. In fact, the non-security role of the military continued to grow during the Guided Democracy period and, in 1965, when the Army held its first seminar, the dual function concept was formally proposed.[2] According to this concept, the Indonesian military is both a "military force" as well as a "socio-political force". In other words, it is legitimate for the military to be involved in both the military and political fields.

After the 1965 coup, the "socio-political" role of the Army was further refined. At the second army seminar held in Bandung in August 1966, military involvement in all aspects of Indonesian life was detailed.[3] In fact, this was the beginning of the large-scale "militarization" process. Government positions at both national and sub-national levels were taken over by military officers.[4] Military personnel even moved into the Ministry of Foreign Affairs. (See the section on MFA.)

It should be stressed here that after the 1965 coup, the military, as represented by General Suharto, became the most important decision-maker in both the domestic and foreign policy of Indonesia. Unlike Sukarno, Suharto has been more concerned with economic development and maintaining friendly relations with the West. The new government, under his leadership, introduced an open-door policy in which foreign investment was encouraged, and loans were sought to rehabilitate Indonesia's economy.[5] He quickly ended the confrontation with Malaysia although he was still concerned with foreign military bases in Southeast Asia. It was during this period that Indonesia paid special attention to regionalism. It actively supported the formation of ASEAN (Association of Southeast Asian Nations) in 1967 to promote economic and political co-operation.[6] The new Indonesian leaders recognized the importance of regional stability for ensuring the success of Indonesia's development programme.

Nonetheless, as during the Sukarno era, Indonesia was concerned with its role and security, as evidenced by the 1967 Bangkok Declaration (or ASEAN Declaration) which included, at Indonesia's request, a statement that foreign military bases should be of a temporary nature.[7] Like Malaysia, Indonesia wanted to set up a Zone of Peace, Freedom and Neutrality (ZOPFAN, 1971). This meant that external powers would be kept out of the region so that Indonesia could play a major role. Only after the fall of Ferdinand Marcos in the Philippines and, in the absence of other alternatives, did Indonesia tacitly agree to the presence of American military bases on ASEAN soil, provided that they were not in Indonesian territory.[8]

The Suharto Government's intervention in East Timor can be attributed to its concern with stability and security. However, one cannot help but think that there may be an element of territorial ambition. (See Chapter 4 for details.) Towards the PRC, however, the Suharto Government was critical at the outset. The PRC was thought by the new Indonesian leaders to have been involved in the 1965 coup although the evidence was inconclusive. The antagonistic attitude of the PRC Government further strained Sino-Indonesian relations, to the point when diplomatic ties were eventually "frozen" (severed) in 1967. The normalization process only started 22 years later, and this was after the PRC had promised that it would not support Communist activities in the region.[9]

Fear of the PRC, coupled with common revolutionary experiences and anti-Chinese feeling, made Indonesia's perception of Vietnam rather different from that of other ASEAN countries. It viewed Vietnam as a smaller threat than the PRC. Nonetheless, because of the importance placed on solidarity within ASEAN, Indonesia continued to support the association's common stand on a number of issues, the International Civil Aviation Policy (ICAP) and Vietnamese occupation of Cambodia for example.

Indonesia's foreign policy after Suharto assumed power was radically different from that under Sukarno. Initially, it had tended to move nearer to the West, evidenced by its relations with the United States and its attitude towards the Communist states. Relations with the Socialist/Communist states, the Soviet Union, and to a certain extent, North Vietnam, were downgraded. After the East Timor issue had lost prominence, and especially in the wake of the 1983 presidential election, Suharto became more confident, and Indonesia's foreign policy took a more outward-looking direction. Indonesia has consciously attempted to project a non-aligned image in order to gain acceptance as a leader of the Non-Aligned Movement. It is clear that Indonesia once again wants to play a leading role in regional and extra-regional affairs. This high profile in foreign policy is related to the personal desire of President Suharto.

President Suharto as a Javanese Ruler

As he is a central figure in Indonesia's foreign policy during the New Order, something must be said about Suharto in order to better understand Indonesia's foreign policy during the post-Sukarno period. Suharto, who was born on 8 June 1921, is the son of a minor village officer in Central Java.[10] His upbringing and marriage to Siti Hartinah (now known as Ibu Tien) who is the daughter of an official of the Mangkunegaran (a small principality in the Solo area), imbued Suharto with the *abangan/priyayi* type of culture.[11] His thinking and behaviour are reflected in the book of quotations that he gave to his children as well as in his recently published autobiography.

His book of quotations was completed on his sixty-fourth birthday (1983) in accordance with the Javanese Calendar.[12] Although the book was given to his children for their "guide in life", it in fact manifests Suharto's personal belief. The quotations in the book are taken from 13 sources, all are from Javanese classics and customs, including books of mystics. None is from Arabian Islamic sources.[13] Not surprisingly, the book contains no section on religion (*agama*), but there is one on spiritual life (*kerohanian*), which is closely identified with Javanese mysticism. For instance, "God is one, omnipresent, eternal, the creator of the universe and all that is therein, and is adored the world over". Another quotation: "God is omnipresent, also with you, but you should not dare to claim that you are God".[14]

Suharto is proud of his Javanese heritage. He has stated in his autobiography that mysticism and religion are similar because both teach men to be close to God.[15] When asked whether he felt different praying in the Ka'bah, the holy shrine of Muslims in Mecca, he said that he did not feel any different. He said that he was able to be close to God wherever he prayed.[16]

His book of quotations and autobiography clearly show that he possesses a deeply rooted sense of Javanese culture. His beliefs are a mixture of pre-Islamic and Islamic ideas, but the pre-Islamic elements are dominant. This explains why he has such a strong sense of Javanese/indigenous nationalism.

For a long time, Suharto did not perform a Haj (pilgrimage to Mecca). He only became a hadji in 1991, when he was 70 years of age, at a time when his support from the military appeared to be falling away, and he needed the support of Indonesia's Muslim population during the upcoming presidential election.

The *abangan* background and strong Javanism of the President have a bearing on Indonesia's foreign policy in the following ways. First, Suharto's foreign policy is not based on Islamic considerations. Second, his strong sense of Javanism leads him to view the world from a Javanese perspective: Java is the centre of the world and Indonesia is destined to play a leading role in world affairs. Third, he has inherited Javanese traditions which have caused him to rule Indonesia in the manner of a Javanese king. He practises a personalized rule.[17] This has affected the decision-making process, not only in domestic politics, but also in foreign policy, a fact which has become increasingly obvious in recent years. Input from those below him has been limited.[18]

Institutions in Foreign Policy-Making

Although Suharto came to power in 1965, it appears that initially he was not closely involved in foreign policy-making. Nonetheless, it is clear that he approved policy that was in accordance with his general priorities. One of the reasons for his initial lack of involvement was that he did not have much experience in foreign affairs and, according to Roeder, was not very interested in foreign policy at that time. In 1961, before coming to power, he had accompanied General Nasution on a short visit to Western countries which had been his only overseas trip.[19] Gradually, however, Suharto began to take an interest in foreign policy. This became clear in the 1970s when Suharto and

Adam Malik clashed over the issue of normalization of Sino-Indonesian relations.[20]

At the beginning of the New Order period, there were at least two groups of foreign policy-makers: the military (in the Ministry of Defence, or Hankam; the Institute of National Defence, or Lemhanas; and the State Intelligence Body, or Bakin), and the Ministry of Foreign Affairs.

Ministry of Foreign Affairs

A brief note on the Ministry of Foreign Affairs (MFA, in Indonesian, Departemen Luar Negeri, or Deplu) is needed here. From the beginning, the MFA has been dominated by civilian career diplomats, and its role has varied from time to time. Prior to the Sukarno era, the MFA played a significant role in foreign policy-making. Its role lessened during the Sukarno era and was further reduced during the New Order period.

During the New Order period, there have been three foreign ministers, all civilian. The first and most influential was Adam Malik who was a successful politician and experienced diplomat in his own right.[21] Using his experience and international standing, Malik was able to exercise considerable influence over Indonesian foreign policy during this initial period. He was gradually pushed out by the military group and Suharto.

Malik's successor, Mochtar Kusumaatmadja, who is a law professor, was less influential.[22] Nonetheless, he too, tried to influence the process of Indonesian foreign policy-making, but found that in some cases he was unable to do much owing to the increasing assertiveness of the military and of Suharto himself. Mochtar's successor, Ali (Alex) Alatas, a career diplomat, has also faced the same problem.[23] In addition to these three ministers, there have been a few other outstanding diplomats/intellectuals in the MFA, for instance, Anwar Sani (UN ambassador), Hasyim Djalal (Law of the Sea expert), and Nana Sutresna (UN). Their work seems to have been confined to very specific areas, however.

The Military

It has been argued that during the New Order period, the military has dominated in foreign policy which touches on security issues. The MFA has dealt only with political issues while security issues have been left to the military (i.e. Hankam).[24] It is often difficult to separate these two kinds of issues.

It should be pointed out that, soon after the 1965 coup, the military moved into the MFA in order to rid it of PKI members or sympathizers. In April 1966, a team was established within the MFA to purge "undesirable elements". It was also used to combat the PKI's activities overseas. This team was later transformed into Laksus (Special Implementer) which reported directly to Kopkamtib (Operations Command to Restore Order and Security).[25] Two military officers were active in this team, Colonel Her Tasning and Colonel Soepardjo Rustam.[26] The role of the military was institutionalized within the MFA in 1970 with the formation of the Directorate of Security and Communications while Laksus also remained in the ministry. Both sections were headed by military officers. (In 1970, the two positions were held by the same man, Her Tasning, who had been promoted to Brigadier-General by then.)[27]

Outside the MFA, other military groups have also been involved in influencing, if not determining, New Order foreign policy. These groups include Hankam (Ministry of Defence and Security), Bakin (Intelligence Body), BIAS (Intelligence and Strategic Organization), Lemhanas (Institute of Defence and Security) and Setneg (State Secretariat).

Hankam, Ministry of Defence and Security, is a general term used to refer to both the ministry and the defence establishment. The Defence Minister is the head of Hankam but he is not always the most influential member. General Panggabean and General Poniman who were Ministers of Defence were not considered influential in either domestic politics or foreign policy. In fact, the Commander-in-Chief of the Indonesian Armed Forces (*pangab*) is often regarded as more powerful. Benny Murdani, who was Defence Minister between 1988-1993, was influential in foreign policy, but he had been a *pangab* prior to the appointment. Deputy Commander-in-Chief, General Sumitro (1970-1974), was also a powerful figure.

Bakin, the Intelligence Body, is another military organization that has input in foreign policy. Bakin was called BPI (Badan Pusat Intelijen) during the Sukarno era. It was headed by Dr Subandrio, a civilian, until the fall of Sukarno. After Suharto came to power, it came to be known as Bakin and headed by a military officer. The most influential have been Sutopo Yuwono (1968-1974) and Yoga Sugama (also known as Yoga Sugomo) (1974-1989). In addition to Bakin, General Benny Murdani himself established the Intelligence and Strategic Centre in 1974 which existed side by side with Bakin. When Benny was made Army Chief of Staff, the Centre was transformed into BAIS.[28] Only after Benny was removed, BAIS was reorganized and used a new name BIA (Badan Intelijen ABRI, Armed Forces Intelligence Body). It no longer falls under the Army Chief of Staff but under the Assistant Head of the Intelligence Service.[29]

Lemhanas, the Institute of National Security (often known as National Defence College), is another organization under Hankam which influences foreign policy. Unlike Seskoad (Sekolah Staf Komando Angkatan Darat) which trains middle ranking officers, Lemhanas has served as the think-tank of the Indonesian armed forces.[30] There were some generals with vision who served as its directors.[31] One of these was Sayidiman Suryohadiproyo.

Finally, Setneg, State Secretariat, is headed by a State Secretary (Sekneg or

Sesneg) who is often a military officer. Sekneg is supposed to play a co-ordinating role with Cabinet Ministers on behalf of the President who is the head of the Cabinet. Because of his access to the President, the power of Sekneg has grown in recent years. A Sekneg has always accompanied the President in meeting Foreign Government leaders, and is often given special duties to perform. In addition, he often serves as the spokesman of the President on many issues, including foreign policy issues. He has a tendency to take over the role of Foreign Minister. General Sudharmono (former State Secretary, 1973-1983) and Brigadier-General Moerdiono (current State Secretary, 1983-present) are known to be powerful men.[32] These two men have been involved in foreign policy-making and have often served as foreign policy spokesmen.

Some of the military officers who were or are influential in foreign policy-making are not necessarily under the umbrella of Hankam. The late generals Ali Murtopo and Sudjono Humardani, for instance, were personal assistants of Suharto and were patrons of the Centre for Strategic and International Studies (CSIS). The CSIS, which was founded in 1971, is run by civilians who were close to the two generals. It has developed into a kind of think-tank for both domestic and foreign policy.

The role of the CSIS in Indonesian domestic politics and foreign policy is a subject of controversy. Some noted that it was the real decision-maker while others stated that it did not play any significant role. Nevertheless, people who held the former view formed the majority. This led President Suharto to devote a chapter in his autobiography to refute the crucial roles of Ali Murtopo and Sudjono Humardani:

> Before Ali Murtopo passed away, some people were fond of passing judgement that it was Ali Murtopo who made the decision ... Ali Murtopo led the CSIS which is located in Tanah Abang, therefore people thought that the CSIS was the kitchen of the government (*dapurnya pemerintah*). This is not true! ... The fact shows that after the death of Ali Murtopo, the government still functions. I can lead. Therefore it is not true that everything depends on him.[33]

This quotation reveals the popular view of the CSIS' dominant role and Suharto's resentment of such a view. There was no doubt that during the initial period of the New Order the CSIS played an important role, both in domestic and international politics, because Suharto was inexperienced and passive, especially in foreign policy matters. However, it is clear that its influence has declined since the demise of Murtopo and Humardani, and Suharto became more assertive in foreign policy matters. Many people believe that, after the death of Murtopo and Humardani, Benny Murdani became a semi-patron of the Institute. The CSIS continued to hold regular seminars that were attended by many generals, active and retired. Nevertheless, its influence was not as strong as during the Ali Murtopo period. With the stepping down of Benny

Murdani as a Cabinet Minister, the influence of the CSIS has been further reduced. Leading figures in the CSIS include Jusuf Wanandi (Liem Bian Kie), Harry Tjan Silalahi, Soedjati Djiwandono and Hadi Soesastro. All of them are civilians.[34]

Committee One

The Komisi Satu (Committee One, which is also known as the Foreign and Defence Committee) in the Indonesian parliament (DPR) is formally responsible for foreign policy and defence matters. The members of this committee include representatives of the three parties (Golkar, PPP and PDI) and the armed forces. Even so, its input into foreign policy decision-making appears to be very limited.

Bappenas

Bappenas is another institution which influences Indonesia's foreign policy. Bappenas (Badan Perencanaan Pembangunan Nasional, The National Development Planning Body), was first established by Sukarno in 1963 and was intended to promote economic development in Indonesia. Interestingly, the organization was only utilized after Suharto came to power.[35] Because of the New Order's concern with economic growth and development, technocrats — most of whom are economists — were asked by Suharto to make policy recommendations. Many economic policies, such as foreign investment laws, were clearly suggested by the technocrats and adopted by Suharto. The implementation of policy has often been a problem. Military entrepreneurs who have vested interests often intervened in the policy implementation. A case in point was their refusal to implement the policy recommended by the Foreign Investment Team.[36] These military entrepreneurs include Ali Murtopo, Sudjono Humardani (that is, the CSIS group) and Ibnu Soetowo of Pertamina, Indonesia's Oil Company.

The Bappenas group, also known as the "Berkeley Mafia" because many of them were University of California at Berkeley graduates, was close to the IMF (International Monetary Fund) and the West, which were the major source of funds for Indonesian economic development. Therefore, the military was not able to completely ignore the technocrats.[37] Since March 1993, Bappenas has been under the control of Ginandjar Kartasasmita, a Japanese-trained engineer who is closed to B.J. Habibie, a German-trained aerospace engineer who is a confidant of Suharto.[38] Habibie has been holding the position of Minister of Research since 1980. He has also served as the Chairman of the Ikatan Cendekiawan Muslim Indonesia (ICMI, the Association of Indonesian Muslim Intellectuals) since 1990 and Adviser-in-Chief of the Centre for Information and Development Studies (CIDES), a think-tank in Jakarta. Since 1992 he has become very active. He was not only able to put his man in Bappenas but was also entrusted by Suharto to reorganize Golkar. His influence in Indonesia's foreign policy can be seen in the purchase of German battleships for the Indonesian navy.[39]

In 1992 Habibie purchased 39 ex-German battleships at the price of US$482 million. However, in 1994 when it was the time to deliver the goods, Mar'ie Muhammad, the Indonesian Minister of Finance, felt that the price was too high. He only agreed to pay US$320 million, leading to conflict with Habibie. It was later revealed that the ships were purchased without the knowledge of the Indonesian navy and that the battleships were not in good condition. *Tempo*, one of the news weeklies which covered the case in detail, even reported that one of the ships sunk in the Biscay Bay near Spain on its way to Indonesia. The purchase of the ships became a scandal and it was extensively covered in the press. Suharto was eventually forced to defend Habibie, saying that he was the one who instructed Habibie to purchase the ships. Soon afterwards, *Tempo*, *Editor* and *Detik* were banned.

In theory there was a division of labour between various departments: the MFA was supposed to handle foreign policy in the political field, the military was supposed to deal with foreign policy which touches on security matters, and Bappenas is supposed to deal with economic matters relating to both domestic and foreign affairs. In practice, in the initial years of the New Order, the military often intervened in every field. Its role in foreign policy was only weakened during the later period.

MFA, the Military and the Increasing Role of Suharto

Up to the mid-1980s, the military group and the MFA did not always agree but they were united on a number of issues. When they were at odds, the military usually got its way. Such disagreements were often conflicts between Adam Malik (MFA) and the military on a number of foreign policy issues.[40] Some of the earlier examples make for a useful study.

The first was the question of Suharto's trip to Japan in 1968. At that time, Indonesia badly needed financial assistance from Japan. Adam Malik learned from the Japanese Government that Japan was not able to commit more aid to Indonesia. He objected on those grounds to Suharto visiting Japan. The military, however, believed that Japan was ready to commit more funds to Indonesia. As it turned out, Malik was right.[41] Suharto went to Japan and was not able to get what Indonesia expected. As a result, Suharto returned without signing an agreement with the Japanese. (Later, however, Japan was able to offer some more aid in order to please Indonesia.)

A second example was Indonesia's China policy in the United Nations. Adam Malik wanted Indonesia to support Albania's proposal to admit the PRC as the only representative of China in the United Nations. The military, however, wanted Indonesia's representative to abstain. The military's desire finally took precedence over that of Malik.[42]

A third example was the handling of the West Irian referendum in 1969. Adam Malik wanted a more tolerant policy towards dissenters but the military's opposing view prevailed.[43]

On one occasion Malik was able to get his way, at a time when he was still important to Suharto. There was a conflict between the military and Malik concerning the Bangkok agreement which ended *konfrontasi* between Indonesia and Malaysia (1963-1966). Suharto and his military group had wanted to end the confrontation against Malaysia so that Indonesia would be able to regain the confidence of the West. In fact, in mid-1964, contacts were made between Ali Murtopo/Benny Murdani and Tun Razak/Ghazali Shafie, when they met first in Hong Kong and later in Kuala Lumpur.[44] The progress was slow, however, because Sukarno was still President and he was unenthusiastic about ending *konfrontasi*. Eventually, Adam Malik was sent by Suharto to settle the matter with his Malaysian counterpart in Bangkok. Malik, who was extremely eager to end the confrontation, signed an agreement (known as the Bangkok Agreement) which recognized Malaysia as a nation even before general elections were held in Sabah and Sarawak. The military, and also Suharto, was unhappy with Malik's action as it could be understood as capitulation. Yet, Suharto and the military did not want to destroy Malik's authority and eventually recognized the agreement. Nonetheless, there was an "annex" in the agreement which required that Sarawak and Sabah to conduct general elections to ascertain the will of the local population. The "annex" was only a formality meant to save face for Indonesia.[45]

It should be pointed out that, increasingly, the military, especially the Ali Murtopo and Benny Murdani group, was making its impact felt in foreign policy-making. A clear example was the East Timor issue. Adam Malik, who had repeatedly stated that Indonesia did not have any designs on East Timor and would not interfere in the area's affairs, was overruled by the military, especially by the Ali Murtopo group.[46] As early as 1973, the Ali Murtopo group had cultivated the friendship of a group of East Timorese so that they would be receptive to Indonesia. One group, which was known as Apoedeti, was believed to have been groomed by the Ali Murtopo group. The sudden departure of the Portuguese and internal conflict in East Timor led to the invasion by Indonesian troops. It is believed that the Ali Murtopo group was responsible for this East Timor policy,[47] perhaps partly owing to the fact that Jakarta considered East Timor to be a strategic area. It was for this reason that the Ministry of Foreign

Affairs, and in this case, Adam Malik personally, was unable to do much about the invasion as it was a *fait accompli*.

The final example is the clash between the military, this time represented by Suharto himself, and Adam Malik over the normalization of relations with China in 1978.[48] Malik was known to have been eager to normalize relations with the PRC, but Suharto and other generals disagreed with him. Suharto wanted the PRC to pledge that it would discontinue support for local communist movements in Southeast Asia while the military demanded that Beijing should acknowledge its involvement in the 1965 coup and apologize for it.[49] Adam Malik, on the other hand, wanted to project an image that Indonesia was non-aligned and could be friendly with a Communist state. In addition, Malik believed that with the normalization of Sino-Indonesian ties, Indonesia would be able to play a prominent role in international affairs. Therefore, when he became Vice-President in 1978, Malik announced that Indonesia was ready to consider the restoration of ties with the PRC.

Suharto was displeased and instructed Mochtar Kusumaatmadja, the newly appointed Foreign Minister, to counter the statement. This example shows that Suharto was gradually asserting himself in foreign policy-making. It seems, however, that he frequently relied on the recommendations of his advisers. These were often made by the military (Hankam, especially the Kopkamtib represented by General Sumitro, and Bakin, represented by Benny Murdani), the MFA (represented by Adam Malik), the CSIS (represented by Ali Murtopo and Humardani), Bappenas (represented by Widjojo Nitisastro and Ali Wardhana), and other institutions which dealt with foreign policy matters. The role of the Foreign and Defence Committee in the DPR (parliament) has been insignificant, however. As Jusuf Wanandi of the CSIS admitted, "the role of the DPR in the formation and implementation of foreign policy is rather limited. Its function is to provide feedback and support to government policies through the institution of hearing (sic)".[50] The role of the mass media and LIPI (Indonesian Council of Sciences) has been equally limited.[51]

It is clear that President Suharto has now become the central figure in the decision-making process in Indonesia's foreign policy. Every major policy requires his endorsement.

However, during this initial period, Suharto was a passive rather than an active decision-maker. The importance of the input from his advisers varied from issue to issue. It seems that, in general, the military (Hankam and CSIS) had the upper hand over the civilians (MFA and Bappenas). This can be seen in the hard-line policy adopted by Indonesia on the West Irian issue, Suharto's visit to Japan in 1970, and Indonesia's attitude towards the PRC in the United Nations. Foreign economic policy was, of course, based on recommendations made by the Bappenas. Even so, the military group occasionally intervened in economic matters as happened when Suharto visited Japan in order to get more aid.

In later years, particularly after 1978, the role of Hankam continued to be significant but the role of the CSIS, represented by Ali Murtopo, declined. Sekneg emerged as a more important institution. Under Sudharmono, it seems that Sekneg was already involved in foreign policy (for instance, the Moro issue)[52] and under Moerdiono, Sekneg's involvement in foreign policy became more conspicuous. Relations with socialist countries, particularly with the PRC, appear to have been within the purview of Sekneg, indicating that Suharto had become more active in foreign policy-making. From available information, it seems that Suharto placed emphasis on questions concerning the PRC and the Middle East. The former was important because of its Communism and political ideology, and the latter was essential because of Islam and Islamic fundamentalism. There are strong domestic implications related to each. Understandably, in both cases, Suharto left a very clear personal imprint. These cases will be discussed in detail in later chapters.

It should be noted that Hankam's views on foreign policy have often coincided with those of Suharto. This was particularly the case during his early years in office. Later, though, differences between the military establishment and the President emerged. Examples of these are the banning of Australian tourists for a short period in 1986, the normalization of relations with the PRC in 1988, the handling of the Dili Affair in 1991 and the Israeli Prime Minister's visit in 1993. When conflicts arose, Suharto's view prevailed. In general, however, the role of the military in foreign affairs was often at the expense of the Foreign Ministry (MFA).

One writer argued that the military was concerned with security and ideology, while the MFA was "trying to be friendly with every country".[53] He also maintained that the MFA was "more involved in the day-to-day, routine conduct of foreign policy, in which institutional interactions of all types and with all types of the government are the norm".[54] It was generally true that the military had been influential in the making of foreign policy, but the role of MFA varied from period to period. So has the role of President Suharto, who cannot be classified simply as a military officer.

As stated earlier, the Ministry of Foreign Affairs had initially been quite influential in foreign policy-making because of Adam Malik's status as a politician and a diplomat. His power was gradually undermined by the military, and he was unable to overrule the military's decisions. When Mochtar Kusumaatmadja, a university professor, assumed office as Foreign Minister, it became clearer that the military was the major actor in foreign policy. When Ali Alatas became Foreign Minister, the military's role was still quite decisive, especially on issues perceived to impinge on security. Three examples will illustrate the crucial role of the military during the 1980s. However, at least one example shows that President Suharto was more influential than any other generals in the foreign policy arena.

The David Jenkins Affair

In 1986 David Jenkins, an Australian journalist who is familiar with Indonesia, published a feature article in the *Sydney Morning Herald* on Suharto's family businesses and compared him to Marcos (see also Chapter 6). The timing of the publication of the article coincided with the Indonesian-Australian meeting in Jakarta. Jakarta considered this an unfriendly act and the military immediately decided to bar Australian tourists from entering Bali. Many tourists were left stranded. The Ministry of Foreign Affairs was unaware of the action which caused embarrassment. Mochtar Kusumaatmadja had to report this to the President, and it was only after Suharto's intervention that the ban on Australian tourists was lifted: an indication of Suharto's major say in foreign relations.

The Military Visit to Vietnam

The military, especially Benny Murdani, was reported to have seen Vietnam as a buffer against the possible expansion of the PRC. (See also Chapter 8.) It was also sympathetic to the Vietnamese, partly because of its belief that Vietnam has shared a similar revolutionary experience to Indonesia's, and they were not happy with the ASEAN stand concerning Kampuchea. In 1982 and 1984, Benny Murdani visited Vietnam, hoping to persuade the government to make some compromises so that the Kampuchean issue could be settled. The Vietnamese refused to budge. While in Vietnam, Benny Murdani made a statement that Vietnam did not pose any military threat to Southeast Asia, thus contradicting the stand of the Indonesian foreign ministry. This created an uproar in some of the ASEAN capitals. He was later asked to "clarify" the statement, but his basic stand did not change.

The Closure of Lombok and Sunda Straits

In September 1988, Benny Murdani declared that the Lombok and Sunda Straits would be temporarily closed for Indonesian naval exercises.[55] He claimed that these Straits were not part of the international waters but were Indonesian territorial waters. Again, this created an international uproar.[56] The international community insisted that the Lombok and Sunda Straits not be closed, but the new Foreign Minister of Indonesia, Ali Alatas, argued that the case of the Lombok and Sunda Straits was different from that of the Straits of Malacca.[57]

Conclusion

In foreign affairs, the military succeeded in undermining other institutions which traditionally dealt with foreign policy matters, including the Ministry of Foreign Affairs, the Committee One in DPR, and Bappenas which was in charge of domestic and foreign economic matters. Initially, there was a conflict between the military and the Ministry of Foreign Affairs, with the former emerging as the victor. The invasion of East Timor in the 1970s, the handling of Indonesia-Vietnam relations, and the nature of Indonesia-Australia relations up to the mid-1980s shed light on the roles of the various players.

The Indonesian military has been particularly concerned with foreign policy issues touching on ideology and security. Up to the mid-1980s, the military was able to assert its initiative in foreign policy. The personal role of President Suharto, however, was becoming increasingly visible in the early 1980s. By the mid-1980s, it was clear that the President played the decisive role.

NOTES

1. Harold Crouch, *The Army and Politics in Indonesia* (Ithaca: Cornell University Press, 1978), pp. 24-25; For a more detailed study on military involvement in politics, see Salim Said, "The Political Role of the Indonesian Military: Past, Present and Future", *Southeast Asian Journal of Social Sciences*, Vol. 15, No. 1 (1987), pp. 16-34.
2. See for instance, David Jenkins, "The Evolution of Indonesian Army Doctrinal Thinking: The Concept of Dwifungsi", *Southeast Asian Journal of Social Science*, Vol. 11, No. 2 (1983), pp. 15-30.
3. Ibid., also Salim Said, "The Political Role of the Military ... ".
4. The positions occupied by the military include most of those that control people: governorship, district officership and village head. See Leo Suryadinata, *Military Ascendancy and Political Culture: A Study of Indonesia's Golkar* (Athens: Ohio University Press, 1989), pp. 29-30.
5. There will be a discussion on this point in the chapter on Indonesia-Superpowers relations.
6. For a discussion on Indonesian interests in setting up ASEAN, see Adam Malik, *In the Service of the Republic* (Jakarta: Gunung Agung, 1980), p. 273.
7. Adam Malik, "The Establishment of ASEAN August 8, 1967", delivered to DPR-GR on 21 August 1967, in *The Association of Southeast Asian Nations [ASEAN]*, Special Issue 039/1969 (Jakarta: Department of Information, Republic of Indonesia), pp. 3-9 (especially p. 5).
8. Dr Kirdi Dipoyudo of the CSIS argues that "Indonesia, for instance, supports the existence of an American military base in the Philippines but it does not want to have it on its own soil", see Leo Suryadinata and Sharon Siddique (eds.), *Trends in Indonesia II* (Singapore: Singapore University Press, 1981), p. 159.
9. For Jakarta-Beijing relations, see Chapter 7 of this book.
10. For Suharto's biography, see Roeder, *Suharto: The Smiling General* (Jakarta: Gunung Agung, 1970). Also *Apa dan Siapa* (Jakarta: Grafiti Pers, 1986), pp. 905-909 and Suharto's own autobiography, *Otobiografi Soeharto: Pikiran, Ucapan, dan Tindakan Saya. Seperti dipaparkan kepada G. Dwipayana dan Ramadhan K.H.* (Jakarta: P.T. Citra Lamtoro Gung Persada, 1989), p. 5.
11. Recently some writers argue that Suharto cannot be classified as *"abangan"* because he went to study at the Muhammadiyah secondary school in Yogyakarta. (This fact is also

12   Suharto, *Butir-Butir Budaya Jawa* (Jakarta, 1990, 3rd edn,).
13   For the references that he used, see *Butir-Butir Budaya Jawa*, pp. 198-203. It is interesting to note that many of the sources cited coincide with Koentjaraningrat's discussion of those of *agami Jawi*, see *Javanese Culture*, pp. 316-445.
14   The term God is a translation of "Pangeran" in the Javanese original, the official Indonesian translation is Tuhan and the official English translation is "The Lord". However, the term Allah is not used throughout the book, p. 3.
15   *Otobiografi Soeharto*, pp. 311-314.
16   Ibid., p. 327.
17   Benedict Anderson, "The Idea of Power in Javanese Culture", in Claire Holt (ed.), *Culture and Politics in Indonesia* (Ithaca: Cornell University Press, 1972), especially pp. 22, 36-38.
18   Koentjaraningrat, *Javanese Culture* (Kuala Lumpur: Oxford University Press, 1985), p. 462.
19   Roeder, *Suharto: The Smiling General*, op. cit., p. 179.
20   For a discussion on this point, see the letter section of this chapter; see also Chapter 7 of this book.
21   For Adam Malik's view regarding Indonesia's foreign policy in general, see his *Mengabdi Republik*, Vol. 3 (Jakarta: Gunung Agung, 1979), pp. 71-166; on ASEAN, see pp. 78-89.
22   For Mochtar's short biography, see *Apa dan Siapa 1986*, p. 424.
23   For Alatas' brief biography, see *Apa dan Siapa 1986*, pp. 41-42.
24   This point was stressed by a university professor in Jakarta in an informal discussion with the author, (1990).
25   *Dua Puluh Lima Tahun Departemen Luar Negeri 1945-1970* (Jakarta: Jajasan Kesedjahteraan Karyawan Deplu, 1971), p. 345.
26   See Hidayat Mukmin, *TNI dalam Politik Luar Negeri: Studi Kasus Penyelesaian konfrontasi Indonesia-Malaysia* (Jakarta: Sinar Harapan, 1991), pp. 149-150. Note that Her Tasning is spelled as Chaerudin Tasning in this book. Tasning was later appointed Ambassador to Singapore while Soepardjo Rustam was made Minister of Home Affairs (1983-1988).
27   "Lampiran E: Pemimpin dan Pegawai2 Pemimpin Departemen Luar Negeri pada Akhir Tahun 1970", ibid., no page number.
28   *Tempo*, 22 January 1994, p. 23
29   Ibid., pp. 22-24.
30   Hein, op. cit., p. 174.
31   The Indonesian term for the director of Lemhanas is *gubernur* (governor).
32   According to *Apa dan Siapa 1983-1984*, (p. 509), Moerdiono was assistant to Sudharmono for many years and took over from him in 1981 as Cabinet Secretary. He was made state secretary officially only in 1983. See also *Apa dan Siapa 1985-1986*, p. 521.
33   *Otobiografi*, pp. 440-441.
34   Soedjati has joined the editorial board of *Suara Karya*, the Golkar daily newspaper.
35   Ateng Winarno (ed.), *Kamus Singkatan dan Akronim Baru dan Lama* (Yogyakarta: Kanisius, 1991), p. 74.
36   The team was headed by Professor Mohammad Sadli, a technocrat. For a brief discussion of this issue, see Harold Crouch, *Army and Politics in Indonesia* (Ithaca: Cornell University Press, 1978), pp. 323-324.
37   F.B. Weinstein, "The Uses of Foreign Policy in Indonesia" (Ph.D. dissertation, Cornell University, 1972), p. 624. See also Harold Crouch, *The Army and Politics in Indonesia* (Ithaca: Cornell University Press, 1978), especially pp. 318-322.
38   For a discussion of the rise of Habibie in the new cabinet, see "Habibie dan Ginandjar: Dua Tokoh Kunci di Kabinet", *Eksekutif*, May 1993, pp. 38-39; Also "Banting Stir atau Pindah Jalur?" *Eksekutif*, May 1993, pp. 32-34.
39   For a detailed account of Gennan ships which led to the confrontation between Suharto Government and the press represented by *Tempo* and *Editor*, see *Tempo*, 11 June 1994,

special report. Also "Suharto Legacy", in *Newsweek*, 4 July, pp. 6-9.
40 Weinstein, *Indonesian Foreign Policy and the Dilemma of Dependence: From Sukarno to Soeharto* (Ithaca: Cornell University Press, 1976), p. 334. A more detailed description was given in his dissertation, "The Uses of Foreign Policy in Indonesia" (Ph.D. thesis, Cornell University, 1972).
41 For a detailed discussion on this, see Weinstein, "The Uses of Foreign Policy in Indonesia", especially pp. 634-535; also Michael Sean Malley, "A Political Biography of Major General Soedjono Hoemardani, 1918-1986" (M.A. thesis, Cornell University, 1990), pp. 72-73.
42 Weinstein, *Indonesian Foreign Policy*, p. 334.
43 Ibid.
44 Hidayat Mukmin, *TNI Dalam Politik Luar Negeri: Studi Kasus Penyelesaian Konfrontasi Indonesia-Malaysia* (Jakarta: Sinar Harapan, 1991), pp. 116-119.
45 Weinstein argues that "diplomatic relations were established before the holding of the election, which did not really constitute a referendum on Malaysia anyway". See Weinstein, *Indonesian Foreign Policy*, p. 340.
46 J. Stephen Hoadley, *The Future of Portuguese Timor: Dilemmas and Opportunities*, Occasional Paper No. 27, (Singapore: ISEAS, 1975).
47 Hamish McDonald, *Suharto's Indonesia* (Victoria: Fontana Books, 1981), p. 195.
48 See *Otobiografi Soeharto*, p. 333.
49 See for instance, *Angkatan Bersenjata*, 8 November 1984.
50 Jusuf Wanandi, "The Correlation between Domestic Politics and Indonesian Foreign Policy", in Robert A. Scalapino, et al. (eds.), *Asia and the Major Powers: Domestic Politics and Foreign Policy*, Research Papers and Policy Studies 28 (Berkeley: Institute of East Asian Studies, University of California, 1988), p. 197.
51 Ibid., p. 198.
52 For a discussion on the Moro issue, see Chapter 5.
53 Gordon Robert Hein, "Soeharto's Foreign Policy: Second-Generation Nationalism in Indonesia" (Ph.D. thesis, University of California at Berkeley, 1986) p. 202.
54 Ibid.
55 Leifer says that the Straits were closed to traffic in late September but *Tempo* says that the closure was during mid-September. See Michael Leifer, "Indonesia Waives the Rules", *FEER*, 5 January 1989, p. 17; *Tempo*, 29 October 1988, p. 34.
56 Leifer, "Indonesia Waives the Rules", p. 34.
57 Ibid.

4

Indonesia's Foreign Policy during the New Order (II)
The Assertive Role of the President

Introduction

The previous chapter considered the role of the military in Indonesia's foreign policy. It showed that initially the President was passive with respect to foreign policy matters. After the 1982 general election, however, Suharto became more active in foreign policy-making as he was interested in projecting a higher foreign policy profile for Indonesia. This chapter focuses on the assertive role of Suharto after the 1983 presidential election. Some examples will be provided, but the main focus will be on the East Timor issue, including the Dili Affair, in which Suharto has played a decisive role.

Suharto and a Higher Foreign Policy Profile

After the 1982 general election, Suharto became more confident. Golkar had scored a landslide victory in the election and, unlike the previous general election, there had been no violence or student demonstrations prior to the polling, signifying that there was no longer any opposition. During the 1983 presidential election, Suharto was nominated by the three parties (Golkar, PPP and PDI) as the only candidate for the presidency. In the previous presidential election, the PPP had only agreed to nominate Suharto at the last minute.[1] In the 1980s also, the East Timor problem was under control. Suharto might have thought that it was time for Indonesia to play an active role again in foreign affairs. Indeed, a number of events from 1984 onwards demonstrate this trend.

The Thirtieth Anniversary of the Afro-Asian Conference

In 1985, Indonesia decided to host the thirtieth anniversary celebration of the Afro-Asian conference in Bandung. About one hundred Afro-Asian states were invited (including the PRC). At the meeting, however, the participants were not able to agree on any major international issues. As a result, no resolution was issued. Some commentators have argued that it was a non-event.[2] From the Indonesian point of view, this was the first step for Indonesia in becoming active again in the international arena.

Chairman of the Non-Aligned Movement and APEC Summit

In 1987, President Suharto sent his Vice-President, Umar Wirahadikusumah, to attend the Non-Aligned conference in Zimbabwe, Africa. Umar was instructed to express Indonesia's desire to be the chairman of the next Non-Aligned conference. The offer was turned down. Apparently, the Non-Aligned Movement, which was dominated by pro-Soviet states, did not agree to Indonesia's leadership. They maintained that Indonesia was too pro-Western. Indonesia's annexation of East Timor had also antagonized many African states. Finally, Indonesia's refusal to allow the Palestine Liberation Organization (PLO) to open an office in Jakarta was cited by observers as a reason for Suharto's failure to win the chairmanship. In 1988, another attempt was made by Ali Alatas, but again Indonesia was not able to win the support of the majority of the countries in attendance. Indonesia did not give up and eventually succeeded in obtaining the chairmanship in 1991. It should also be noted that only in the 1990s was Indonesia eager to advocate free trade both in ASEAN and APEC to portray its leadership role. (See Chapters 5 and 11 for further discussion.)

Mediator between Singapore and Malaysia

In November 1986, a dispute occurred between Singapore and Malaysia over the visit of Israeli President Chaim Herzog. Malaysia protested his visit by recalling its ambassador to Singapore. However, Singapore stated that it had the right to invite any head of state to visit, though Prime Minister Lee Kuan Yew did admit that, had he known how Prime Minister Mahathir would react, he would have postponed the visit. Soon after this, when Suharto was invited to visit Malaysia, he met Mahathir in Johor rather than at Subang airport. After the meeting, Suharto travelled by car rather than air to Singapore and was met by Prime Minister Lee at the causeway. This has been interpreted by some observers as the Indonesian way of showing regional leadership.[3]

The ASEAN Summit

When Mrs Aquino became President, the Philippines needed the support of other ASEAN countries and, for this reason, proposed that the third ASEAN summit be held in Manila. Security was a problem in Manila at the time. Nonetheless, President Suharto decided to attend against the recommendations of his advisers. Owing to this gesture of leadership on Indonesia's part, the third ASEAN Summit was successfully held in December 1987.[4] It was a boost to the solidarity of ASEAN and has been seen as securing the stability of the region. This event confirmed Suharto's leadership among ASEAN leaders.[5] It was also Indonesia that set the agenda of the fourth ASEAN summit in 1992.

New Foreign Policy Statement of Ali Alatas

In August 1988, at a forum on Indonesia's foreign policy in Yogyakarta, Ali Alatas presented a paper stating that Indonesia should continue to play a major role in both regional and international affairs and should project a higher profile. Many observers interpreted the speech as new official policy. (See Chapter 11 for details.)

Jakarta Informal Meeting (JIM)

Indonesia wanted to show its leadership in regional affairs by attempting to help solve the Kampuchean problem. Thus in 1980, Suharto visited Prime Minister Hussein Onn in Malaysia. The Kuantan Principle was drawn up, aimed at urging Vietnam to withdraw from Kampuchea. In return, Vietnam would be given economic aid. Thailand was very displeased and the Kuantan Principle was quietly abandoned.[6] Later, a "Cocktail Party" was proposed but Vietnam did not respond favourably. The venture was a failure. In 1987, the Jakarta Informal Meeting was proposed. This time, as a result of changes in the international environment, Vietnam agreed to attend. This made Indonesia the focus of international attention.[7]

Beijing and Dili

It seems that Suharto's high foreign policy profile has not always been supported by the military. Suharto appeared to be able to get his way, however, as evidenced, for example, by the restoration of diplomatic ties between Jakarta and Beijing. Suharto made a surprise announcement in February 1989 that Indonesia would start the process of normalization with the PRC. The military was not enthusiastic about this "early normalization". (See Chapter 7 for details.)

Another example of Suharto's foreign policy initiative was his response to the Dili Affair on 12 November 1991. Suharto was in full control and he wanted to keep his distance from the military establishment.

Since the annexation of East Timor is one of the most important issues in Suharto's foreign policy, greater detail on Indonesia's involvement in East Timor is required here. Apart from the "integration" of East Timor, Suharto's subsequent role on the Dili Affair and its impact on Indonesia's foreign policy will be discussed.

Origins of the East Timor Issue

Many observers argue that Suharto's foreign policy is different from that of Sukarno in that Sukarno was aggressive, as evidenced in his campaign to recover West Irian from the Dutch and *Konfrontasi* (confrontation) with Malaysia, while Suharto is benign because his Government is more interested in developing Indonesia's economy. The only exception, according to this view, is the annexation of East Timor, the former Portuguese colony.

Why did Indonesia invade and eventually incorporate East Timor into its territory? The reasons are complex, but the development of events in East Timor and Indonesia's intention to include their Timorese "brothers" in a big Indonesian family appear to be motivated by two major factors. Many people argue that Indonesia had been interested in East Timor long before open conflict arose among the East Timorese. When Indonesia was preparing for its own independence, both Mohammad Yamin and Sukarno attempted to include East Timor as part of Indonesian territory. The idea was eventually abandoned due to opposition within Indonesia and change in the international situation.[8]

For several decades there was no clear evidence that Indonesia was concerned with East Timor. This was partly due to the fact that East Timor was quite peaceful and did not present a threat to Jakarta. The situation began to change in the 1970s when new developments in Portugal began to affect its colony. This point will be elaborated later.

The attitude of Indonesian leaders towards East Timor was divided. Indonesian Foreign Minister, Adam Malik, for instance, made a statement that Indonesia would support the liberation movement of East Timor if the Timorese wished it.[9] It was also reported that, as late as June 1974, Malik wrote to Jose Ramos-Horta, the representative of the Timorese Social Democratic Association (ASDT, which later became Fretilin), "assuring him that Indonesia supports independence of East Timor".[10] Malik later changed his mind on this question.

The military leaders, including President Suharto and Ali Murtopo, were not in favour of independence for East Timor. In fact, in September 1974, when Australian Prime Minister Gough Whitlam visited Suharto in Indonesia, he agreed that the eventual integration of East Timor into Indonesia was the best solution.[11] However, he also stated that the views of the East Timorese should be respected and that "public reaction in Australia would be hostile if Indonesia used force".[12] In October 1974, Ali Murtopo visited Lisbon and conducted secret talks with the Portuguese at which he noted that Jakarta only accepted East Timor linked to either Portugal or Indonesia.[13] Apparently, Indonesia was concerned with the future of East Timor. This was a result of the April 1974 "Flower Revolution" in Portugal and Portugal's subsequent declaration allowing its overseas provinces (East Timor was one of its "overseas provinces") the right of self-determination and independence.

Indonesia had some supporters in East Timor who had been trained in Indonesia, and on 27 May 1974 they established a minor pro-Indonesian party called the Timorese Popular Democratic Party (Apodeti).[14] The central demand of this party was the integration of East Timor into Indonesia. Two weeks earlier, two major parties were also formed, indicating that the Portuguese had not prepared the East Timorese for their independence. The two parties formed were the Timorese Democratic Union (UDT), which was a right-wing party, and the left-wing revolutionary front for the Independence of East Timor, known as Fretilin.[15] The UDT initially favoured continuing links with Lisbon but later supported independence after several years of preparation. Fretilin on the other hand, demanded immediate independence. In January 1975, a coalition government consisting of the UDT and the Fretilin was established. The Indonesian Government was closely watching developments in East Timor.

Given the international political situation during the Cold War, it is not possible to know whether East Timor could have been developed into an independent state, free from external interference. Indonesia was concerned with the possibility of East Timor turning into a Southeast Asian Cuba. It seems likely that an independent East Timor would have become unstable and, sooner or later, would have had to submit to Indonesia. But the process would have been peaceful, however, if East Timor was in the hands of a government acceptable to Indonesia.[16] It is also possible that Indonesia feared that an independent East Timor would set an example for other ethnic groups in Indonesia who might demand independence.

The coalition between the right-wing UDT and left-wing Fretilin was precarious. Fretilin became more militant and the UDT feared that the new left-wing government in Portugal might favour Fretilin over the UDT.[17] Indonesians were suspicious of Fretilin links with Communists in Portugal as well as with the defunct PKI.[18] UDT leaders appeared to be responsive to Indonesian pressure. In July 1975, the UDT chairman was even quoted as saying that "UDT would accept the union of East Timor with Indonesia if the people of East Timor so wished".[19] Not surprisingly, civil war broke out in August 1975, and the Fretilin succeeded in getting the upper hand. Indonesia, backing the UDT and Apodeti, began a pacification campaign. Indonesia sent so-called "volunteers" to East Timor to carry out military operations. General Ali Murtopo, then personal assistant of President Suharto, was in charge of the East Timor plan.[20] He was later replaced by Benny Murdani, then the Army Chief of Staff.

Contrary to their expectations, the Indonesian military operation was neither smooth or speedy. It encountered stiff resistance from the Fretilin. The Indonesian side suffered many casualties, but Jakarta was determined to take over East Timor and continued to send in additional "volunteers" who remained there to control the local population.

The East Timor Issue at the UN

The UN Trusteeship Committee called for Indonesia to withdraw from East Timor and to respect the integrity of East Timor's territory. This resolution passed by 69 votes (including China, the Soviet Union, and Australia) to 11 (including Indonesia, Malaysia, Thailand, and the Philippines), with 38 abstentions (among them Singapore, USA, and the EEC countries). Adam Malik, then Indonesian Foreign Minister, responded that his Government would not be bound by the resolution because Indonesia had no troops in East Timor, only "volunteers". The fight continued and on 28 November 1975, the Fretilin unilaterally declared the independence of the Democratic Republic of East Timor.[21]

More Indonesian "volunteers" were sent to East Timor soon afterwards. Portugal protested Indonesia's military intervention resulting in the severance of diplomatic ties between the two countries. On 12 December 1975, the General Assembly of the UN passed a resolution by 72 votes to 10 calling for Indonesia to withdraw from East Timor. Ten days later, the UN Security Council passed a unanimous resolution to the same effect. These resolutions had little effect on Indonesian actions in East Timor. Indonesian "volunteers" remained in East Timor on the grounds that they had been requested to do so by their East Timorese brothers in order to keep law and order.[22]

The Indonesian Press and East Timor

The Indonesian press reaction towards Indonesian policy in East Timor was generally favourable. *Kompas,* a leading Jakarta daily, urged the public to give full support to the Government. It blamed Portugal for the turbulence in East Timor and justified Indonesian involvement in the area as a means to secure

Indonesian national interest. It criticized the UN for failing to understand the origins of the Timor problem. The only newspaper which was critical of Indonesian foreign policy in general, and "Malik's policy" in particular, was *Merdeka,* a daily edited by a former Sukarnoist, B.M. Diah. Diah's articles, serialized in *Merdeka* in January 1976, were one of the sharpest public attacks on a Cabinet Minister (that is, Adam Malik) for several years.

Diah agreed that it was in the Indonesian national interest to send volunteers to East Timor. Like many other Indonesians, Diah believed that an unstable East Timor presented a threat to Indonesian security. Diah regretted that Indonesia had been isolated in the world. The West had not backed Indonesia during the Timor crisis, Communist states were hostile towards the New Order, and Third World countries were critical of Indonesia. Diah attributed this isolation to Indonesia's complete dependence on the West. He maintained that this situation could only be remedied if Indonesia pursued an independent economic policy, refusing imperialist aid and foreign investment.

Responding to this criticism, Malik argued that the fact the West did not side with Indonesia on the Timor issue indicated that Indonesia had pursued an independent policy. He also commented that the luxurious Arya Duta Hotel (in Jakarta), which was owned by Diah, had received foreign aid and had benefited from it. Malik argued that Fretilin was controlled by Communists. "If we recognize Fretilin, it is possible that our name will rise in the world. But this would mean that we have betrayed our nation".[23] Malik later tried to intimidate Diah: "If anyone dares to [recognize Fretilin], let him try. Such action will infuriate the public and his newspaper will surely be shut down".[24] Because of the series of articles, Diah was questioned by the authorities. He was warned but not detained. The articles were published as a book in June 1976 and immediately banned by the Government.

With the help of Indonesian "volunteers", the UDT and Apodeti eventually defeated the Fretilin. Leaders of the Fretilin fled and established a government in exile. Their chances of success appeared to be very slim. Since Timor is small and is remote from the area of interest of any major power, it was not likely to become a world concern. Understandably, by the first half of 1976, the anger of many countries in the UN in December had largely subsided. On 1 June 1976, a pro-Indonesian 28-member Assembly of East Timor approved a petition to integrate the territory into Indonesia. On 15 July, the Indonesian Parliament passed a bill concerning the formal integration of East Timor into Indonesia as its twenty-seventh province.

Indonesian intervention in East Timor at first caused an international outcry, but this did not affect Indonesia's relations with other ASEAN countries. Three out of the four other ASEAN nations supported Jakarta on the East Timor issue while Singapore abstained from voting. In January 1976, before the first Summit of ASEAN countries in Bali, Adam Malik, in an interview with *Tempo,* a leading

Jakarta news magazine, noted that "Singapore is afraid of being Timorized by Indonesia or Malaysia".[25] It was the way that Indonesia had stepped in and annexed East Timor that caused concern to Singapore. In the following year, however, when the East Timor issue was discussed again in the UN, the Singapore delegation voted with other ASEAN members in a demonstration of ASEAN solidarity. President Suharto sent a cable to the Prime Minister of Singapore expressing his appreciation of Singapore's support for Indonesia.

The East Timor issue is far from settled. Every year there is a debate in the UN and a vote on the issue. In 1982, Indonesia, supported by friendly nations, wanted to delete the item from the UN General Assembly agenda once and for all, but the attempt was not successful. The support for the resolution, which had been proposed by Fretilin and Portugal, was lessened, however. In 1981, 54 countries voted for Fretilin, while 42 supported Indonesia. Another 46 countries abstained. In 1982, the Fretilin votes were reduced to 50, while Indonesia gained 46, and the number of abstentions increased to 50 (See table below.) The Indonesian Government hopes that, as time passes, the issue will either be forgotten or dropped. After 1982, no vote on East Timor was taken in the UN General Assembly as the issue was handled by a UN committee. This was considered as a victory by Jakarta.

Votes on the East Timor Issue in the UNGA (1975-1982)

Year	For	Against	Abstained
1975	72	10	43
1976	68	20	49
1977	67	26	47
1978	59	31	44
1979	62	31	45
1980	58	35	46
1981	54	42	46
1982	50	46	50

Sources: Dusan J. Djonovich (ed.), *United Nations Resolutions: Series II*, Vols. IX & XI (New York: Oceana Publications, 1990).

Since Alatas became Foreign Minister in 1988, Indonesia has intensified its efforts to persuade Portugal and other countries in the United Nations to accept the annexation of East Timor as a *fait accompli*. In September 1991, Alatas told the Indonesian Parliament that two delegations — one of Portuguese legislators and another of UN Ambassadors from countries selected by the UN Secretary-General — would visit East Timor at the end of the year.[26] Alatas said that "with the visit, we will get closer to an overall settlement, especially at the United Nations".²⁷

The unexpected occurrence of the anti-Jakarta demonstration in Dili on 12 November 1991, which resulted in the death of more than 100 people, shattered Alatas' efforts to make the world accept East Timor as Indonesian territory.²⁸ Jakarta was criticized by the international community for the alleged massacre of the East Timorese. Canada, the Netherlands and Denmark decided to suspend aid to Indonesia as a result of the shootings.²⁹ Australia did not follow suit but threatened to recall its envoy if the investigation committee formed by Indonesia to study the incident did not produce a credible report. Gareth Evans, Foreign Minister of Australia, was dispatched to Jakarta to show Australia's concern over the incident.³⁰ However, no concrete action was taken to warn Indonesia. At the July 1992 meeting of the Consultative Group on Indonesia, consisting of 18 aid donor governments, the donor agencies and the governments (including US and Japan) pledged $4.95 billion in new annual economic aid to Indonesia. This was higher than that of 1991.³¹ According to a report, during the meeting "only U.S. delegation raised the East Timor issue, and no government responded to this initiative".³² Nevertheless, the East Timor problem is still far from being solved.

East Timor under Indonesian Rule

In order to put the problem in perspective and to show the increasing role of President Suharto in both domestic and foreign policy, developments in East Timor after Indonesian annexation must be considered. General Ali Murtopo, who was in charge of matters relating to East Timor, was replaced by General Benny Murdani (who was Minister of Defence from 1988-1993) in 1978.³³ Murdani was very firm about the East Timor issue and was determined not only to keep East Timor in Indonesian hands, but also to speed up the Indonesianization process.³⁴ He used both the carrot and stick in order to pacify the East Timorese. Economic development has begun and an Indonesian system of education was introduced. Money was poured in to sustain the backward ex-Portuguese colony. At the same time, the military operation was continued in order to wipe out Fretilin. The military operation was not completely successful, however. One source indicates that in 1981 Fretilin had between 150 and 600 members. In 1989 another gives the number as 1,500.³⁵

Although Indonesian troops have used violence to subdue East Timor, they have failed to get rid of the armed Fretilin completely. Nonetheless, there is little chance for the Fretilin to succeed in its bid for power. The Suharto Government has appeared to be confident. By the end of 1988, the Indonesian

Government felt that it had fuller control over East Timor and it decided to open East Timor to outsiders. Some maintain that the group which was eager to open up East Timor was made up of civilians, among whom was the Minister of Foreign Affairs.

The decision to open up East Timor might also be connected with Suharto's desire for Indonesia to play an expanded role and particularly with its intention to become the Chairman of the Non-Aligned Movement (NAM). Many NAM countries were critical of Indonesia's action in East Timor, and the Indonesian Government wished to pacify these countries so that they would support Indonesia as Chairman. In addition, Indonesia wanted the world, especially the UN, to accept that East Timor under Indonesian rule is becoming stable and prosperous. In October 1989, the Pope was invited to Indonesia for a six-day visit. It was reported that the Portuguese President pleaded with the Pope to skip East Timor but failed to convince him. An Indonesian commentator interpreted this as an indication that the Pope favoured East Timor's integration into Indonesia.[36] It was in fact Jakarta's intention to gain the support of the Vatican on the East Timor problem. It was also reported that there was a demonstration by students from the Technological High School in Dili urging the Pope's support of their position against the "integration" of East Timor.[37]

Perhaps the Indonesian Government thought that the resentment of Jakarta was confined to only a few individuals.[38] As economic development proceeded in East Timor, it was hoped that the Timorese would eventually accept Indonesian rule. The Indonesian press argued that East Timor was backward under Portuguese rule: there were only 12 kilometres of road; 70 primary schools, and one secondary school. Ninety-two per cent of the population was illiterate. After "integration" with Indonesia, roads were built in every district. There are 569 primary schools, 90 junior middle schools, and 33 senior middle schools.[39] These material developments gave new confidence to the Suharto Government.

It was not surprising that, through the good offices of the UN, Indonesia eventually agreed to invite 13 Portuguese members of parliament to visit East Timor.[40] These members of parliament would also be allowed to go anywhere and to talk to anybody.[41] The scheduled visit of the Portugal parliamentary delegation was eventually aborted at the last minute because of a journalist. It was reported that Portugal insisted on including an Australian journalist named Jill Jolliffe in the Portuguese delegation. Alatas argued that Indonesia had made many concessions to Portugal but refused to allow a journalist, who was a "Fretilin Propagandist", to join the Portuguese team.[42]

It was reported that the military disagreed with the opening up of East Timor, especially with the visit of Portuguese parliamentarians.[43] Even the Governor of East Timor, Mario Viegas Carrascalao, was quoted as saying that he was against the visit. In his view, this would only provoke the anti-integration group.[44]

The Dili Tragedy and President Suharto

The planned visit of the Portuguese parliamentarians to East Timor excited East Timorese youth. On 28 October 1991 during the Indonesian Youth Pledge Day there was a demonstration in Dili which led to physical conflict. Two of the demonstrators were killed.[45] On 12 November 1991, a large group of East Timorese visited the grave of the two victims to lay wreaths on them. Security forces were taken by surprise. The army was reported to have responded violently, resulting in many casualties.

After the incident, General Try Sutrisno made a statement that the army had been attacked by the mob and, when they reacted, 19 people were shot dead.[46] The East Timorese claimed that the army had begun shooting without provocation. They said that more than 200 people were killed, and a larger number were wounded. There were video tapes of the incident made by a British journalist and an Italian priest which were shown on TV all over the world.[47] The world was shocked.

It should be noted that the situation in the 1990s is different from in the 1970s when Indonesia took over East Timor. In the 1970s the Cold War was still on and the Communists were still aggressive. In the mid-1970s, Communists scored a major victory in Indochina which caused concern among the Western states. Therefore, Indonesian action in East Timor, which was seen as a means to stop a left-wing group from coming to power, was tolerated. In the 1990s, however, with the Cold War over, and Communism no longer a threat, the West became more concerned with human rights issues.

Many Western countries criticized Indonesia and some of them decided to hold back economic aid to Indonesia, demanding a proper investigation of the event. The Netherlands, Australia, Denmark and Canada were among these countries. Even the United States and Japan were reported to have pressured Indonesia. An end to foreign aid might have affected the Indonesian national budget for 1992/1993.[48]

When the incident took place, President Suharto was on an overseas trip. Probably due to international pressure, he gave in to external demands that a national commission (Komisi Penyelidik Nasional) be formed to investigate the event. The commission, headed by Supreme Court Judge M. Djaelani, was made up of civilians and was said to be independent of the Government.[49] When the preliminary findings were released, they were different from the army version. The report stated that the army had overreacted to the incident and that 50 people were killed while 90 were still missing. The report was submitted to President Suharto. The President, as the supreme commander of the Indonesian armed forces, instructed that the territorial commanders who were in charge of East Timor, Major General Sintong Panjaitan and Brigadier General R.S. Warouw, be removed.[50] It was later reported that six officers had been found guilty of negligence for their actions during the 12 November shootings and eight others would face court martial. The action of President Suharto put the armed forces in a defensive position. It was reported that the armed forces wanted to fight back through its "spokesman", Benny Murdani, by arguing that it should not shoulder full blame for the Dili tragedy,[51] but the fact remains that the armed forces accepted the President's decision. The report and the removal of the officers served to pacify the anger of some donor countries. Ali Alatas was sent overseas to engage in dialogue with foreign leaders and his mission was reported to have been quite successful.

The Dili Incident shows that the East Timor problem is still far from being solved. The pro-liberalization group in the Suharto Government has underestimated the strength of East Timorese nationalism. They were overly optimistic concerning the achievement of economic development in this newly acquired province. In fact, at the time East Timor was still very economically poor, with the average monthly salary only Rp.20,000, enough to live for just 10 days.[52] These two factors were at the roots of the Dili tragedy.

The Indonesian Government, under international pressure, was forced to make concessions. It appears that President Suharto fired the military officers in order to pacify the international community. There was also speculation that, in fact, it was a superb strategy on the part of the President to undermine the strength of the military in domestic politics. As the 1993 presidential election was approaching, it was rumoured that a group within the military did not want to see Suharto stand for election again. According to this argument, the Dili affair, in fact, gave the President an opportunity to strengthen his own position *vis-a-vis* the military.

It should also be noted that while the Indonesian Government was making concessions to the international community, Jakarta also attempted to fight back. Indonesia was annoyed by continuous Dutch criticism of Indonesia's human rights records and the linking of aid to human rights issues. In March 1992, Jakarta rejected Dutch assistance to Indonesia and also demanded that the IGGI, an organization of which the Netherlands was chairman, be replaced by a new organization.[53] Indonesia was able to do this because the Netherlands only contributed 1.9 per cent of total IGGI aid to Indonesia.[54]

In addition to its counter-offensive, there was also a tightening up in East Timor. People who were suspected of opposing the integration of East Timor were arrested and tried. Some who were accused of subversion were threatened with the death penalty, but were actually given heavy jail sentences.[55] The Indonesian army scored a victory on 20 November 1992, one year after the Dili Affair, when it arrested Xanana Gusmao, the leader of Fretilin. The capture of Xanana has undermined the strength of Fretilin significantly.[56]

It is worth noting that Suharto's eldest daughter, Mrs Siti Hardiyanti Hastuti Rukmana (better known as Mbak Tutut), has been active in attempting to help solve the East Timor issue since the re-election of Suharto as President in 1993. On 17 December 1993, she surprised the Indonesian public when she met Abilio Araujo, an ex-Fretilin leader, in the Indonesian Embassy in London. At the meeting, she was accompanied by Indonesian Ambassador, J.E. Habibie and Ambassador-at-Large, Lopez da Cruz, while Abilio was accompanied by Manuel Joaqim Rodriques Macedo, the President of the Portugal Indonesia Friendship Asociation.[57] Soon after the meeting, on 3 January 1994, she established the Perhimpunan Persahabatan Indonesia Portugal (PPIP, Indonesia-Portugal Friendship Association).[58] Four days after the formation of the PPIP, she received General Carlos Galva de Melo from Portugal which was widely publicized, giving the impression that Jakarta-Lisbon relations were improving.[59] Nevertheless, the East Timor issue remains unresolved.

Opposition to Indonesia persisted and Indonesian troops continued to come into conflict with the local population, especially with the anti-integration group. The most serious conflict which drew renewed international criticism was the slaying of six East Timorese on 12 January 1995 by the security forces at the Liquisa district, a village which was 37 kilometres from Dili.[60] Initially it was reported that the six East Timorese were armed rebels who were killed during the firefight, but a fact-finding mission of the Indonesian Human Rights Commission subsequently reported that they were unarmed civilians. The Indonesian military was forced to admit that there was a "violation of procedures" by the troops involved in the incident and two of them were eventually tried.[61] However, peace has not really returned to the land. East Timorese nationalism is likely to exist for some time.

Conclusion

After the 1983 presidential election, there is no doubt that Suharto became more assertive in foreign policy-making. He was not always in agreement with the military establishment over foreign policy issues. A number of examples have been cited in this chapter to illustrate the point. The actual "confrontation" between the President and the military establishment was on the East Timor issue when he expressed his disagreement over the military's handling of the Dili Affair. It seems that the military accepted his verdict. The concessions Suharto made in the Dili Affair do not mean that Indonesia did not want to integrate East Timor.

In retrospect, East Timor has become one of the most important issues in Suharto's foreign policy. It shows that Suharto's Indonesia is concerned with security issues but is also very nationalistic. Indonesia believed it had the right to include East Timor as part of Indonesia because the East Timorese population are Indonesian brothers. This is a prime example in which the problems of security and nationalism have been fused into one. The East Timor example was perhaps unique in the sense that East Timor was a colony. It achieved "independence" through "merger" with Indonesia. But critics of Indonesia have argued that it was a form of "internal colonialism". They have even wondered whether this would set the pattern for Indonesia's future behaviour.

The East Timor issue is also important in the sense that it was one of the major issues affecting Jakarta-Canberra relations. Australian acceptance of annexation as a *fait accompli* has gradually improved Indonesian-Australian relations. Future friction over East Timor may still occur due to the issue of refugees and other problems.

An important point concerning the East Timor issue, especially the Dili tragedy, is the active role played by President Suharto. He was able to take the initiative in pacifying international critics and to show his extraordinary skills in dealing with both domestic and international politics. Alatas continued to enjoy the confidence of the President in dealing with the East Timor issue even after the Dili affair, and this was often at the expense of the military. There is no doubt that it has enhanced the prestige of the Minister of Foreign Affairs. This has, at times, been misread as the Foreign Ministry being able to overrule the military establishment. In fact, President Suharto called all the shots. It is worth noting that Suharto's daughter has also involved herself in the diplomacy concerning East Timor.

It has been suggested that one of the possible solutions of the East Timor issue is to conduct a referendum. This has been strongly opposed by Jakarta. Mochtar Kusumaatmadja argued recently that conducting a referendum was tantamount to "denying what we already have for almost twenty years". He maintained that integration is a form of self-determination which has not been well explained by the Indonesians.[62]

NOTES

1. Leo Suryadinata and Sharon Siddique (eds.), *Trends in Indonesia II* (Singapore: Singapore University Press, 1981), p. 26.
2. See "Bukan Sekadar Memutar Film Lama, Bukan?", *Tempo*, 27 April 1985, pp. 12-15.
3. I heard this argument in Jakarta. However, Chan Heng Chee noted that this was "clearly a symbolic act uniting the two countries". See her article in "Singapore Foreign Policy and Domestic Politics", in Robert Scalapino et al. (eds.), *Asia and the Major Powers*, p. 302.
4. *Straits Times Weekly Overseas Edition*, 19 December 1987, p. 10.
5. Ibid.
6. Liefer argues that the Kuantan Principle was eventually abandoned because "it also proved unacceptable to Vietnam, because the statement failed to take account of the asymmetry in the relations with China and the Soviet Union". See Michael Leifer, *Dictionary of the Modern Politics of South-East Asia* (London and New York: Routledge, 1995), p. 135.
7. For a discussion on JIM I, see Chang Pao-min, "Kampuchean Conflict: The Diplomatic Breakthrough", *Pacific Review*, Vol. 1, No. 4, pp. 429-437.

8   For a discussion on the issue, see Chapter 1.
9   J. Stephen Hoadley, "Indonesia's Annexation of East Timor: Political, Administrative, and Developmental Initiatives", *Southeast Asian Affairs* 1977, p. 134.
10 Cited in John G. Taylor, *Indonesia's Forgotten War: The Hidden History of East Timor* (London and New Jersey: Zed, 1992), p. 200.
11 Ibid., p. 200. Also Hamish McDonald, *Suharto's Indonesia* (Australia: Fontana Books, 1980).
12 Ibid.
13 Ibid., p. 36.
14 Ibid., pp. 134-135.
15 The UDT was formed on 11 May 1974. The Timorese Social Democratic Association (ASDT) was formed on 12 May 1974 but it changed its name to Fretilin (Frente Revolucionara do Timor Reste Independence) on 12 September 1974. Ibid.
16 Recently one writer argued that there was a difference between Suharto and the Murtopo-Murdani group over the East Timor issue. He argued that Suharto was not in favour of taking East Timor by force. It was the Murtopo-Murdani group which was eager to use force. See Riwanto Tirtosudarmo, "Indonesia 1991: Quest for Democracy in a Turbulent Year", *Southeast Asian Affairs 1991*, p. 137. However, it is difficult to believe that the Murtopo-Murdani action was not endorsed by the President.
17 Finnqeir Hiorth, *Timor: Past and Present*, South East Asian Monograph No. 17, (Townsville James Cook University of Northern Queensland, 1985), p. 25.
18 Ibid., p. 24.
19 Hiorth, p. 26.
20 Hamish McDonald, *Suharto's Indonesia*, p. 195.
21 See Leo Suryadinata, "Indonesia in 1976: A Year of Challenge", *Southeast Asian Affairs* 1977, p. 117.
22 Ibid.
23 See "Terpencil Atau Bagaimana", *Tempo*, 24 January 1976, p. 5.
24 Ibid.
25 "Adam Malik Menjawab", *Tempo*, 7 February 1976, p. 5.
26 *Straits Times*, 19 September 1991. However, in October 1991, there was a report that the scheduled visit of Portugal's parliamentary delegation was postponed. *Straits Times*, 29 October 1991.
27 Ibid.
28 On the 12 November 1991 affair, see special reports in *Tempo*, 23 November 1991, pp. 21-32; 30 November 1991, pp. 22-23. See also Adam Schwarz, "Over the Edge", *Far Eastern Economic Review*, 28 November 1991, pp. 15-16.
29 "Ancaman itu Bukan Yang Pertama", *Tempo*, 21 December 1991, p. 90. Jakarta was divided on the issue of aid. One group did not think that the suspension of aid would affect Indonesian economy while the other was very concerned. Suharto stated that economic aid should not be tied to human rights issue.
30 "'Konsep' Untuk Jakarta", *Tempo*, 28 December 1991, p. 15.
31 According to Richard Borsuk, Jakarta's New Aid Group commitment was higher than $4.75 billion pledged in 1991 and the $4.8 billion recommended by the World Bank. Reported in *Asian Wall Street Journal*, 20 July 1992, cited in Larry Niksch, *Indonesian-U.S. Relations and Impact of the East Timor Issue*, CRS Report for Congress (Washington DC: The Library of Congress, 15 December 1992), p. 16.
32 Ibid., p. 16.
33 Hiorth, p. 68.
34 Donald Weatherbee, "Indonesianization of East Timor", *Contemporary Southeast Asia*, Vol. 3, No. 1 (June 1981), pp. 1-24.
35 An American scholar who visited East Timor in 1981 noted that there were between 150 and 600 Armed Fretilin (Interview). However, in 1988, the IISS in London estimated that the Fretilin had 1,500 men. (IISS, *Military Balance 1988-1989*), p. 164. In November 1992, Xanana, the leader of Fretilin, was arrested by the Indonesian security force. It was

reported that some of his followers also surrendered. This has undoubtedly weakened the resistance movement, but did not necessarily eradicate Fretilin.

36 Daniel Setyawan, "The Visit of Pope John Paul II to Indonesia", *Indonesian Quarterly*, Vol. XVII, No. 4 (1989), pp. 290-295 (especially p. 293.)
37 Ibid.
38 It is interesting to note that Alatas, in an interview with *Tempo* after the Dili Shootings, argued that the silent majority has been in favour of Indonesia while only hundreds of outspoken East Timorese have rejected the integration of East Timor into Indonesia. See "Saya Tidak Mau Dirongrong", *Tempo*, 28 March 1992, pp. 22-23.
39 "Antara Trauma dan Kecemburuan", *Tempo*, 23 November 1991, p. 27.
40 "Tim-Tim Siap Buka-Bukaan", *Tempo*, 26 October 1991, p. 43.
41 Ibid., p. 44.
42 *Straits Times*, 29 October 1991; *Tempo*, 2 November 1991, p. 28.
43 *Far Eastern Economic Review*, 9 January 1992, p. 8.
44 "Letupan Kecil di Gudang Isu", *Tempo*, 9 November 1991.
45 Ibid.
46 *Far Eastern Economic Review*, 9 January 1992, p. 8.
47 "Menunggu Hasil Komisi Djaelani", *Tempo*, 30 November 1991, pp. 24-25.
48 "Peristiwa itu Tak Jatuh Dari Langit", *Tempo*, 7 December 1991, pp. 22-23.
49 "Komisi Tanpa Hak Menindak", *Tempo*, 30 November 1991, p. 24.
50 "Dan Panglima Tertinggi pun Memutuskan", *Tempo*, 4 January 1992, pp. 14-15; Also *FEER*, 9 January 1992, p. 8.
51 Paul Jacob, "Murdani Speaks Up for Military, Warns of Economic Inequities", *Straits Times*, 24 March 1992.
52 "Saya Ingin Menulis Buku", *Tempo*, 30 November 1991, p. 27.
53 "IGGI Bubar, Binnenhof pun Terkejut", *Tempo*, 4 April 1992, pp. 14-17; See also Chapter 9 for a discussion of this issue.
54 "Kembali Ke Sistem Normal", *Tempo*, 4 April 1992, pp. 22-23.
55 *Straits Times*, 19 March 1992.
56 Xanana was put on trial in Dili and was sentenced to life imprisonment. See *Straits Times*, 28 May 1993.
57 *Forum Keadilan*, Vol.3, No.5, 23 June 1994, p. 23.
58 Ibid., p.24, also *Sinar*, 24 January 1994, p. 29.
59 *Forum Keadilan*, 23 June 1994, p. 24.
60 "Ninja Politis di antara Dili-Liquisa", *Sinar*, 25 February 1995, p. 10.
61 *Straits Times*, 4 June 1995.
62 "Sudah Kasip Menutup Timtim Lagi", *Tiras*, Vol. 1, No. 6 (9 March 1995) p. 50.

5

Indonesia's Relations with the Ase An states
Regional Stability and Leadership Role

Introduction

In the previous chapter Indonesia's foreign policy under Suharto has been discussed to show the increasing role of the military and the President himself in the decision-making process. From the early 1980s, Suharto was the major foreign policy-maker. In this chapter, discussion focuses on the rise of the Association of Southeast Asian Nations (ASEAN) and Indonesia's role in this regional grouping. The role of the military and the President in Indonesia's bilateral relations with individual ASEAN states (except Vietnam) will also be examined.

The Rise of Ase An

It has been argued by many Indonesian leaders, at least prior to 1988, that ASEAN is the cornerstone of Indonesia's foreign policy.[1] In other words, the ASEAN states are crucial to Indonesia's national interests, that is, its stability and security. It is not surprising, then, that Indonesia was instrumental in establishing this regional organization.

When Suharto came to power in 1966, he immediately ended the confrontation with Malaysia and began to show to the world,[2] especially to the West, that he would abandon the aggressive policy of Sukarno. He was convinced that, with political stability, he would be able to develop Indonesia's economy through foreign investment and foreign aid. The economy during the Sukarno era was seriously troubled. This partly accounted for the political instability of that time. Economic rehabilitation was perceived by the new leadership as a way to legitimize their new regime. Thus, the major concern of the new elite was to create political stability in the region, particularly among the non-Communist ASEAN states. ASEAN, as a regional organization, would serve this purpose. Only under stable conditions would Indonesia be able to develop economically.

As a matter of fact, ASEAN was not the first regional organization in Southeast Asia. As early as 1955, the Southeast Asian Treaty Organization (SEATO) was established by the United States to combat Communism in the region. But only two (namely, the Philippines and Thailand) out of its eight members were from Southeast Asia.[3] This military pact failed to achieve its goal because the threat posed by Communism took the form of subversive activities and could not be solved through conventional military means. In addition, most of the members were not committed to the goal. Like the Communist states, anti-colonialist Indonesia was hostile towards this organization. Malaya, a British ally but not a member of SEATO, was fully aware of SEATO's unpopularity among some states in the region and wanted to establish a security organization outside SEATO. It was not successful. By 1961, with the support of the Philippines and Thailand, Malaya eventually formed an economic and cultural organization known as the Association of Southeast Asia (ASA) aimed at promoting economic and cultural co-operation.[4] Tunku Abdul Rahman of Malaya was eager to invite other Southeast Asian nations to join, but none showed any interest. Indonesia, under Sukarno, was suspicious of ASA and regarded the organization as serving the interests of Western imperialists.

ASA was underdeveloped due to conflicts among the member states. The Philippine claim over Sabah in 1962 eventually killed this embryonic regional grouping. Another regional (racial) grouping known as Maphilindo (Malaya-Philippines-Indonesia) was formed for a brief period in August 1963, but it disintegrated as soon as Indonesia revived its confrontation with Malaysia.[5] ASA was revived and resurrected in March 1966 after Ferdinand Marcos modified his policy towards Sabah. Nonetheless, Indonesia refused to join ASA partly because of its "pro-West" image and partly because of Indonesia's desire to form a new regional grouping with a broader base.[6] ASEAN was proposed in place of ASA. Adam Malik, the Indonesian Foreign Minister, failed to interest Burma (now Myanmar) and Cambodia in joining, but membership was declared open to all Southeast Asian states which subscribed to ASEAN's principles and aims.

It is possible to argue that, through ASEAN, Indonesia should be able to play a leading role in the region as it is the largest country in the grouping. Indonesia's leadership has been realized to a certain extent, although it has not always had its own way. On many fundamental issues, however, Indonesia's views have been taken into consideration. For instance, it was upon the insistence of Adam Malik, then Foreign Minister, that a clause on the temporary and defensive nature of foreign military bases in the region was inserted into the ASEAN declaration.[7] Indonesia has always considered foreign military bases in Southeast Asia a threat to the independence of Southeast Asia, particularly its own. Foreign military bases are also perceived as a constraint on Indonesia's role in regional affairs. Nonetheless, Indonesian leaders (including Adam Malik) realized that it was unrealistic to demand the immediate removal of foreign (namely, American) bases, and hence, a compromise was made among the member states.

The formation of ASEAN was supported by five regional states as it was seen to serve the national interests of each member. Malaysia, under Tunku Abdul Rahman, was eager to join the organization because it saw this as a means to promote regional co-operation, especially with Indonesia.[8] After one confrontation with Jakarta, Kuala Lumpur could not afford another. Ethnic Chinese-dominated Singapore, which had been part of Malaysia (1963-1965), expressed its wish to become a member, partly because of a desire to emphasize its Southeast Asian identity.[9] The regional organization would also guarantee the sovereignty of small states. Thailand was keen to join ASEAN as it considered the new organization to be a continuation of ASA with a larger membership. It perceived ASEAN as a collective political defence against hostile countries, presumably its Communist neighbours in the north.[10] The Philippines under Marcos was equally eager to establish its Southeast Asian identity through a regional organization because, as a Catholic state and an ex-American colony, it was often perceived by other Southeast Asian states as non-Southeast Asian. Perhaps, it was also the intention of the Philippines to have more cordial relations with its neighbours in an effort to solve regional disputes. It is reasonable to say that ASEAN was able to serve each country's national interests and hence gained the initial support of the states concerned.

There appears to have been a convergence of national interests among the non-Communist and development-oriented ASEAN states with regard to regional political stability in order to develop their respective economies. Other national interests have not always been harmonized. Most of the ASEAN states have similar agricultural and mineral products. They are also in different stages of economic development. Not surprisingly, economic co-operation among the ASEAN states has developed very slowly. Some have argued that the lack of economic co-operation among ASEAN members was not due to economic factors but to lack of strong political will. It was also due to the complacent attitude of ASEAN political leaders who have not seen the urgency for such co-operation, at least before 1992.[11] For one thing, many countries continue to enjoy high economic growth rates despite the lack of economic integration. It seems that the combination of economic and political factors has contributed to the absence of economic integration.[12]

In addition to their dissimilar perceptions of economic integration, the ASEAN countries have had different perceptions of external threat. This is due to their different geographical locations, historical experiences and population compositions. For instance, Thailand has seen Vietnam as its major threat while Indonesia has regarded Beijing as its most serious challenge. Indonesia went along with Thailand (and also Singapore) because this would lend political stability to the ASEAN states. In turn, Indonesia was able to develop its economy, because economic development required political stability in the region. It would seem that the ASEAN states co-operate closely when this serves their interests but they are less co-operative when their national interests conflict. In some cases, Indonesia's self-perception of being a major power has affected its relations with its neighbours. Indonesia's relations with the ASEAN states in terms of bilateral relations, as well as Indonesia's position in the ASEAN context, will be examined below.

Indonesia-Malaysia Relations: Big and Little Brothers

Factors which explain relations between Indonesia and Malaysia are complex, but there is one element which is often present and has to be taken into account when considering the issue. It is that Indonesia has a tendency to act like the big brother and wants to be treated as such. Of course, different political systems, cultures and economic interests are equally important, but these factors alone are unable to account for some Indonesian foreign policy behaviour towards Malaysia.

When Sukarno was still in power, relations between Jakarta and Kuala Lumpur were far from cordial. Indonesia took an anti-colonialist and imperialist stand which contrasted with Malaya's attitude. Nonetheless, Sukarno was interested in forming Maphilindo, an embryonic organization, which was supposed to hold the Malay world (Malaya-Philippines-Indonesia) together. This concept may have originated in the Indonesian nationalist idea of Indonesia Raya. That is, before Indonesia's independence, many leaders hoped to establish an Indonesian state extending beyond the boundaries of the Dutch East Indies (see Chapter 1). But Maphilindo was abandoned when Malaysia was formed and Jakarta renewed confrontation with Kuala Lumpur.

After Suharto came to power and the confrontation with Malaysia ended, socio-cultural relations between the two countries were restored. Many Indonesian teachers and lecturers were sent to Malaysia to teach in Malay schools and at the newly established Universiti Kebangsaan Malaysia. In 1972, the Malay language and Bahasa Indonesia were united by a common spelling system.[13]

Joint security exercises were launched in order to combat Communist activities in Sabah and Sarawak, and an agreement on the Straits of Malacca was signed by Indonesia, Malaysia and Singapore. While Indonesia's view and that of Malaysia were identical as far as the status of the Straits of Malacca was concerned, each considered the Straits a part of its internal waterways.[14]

When Tun Razak became Prime Minister of Malaysia, relations between the two countries improved somewhat. Tun Razak began to reorient Malaysia's foreign policy to advocate neutralization and the establishment of a Zone of Peace, Freedom and Neutrality (ZOPFAN), and opposed the presence of foreign military bases in the region.[15] This concept was eventually adopted by ASEAN as the ideal the ASEAN states should achieve in the future. Jakarta-Kuala Lumpur relations improved further when Hussein Onn became the Prime Minister of Malaysia. This was perhaps related to international developments at the time. In 1975, the three Indochinese states became Communist and, in early 1976, ASEAN leaders held the first ASEAN summit in Bali at which the Treaty of ASEAN Concord and Bali Declaration were generated.

Indonesian and Malaysian perceptions of external threat were quite similar. Although Malaysia had established diplomatic ties with the PRC in 1974 (during the tenure of Tun Razak), Kuala Lumpur's relations with Beijing were less than cordial. China was still considered a major threat to the security of Malaysia because of its support for the Malayan Communist Party.[16] Indonesia, under Suharto, also harboured suspicions of Beijing and considered the PRC a major threat to its security because of Beijing's support for the PKI. It is not surprising then that when the PRC invaded Vietnam to punish the Vietnamese for Hanoi's occupation of Kampuchea, Jakarta strengthened its security co-operation with Kuala Lumpur. In March 1980, Suharto met with Hussein Onn and produced what was known as the Kuantan doctrine.[17] The doctrine assumed that Vietnam was under Chinese pressure and, as a result, it was moving closer to the Soviet Union, which would be dangerous for regional security. It was believed that Vietnam was basically very nationalistic and, if it had a choice — for instance, if assistance was forthcoming from the ASEAN states — it would gradually move away from its Soviet allies. Therefore, the Kuantan Doctrine offered to assist the Vietnamese. The Thais felt that this policy position was at their expense, however. The Kuantan Principle thus created friction within the ASEAN states and, as a result, was quietly abandoned.

The Malaysian concept of ZOPFAN (Zone of Peace, Freedom and Neutrality) was accepted by ASEAN Foreign Ministers in 1971. It became the ASEAN doctrine in 1976 when it was accepted at the ASEAN summit. While supporting the ZOPFAN concept, Indonesia introduced another doctrine in 1983, the Nuclear Weapons Free Zone (NWFZ), as part of ZOPFAN.[18] The Nuclear Weapons Free Zone was meant to complement, not replace, ZOPFAN. It was argued by the Indonesians that, since ZOPFAN could not be achieved, the Nuclear Weapons Free Zone should be implemented first.[19] In fact, the Indonesians argued that "if put into effect, a NWFZ for Southeast Asia would give substance to the Kuala Lumpur Declaration of 1971 on ZOPFAN".[20] This was a reflection of Indonesia's desire to play an active role on the regional scene. The Nuclear Weapons Free Zone was eventually included in the ASEAN Manila Declaration in 1987, but actual implementation was a problem because of American disapproval.

There was growing security co-operation between Jakarta and Kuala Lumpur from the time Suharto came to power. Initially, the co-operation was confined to the Joint Border Committee (JBC) which was established in 1972 to deal with communist insurgency along the borders of East Malaysia. Later, it was developed to cover other areas, including intelligence exchange, joint exercises and exchange of officers to attend military colleges.[21] In 1984, the 1972 security arrangement was revised to include joint naval and air patrols along the common borders of Indonesia and Malaysia, and the Straits of Malacca. The earlier agreement was confined to dealing with Communists who were operating in the target areas, but the 1984 revised agreement also included smugglers, drug traffickers and counterfeiters.[22]

As the Communist threat declined and the Cold War ended, Indonesia became more confident in both domestic politics and foreign affairs. Indonesia-Malaysia relations began to have some problems again. Five events occurring in the 1990s attest to this.

The first example was Jakarta's offer of army training facilities to be used by the armed forces of Singapore. The Malaysian Government was initially critical of this and regarded it as a threat to Malaysian security. But Jakarta did not share this view.[23] Later, however, a Malaysian military spokesman stated that Malaysia did not actually think that it constituted a threat.[24]

The second example concerned the hanging of Basrie Masse, an Indonesian, in Sabah for drug trafficking. Before the hanging, Jakarta failed in last minute efforts to save the condemned man.[25] Basrie's execution prompted a series of protests in Jakarta while the Indonesian Government expressed regret that its appeal for a stay of execution had been denied. Foreign Minister Alatas commented that Indonesia was told after Basrie was sentenced, "earlier action would have allowed the Indonesian council there to seek legal assistance".[26] Alatas finally noted that numerous Indonesians worked in Malaysia and a prompt notification of any arrest would help Indonesian consulates to take the necessary action.[27]

The third example was that of illegal Indonesian immigrants to Malaysia. It has been a public secret that since 1970, the number of Indonesians in Peninsular Malaysia has been increasing. Many of them entered illegally. It was estimated that, in Johor alone, there were 100,000 Indonesian workers. According to the 1990 estimate, there were more than 500,000 Indonesian workers in West

Malaysia.²⁸ The total number of Indonesian illegal immigrants may reach 1.2 million by 1994.²⁹ The presence of this large number of illegal immigrants has created problems because the situation aggravates Malaysian unemployment. It has also angered some Malaysians because the incidence of criminal activity and disease among these Indonesian immigrants is high.³⁰ When the problem became serious, Kuala Lumpur and Jakarta negotiated and eventually reached an agreement to resolve the issue. However, the Malaysian Government's attempts to stem the flow of the illegal immigrants has not been very successful. Some argue that the Indonesian Government has not been very co-operative in stopping the flow of illegal workers to Malaysia.³¹ In September 1994, Mahathir visited Jakarta to discuss the illegal labour problem as well as the disputed islands. However, Mahathir was quoted as saying that Malaysia still needed 17,000 plantation workers from Indonesia. The Indonesian Army daily, *Angkatan Bersenjata,* stated in its editorial that the pay in Malaysia is high and many Indonesians were attracted to work there legally or illegally. "Perhaps in Malaysia there is still a lot of illegal immigrants. If this is true, it will be very good should these people be recruited and are given the legal status. If more is needed, then [Malaysia] could recruit directly from Indonesia."³² The Indonesian military does not see any problem of illegal immigrants in Malaysia.

The fourth example involves the two small disputed islands of Sipadan and Ligitan. In June 1991, Malaysia attempted to develop the two islands for tourist purposes. Indonesia asked Malaysia to stop developing the islands and criticized Kuala Lumpur for violating the previous agreement (1969) in which both sides agreed to maintain the status quo. However, Malaysia did not stop developing the islands and in retaliation Indonesia detained a 100-ton Malaysian fishing vessel with its 13-member crew. There was tension but both sides decided to negotiate. In July 1991, Ghafar Baba met Suharto to discuss the issue, leading to the formation of a joint commission.³³ It made little progress as evidenced in the disagreement on solving the disputed islands issue in September 1994. The Malaysian delegation wanted to submit the case to the International Court of Justice while the Indonesian delegation insisted that the ASEAN High Council should handle the matter. The Malaysians argued that the International Court would be unbiased while the Indonesians maintained that both Kuala Lumpur and Jakarta should settle the issue in the ASEAN spirit.³⁴ In October 1994, Aminullah Ibrahim (representing ABRI faction), the Deputy Chairman of Committee One in Indonesian parliament, stated in parliament that the Indonesian ministry "should contact the Malaysian government to query about its provocative attitude regarding the disputed islands".³⁵ He claimed that in January 1994, Kuala Lumpur had agreed that Malaysia would not allow the development of the disputed islands as tourist attractions. Kuala Lumpur, however, did not keep the promise and unilaterally developed the two islands. It appears that the Indonesian military is very rigid in its stand on the two islands. In June 1995, however, Datuk Abdullah Ahmad Badawi, the Foreign Minister of Malaysia, negotiated with his Indonesian counterpart and announced that Malaysia was no longer considering its proposal of submitting the case to the International Court of Justice.[36] He said that Kuala Lumpur wanted to have a quick and peaceful resolution of the long-standing dispute. The dispute has yet to be settled.

The fifth example has to do with Prime Minister Mahathir's proposal for an East Asian Economic Grouping (EAEG). He first expressed his idea in December 1990 at a banquet for visiting Chinese premier Li Peng and reiterated it at a conference in Bali in early March 1991.[37] Prior to the conference, Mahathir visited Suharto to discuss a number of issues, including the EAEG proposal. In his usual Javanese style, Suharto stated the proposal would require further study by senior officers of the two countries.[38] This was a subtle way of saying that Indonesia had reservations about the proposal.

On 3 March 1991 when opening the conference in Bali, Suharto delivered a speech stressing that Indonesia was not in favour of "a closed trade bloc".[39] There was no mention of the EAEG proposal but it was clear that Suharto was referring to it. Jakarta felt that no more regional economic groupings, which would harm international co-operation, were needed. In addition, Jakarta felt that Mahathir's proposal would exclude the United States from the group and did not want to antagonize the United States when the country still badly needed American assistance and foreign investment. Some Indonesians maintain that APEC would be more beneficial to Indonesia and other ASEAN countries than EAEG.[40] Therefore Indonesia should get involved in APEC actively in order to promote investment and trade.[41] Indonesia also wanted to use the United States to counter-balance Japanese economic domination in Southeast Asia.[42]

Perhaps the unspoken factor in the disagreement was the competition between Indonesia and Malaysia for leadership of the "Malay World". Jakarta perceived itself to be the natural leader, and the fact that the EAEG was proposed by Malaysia without Jakarta's prior endorsement was seen an act of disrespect towards Indonesia. On 4 March, Mahathir made a speech denying that his proposal was intended to form a trade bloc, but he noted that the East Asian region was most active economically and that East Asian states should speak with one voice.[43] He insisted on forming the EAEG, but Jakarta did not give in. The Malaysians worked hard to persuade ASEAN to accept the proposal. After long negotiations, the Malaysian proposal was finally accepted at the ASEAN Economic Ministers' Meeting in October 1991 as one of ASEAN's proposals. This was after Malaysia accepted an Indonesian suggestion to change the term "grouping" to "caucus".[44] Now the name is officially EAEC (East Asian Economic Caucus) and is a forum rather than an economic bloc. In addition, it is no longer an independent unit but rather a small group within the larger organization, the Asia Pacific Economic Co-operation (APEC). This was not the original idea of the Malaysian proposal. Still, the issue was far from being solved, for just before the ASEAN summit in Singapore, Indonesia called for further revisions to the proposal.[45] Mahathir was irritated and raised the issue before the summit demanding that EAEC be endorsed fully by ASEAN.[46] Alatas was quoted as saying that "EAEC is a very important topic but there are many more important topics".[47] Mahathir and Suharto met again during the ASEAN summit, presumably to discuss the proposal. After the meeting, Alatas was reported to have said that "Indonesia had no difficulties with [the] fundamentals of EAEC".[48]

The issue of EAEC was discussed again during Suharto's visit to Kuala Lumpur in July 1993. However, Suharto stuck to Indonesia's original stand, i.e. EAEC should be placed under APEC.[49] Indonesia would be the chairman of APEC in 1994 and was concerned with the effectiveness of the grouping. It was reported that no agreement was reached and Suharto decided to cut short his stay in Malaysia. When President Bill Clinton announced an APEC meeting to be held in Seattle (Washington), Suharto agreed to attend while Mahathir rejected. (See Chapter 11 on NAM and APEC.)

These examples show that there are still communication gaps between the two countries. Each appears to have taken things for granted because both Malaysian Malays and indigenous Indonesians come from the same racial stock and "Malay" culture. Jakarta feels that Kuala Lumpur sometimes forgets to give it "due respect". In addition to the bilateral issues mentioned above, there are still a number of pending bilateral problems to be solved that could become a source of conflict. For instance, the problem of delineation of the common border in Kalimantan, the overlapping claims to the two small islands in the South China Sea and the question of fishing rights for Indonesians. Obviously, Indonesia and Malaysia need to improve their channel of communication, and Indonesia desires that its role as a leader be recognized.

Indonesia-singapore Relations: Mutual Benefit

Indonesia-Singapore relations during the Sukarno era were not cordial. The Jakarta authorities had considered Singapore as a place which foreign powers and Indonesian rebels used as a stepping stone. The Jakarta Government also saw Singapore as a place where Indonesian smugglers resided. During the confrontation with Malaysia, Singapore, as an integral part of Malaysia, was under severe attack. Undercover troops were sent to Singapore to carry out subversive activities.

In August 1965, Singapore left the Federation of Malaysia and became independent. It also normalized diplomatic ties with Indonesia. Relations turned sour in 1968 when two Indonesian marines were sentenced to death.[50] The two marines, who had been sent by the Sukarno Government during the confrontation period, had planted a bomb in MacDonald House on Orchard Road. The bomb exploded, killing a few people and injuring many. In accordance with Singaporean law, the marines were tried as criminals and sentenced to death by a court. After the sentence, the Indonesian leaders, Suharto and Adam Malik, requested that the Singapore Government commute the death penalty to life imprisonment. However, the Singapore authorities refused and the two marines were hanged. Riots occurred in Jakarta and Surabaya as a result. The Singapore Embassy in Jakarta was ransacked, and there was an anti-Chinese demonstration.[51] The mobs believed Indonesian Chinese to be sympathetic to the ethnic Chinese in Singapore who formed the majority of the nation's population.

The new Indonesian Government considered Singapore's action very unfriendly, and some leaders advocated "punishing" Singapore with another confrontation. Others even advocated sending troops. Suharto, who was concerned with economic rehabilitation and economic development refused to take any drastic measures however.[52] He overruled the intention of some hawkish generals and projected an image that Indonesia was really serious about economic development.[53] Although no armed conflict occurred, relations between Indonesia and Singapore were at an all-time low. It took five years for Singapore to mend its relations with Indonesia.

In May 1973, Prime Minister Lee Kuan Yew was invited by the Indonesian Government to visit Indonesia, paving the way for better Jakarta-Singapore relations. Upon the advice of the Singapore Ambassador in Indonesia, Lee Khoon Choy, Prime Minister Lee went to sprinkle flowers on the graves of the two marines.[54] This friendly gesture won the goodwill of many Indonesians, particularly Suharto. The Indonesian press considered this to be proof of Singapore's sincere desire for friendship with Indonesia and a new phase of Indonesia-Singapore relations began. Soon after, Suharto paid a visit to Singapore. An understanding between the two leaders developed and Singapore became responsive to the Indonesian Government. Singapore even released bilateral trade information concerning the two nations to top Indonesian leaders, indicating that it had nothing to hide. Earlier, Indonesia had suspected that Singapore had not released these figures because of irregularities (smuggling) in Jakarta-Singapore trade.

The Indonesian authorities, especially some military leaders, have been suspicious of Singapore. In the past, they considered Singapore to be a Chinese city which had the potential to be used by the PRC as a front post.[55] Because of this fear, Jakarta kept a close eye on Singapore-PRC relations. Indonesia would not tolerate Singapore if it were allied with Beijing. When Malaysia and two other ASEAN states decided to establish diplomatic relations with the PRC, Singapore did not follow suit. Prime Minister Lee stated repeatedly that his country would only normalize relations after Jakarta because Singapore did not want to project an image that it was eager to establish diplomatic ties with the PRC.[56]

When Indonesia invaded Portuguese East Timor in 1975 and incorporated the ex-colony into Indonesian territory, Singapore abstained from the vote in the United Nations.[57] The Indonesian Foreign Minister, Adam Malik, commented that Singapore was afraid that it might be "Timorized" by Malaysia or Indonesia.[58] It appears that Singapore was concerned by Indonesia's action and registered its reservation but eventually, in November 1977, sided with other ASEAN states in supporting Indonesia. After the vote, Suharto, as President of Indonesia, sent a personal message to Prime Minister Lee expressing his appreciation.

The prosperity of Singapore has led to jealousy among some Indonesian leaders. There were discussions about developing an Indonesian port so that Indonesia could bypass Singapore in dealing with foreign countries. Sabang, in Sumatra, was chosen as the site, but the plan did not take shape for various reasons. Also, during the New Order period, Indonesia had wanted to develop Batam as a port. In fact, the Suharto Government requested Singapore's aid and the latter saw that this would be of mutual benefit. Some labour-intensive industries could be moved to Batam rather than being phased out, and this would definitely benefit Singapore too.

The Batam project, which was first announced in 1978, progressed slowly, however.[59] Both sides were reluctant to compromise. Indonesia was concerned about its sovereignty and had high expectations from Singapore. Singapore was concerned with its investment profit and Indonesia's sensitivity over its own sovereignty. A major breakthrough came in 1989 when Lee Kuan Yew met Suharto again. (The factors contributing to this change will be discussed later in this section.) In January 1990, a deal was signed between Indonesia and Singapore on the establishment of the Batam Industrial Park which would cost S$400 million. Two companies owned by the Government of Singapore and major Indonesian companies belonging to the Liem Sioe Liong Group, which is closely associated with President Suharto, were involved.[60]

Following this, both countries signed a tax treaty aimed at eliminating double taxation and promoting greater cross-flow of trade.[61] A joint effort to promote tourism was also publicized. Even the possibility of Singapore buying drinking water from Bintan island in Indonesia was discussed.[62] Indonesia-Singapore relations thus entered a honeymoon period.

The Batam project was later expanded by Prime Minister Goh Chok Tong as a Growth Triangle to include Riau (including Batam), Singapore and Johor, Malaysia. This plan is known in Indonesian as Sijori. It is quite clear, however, that there are only two links: Singapore-Riau and Singapore-Johor. The Johor-Riau link is still very tenuous, if not completely absent.

The closer ties between Singapore and Jakarta had not come about suddenly in 1989, however. Since 1986, especially after the President Chaim Herzog visit, Singapore had shown its eagerness to develop closer relations with Indonesia. It should be noted that when Singapore invited President Herzog of Israel to visit the island state in 1986, Malaysia had reacted emotionally. There was also talk of reviewing Malaysia-Singapore co-operation, including Malaysia's provision of water. The Malaysian Ambassador to Singapore was recalled for consultations. Indonesia, with its large Muslim population, also recalled its Ambassador. But Indonesia's reaction was unemotional. Indonesia has not been very Islamic in its foreign policy, but, because of Malaysia's reaction, it reluctantly recalled its Ambassador to pacify Indonesian Muslims.[63] Singapore, realizing that it should not depend too heavily on Malaysia, decided to move closer to Indonesia. Indonesian leaders, especially the Suharto group, wanted to further develop Indonesia and had a special interest in Batam. They were also eager to tap Singapore's capital and expertise. Each nation thus appeared to be responsive to the other's needs, resulting in a closer economic and security relationship.[64]

These mutual interests may explain the closer security relations between Jakarta and Singapore. In February 1989, a Memorandum of Understanding (MOU) was signed allowing Singapore to train its troops in Indonesia. In return, the Indonesian military would be given access to Singapore's military technology. In addition, an air weapons range, jointly developed by Indonesia and Singapore, was opened in Pekan Baru, Sumatra, allowing the air forces of the two countries to conduct effective training.[65] Since 1989, there have been regular joint exercises between the armies, navies and air forces of the two countries, reflecting the close relationship. Closer military co-operation between Jakarta and Singapore was made by top leaders on both sides, but some Indonesian military leaders may not share the same view. Nonetheless, as long as the Suharto group is in power, Suharto's view will prevail.

It is interesting to note that, in August 1989, when Singapore announced that it would offer use of its military facilities to the United States, there were divided reactions. While Suharto was reported to have said that he had no objection as long as this was not a military base, Indonesian newspapers and some army generals were very critical.[66] It is known that Indonesia is against foreign military bases in principle but realizes that, for the time being, there is no alternative but to recognize the need for American military bases. The Indonesian Government has refused to endorse them publicly, however.

Since the mid-1980s, it seems that Indonesian-Singaporean relations have improved and there have been frequent mutual visits between the country's top leaders, especially between Suharto and Lee Kuan Yew. In fact, Lee has repeatedly praised Suharto for his able leadership and his contribution to Southeast Asian political stability and development.⁶⁷ Closer co-operation has also been reflected in other fields: in 1994 Jakarta and Singapore signed the Tourism Co-operation Agreement and the Air Service agreement, which enable the two countries to benefit from the booming tourist industry.⁶⁸ In 1995 Singapore has become Indonesia's sixth largest cumulative investor, after Japan, Hong Kong, Taiwan, the United States and the United Kingdom.⁶⁹ Singapore is also the third largest Indonesian trading partner, after Japan and the United States.⁷⁰

Indonesia-Philippines Relations: Close Yet Distant

In the early 1960s, President Macapagal of the Philippines proposed the concept of Maphilindo which was intended to establish solidarity in the Malay world. The concept was taken over by Sukarno. It was short-lived, however, partly because of the conflict between Manila and Kuala Lumpur over Sabah and partly because of the Indonesian confrontation with Malaysia.

After Suharto came to power, Indonesia's relations with the Philippines returned to normal. Manila and Kuala Lumpur were still in conflict over Sabah and, at one time, diplomatic ties were even suspended. Later, the ties were resumed due to the good offices of Indonesia and other ASEAN states. The Sabah Government, under Tun Mustapha, supported Muslim (Moro) rebels in the southern Philippines resulting in the intensification of the conflict between Manila and the Moro.⁷¹ Manila and Kuala Lumpur accused each other of engaging in subversive activities to destabilize the other's government. It was revealed in a recent Indonesian publication that Marcos requested Suharto's help at this time.⁷² Suharto then instructed Yoga Sugomo, the chief of the intelligence body Bakin, to look for a possible solution.

Yoga was assisted by Benny Murdani, then Deputy Chief of Bakin, to get in touch with the Muslim guerrillas who were members of the Moro National Liberation Front (MNLF). On 3 January 1974 Yoga and Benny succeeded in organizing a meeting of the three parties in conflict outside Manila, but Nur Misuari, the leader of the MNLF, was not present because he was then overseas.⁷³ Nonetheless, Yoga continued his efforts, and eventually a meeting of Nur Misuari and Suharto took place.⁷⁴ It is not known where the meeting was held, but it is clear that, only after the meeting, an informal discussion between Marcos and Suharto was held on 29 and 30 May 1974 in Manado, a northern Indonesian town in a Christian area. The selection of the venue was arguably intentional. Suharto wished to show that, in Indonesia where a majority of the population was Muslims, it was possible for Christians to live in peace.

It was reported that, at the meeting, Suharto put forward four proposals to solve the Moro problem. First, there would be a guarantee of religious freedom and the Muslims in the southern Philippines would be provided with protection; second, Islamic culture and tradition would be cherished; third, the lands owned by the ancestors of the Moros would be returned; and fourth, Muslims would be given greater opportunities to participate in national development.

Marcos accepted three of the four proposals rejecting the one concerning the return of Muslim ancestral lands.[75] Apparently, it was impossible for Marcos to return the "Moroland" to the Muslims because most of those lands were in the hands of Christians who make up the majority of the population in the south.[76] This was one of the key issues in the Moro problem.

Suharto was a little disappointed with the outcome of the meeting but could not support the separatist movement staged by the Moro. This was because Indonesia itself had experienced many Islamic rebellions and it would not have been in the interests of Indonesia to favour a radical movement such as the Moro National Liberation Front. It was also due to the pressure of Indonesia and Malaysia at the Organization of Islamic Conference (OIC) that the MNLF was forced to abandon its demand for independence for the Moros. This was acknowledged by the Philippines Foreign Minister Romulo.[77]

The Indonesian mediation of the Moro issue is revealing in terms of the nation's foreign policy-making. Those who were involved in the negotiations were mostly military officials (such as Yoga and Benny etc.) rather than people from the Ministry of Foreign Affairs. Suharto himself also took a special interest in the issue. In addition, at the Manado meeting, General Sudharmono, then State Secretary (Mensesneg), played a role as well. He was the one who made the press statement at Halim airport announcing the informal meeting in Manado.

The Manado talks were not confined to the Moro problem. Suharto also wanted to mediate between Kuala Lumpur and Manila. Suharto had met Tun Razak in Palembang, Sumatra, in May 1973 and, in early May 1974, they met again in Penang. Prior to the Penang meeting, in April 1974, Mrs Imelda Marcos had visited Indonesia and had met Suharto. It is not surprising then that the Armed Forces daily newspaper concluded that the Manado meeting was a continuation of this series of meetings.[78] There was no report concerning discussions on the Sabah issue, but it is possible to guess that Suharto must have attempted to convince Marcos to give up Manila's claim to Sabah in order to promote ASEAN solidarity. It was reported that Suharto made an effort to arrange a meeting between Hussein Onn and Marcos.[79] This time Suharto seemed to have made some headway because Marcos stated during the ASEAN summit in Kuala Lumpur (in 1977) that Manila intended to give up its claim over Sabah.

It seems, however, that the Manado talks were not entirely successful after all. In his memoirs, General Yoga has noted that Marcos did not follow the steps recommended by Suharto. Marcos later pushed Indonesia aside and attempted to approach the Middle Eastern countries and the Organization of Islamic Conference to solve the Moro issue.[80] Yoga also commented that because of Marcos's attitude, Indonesia (read: Suharto) was no longer willing to extend a helping hand.[81] On the Sabah issue, Marcos did not make any concessions to Malaysia during the Bali summit, which caused disappointment in Indonesia.[82]

The Sabah issue has been a continuing cause of friction between Jakarta and Manila. In 1981, the Indonesian Ambassador in Manila, General Leo Lopulisa, was reported by the Philippine press to have urged the Philippines to negotiate with Malaysia on the Sabah issue and was said to have called for the Manila National Assembly to pass a resolution to convince Malaysia that the Philippines would not pursue its claim to Sabah.[83] The Philippine Government considered this blatant interference in its internal affairs and protested to the Indonesian Government. As a result, the Indonesian Ambassador to the Philippines was recalled and, between January 1982 and April 1984, no Indonesian Ambassador was posted to Manila.[84]

It appears that the relationship between Marcos and Suharto was not particularly cordial. After the assassination of Ninoy Aquino, Marcos was faced with a legitimacy crisis. He wanted to use ASEAN to legitimize his position by proposing a third ASEAN summit. The summit, if it had been held, would have been held in Manila. Suharto resisted the idea, saying that he did not think it was time to hold such a meeting.

When Marcos was overthrown and Corazon Aquino became President, Indonesia's attitude towards the Philippines changed. Suharto believes that the stability of the Philippines is important for the region. For this reason, he supported the proposal that an ASEAN summit be held in Manila in December 1987.[85] Against the advice of his security advisers, Suharto attended the summit in Manila, thus boosting Aquino's position.

Nonetheless, this did not mean that Indonesia had been offering unlimited support to Mrs Aquino. In the 1980s, the Indonesian Government still supported Marcos and preferred him to other opposition candidates. Prior to the 1986 Philippine election, a high ranking Indonesian officer was quoted as saying that "we prefer that Marcos win because we already know his policy well".[86] The Indonesian military's relations with the Marcos regime were especially close. Military assistance was given to the Marcos Government. For instance, on 9 January 1986, General Benny Murdani delivered two Indonesian-made Casa CN-212 aircrafts to the Philippine General Fabian Ver.[87] Only after the collapse of the Marcos regime did Indonesia clearly express its support for the new government.

Although there were foreign military bases in the Philippines until very recently, the New Order Government had never openly stated that it desired that the American bases be removed. In fact, when Manila wanted to review the bases treaty and requested ASEAN support, there were two conflicting views in Jakarta. Army Chief of Staff, General Try Sutrisno, was reported to have said that the American military bases in the Philippines were beneficial for the security of Southeast Asia.[88] On the other hand, Foreign Minister Mochtar Kusumaatmadja continued to promote an "independent and active" foreign policy and refused to make any commitment on the bases issue.[89] Nonetheless, each realized that, in the short run, Indonesia benefited from the presence of these bases. They also knew that there was no alternative for Manila at that time.[90] However, in the long run, Jakarta still prefers the absence of American military bases in Southeast Asia.[91]

Jakarta-Manila relations during the Aquino administration improved. Soon after becoming President, Aquino visited Indonesia. She discussed various issues with Suharto, including the problem of Communism, the Moro issue and economic development.[92] It was reported that Suharto lectured Aquino on the danger of Communism, telling her not to be soft towards the Communists. He also told her that it would take a long time to rebuild a country, therefore she needed to be patient. On the Moro issue, Suharto restated that "Indonesia was ready to help the Philippines solve the problem, which is the wishes of the Moro people for autonomy, not for secession".[93] Sudharmono, then the State Secretary, quoted Suharto as saying that the problem could be solved provided the Philippine Government gave "some attention to the aspirations of the Muslims in the area and improve their well being".[94] However, there was no longer any mention of returning Moro lands to the Muslims as suggested at the Manado Talks in 1974.

Jakarta continued to offer its good offices to the Philippines. After Fidel Ramos was elected President, a meeting was arranged between Manila and the Moro at Cipanas, a hill resort in West Java. The three-day meeting (14-16 April 1993) resulted in an agreement that the parties in conflict would hold further talks to reach peaceful settlement.[95] It was reported that Ramos thanked Suharto for his effort to arrange the meeting.[96] On 25 October 1993, there was another talk between MNLF and the Ramos Government in Jakarta. The MNLF was represented by Nur Misuari himself, while the Philippine Government delegation was led by Ambassador Manuel Yan. An agreement for cease-fire was eventually reached but more talks were scheduled for April 1994.[97] Alatas noted that the Moro problem was still far from being solved.

In May 1994, there was an event which had a bearing on Manila-Jakarta relations. A Philippine non-governmental organization (NGO) scheduled an international conference on East Timor. When the time for the conference drew near, Jakarta pressured the Philippine Government to bar the conference from being held. When Manila said that it could not ban an NGO meeting, Jakarta announced that the Indonesian delegation would not attend the East ASEAN Business Conference to be held in Davao. Indonesia also threatened that it might not want to continue to serve as mediator between the Moro and Manila.[98] There was, in addition, a report that a pro-government Muslim organization in Jakarta suggested holding "a counter conference" on the MNLF's move for autonomy.[99] Jakarta-Manila relations became tense.

President Ramos sent Raul Manglapus, former Foreign Secretary, to explain Manila's position on East Timor to Indonesia. Manglapus maintained that Manila did not condone the staging of the conference and that it "fully and unequivocably" accepted East Timor as part of Indonesia.[100] He also told Jakarta that the Philippine constitution allowing for the freedom of association and speech prevented the Government from ordering that the conference be cancelled.[101]

However, Jakarta was of the view that the conference was "part of a larger and on-going political campaign being waged against Indonesia by East Timorese exiles" and the staging of such a conference in Manila would affect Philippine Jakarta relations. Under Jakarta's continuing pressure, Ramos eventually ordered that the non-Filipino delegates be barred from entering the Philippines for the conference on the grounds that they would jeopardize Philippine national interest.[102] Indeed, a few foreign delegates were refused entry and Indonesia hailed the Philippine decision.[103]

The event showed the precarious nature of the relationship between Manila and Jakarta. There may be political frictions in the future between the two countries due to their different political traditions.

Indonesia-Thailand Relations: The Front-Line state

As is the case with the Philippines, Jakarta's relations with Bangkok are not very close.

During the Sukarno era, because of Thailand's close relations with the United States, Jakarta kept its distance from Bangkok. When Suharto came to power and wanted to promote regional co-operation, however, Bangkok-Jakarta relations improved.

Thailand and Indonesia have had different perceptions of threat. This was especially the case before Chatichai Choonhavan became Thai Prime Minister. Thailand considered Vietnam its major enemy and intended to keep the Vietnamese at bay.[104] When Vietnam invaded Kampuchea, Bangkok became very hostile towards Hanoi. The Thai government feared that Vietnam would subvert, if not invade, Thailand and therefore, took a hardline stand on the Kampuchean issue.[105] Indonesia, being further away from Vietnam and suspicious of the PRC rather than Vietnam, did not share Thailand's intense hostility towards Vietnam. On the contrary, some Indonesian military and civilian leaders were sympathetic to Vietnam because of the nations' common revolutionary past and nationalist struggle. For this reason, Indonesia's attitude towards Vietnam was benevolent (see Chapter 8). It is interesting to note that in 1980, when Suharto and Hussein Onn wanted to woo Vietnam away from the Soviet Union, Thailand was displeased because it saw this move coming at the expense of the Thais. In order to show ASEAN solidarity, Jakarta quietly abandoned the Kuantan Doctrine and put Thai interests foremost. Perhaps, it was also Indonesia's intention not to push Thailand further into the arms of the PRC.

In public forums, ASEAN managed to make a common stand on the Kampuchean issue. Domestic developments in Thailand and Chatichai's stand on the Kampuchean issue — to transform Indochina from a war zone to a market place — caught Indonesia off balance, however.[106] Although Thailand eventually began to move back slowly to the original ASEAN stand, Indonesian-Thai relations have been somewhat strained.

Chatichai's downfall resulted in the improvement of Indonesian-Thai relations. In early 1991, Anand Panyarachun, the new Thai Prime Minister, revived the idea of an ASEAN Free Trade Area (AFTA) and received the full support of Singapore and later Malaysia as well. Both the Philippines and Indonesia had some reservations about the idea but were eventually convinced that it would be good for the development of the region.[107] It is interesting to note that before AFTA was put forward as an ASEAN proposal, the Thais were actively lobbying for support. Only after Indonesia's full endorsement was given was the proposal taken up as an ASEAN proposal. Its official acceptance took place in early 1992 during the fourth ASEAN summit in Singapore. It should be noted that while AFTA was fully supported by Indonesia, EAEG was not, indicating the uneasy nature of Indonesian-Malaysian relations.

Jakarta-Bangkok relations further improved after Chuan Leekpai assumed the premiership. Chuan visited Indonesia and agreed to study the Northern Triangle project to foster Indonesia-Thailand-Malaysia economic co-operation. It was proposed that Indonesia, although initially lukewarm towards the proposal, has become more enthusiastic after the PRC's efforts to attract foreign investment.

Indonesia-Brunei Relations: A Rich Brother

When Sukarno was in power, Brunei was still a British protectorate. In 1962, there was a rebellion in Brunei which aimed at overthrowing the Sultan. This rebellion was supported by the Sukarno Government.[108] After the failure of the rebellion, the rebels were given sanctuary in Indonesia.

When Suharto came to power, some Bruneian rebels were still in Indonesia (others were in Kuala Lumpur) but they were inactive. On becoming an independent state in January 1984, Brunei immediately joined ASEAN. This suggests its concern with security: Brunei would be more secure if it were a member of a regional organization. Brunei's relations with its neighbouring countries also improved as evidenced by visits between Suharto and the Sultan. In fact, Suharto has visited Brunei twice. His first trip took place in 1984 when Brunei celebrated its independence, the second was in 1989 during the *berkhatan* ceremony.[109] The Sultan also paid a visit to Jakarta in 1988 and "gave a soft loan of US$100 million to the Indonesian projects, half of it went to financing a proposed toll road".[110] It was reported that this soft loan benefited the associates of President Suharto.[111]

Indonesia and the Ase An Regional Forum

There is no doubt that Indonesia has been a crucial actor in maintaining ASEAN as a viable organization. However, it is also clear that Indonesia has attempted to maximize its role in ASEAN in recent years. One of the indicators was the promotion of ZOPFAN and SEANWFZ through ASEAN. Even in the recently established ASEAN Regional Forum (ARF), it appears that Indonesia has been trying to promote its concept of regional order and security.

The ARF was first launched during the ASEAN Post-Ministerial Conference (PMC) meeting in July 1993 in Singapore which aimed to build "mutual confidence, preserve stability and ensure growth in the Asia-Pacific by creating a network of constructive relationship".[112] It had its first inaugural meeting in Bangkok in the following year. It is not clear which country initiated the ARF, but Indonesia has gone along with the idea signifying its support, albeit limited, to this new forum. Nevertheless, it appears that the development of the ARF is likely to be slow. Apart from differing views on the security issues among the members, perhaps it is also due to Indonesia's own perception of its security role.

The ARF which consists of 18 members, including four major powers (United States, China, Russia and Japan), is still in its embryonic stage.[113] Since Indonesia continues to hold the idea of an active and independent foreign policy, it is uncomfortable being locked into a security institution in which there are major non-Southeast Asian powers. Perhaps, Jakarta is worried about being overwhelmed by these major powers. It is not surprising that Alatas was quoted as saying that the ARF is not a problem-solving tool. It is "not meant as an instrument to solve problems. It's meant as a consultative forum. Its utility, its success should be judged from that angle".[114]

This forum would continue to discuss key issues such as confidence-building measures, the arms race, the Korean crisis, rival territorial claims in the South

China Seas and Cambodia's future. However, for Indonesia, Alatas stated that in the Senior Official Meeting preceding the ARF conference in Brunei this year, ASEAN will submit papers on ZOPFAN, SEANWFZ and the Treaty of Amity and Co-operation.[115] All of these concepts are being promoted by, if not closely linked to, Indonesia. One can argue that Jakarta sees the usefulness of the ARF in promoting Indonesian foreign policy in such a format.

Conclusion

Suharto and the military have been instrumental in formulating foreign policy towards the ASEAN states. It was through the initiative of Suharto and the military that Indonesian confrontation with Malaysia was terminated and regional co-operation was promoted. It was also under them that Indonesia attempted to help the Philippines solve the Moro and Sabah problems. Improved relations between Indonesia and Singapore were the result of actions by Suharto and the military. Indonesia's relations with the ASEAN states reflect its desire to play an active role in regional affairs which has often led to tension and even friction. In the early years of the New Order, however, Indonesia tended to be more accommodating.

Indonesia under Suharto has been eager to promote regional co-operation within the context of ASEAN in order to achieve regional stability. This, in turn, has provided Indonesia with the opportunity to enjoy economic growth and development. Jakarta's desire to project a higher foreign policy profile may affect its relations with other ASEAN states, however.

Some groups in Indonesia have held the view that the nation has not benefited much from ASEAN. They maintain that Indonesia should not be led by ASEAN; on the contrary, Indonesia should lead the other ASEAN states. Friction has occurred between Indonesia and other ASEAN nations, the most recent example of this being the EAEG issue involving Jakarta and Kuala Lumpur. Nonetheless, Indonesia is gradually emerging as the leader. Indonesian leaders have openly stated that ASEAN is one of the cornerstones, not the only pillar, of Indonesia's foreign policy. This is significant because Indonesia no longer wants to be constrained by ASEAN. This point will be discussed again later.

It is also worth noting that Indonesia is sensitive to major powers military bases in Southeast Asia. It has been reluctant to accept any US military bases in the Southeast Asian region. The recently proposed ASEAN Regional Forum, in which four non-Southeast Asian major powers are members, may have problems if it develops into a security organization. Jakarta prefers to stay away from a security organization which may be dominated by foreign powers.

nOTes

1. It is interesting to note that, in 1988, Suharto began to refer to ASEAN as *a* (not *the*) corner stone of Indonesia's foreign policy. See his independence day speech, *Kompas*, 18 August 1988. A study of various GBHNs (General Outline of State Direction) from different periods shows that Indonesia's foreign policy is shifting its focus from just ASEAN to the World. See also Chapter 11 of this book.
2. The best study on this subject is J.A.C. Mackie, *Konfrontasi: The Indonesia-Malaysia Dispute* (Kuala Lumpur: Oxford University Press, 1974).
3. For a comprehensive study on SEATO, see Leszek Buszynski, *S.E.A.T.O.: The Failure of an Alliance Strategy* (Singapore: Singapore University Press, 1983).
4. For a good discussion on the initial idea proposed by Malaya, see J. Saravanamuttu, *The Dilemma of Independence: Two Decades of Malaysia's Foreign Policy, 1957-1977* (Penang: Penerbit Universiti Sains Malaysia, 1983), pp. 41-44. For another version of ASA, see Bernard Gordon, *Dimensions of Conflict in Southeast Asia* (New Jersey: Prentice-Hall, 1966), pp. 162-187.
5. For a discussion on Maphilindo, see J.A.C. Mackie, *Konfrontasi: Indonesia's Dispute against Malaysia* (Kuala Lumpur: Oxford University Press, 1974), especially pp. 165-170.
6. For a discussion of Indonesia's relations with ASA, see Roger Irvine, "The Formative Years of ASEAN: 1967-1975", in Alison Broinowski (ed.), *Understanding ASEAN* (London: Macmillan, 1982), pp. 10-11.
7. On Indonesia's initiative, see *The Association of Southeast Asian Nations (ASEAN)* (Jakarta: Dept. of Information, 1969, p.5. Cited in Michael Leifer, *Indonesia's Foreign Policy* (London: Allen and Unwin, 1983), p. 122.
8. Frank Frost, "Introduction: ASEAN Since 1967 — Origins, Evolution and Recent Developments", in Alison Broinowski (ed.), *ASEAN into the 1990s* (London: Macmillan), p. 4
9. The desire to project this identity can be found in the speeches made by Lee Kuan Yew during Deng Xiaoping's visit in 1978 and also in Lee's repeated statements that Singapore would only establish diplomatic ties with Beijing after Indonesia. See Leo Suryadinata, *China and the ASEAN States: The Ethnic Chinese Dimension* (Singapore: Singapore University Press, 1985), pp. 112-113.
10. Charles Morrison, "Progress and Prospects in Foreign Policy and Cooperation among the ASEAN Countries", in R.P. Anand and Purification V. Quisumbing (eds.), *ASEAN: Identity, Development and Culture* (Quezon City: UP Law Center & East West Center, 1981), pp. 356-377.
11. Bernardo Villegas, "The Challenge to ASEAN Economic Co-operation", *Contemporary Southeast Asia*, Vol. 9, No. 2 (September 1987), pp. 120-128.
12. Bernard M. Villegas maintains that there are four levels of economic integration: the lowest level is the creation of a free trade area, followed by the establishment of custom union and then common market. The highest level is the realization of a full economic union. "But ASEAN is still miles away from arriving at this stage, if it gets there at all", ibid., p.121.
13. Despite this unification, some differences in spelling remain. See Leo Suryadinata, *A Comparative Dictionary of Malay and Indonesian Synonyms* (Singapore and Kuala Lumpur: Times Editions, 1991).
14. For a detailed study on the Straits of Malacca, see Michael Leifer, *Malacca, Singapore and Indonesia* (Vol. II, *International Straits of the World*) (Alphen van den Rijn, Netherlands: Sijthoff and Noordhoff, 1978).
15. See J. Saravanamuttu, *The Dilemma of Independence*; also Alison Broinowski (ed.), *Understanding ASEAN*, pp. 23-33; 294-296, on the Kuala Lumpur Declaration, which was later known as ZOPFAN.
16. For a brief discussion on Kuala Lumpur-Beijing relations, see Suryadinata, *China and the ASEAN States*, pp. 101-108.
17. For a brief discussion on the Kuantan Principle, see K. Das, "The Kuantan Principle", *Far

Eastern Economic Review, 4 April 1980, pp. 12-13; David Jenkins, "Second Thoughts on Kuantan", *Far Eastern Economic Review*, 10 October 1980, pp. 27-28.

18 "Speech by Indonesian Foreign Minister, Professor Dr Mochtar Kusumaatmadja, at the 16th ASEAN Ministerial Meeting in Bangkok, 24-25 June 1983" (Jakarta: ASEAN Secretariat, 1983), p. 13. For a discussion of this concept by an Indonesian official, see Hasjim Djalal, "Gagasan Zopfan — KBSN-AT dalam Upaya Peningkatan Stabilitas Kawasan Asia Tenggara", in *Jurnal Luar Negeri*, No. 12 (April 1989), pp. 128-152.

19 See Soedjati Djiwandono, *Southeast Asia as a Nuclear Weapons Free Zone* (Kuala Lumpur: ISIS, 1986), p .2.

20 Ibid., p. 6.

21 Jusuf Wanandi, "Indonesia-Malaysia Bi-lateral Relations", *Indonesian Quarterly*, Vol. 16, No. 4 (1988), pp. 454-463.

22 Khong Kim Hong and Abdul Razak Abdullah, "Security Co-operation in ASEAN", *Contemporary Southeast Asia*, Vol. 9, No. 2 (September 1987), pp. 129-139, especially pp. 131-132.

23 The statement made by Indonesia's Ambassador to Kuala Lumpur, Soenarto Djajusman, was first published in *Utusan Malaysia*. Part of this statement was translated into English and published in the *Straits Times*, 10 February 1990.

24 The statement was made by General Tan Sri Yaakob Mohamad Zain to *Utusan Malaysia*. Translated and published in *Straits Times*, 3 and 6 March 1990.

25 *Straits Times*, 6 February 1990.

26 Ibid.

27 Ibid.

28 *Straits Times*, 6 December 1990.

29 This figure is given to me by a Malaysian military officer in April 1994.

30 Graeme Hugo, "Population Movements in Indonesia: Recent Developments and Their Implications", paper submitted to the International Conference on Migration, National University of Singapore, 8 February 1991, p. 6. See also the statement made by Malaysian Deputy Home Minister in April 1994, published in *Lianhe Zaobao*, 6 April 1994, p. 12.

31 Comments made by Malaysian military officers, 1990.

32 "Tajuk rencana", *Angkatan Bersenjata*, 19 September 1994.

33 In September 1991, Jakarta offered to develop jointly those islands but Kuala Lumpur did not accept the offer. *Straits Times*, 12 September 1991. In the following month, however, a joint committee was formed to discuss bilateral issues (especially on the territorial dispute). *Kompas*, 11 October 1990.

34 "RI-Malaysia belum sepakati penyelesaian Sipadan", *Angkatan bersenjata*, 10 September 1994.

35 "Malaysia sudah lakukan provokasi", *Angkatan Bersenjata*, 12 October 1994.

36 Paul Jacob, "Indonesia and Malaysia to work towards quick, peaceful solution", *Straits Times*, 10 June 1995.

37 The proposal was officially suggested by Mahathir on 10 December 1990 at a banquet in honour of Li Peng, the visiting PRC Prime Minister. See the "Text of the Speech by the Malaysian Prime Minister" (mimeograph). In March 1991, he discussed the proposal again in his paper entitled "ASEAN Countries and the World Economy: Challenge and Change", delivered at the conference on "ASEAN Countries and the World Economy", held in Bali. See *Straits Times*, 5 March 1991.

38 Referring to the EAEG, Moerdiono (the Indonesian State Secretary) made the following statement to the press: "Presiden Soeharto menanggapi itu dengan mengemukakan bahwa gagasan tersebut perlu ditelaah oleh pejabat-pejabat tinggi kedua belah pihak, dan khususnya perlu ditelaah bersama-sama dengan para anggota lainnya." (Responding to the [EAEG] proposal, President Soeharto suggested that it should be studied by senior officers of the two countries, and more important, by other members of ASEAN.) *Kompas*, 2 March 1991.

39 *Kompas*, 4 March 1991.

40 For a discussion of Indonesian view regarding EAEG, see Hadi Soesastro, *The East Asian Economic Group (EAEG) Proposal and East Asian Concepts of the Pacific Basin* (Jakarta: Centre for Strategic and International Studies, 1991). According to Soesastro, the concept of EAEG is similar to the proposal put forward by Dr Phisit Pakkasem of the National Economic of Thailand who called for the creation of Western Pacific Economic Co-operation scheme or WESPEC, but the "proposal was found unacceptable". However, EAEG differs from WESPEC in the sense that, for the first time after World War II, Japan was offered a leadership role by Malaysia, another Asian country, "on a silver plate". Ibid, p. 13. He also predicted that EAEG at the end will "take the form of an East Asian caucus that operates with the objective of strengthening the position of ASEAN and other developing East Asian countries in APEC. This may be the only modality that is acceptable to Japan", p. 14.
41 Djisman S. Simandjuntak, "ASEAN Si Bungsu APEC", *Tempo*, 20 November 1993, p. 89.
42 For a brief analysis of the EAEG and the Indonesian view, see "Prospek Ekonomi Asia Timur", in *SWA Sembada*, Vol. 7, No. 1 (1991), pp. 120-121.
43 *Kompas*, 5 March 1991.
44 *Straits Times*, 9 and 10 October 1991. Also *Lianhe Zaobao*, 10 October 1991.
45 *New Straits Times*, 16 January 1992, p. 4.
46 *Straits Times*, 18 January 1992, p. 26.
47 *Straits Times*, 27 January 1992, p. 24.
48 *Straits Times*, 28 January 1992, p. 23.
49 "Oleh-Oleh dari Langkawi", *Tempo*, 24 July 1993, p. 33.
50 For a detailed study of the affair, see Andrew Wong Hup Wah, "Singapore-Indonesia Relations, 1973-1984" (B.A. Honours thesis, Department of Political Science, National University of Singapore, 1985), pp. 8-9. For an interesting view of the incident and its development, see Lee Khoon Choy, *An Ambassador's Journey* (Singapore: Times Books International, 1983), pp. 187 ff.
51 Ibid.
52 A Correspondent, "Adam Says 'Cool It'", *Far Eastern Economic Review*, 31 October 1968, p. 226; Lee Khoon Choy, op. cit., p. 202.
53 Lee Khoon Choy, op. cit., p. 202.
54 Ibid., pp. 213-214.
55 For a discussion of Indonesia's view of Singapore, see Lie Tek Tjeng, *R.R.T dan Singapura: Suatu Pandangan*, Jakarta Lembaga Research Kebudayaan Nasional-LIPI, 1970. Seri no. IX/4, pp. 7-8. In fact, Mohammad Hatta in 1965 also expressed Indonesia's fear of the PRC which might use the Chinese in Singapore and Malaysia to "encircle Indonesia". Hatta noted that "the creation of 'Malaysia' is nothing but the creation of a second China using the mask of 'Malay', a new colony dominated by Chinese capitalists, oppressing the Malay nation". See Hatta, "One Indonesian View of the Malaysian Issue", *Asian Survey*, Vol. 5, No. 3 (1965) p. 143. Although the Suharto Government has become more friendly with that of Singapore, certain sectors continue to be critical of Singapore. For instance, *Merdeka*, a pro-Moscow newspaper, has been most outspoken. B.M. Diah, (Editor-in-Chief) of *Merdeka*, has criticized Singapore in an interview published in *Prisma*, "Kita Tidak Lagi Bebas Aktif", *Prisma*, 9 (September 1977) pp. 42-46 (especially pp. 44-45). It should be noted that Indonesia's concern with Singapore becoming "the third China" was disappearing in the 1980s, at least in the public eye, as a result of improved Singapore-Indonesia relations.
56 Lee Kuan Yew made this point in an interview with *Tempo*, see "Generasi Kedua: Gaya Pemerintahan Harus Berubah", *Tempo*, 5 July 1980, p. 17. Also *Straits Times*, 4 July 1980, for the English version of the same interview.
57 Singapore was one of the 38 countries which abstained. See Dan Coggin, "Angry Words after the Bloodshed", *Far Eastern Economic Review*, 2 January 1976, p. 10; See also Andrew Wong, "Singapore-Indonesia Relations 1973-84", pp.32-36.
58 See Malik's interview with Tempo, "Adam Malik Menjawab", Tempo, 7 February 1976, p. 5.

59 See Leo Suryadinata," Indonesia: A Year of Continuing Challenge", in *Southeast Asian Affairs* 1979, pp. 139-140.
60 See *Straits Times*, 12 January 1990. Also a special report in *Editor* (a Jakarta weekly), No. 51 (1 September 1990), pp. 11-21.
61 *Straits Times*, 8 May 1990.
62 *Straits Times*, 18 and 20 August 1990.
63 For a discussion on Indonesia's foreign policy and Islam, see Chapter 10.
64 It was later developed into the growth triangle concept, see *Straits Times*, 5 June 1990, p. 2.
65 *Straits Times*, 11 and 14 December 1989. See also Tommy Koh, "Indonesia-Singapore Relations: A Singapore Perspective", in *Indonesia 50 Years* (Singapore: Embassy of the Republic of Indonesia, 1995), p. 93.
66 See for instance, *Straits Times*, 8 and 15 August 1989; 21 and 24 December 1989; also *Jakarta Post*, 8 December 1989.
67 On at least two occasions, Lee praised Suharto. One was in a speech to the National Press Club in Canberra in April 1986, the other was in Singapore National Day speech. See *Tempo*, 24 April 1986, p. 14; *Straits Times*, 15 September 1989. In his National Day speech, Lee said that Suharto "was the most important factor determining the stability and progress of the ASEAN region".
68 Koh, op. cit., p. 92.
69 Ibid.
70 *Straits Times*, 22 June 1995. Previously it was fifth, next to Japan, United States, South Korea and Germany.
71 W.K. Che Man, *Muslim Separatism: The Moro of Southern Philippines and the Malays of Southern Thailand* (Kuala Lumpur: Oxford University Press, 1990), especially pp. 82-83; 139.
72 Yoga Sugomo, *Memori Jenderal Yoga (Seperti Diceritakan Kepada Penulis B. Wiwoho dan Banjar Chaeruddin)* (Jakarta: Bina Rena Pariwara, 1990), p. 209.
73 Yoga was incorrect when he said that the meeting was held on 3 January 1975. See Sugomo, op. cit., p. 210. The Manado Talks were in May 1974, therefore the meeting should have been held on 3 January 1974.
74 Ibid., p. 210.
75 Department of Public Information, Bureau of National and Foreign Information, The Philippine Government, *Manado Talks* (Manila 1974).
76 Out of 23 provinces in the Moroland, only five still have a Muslim majority. The rest are dominated by the Christians. See Peter Gowing, *Muslim Filipinos — Heritage and Horizon* (Quezon City: New Day Publishers, 1979), pp. 212-213.
77 *Straits Times*, 28 May 1977 and 14 July 1977.
78 "Pertemuan Manado", (editorial), *Angkatan Bersenjata*, 1 June 1974 .
79 *Sinar Harapan*, 11 January 1982.
80 Sugomo, op. cit., p. 211
81 Ibid.
82 Marcos only stated that the Philippines would give up its claim to Sabah at the second ASEAN summit in 1977.
83 *Straits Times*, 9 January 1982; *Sinar Harapan*, 11 January 1982.
84 Ibid. Also Michael Antolik, *ASEAN and the Diplomacy of Accommodation* (Armonk, New York: M.E. Sharpe, 1990), p. 79.
85 For Suharto's decision to attend the summit, see his *Otobiografi Soeharto*, pp. 517-518.
86 *Tempo*, 1 March 1986, p. 12.
87 Ibid.
88 For the statement, see *Kompas*, 21 November 1987.
89 Mochtar stated that the Subic and Clark bases were the internal problem of the Philippines. He also stated that Indonesia would not support any military bases. See *Jakarta Post* and *Kompas*, 14 November 1987.
90 See also Chapter 3, footnote 8 for the relevant argument.

91 The most recent statement by Ali Alatas on the US military bases was made in November 1994. He said that Indonesia "agreed that a US presence in Asia was necessary as a balancing factor, this should not take the form of military bases in Southeast Asia". See "Jakarta says it again", *Straits Times*, 3 November 1994.
92 *Jakarta Post*, 26 August 1986.
93 Ibid.
94 Ibid.
95 *Kompas*, 16 April 1993. However, Paul Jacob, the *Straits Times* correspondent in Jakarta maintained that the talk "was brokered by the Organization of Islamic Countries (sic) and hosted by Indonesia", *Straits Times*, 17 April 1993.
96 *Kompas*, 16 April 1993.
97 *Sinar Harapan*, 1 and 2 November 1993.
98 *Straits Times*, 18 and 22 May 1994.
99 *Straits Times*, 18 May 1994.
100 *Straits Times*, 17 May 1994.
101 Ibid.
102 *Straits Times*, 21 May 1994.
103 It is worth noting that the Front Aksi Malaysia, a Malaysian NGO, also planned to hold a forum on East Timor in June 1994. It failed to materialize as a result of the ban imposed by the Malaysian Government, presumably under Jakarta's pressure. See *Suara Pembaruan*, 27 June 1994.
104 For a good discussion on the ASEAN perception of threat, see Robert Tilman, *Southeast Asia and the Enemy Beyond: ASEAN Perceptions of External Threats* (Colorado: Westview Press, 1987).
105 See Werner Draguhn, "The Indochina Conflict and the Positions of the Countries Involved", *Contemporary Southeast Asia*, Vol. 5, No. 1 (June 1983), pp. 95-116.
106 For a discussion of Chatichai's policy on Kampuchea, see David Koh Wee Hock, "The Indochina Policy of Chatichai Choonhavan: An Application of National Role Conception Analysis" (B.A. Honours thesis, Department of Political Science, National University of Singapore, 1990).
107 For a brief discussion on the proposal, see Tan Kong Yam, "Whither ASEAN?", in *Asean-ISIS Monitor*, No. 2 (January 1992), pp. 6-10, especially p. 8.
108 Haji Zaini Haji Ahmad, the Acting Vice President of The Peoples' Party of Brunei in Exile, admitted "Indonesian blatantly gave support and involvement in the Bruneian Revolution". He also noted that "a policy to liberate Northern Borneo had always been pursued by the Indonesian Government. It was essential for Indonesia to view the Northern territory as an area rightfully under her sphere of influence". See Haji Zaini Haji Ahmad (ed.), *Partai Rakyat Brunei, The People's Party of Brunei: Selected Documents*, (Kuala Lumpur: Insan, 1987). p. 45. Also see Michael Leifer, *Indonesia's Foreign Policy*, (London: George Allen and Unwin, 1983), p. 81.
109 *Berkhatan* (or *berkhitan*) means to be circumcised, one of the obligations for a Muslim.
110 James Bartholomew, *The Richest Man in the World: The Sultan of Brunei* (London: Penguin Books, 1989), pp. 184-185.
111 Ibid.
112 Lee Kim Chew, "ASEAN sees success at security discussions", *Straits Times*, 11 June 1994.
113 The ARF consists of six ASEAN states, United States, China, Russia, Japan, South Korea, Canada, Australia, New Zealand, the European Union, Vietnam, Laos and Papua New Guinea.
114 See Yang Razali Kassim's interview with Ali Alatas in *Business Times*, 27 July 1994.
115 Ibid.

6

Indonesia's Relations with Australia and Papua New Guinea
Security and Cultural Issues

Introduction

Although Indonesia's relations with Australia are not as important to it as its relations with the ASEAN states, it is clear that Indonesia has been concerned with Australia. This has become particularly evident after the "liberation of West Irian" (now Irian Jaya) and more recently, since the annexation of East Timor. Two issues have coloured Jakarta-Canberra relations — the East Timor problem and Indonesia's policy towards Papua (i.e. eastern) New Guinea (PNG). This chapter examines recent relations between Indonesia and Australia during the New Order period, especially after the annexation of East Timor, and also considers Indonesia's relations with PNG.

Indonesia-Australia Relations

Early relations between Jakarta and Canberra were cordial. Australia was among the few Western nations which were sympathetic to Indonesia's claim for independence. The relationship began to cool once Jakarta adopted a militant foreign policy. Indonesia's campaign to "liberate West Irian" caused tension between Jakarta and Australia because Canberra was concerned with the security of Papua New Guinea, then Australian "territory". Australia was suspicious of Sukarno's policy as the Government feared he might not stop in West Irian. Australian suspicions were strengthened by Indonesia's *konfrontasi* policy with Malaysia. Relations between Indonesia and Australia began to improve after the fall of Sukarno and the emergence of Suharto, before the East Timor problem became the major issue between Jakarta and Canberra.

In 1974, Portugal underwent a "revolution" which resulted in its decision to grant self-government to its colony, East Timor. The decolonization process was far from smooth. Internal conflict and the emergence of the left-wing Fretilin were perceived by Suharto's Indonesia as a threat to Indonesian political stability. Jakarta was afraid that an independent East Timor under Fretilin might become the Cuba of South east Asia. In addition, Indonesia also saw the East Timorese as their "lost brothers". As a result, Indonesia intervened and eventually incorporated the Portuguese ex-colony into the Republic.[1]

In 1974, when Labor Prime Minister of Australia, Gough Whitlam, visited Indonesia, Suharto sounded him out on the East Timor issue. It was reported that Australia would have no objection if the territory was peacefully integrated into Indonesia.[2] When Indonesia annexed East Timor by force, however, the Australian public was not willing to accept the situation. Even the Labor Government was critical of Indonesia's action and Australia criticized Indonesia in the United Nations.

Major criticisms came from Australian labour unions and a number of left-wing groups. Perhaps the event which soured Jakarta-Canberra relations was the death of five Australian journalists who were covering a story in East Timor.[3] They witnessed the Indonesian invasion and are believed to have been killed by Indonesian soldiers.[4] Understandably, the Australian press continued to be critical of Indonesia and especially of Indonesia's policy towards East Timor.

Australian attitudes concerning the plight of the East Timorese were sympathetic. The Government allowed refugees to enter Australia and urged Indonesia to allow those East Timorese who had families in Australia to migrate. Nevertheless, Canberra attempted to improve relations with Jakarta. In August 1976, soon after Indonesia's integration of East Timor, Liberal Prime Minister, Malcolm Fraser, made a remark about ineffective Indonesian leadership while he was in Beijing. This upset the Indonesian Government although Canberra maintained that a misunderstanding had occurred. The matter was dropped in the hope of preventing further embarrassment.[5] Australia, conscious of the damage done, moved to patch up its relations with Indonesia. Fraser decided to visit Jakarta. Immediately prior to his visit, the Australian Government closed the Fretilin exile radio in Darwin and made a contribution to the Indonesian Red Cross for East Timor. While in Indonesia, the Australian Prime Minister was full of praise for President Suharto and made statements which were interpreted by the Indonesian Government as recognition of East Timor's integration into Indonesia.[6] Some analysts argue that Fraser had no interest in Indonesia at all, and that his main foreign policy thrust was to associate closely with China against the Soviet Union, even at the cost of neglect of ASEAN, for which he had little respect.[7] Yet he decided to give *de jure* recognition of Indonesia's acquisition of East Timor in 1978, to enable talks to be started over the Timor Gap in the seabed boundary; Jakarta had refused to start talks until its sovereignty was recognized.[8]

In March 1977, when the former Australian consul in East Timor, James Dunn, testified before the American Senate on Indonesian atrocities in East Timor, the Indonesian Government protested. The Australian Government argued that Dunn was appearing in the Senate hearing as a private citizen. The event further affected Jakarta-Canberra relations. By the early 1980s, Canberra had "accepted and recognized the integration of East Timor into Indonesia as a reality".[9] In November 1982, Australia's Foreign Minister, Anthony Street, said that it was time for the international community to put the Timor issue behind it.[10] Australia also actively opposed the Portuguese resolution on East Timor in the UN General Assembly. The Australian attitude was appreciated by Jakarta.

In 1984, however, Jakarta again became angry with Canberra over the visit of the Fretilin Foreign Minister to Australia. Jakarta considered the granting of a visa to Jose Ramos Horta a hostile act.[11] The situation worsened when Australian Foreign Minister, Bill Hayden, commented in a television interview that Australia would continue to criticize Indonesia as long as "death squad" activities were going on in the ex-Portuguese colony.[12]

The interpretation of democracy by the Australians was very different from that of the Indonesians. It is worth noting that Jakarta has always been critical of the Australian Broadcasting Corporation which broadcasts in Bahasa Indonesia and has been critical of the Indonesian Government. The Jakarta authorities have often complained that this is an unfriendly act, but the Australians, who traditionally practise democracy, argue that the Government is not be able to control Australian journalists.[13] It seems that the antagonism between the Indonesian Government and the Australian press hindered better relations between the two countries.

Since 1976 when East Timor became an issue, many Australian journalists have been barred from entering Indonesia. In early 1986, two Australian journalists who were working for the US media were forbidden to cover President Reagan's visit to Indonesia as a result of the so-called "David Jenkins Affair" that had taken place just before Reagan's scheduled visit. Jenkins, foreign editor of the *Sydney Morning Herald*, published a two-part article (10 April 1986) which purported to reveal the business dealings of the Suharto family. The introduction compared Suharto to Marcos of the Philippines, particularly the indulgent attitude of the two leaders concerning the accumulation of wealth by their friends and family members.[14]

The article angered Indonesian authorities who took retaliatory measures. All Australian journalists were barred from entering Indonesia to cover the Reagan visit.[15] Any Australian journalist whose permit had expired would not have it renewed and Australian tourists attempting to enter Bali without visas, as had previously been allowed, were turned away. This created an uproar, but, within 24 hours the authorities had reversed their order and Australian tourists were once again permitted to enter the country without visas.[16] It was reported that the reversal came by order of President Suharto himself.[17] There was speculation that this incident had been caused by competition among government officers (especially the military) who wanted to show their loyalty to the President and some of them had gone overboard in the process. Apparently, the Indonesian Foreign Ministry was embarrassed by the affair and wanted to keep it low key.

While Mochtar Kusumaatmadja stated that "Indonesia realized that what was said in the article is not the position of the Australian Government", Benny Murdani was quoted as saying "we are deeply hurt and very offended" by the *Herald's* article.[18] Murdani also noted that "as in the case of 1948 [when Indonesia was attacked by the Dutch], the Indonesian Armed Forces also feel obliged to defend the honour of the Indonesian head of state and family".[19] This incident shows that there was disagreement between the army (security authorities) and the Ministry of Foreign Affairs. The military usually took a harder line.

Following the appearance of the *Sydney Morning Herald* article, Dr B.J. Habibie, Minister for Research and Technology, cancelled a scheduled visit to Australia.[20] It was also reported that the defence co-operation programme between Jakarta and Canberra was frozen.

Another incident occurred in September 1986. The Indonesian authorities forbade the Royal Australian Air Force to land in Jakarta to refuel. This refusal coincided with the publication of a book by Richard Robison, an Australian scholar, which criticized the economic development policy of the Suharto Government. Like Jenkins, Robison discussed Suharto and his family businesses and this annoyed the authorities.[21] Jakarta's strong action was attributed to the Ministry of Defence as a form of protest against Robison's book.[22] Five days after the landing ban, Australian Ambassador Bill Morrison and Benny Murdani met to discuss the matter and the ban was lifted.[23] Towards the end of October of the same year, the Australian Primary Industries Minister, John Kerin, visited Indonesia and held discussions with President Suharto. This was seen as indicative of an improvement in relations between the two countries.

However, a revelation of two reports caused some tension between the two countries again: the Paul Dibb Report and the "White Paper" of the Australian Ministry of Defence. Paul Dibb is an expert who was commissioned by the Australian Ministry of Defence to investigate the Australian defence capability. He suggested that Australian defence should also take into account potential threats, one of which would come from Indonesia. The White Paper suggested that Australia should defend its northern areas by establishing naval units capable of operating long distance. This was considered by Jakarta to be a provocative move.[24] After Ali Alatas became Foreign Minister in March 1988, Jakarta-Canberra relations appeared to improve considerably. One of the reasons was good personal relationships between Alatas and some Australian leaders, particularly Foreign Minister Gareth Evans. Australian ministers began to visit Indonesia again, and, eventually the Australian Chief of Staff was invited to Jakarta which was reciprocated by a visit of the Indonesian Army Chief of Staff to Australia. Alatas also made a trip to Australia to engage in dialogue with the Australian press.[25] It was also reported that Indonesia might hold a joint military exercise with Australia.[26] The Indonesian military seemed to have adopted a more pragmatic policy towards Indonesia's southern neighbour. Some observers in Jakarta argued that the change of the policy may have been due to the new Army Chief of Staff, Try Sutrisno, who wanted to show that he was quite different from his predecessor. In fact, even Minister of Defence Benny Murdani mellowed in his attitude towards Australia. He stated that Australia was not a threat to Indonesia.

The major breakthrough in relations between Jakarta and Canberra took place when the Foreign Ministers of the two countries signed the Timor Gap Agreement in December 1989.[27] As mentioned earlier, the talk on Timor Gap was attempted during the Fraser administration, but because of the East Timor issue the Indonesians refused to negotiate. When Bob Hawke was Prime Minister, he was also eager to talk about the issue, but again, the strained relations over East Timor, Papua New Guinea and the Australian press made any fruitful discussion impossible. It was only after Suharto's move to play a more active role in foreign affairs and Alatas' succession as Foreign Minister, that the Agreement was eventually concluded.

The Agreement allows the two countries to explore and exploit the Timor Gap, which is rich in oil, pending a settlement of their overlapping boundary claims. They are required to share the products of such exploration evenly. Alatas was of the opinion that the two nations have succeeded in turning "prolonged and fruitless negotiations on sea boundaries into an area of practical co-operation".[28] Alatas also commented that the Timor Gap Agreement "will confirm Australia's *de jure* recognition of East Timor's integration into Indonesia".[29]

The issue of East Timor emerged yet again when a massacre of East Timorese occurred in November 1991. The event drew world attention to Indonesia once more. (For a discussion of the event, see Chapter 4.) A demonstration took place in front of the Indonesian Embassy in Canberra. The demonstrators burned the Indonesian flag which caused some tension to enter Canberra-Jakarta relations. Australian Foreign Minister, Gareth Evans, was sent to Indonesia to show Australian concern. It was reported that he failed to see President Suharto, Minister of Defence, Benny Murdani and Chief of Staff, Try Sutrisno.[30] However, after Indonesia set up a national commission to investigate the shooting and a preliminary report was released, the international community seemed pacified.

Nonetheless, the East Timor issue did not disappear. Portugal and the East

Timorese wanted to draw international attention to the Indonesian occupation of the island. Soon after the Dili Affair, it was reported that a peace boat full of East Timorese activists sailed to Australia from Portugal, but their eventual destination was East Timor. They wanted to lay wreaths on the graves of the people killed by the Indonesian army during the incident. Indonesia was critical of this action and claimed it was provocative. The boat was sent back to Darwin.

The Dili Affair strained the relationship between the two countries. The new Prime Minister, Paul Keating, was eager to improve ties between Australia and Indonesia. It was announced that from 21 to 24 April 1992, Keating would visit Indonesia to discuss the establishment of "a firm base for the long term development of relations between the two countries".[31] The visit was taken to mean that Australia accepted Indonesia's report on the shooting in Dili.[32] At the end of his visit, Keating also pledged A$11.5 million to be used for the development assistance of East Timor.[33]

Keating appears to be fond of Indonesia. Within 18 months of becoming Prime Minister, he visited Indonesia three times. When the newly designated Indonesian Ambassador, Lt.-Gen. Herman Mantiri, who had made a controversial statement soon after the Dili massacre, was about to be sent to Canberra, there was strong opposition in Australia. Nevertheless, Keating refused to veto the appointment, although it was hinted that it would be difficult for the new envoy to perform his tasks under the circumstances.[34] Jakarta, under pressure, gave in. Mantiri himself was angry but he said that as a military man, he would accept the Government's decision.[35]

Perhaps, Keating's accommodating position concerning Indonesia has been influenced by his perception of Australia's national interest. He believes that "there was a natural link up of interests between Indonesia, Vietnam and Australia".[36] The defining elements of Indonesia and Vietnam's foreign policy, are their suspicions of China. Keating is of the view that it is important to set up "a non-China bloc of economic interests" which includes Indonesia, Vietnam and Australia, as Australia does not want to come within the Chinese orbit. However, he quickly adds that this is not "a primary objective of Australian foreign policy because we have nothing to fear from China".[37]

Keating's pro-Indonesia attitude bore fruit. On 18 December 1995, Australia signed a security agreement with Indonesia, committing the two countries to consult regularly on common security concerns and to promote security co-operation. The agreement also states "their security respect for the sovereignty, political independence and territorial integrity of all countries".[38] This is the first time that the Suharto Government has signed a security agreement (not a treaty) with a Western country, signifying improved Canberra-Jakarta relations and Suharto's admission that Indonesia shares common security interest with Australia.

Indonesia and Papua New Guinea

Indonesian relations with Australia's neighbour, Papua New Guinea (PNG), is also a factor in the Indonesian-Australian relations. Papua New Guinea was, at one time, under Australian control. In September 1975 it became an independent state.[39] The Indonesian Government has been very concerned with Papua New Guinea partly because of the presence of the Free Papua Movement (OPM). Rebels often used Papua New Guinea as a sanctuary after harassing Indonesian troops. The Papuan government in Port Moresby also fears possible invasion by Indonesian troops.

After a number of border conflicts, Indonesia eventually signed a border treaty with Papua New Guinea in 1979. It is interesting to note that the treaty was signed in Port Moresby by President Suharto.[40] Tensions continued to arise over border-crossers, however. In March 1984, there was a confrontation between Jakarta and Port Moresby over Indonesian border violations.[41] An Indonesian chartered plane landed in Papua New Guinea and was ambushed by OPM guerillas. Indonesian air force exercises were going on near the border at the time, and when the plane was discovered missing, Indonesian jets flew into Papuan territory and either dropped a bomb or fired a rocket.[42] Port Moresby protested the violations of its border and condemned Indonesia for undertaking "a major military exercise in the border region without first notifying the Papua New Guinea Government of their intention".[43]

Initially, Jakarta's response was mixed. Mochtar Kusumaatmadja was reported to have said that it would be better if military exercises were conducted farther away from the border but he was unable to give further information.[44] However, the military denied that any border violations had occurred. Port Moresby was dissatisfied with the reply and expelled the Indonesian military attache. The Indonesian response to this was restraint. When Namaliu, the Papuan Foreign Minister, requested a meeting with Mochtar and the Defence Minister, Benny Murdani, he was refused.

Despite the tension, negotiations continued. The PNG and Indonesian Governments eventually reached an agreement. Real improvement only took place when Paias Wingti took office in November 1985. He adopted a more co-operative attitude towards Jakarta. It was under Wingti's premiership that the Treaty of Mutual Respect, Friendship and Co-operation between Jakarta and Port Moresby was signed in October 1986.[45] The Indonesian military courted the Papuan military: it was later revealed that General Murdani had given nearly A$200,000 to Ted Diro, the former military commander of the PNG army, for his political campaign.[46] Indonesia-Papua New Guinea dialogues were reported to be conducted regularly, involving high-ranking officials and scholars. In July 1988, Namaliu took over the government from Wingti and Jakarta-Port Moresby relations improved further. Consulates were established in Jayapura, Irian Jaya, and Vanimo, PNG.[47] In April 1990, Alatas visited Port Moresby, renewing the current five-year border accord and extending it to ten years. He noted that the renewal of this treaty for ten years showed that "both sides were satisfied with the existing arrangements on the border".[48]

The most important agreement was the Status of Forces Agreement (SOFA) signed by Namaliu during his visit to Jakarta. This agreement "provided further co-operation in defence activities, including joint military training and exchanges of military personnel and civic missions".[49] PNG's changing attitude towards Indonesia was based on a realistic assessment of the situation. Each side needed the other's co-operation to maintain political stability. SOFA would enable PNG to concentrate on domestic issues, including the solution of the separatist problem on Bougainville island. SOFA is also important for Indonesia because it raises the possibility of PNG allowing Indonesian the right of 'hot pursuit' of OPM across the border.[50]

During the 1980s, Indonesia had become more concerned with the South Pacific. In addition to Papua New Guinea, Indonesia also recognized the possibility of having more influence on other Pacific islands. When a military coup, led by Colonel Setiveni Rabuka, took place in Fiji and the elected government was overthrown, many countries boycotted the new regime. However, Indonesia continued to support the junta.[51] Representatives of the Rabuka regime were dispatched to visit Indonesia. It was reported that Rabuka and his officers admired Suharto's Indonesia because of the central role played by the Indonesian military in both political and economic affairs. The new Fiji authorities wanted to use the Indonesian constitution as a model.[52]

An unofficial Indonesian trade mission was sent to Fiji. President Suharto offered Fiji 25,000 tons of rice on credit and special financing facilities. Benny Murdani also announced in Jakarta that he had approved a high level military delegation to Fiji in order to form some kind of alliance.[53] Indonesian Foreign Minister Mochtar also called for closer ties with Fiji. Apparently Indonesia wanted to play a greater role in the South Pacific through cultivating the military leaders in Papua New Guinea and Fiji.

Conclusion

Indonesia's relations with Australia and Papua New Guinea have been influenced by Indonesia's concern with its security and influence in the southern region. Understandably, the Indonesian military has been heavily involved in foreign policy-making. It appears that the approach of the Indonesian Foreign Ministry and that of the Ministry of Defence often conflicted. Although the picture is not entirely clear, there is evidence that, initially, the Indonesian military had the upper hand. Gradually, however, the Ministry of Foreign Affairs, supported by President Suharto, was able to assert more influence. The concessions made by the Australians and Papuans to Indonesia made it possible for Indonesian relations with the two countries to improve. The position has been especially cordial after Paul Keating became Prime Minister, partly due to his strategic concept — he saw Indonesia and Vietnam as Australia's natural political and economic partners. Nevertheless, the different cultures of these countries, Western democracy and Asian authoritarianism may still be a major source of conflict between Indonesia and Australia in the future.

NOTES

1 For an in-depth discussion of the East Timor issue, see Chapter 4.
2 According to Hamish McDonald, "Whitlam told Suharto that he thought the best solution would be for East Timor to join Indonesia, adding with somewhat less emphasis that the wishes of the Timorese should be respected and that the public reaction in Australia would be hostile if Indonesian used force", McDonald, op. cit., p. 195. Also Hiorth, op. cit., p. 41.
3 *Kompas*, in its editorial noted that one of the reasons for the Australian press's negative reports on Indonesia was the five Australian journalists killed during the conflict in East Timor. "Indonesia dan Australia Sepakat untuk Membarui Hubungan", 2 March 1989.
4 Another source said that they were killed in Balibo at the height of the fighting between pro-Indonesian forces and the leftist Fretilin group. See Lim Yoon Lin, "A History of Suspicion", *Straits Times*, 28 April 1986.
5 Leo Suryadinata, "Indonesia in 1976: A Year of Challenge", *Southeast Asian Affairs 1977*, p. 120.
6 Leo Suryadinata, "Indonesia under the New Order: Problems of Growth, Equity, and Stability", in Leo Suryadinata and Sharon Siddique (eds.), *Trends in Indonesia II* (Singapore: Singapore University Press, 1981), especially pp. 38-39.
7 A comment by a leading scholar on Australian-Indonesian relations.
8 Ibid.
9 H.D. Anderson, "Australia-Indonesia Relations", in *Regional Dimensions of Indonesia-Australia Relations* (Jakarta: CSIS, 1984), p. 13.
10 Ibid.
11 *Suara Karya*, 16 July 1984.
12 Donald Weatherbee, "Indonesia: The Pancasila State", *Southeast Asian Affairs 1985*, p. 146.
13 It is worth noting that, in 1980, Jakarta demanded that Radio Australia stops its broadcasts on Indonesian politics in Bahasa Indonesia. (See *Tempo*, 5 July 1980, p. 10.) From Jakarta's point of view, the broadcasts were aimed at the Indonesian people and hence represented an unfriendly act.
14 The title of Jenkins article was "After Marcos, Now for the Soeharto Billions".
15 "Indonesia Bans 12 Journalists", *International Herald Tribune*, 29 April 1986.
16 Max Karundeng, "Kasus David Jenkins: Kerapungan Hubungan RI-Australia", *Rekaman Peristiwa '86* (Jakarta: Sinar Harapan, 1987), p. 20; *Asia 1987 Yearbook* (Far Eastern Economic Review Annual Publication), p. 155.
17 Hamish McDonald, "Strained Relationship", *Far Eastern Economic Review*, 22 May 1986, p. 42.
18 *Straits Times*, 22 April 1986.
19 Ibid.
20 *International Herald Tribune*, 30 April 1986; also *Asia 1987 Yearbook*, p. 155.
21 Richard Robison, *Indonesia: The Rise of Capital* (Sydney: Allen and Unwin, 1986).

22 *Tempo*, 13 September 1986, p. 21.
23 Ibid.
24 Hilman Adil, *Hubungan Australia Dengan Indonesia 1945-1962* (Jakarta: Djambatan, 1993), p. xiii.
25 *Suara Karya*, 1 and 4 March 1989.
26 *Jakarta Post*, 27 February 1989.
27 *Straits Times*, 9 December 1989.
28 *Straits Times*, 12 December 1989.
29 *Jakarta Post*, 6 December 1989; *Straits Times*, 7 December 1989. It is worth noting that in early 1995, Ali Alatas received the Order of Australia award in recognition of his role in boosting ties between Indonesia and Australia. Bill Hayden, the Governor General of Australia commented that "Alatas made a personal and political commitment to the development of a relationship with Australia based on practical cooperation for mutual benefit". *Indonesia Business Weekly*, Vol. VIII, No. 18 (17 April 1995), p. 28.
30 Hilman Adil, *Hubungan Australia Dengan Indonesia*, p. xiv.
31 *Straits Times*, 19 March 1992.
32 Ibid.
33 Adil, *Hubungan Australia Dengan Indonesia*, p. xv.
34 He made a remark in *Editor*, a weekly which is now defunct, that the Dili massacre was "quite proper". *Strait Times*, 30 June 1995. Lt.-Gen. Mantiri later told the Australian Broadcasting Corporation radio that he was sorry about the incident. *Sunday Times*, 2 July 1995.
35 "Wawancara: Mantiri siap mati", *Gatra*, 15 July 1995, p. 34.
36 Laura Tingle, "PM tells Asia to get tough on trade", *Australian*, 11 July 1994.
37 Ibid.
38 *Straits Times*, 19 December 1995; *Gatra*, 23 December 1995, p. 23.
39 For a short discussion on Indonesia-PNG relations up to early 1982, see Donald Weatherbee, "Papua New Guinea's Foreign Policy: A Bridge to Indonesian Shores", *Contemporary Southeast Asia*, Vol. 4, No. 3 (December 1982), pp. 330-345 (especially pp. 333-334).
40 *Asia Yearbook 1987*, op. cit., p. 220.
41 For a good discussion of the problem, see Stephen V. Harris and Colin Brown, *Indonesia, Papa New Guinea and Australia: The Irian Jaya Problem of 1984* (Australia-Asia Papers No. 29) (Nathan: Centre for the Study of Australian-Asian Relations, Griffith University, February 1985).
42 Ibid., p. 16.
43 Ibid., p. 17.
44 Ibid.
45 Ikrar Nusa Bhakti, "Learning to Live Together", *Far Eastern Economic Review*, 12 March 1992, p. 14.
46 Michael C. Howard, *Fiji: Race and Politics in an Island State* (Vancouver: UBC Press, 1991), p. 337.
47 Ibid.
48 *Straits Times*, 9 April 1990.
49 Ibid.
50 Ibid.
51 Howard, op. cit., p. 337.
52 Ibid.
53 Ibid.

7

Indonesia-China Relations
Ideology, Ethnic Chinese and the President

Introduction

This chapter examines Indonesia's policy towards China under Suharto. It explains why it took so long for Jakarta to normalize relations with Beijing and what obstacles arose in the process. What were the factors that contributed to the diplomatic breakthrough in 1989? What were the roles of the military and the President in this normalization process? Are there any issues which may affect the relations?

Sino-Indonesian Relations under Sukarno

It is a well-known fact that, during Sukarno's time, Indonesia was on good terms with the PRC, especially in the mid-1960s when Indonesia, together with the PRC, attempted to set up the Conference of New Emerging Forces (CONEFO) headquartered in Jakarta. CONEFO was supposed to be a United Nations of poor countries because at the time, the PRC had not yet been admitted to the UN, and Indonesia had just left the organization.[1] This did not mean, however, that all socio-political forces in Indonesia were in support of close Beijing-Jakarta relations. On the contrary, the army was worried about a Beijing-Jakarta axis but was not able to move Indonesia away from the PRC anti-colonialist coalition.

In the 1960s, prior to the emergence of the New Order, there were three political forces competing for influence in domestic politics. Communist influence continued to grow after the 1957 by-elections and the Army also gained in strength after crushing the 1958 regional rebellions in Sumatra and Sulawesi. The President, who was becoming more left-wing in his political orientation, initially attempted to balance the PKI against the Army and vice-versa, but gradually he moved closer to the PKI. Fearing the rise of the military, the PKI wanted to establish a Fifth Army under its control made up of peasants and workers. Sukarno lent his support to the idea and sent Omar Dhani, the chief of the Air Force, to negotiate with the PRC in the hopes of getting small weapons for the Fifth Force. Apparently, the President wanted to balance the army's strength by aligning himself with the PKI and the Air Force.

This balance of power game came to a sudden end on 30 September 1965 when an alleged communist coup took place.[2] Six generals were kidnapped and slain, but General Nasution escaped. General Suharto, who was the commander of the Strategic Unit in Jakarta, was not on the list. The coup resulted in the liquidation of the PKI, the downfall of Sukarno and the triumph of the Indonesian Army. Suharto emerged as Indonesia's new strongman. He succeeded in manoeuvring other groups and, in 1966, became the most influential leader.

The Coup and Sino-Indonesian Relations

The coup changed the direction of Indonesia's foreign policy. New Indonesian leaders who were anti-Communist began to abandon the previous left-leaning policy. The first target of the new Indonesian foreign policy was the People's Republic of China (PRC) which was believed to have been involved in, if not behind, the abortive coup.

The role of the PRC in the coup is still unclear. Two views are worth mentioning. The first is that China endorsed the coup and supplied the PKI with weapons "outside the knowledge and control of regular Indonesian army authorities". Chinese officials in Beijing knew about the coup six hours after it occurred and possessed a list of all the Indonesian generals supposed to have been assassinated. Moreover, it was a team of Chinese physicians brought from Beijing who had informed D.N. Aidit, the leader of the PKI, of Sukarno's precarious health, and it was this information that led to the PKI's abortive coup.[3] A CIA report released later argued that there was no hard evidence to suggest that the PRC was behind the coup but it suggested that "because of the timing of [Chairman] Aidit's visit to China and the start of PKI's preparations for the coup almost immediately upon his return from China, a case can be made on the basis of circumstantial evidence that the Chinese must have inspired the Indonesian coup".[4]

Another view holds that Beijing did not endorse the coup for the following reasons. First, the situation prior to the coup was favourable to Beijing and it is difficult to comprehend why Beijing would plan a coup which would jeopardize this situation. The seizure of only a small number of Chinese-made weapons after the coup also suggested that China was not involved. Second, it is not likely that a strong Communist party like the PKI would have taken orders from Beijing.⁵

The true role of China in the coup may not be known for some time because of the limited evidence available. But, for the purpose of this discussion, it is not really important whether or not China was involved in or behind the coup. What is important is how the new Indonesian authorities (the army and the anti-communist elite who came to power after the coup) perceived China and what the Chinese attitude was towards them.

The new Indonesian authorities believed that China was behind the coup. They were not only suspicious but were also hostile towards the PRC. The PRC, in turn, was equally hostile towards them. The Chinese called the Indonesian army "reactionary" and "fascist". In addition, Beijing defended the PKI and gave some of its leaders political asylum. Relations between Indonesia and the PRC continued to deteriorate and in October 1967, Jakarta suspended diplomatic ties with Beijing.⁶ Relations remained frozen for 22 years. Suharto also ended direct trade links with China. Although China continued to sell goods to Indonesia and vice-versa, the exchanges took place through a third party.

With the deterioration of relations between Jakarta and Beijing, Indonesia's relations with Taiwan improved, although Indonesia continued to pursue a one-China policy and refused to establish diplomatic ties with Taiwan. At one time, Adam Malik said that, if Taiwan changed its name to the Republic of Taiwan, Indonesia would recognize it.⁷ Although there were no diplomatic ties, Taiwanese leaders and trade delegations made frequent informal visits to Indonesia. The volume of trade between Jakarta and Taipei also increased.

Sino-Indonesian Relations under Suharto

As soon as Suharto assumed power, he terminated Indonesia's policy of *konfrontasi* with Kuala Lumpur and introduced a good neighbour policy. On the one hand, Indonesia made an effort to improve its relations with Western countries and on the other hand, it kept its distance from the socialist states. Soon after the inception of the New Order, Indonesia was readmitted to the United Nations (UN). Whenever the PRC's UN seat was discussed and votes were taken on the issue, Jakarta abstained. This was different from the situation before the 1965 coup.⁸ In 1971, when the PRC was admitted as a member of the United Nations, Chinese representatives began to woo their Indonesian counterparts at the UN and expressed a desire to be friendly. Jakarta was not responsive. Malik, in a radio interview in the Netherlands, reiterated that the PRC had been involved in the 1965 coup and that it continued to support PKI leaders in exile, thus showing an unfriendly attitude towards the new Indonesian Government.[9]

In the 1970s, the PRC began to adopt a more moderate foreign policy aimed at cultivating friendship with Third World countries in the hope of exercising more influence over them. In 1974 and 1975, China succeeded in establishing diplomatic ties with three ASEAN nations, Malaysia, the Philippines and Thailand. Indonesia remained adamant. In order to avoid Indonesian suspicion, ethnic Chinese-dominated Singapore decided not to normalize relations with Beijing before Jakarta did.

Deng Xiaoping's rise to power in 1977 led to further moderation in the PRC's foreign policy. It embarked on the "Four Modernizations Programme" which required foreign investment, high technology and a stable political situation. Friendly relations with non-Communist countries were actively pursued. This was especially noticeable after the Vietnamese invasion of Cambodia in 1978 and the Sino-Vietnamese war in early 1979, when Beijing began to pay greater attention to Southeast Asia. It decided that having good ties with Indonesia, the largest country in the region, would enhance its position and also benefit the PRC. ASEAN's stand on the Kampuchean issue was also closer to that of Beijing than that of Hanoi, and Beijing wanted the continued support of the ASEAN states and the friendship of Indonesia.

Indonesia was still suspicious of the PRC, however. In 1967, Suharto noted in his National Day speech that Chinese involvement in the 1965 coup and its continuing support for the PKI had resulted in abnormal relations between the two countries.[10] In 1973, he stated that Indonesia would normalize relations with the PRC if China were truly friendly and "ceases to render assistance and facilities to the former PKI leaders".[11] It was clear that Jakarta was not yet ready to restore relations with Beijing.

In fact, Indonesian leaders were divided in their views of Sino-Indonesian relations. This division became conspicuous after the rise of Deng Xiaoping. Some saw advantages while others saw disadvantages in normalizing relations between Jakarta and Beijing. The pro-normalization group included businessmen and officials in the Ministry of Foreign Affairs, especially Adam Malik and Mochtar Kusumaatmadja. The Indonesian businessmen felt that normalization would encourage Indonesian exports to the PRC and this would help stimulate business in Indonesia. The Ministry of Foreign Affairs felt that normalization would project Indonesia's image as a non-aligned nation overseas. It would be easier for Indonesia to deal directly with the Chinese on a number of international problems. The pro-normalization group was defeated.

The anti-normalization group was much larger and stronger than the pro-normalization group. It consisted of President Suharto himself, the military in Hankam, the *Merdeka* group (based on a newspaper owned by B.M. Diah, an

Indonesian nationalist, who was pro-Moscow and anti-Beijing), the Islamic group, and the Taiwan lobby in Indonesia. The military, which was concerned with internal security, regarded the PRC as a major security risk. It was afraid that the PRC would assist the banned PKI to subvert the New Order once it was allowed to establish an embassy in Indonesia. The military feared that Beijing would make use of the overseas Chinese in Indonesia to promote its own interests.[12] It is also possible that some of the generals were benefiting from indirect trade with mainland Chinese as the situation allowed them to gain commissions. (This point will be discussed later.) Meanwhile the *Merdeka* group was actively spreading anti-Beijing propaganda.[13]

The Islamic group which was fundamentally anti-Communist, was also worried about the PRC. The Muslims were afraid that Beijing would again support the left-wing movement in Indonesia after it established normal ties with Jakarta. Muslims who were active in business were also concerned about the changing position of the overseas Chinese. Once Beijing-Jakarta relations were restored, Jakarta would grant citizenship to these alien Chinese in order to avoid Chinese intervention in its internal affairs. Granting citizenship to alien Chinese would strengthen the hold of this minority group on the Indonesian economy. This was perceived as being at the expense of the indigenous Indonesian business group. The Taiwan lobby in Jakarta was worried that normalization would affect its relations with Jakarta.

The most significant figure in determining Sino-Indonesian relations was President Suharto himself. In fact, Suharto had clashed with Adam Malik over the normalization issue. Adam Malik had appeared to be interested in resuming ties with the PRC since August 1976. Reviewing New Order foreign policy, Malik had argued that there were no problems between Jakarta and Beijing, and they could normalize relations "any time".[14] In January 1977, he told the press that he had met abroad with Chinese officials in recent years "and all obstacles to re-establishing relations have been eliminated". He said that the PRC "has stopped anti-Indonesian propaganda and no longer supports PKI" and suggested that diplomatic ties could be resumed after the general elections of May 1977.[15] In March 1978, Vice-President Malik announced to the foreign press that "Indonesia had already reached a decision on the question and said the resumption of ties would not be so difficult". He noted that normalization "will not be too long off".[16]

Suharto, however, disapproved of what Malik said. In his autobiography, Suharto clearly expressed his disagreement with Malik on this question although, in general, the two got along well. The President mentioned that Malik often made statements which did not coincide with the governmental policy on political issues, although Malik himself was part of the Government.[17] Suharto specifically mentioned the normalization issue. He said that Indonesia was still restrictive (*membatasi*) in its relations with the PRC, but Malik's statements conveyed the impression that diplomatic ties would be restored in the coming year.[18] This created difficulties for the Government. In fact, Suharto still held the view that the PRC had backed the PKI and saw this as interference with Indonesia's domestic affairs. He demanded that the PRC suspend its links with Communist parties in the region before diplomatic ties could be normalized.[19]

The military was even more rigid in its demands. As late as 1984, the army newspaper *Angkatan Bersenjata*, demanded that the PRC sever links with the PKI, acknowledge its involvement in the coup and apologize to Indonesia.[20] These conditions would be impossible to fulfil and indicated that the military group was not yet ready for normalization. It appears that there was a difference of opinion between Suharto and the military concerning their conditions for normalization, although both were concerned with the question of security posed by the PKI. In the case of Suharto, it appears that since 1984 he had decided on a more liberal policy towards the PRC due to economic pressures and also his desire to play a major role in foreign affairs.

Direct Trade and Improvement of Relations

Indonesia began to make concessions to the PRC when oil prices declined. As oil constituted 60 per cent of its state revenues, Indonesia needed to promote its non-oil exports. The Suharto Government thus decided to expand its export markets, especially for its non-oil commodities. In addition to Japan and the West, Jakarta also wanted Indonesian products to enter the markets of the socialist states, in particular the Chinese market. Indonesian businessmen, especially those in Kadin (Chamber of Commerce and Industry), were particularly enthusiastic. Kadin is a semi-official organization which was once headed by Suharto's brother-in-law, Sukamdani. It was under his leadership that Kadin board members joined Golkar, the governing political party.[21]

In November 1984, Mochtar Kusumaatmadja announced Indonesia's intention to resume direct trade with the PRC.[22] He pointed out that this would not be linked with the re-establishment of diplomatic ties, however, because Jakarta was not ready for overall normalization. Apparently, the military was still wary of the PRC. Beijing welcomed the Indonesian initiative. Representatives of the two countries began to negotiate in Singapore on direct trade links. In April 1985, Wu Xueqian, Chinese Foreign Minister, was invited to attend the thirtieth anniversary celebration of the Afro-Asian Conference in Bandung. The presence of Wu Xueqian at the conference was a friendly gesture by the PRC and helped to smooth trade negotiations. In July 1985, a trade memorandum between China and Indonesia was signed in Singapore.[23] It was the first time that an agreement on direct trade had been reached. In the same month, an Indonesian trade delegation visited China. Soon after, China sent a trade delegation to Indonesia. Direct trade had nominally started, but Indonesia continued to refuse to let the PRC establish a trade office within its borders as the military was still afraid that the PRC might use such an office to carry out subversive activities.

Direct trade moved slowly as problems arose. The facilities for direct trade had not been well developed and some argued that Sino-Indonesian trade might be better conducted through a third party, that is, through Hong Kong and Singapore, due to the "apparent weaknesses of both countries in managing international trade".[24] It has also been argued that the Indonesian military and the PRC bureaucrats preferred to conduct trade through a third country because it allowed them to take kickbacks. It was difficult for the military and Chinese bureaucrats to profit from direct trade.[25]

Although direct trade was not smooth, its volume continued to grow. According to Indonesian statistics, exports to China increased from US$110 million in 1985 to US$361 million in 1987. Chinese exports to Indonesia increased from US$72 million in 1985 to US$250 million in 1987. According to the same source, when imports from Hong Kong were included, Chinese exports to Indonesia exceeded Indonesia's exports to China.[26]

If Sino-Indonesian economic relations improved slowly, the improvement in political relations was even slower. As noted, Wu Xueqian, Foreign Minister of the PRC, was present at the thirtieth anniversary celebrations of the Afro-Asian Conference in Bandung. It was reported that Wu Xueqian wanted to meet Suharto privately on this occasion, but Suharto was only able to see him on the day when Wu was to depart. Wu decided to leave on schedule.[27] Later, Mochtar commented that had Wu gone to see Suharto, the President "could have forgiven China and relations between the two countries would have been normalized then".[28]

It is possible that Suharto intentionally scheduled the meeting on the day of Wu's departure as a hint that Indonesia was not yet ready to normalize relations with the PRC. Even if Wu had gone to see Suharto, he would not have been able to get what he wanted. There was also a rumour circulated at the time that the odd scheduling was intentional as there were some military leaders who wished to humiliate the Foreign Minister of the PRC.

During his visit to Bandung, Wu Xueqian was quoted in the Indonesian press as saying that China had stopped supporting the PKI.[29] He also noted that most of the PKI leaders who took refuge in China after the 1965 coup had left China for Europe. China, however, refused to sever all links with the Communist parties of the same ideology.[30] Indonesia and other ASEAN countries considered the Communist party illegal. To maintain contact with illegal political parties was seen as an intervention in the internal affairs of the ASEAN states.

Sino-Indonesian relations continued to improve after the thirtieth anniversary of the Afro-Asian Conference. In March 1987, for instance, Ali Alatas, then the Indonesian Ambassador to the United Nations, and Nana Sutresna, then Political Director at the Indonesian Foreign Ministry, went to China to attend the UN disarmament conference in Beijing. In mid-1988, Chinese Deputy Foreign Minister Liu Shuqing was invited to attend the UN Asia-Pacific Economic Community Conference in Jakarta. Many observers suggested that Indonesian-Chinese relations would soon be normalized, but there was no sign of a complete normalization until February 1989.

The 1989 Breakthrough

In early 1989, Suharto decided to attend the funeral of Japanese Emperor Hirohito in Tokyo. During this visit, on 23 February 1989, Indonesia suddenly announced that it was possible for Jakarta and Beijing to restore diplomatic ties. This came as a surprise to many because the secret had been closely guarded. It was later reported that Chinese representatives had contacted the Indonesian representatives in the United Nations and expressed their wish to meet with Suharto in Tokyo. Indonesia responded favourably. It was also reported that at least ten meetings were held before the decision was made.

What were the factors which contributed to Indonesia's decision to normalize relations with the PRC? After the re-emergence of Deng Xiaoping, China became more benign and inward-looking, and many argued that China was no longer exporting revolution. In fact, the PRC's support for ASEAN Communist parties had decreased significantly after Deng assumed power.[31]

The so-called overseas Chinese problem which was frequently viewed as one of the major obstacles to normal Sino-Indonesian relations was under control. In the 1970s, at least one million Chinese in Indonesia were either PRC citizens or stateless. The presence of this large number of foreign Chinese, who were PRC citizens under Chinese law, was seen as detrimental to Indonesia's national interest as it would allow the PRC to interfere with Indonesian domestic affairs through these ethnic Chinese. Not surprisingly, Jakarta quickly introduced a mass naturalization plan and many Indonesian Chinese took the opportunity to become Indonesian citizens. By 1986, according to Indonesian official figures, there were only 350,000 foreigners in Indonesia of whom 250,000 were PRC citizens. In 1987, the number was slightly higher, 273,000, due to births and other factors.[32] The ethnic Chinese were no longer a problem even though their presence was later used by the contra-normalization group as a reason for not agreeing to "early normalization".

Members of the Suharto group, especially those in Kadin (Chamber of Commerce and Industry), were eager to further improve economic links with the PRC through diplomatic ties. Sudwikatmono, who was a leader of Kadin, is related to Suharto. He also has business connections with Chinese *cukongs* (a term used to refer to Chinese businessmen who collaborate with power elite) such as Liem Sioe Liong,[33] who are interested in expanding Sino-Indonesian trade. Direct trade was often hampered by the absence of political relations.

The decision to normalize relations seems to have been closely connected to Suharto's desire to play a major role in world politics in general and in the Asia-Pacific region in particular. For instance, in 1985, Indonesia's hosting of the thirtieth anniversary of the Bandung Conference showed to the world that Indonesia was ready to play a more active role in international politics. Sponsoring the Bandung Conference anniversary was also a step in Indonesia's preparations to propose to host the upcoming conference of the Non-Aligned Movement (NAM).

From 1986, Jakarta expressed a strong interest in becoming the chairman of NAM.[34] In addition, Indonesia was eager to play a leadership role in the settlement of the Kampuchean issue. This prompted the decision to hold the Jakarta Informal Meeting (JIM) in 1987 in the hope of finding a solution to the Kampuchean problem. Indeed, since 1984, the Indonesian Government under Suharto had begun to establish closer relations with Hanoi as evidenced by the visit of Nguyen Co Thach, the Vietnamese Foreign Minister, to Indonesia and also by General Murdani's visit to Hanoi. The Vietnamese Defence Minister, Van Tien Dung, visited Indonesia in April 1985.[35] Indonesia was anxious to solve the Kampuchean problem quickly and, in this way, establish its leadership role, but Hanoi was not ready to compromise.

Since 1987 a new development has taken place. The Soviet Union under Gorbachev decided to come to terms with the PRC and a summit was planned for May 1989. In light of this, the Indonesian Government felt that if relations with the PRC were not restored, Indonesia might be left behind in the international game.

Nonetheless, the crucial factor was still Indonesia's desire to play a major role in international affairs and especially its wish to host the NAM meeting and solve the Kampuchean issue through its leadership. Without diplomatic relations with China, Indonesia would not be able to do much, as many countries which were friendly to the PRC or the former Soviet Union perceived Indonesia as not completely non-aligned. Normalizing relations with the PRC would project the image that Indonesia was really non-aligned and thus enhance its chance of hosting the NAM meeting. (For Indonesia and NAM, see Chapter 11.)

It should be noted, however, that Suharto wanted to maintain an equidistant policy towards Moscow and Beijing. Since he had scheduled a visit to Moscow, he felt that diplomatic relations with Beijing should be restored. In addition, Suharto's visit to Moscow was intended to gain the support of the "Soviet bloc" in NAM. It was likely that the decision on normalization was aimed at securing the PRC's concession on the Kampuchean issue. In fact, a few analysts maintain that, with normalization, the PRC will be more likely to co-operate with Indonesia to find a quick solution to the Kampuchean problem.[36]

It appears that Suharto would like to be remembered as the architect of Indonesia's foreign policy as well as the "Father of Development". Suharto knew that it was under his rule that Indonesia suspended diplomatic ties with the PRC and wished to see ties restored while he was still in power. Indeed, Suharto was instrumental in the normalization decision. To oversee direct trade with China, for instance, he appointed Moerdiono, a military officer and Minister of State for the State Secretariat (Mensesneg). In other words, this function was taken away from the Ministry of Trade and the Ministry of Foreign Affairs.[37] When Suharto decided to announce the start of the normalization process, he did it through Moerdiono.[38]

What about the conditions that had been set by the Indonesian Government for Sino-Indonesian normalization? There was neither a public statement from Beijing admitting involvement in the 1965 coup nor a declaration that it would sever all links with the PKI. Beijing did state, however, that it would abide by the principles of the Bandung Conference which denounce intervention in another country's internal affairs.[39] Moerdiono explained to the Indonesian press that the Bandung principles also included party-to-party relations.[40]

After the announcement of the normalization, President Suharto told the Japanese Prime Minister that China had "confirmed that it will not support the Communist Party of Indonesia" and that relations between the two countries would be based on "such principles as mutual respect of each other's sovereignty, non-interference in domestic affairs and peaceful coexistence."[41] The international community welcomed Jakarta's decision to normalize relations with Beijing as many felt that this would contribute to peace and prosperity in Asia.

Indonesia's Reactions

The reactions of Indonesian leaders to the decision to normalize relations with China varied. Some were enthusiastic while others were not. For instance, the deputy speaker of the House (the DPR or House of Representatives) representing Golkar, R. Soekardi, said that the President's decision should be supported by the Indonesian people because it was important for Indonesia to have diplomatic ties with all nations.[42]

Civilian newspapers, such as *Kompas* and *Suara Pembaruan*, hailed the decision as being in the national interest. *Kompas*, in an editorial, held that, from both strategic and practical points of view, normalization would benefit

Indonesia because it would allow Indonesia more freedom in implementing foreign policy.[43] It would also help to resolve regional problems such as the Kampuchean and Spratly issues. The army dailies, *Angkatan Bersenjata* and *Berita Yudha*, however, did not show their support clearly.[44] The two newspapers simply reported what had happened in Tokyo, together with the Government's statement and Moerdiono's explanation of normalization. They noted that Moerdiono had had many meetings with PRC representatives before the decision was made. There were no interviews with military leaders on the issue, and the language used in *Angkatan Bersenjata's* editorial was non-committal.

In fact, there were many comments and interviews in the press which expressed doubt concerning the benefits of Sino-Indonesian normalization. For instance, *Suara Karya*, the Golkar newspaper, commented in an editorial that there were still many questions to be answered about the normalization issue.[45] It noted that, although the PRC had promised through its Foreign Minister that it would no longer intervene in the domestic politics of Indonesia, the policy was not made by the Foreign Minister himself. It also argued that, although the PRC had shown signs of change in its orientation, there was no guarantee that it had really changed.

The "opposition party" (Partai Persatuan Pembangunan or PPP) and the pro-Soviet newspaper *Merdeka* also had reservations. The view of H.J. Naro, the deputy speaker, who represented the Muslim PPP party, was similar to that of *Suara Karya*.[46] He added that the PRC should allow Indonesia to question those PKI members who had been hiding in China. Despite their advanced age, they had to be watched. He also noted that the problem of Chinese illegal immigrants still existed and should be well thought out before normalization took place. Finally, he demanded that "the DPR should be involved in the process of normalization".[47]

The chairman of the DPR foreign relations committee from the PPP (Komisi Satu), H. Imron Rosyadi, said that there was no need to rush the normalization of ties between China and Indonesia because trade relations had already been reactivated.[48] He suggested that the decision made in Tokyo be expanded and made into a formal agreement. Noting that there were still problems to be solved, he pointed to the status of ethnic Chinese in Indonesia on which clarification was still required. The pro-Moscow newspaper *Merdeka*, in its editorial, also stated that the PRC could not be trusted. China had stabbed Indonesia in the back many times since the time of Kublai Khan.[49] *Merdeka* noted that Sino-Indonesian normalization was welcome but stressed that, in view of historical experience, Indonesia "should be fully watchful".

At an ASEAN seminar that closed on 1 March 1989 in Jakarta, the director of Lemhanas (Institute of National Defence), General Subiyakto, noted that the ASEAN countries still considered China a potential threat.[50] His assistant, Brigadier-General Santo Budiyono, expressed a similar view.

It is clear then that there were people in Indonesia who opposed "early normalization". Some were concerned with security issues while others had a vested interest maintaining the absence of normal ties. It appeared that the Government had fallen into its own trap by overemphasizing the security risk presented by the PRC. Many military officers still use the same argument in their opposition to normalization. Many politicians felt that the timing was not right and that they had not been informed or involved in the decision-making process. Although Soekardi, a spokesman for Golkar in the DPR, praised Suharto's decision, he, too, wanted the Government to brief parliament on the issue. He said that the President's assistant, Moerdiono, could provide an explanation.[51]

Largely in response to the rather negative reaction, on 1 March 1989, General Try Sutrisno, then the Army Chief of Staff, told the Indonesian people that they should support the Government's decision on normalization and that they should be confident enough to handle the normalization issue.[52]

A number of questions had to be settled before an exchange of ambassadors could take place. In fact, it had not been clear earlier whether relations between the two nations would be at the ambassadorial level. There was also the problem of the stateless Chinese and other technical issues that were yet to be solved. Many observers believed that the actual normalization (that is, the exchange of ambassadors) would take place within a year. The Indonesian Government, itself, did not set a date.

After the Tiananmen Square incident in June 1989, some Indonesian military leaders, including General Subiyakto, again called for a review of the normalization process.[53] Quoting Suharto, Ali Alatas responded that the Tiananmen affair would not affect the process of normalization.[54] Nonetheless, opposition to normalization still existed. The former head of the State Intelligence Body (BAKIN), Yoga Sugama, expressed his reservations about "early normalization". He noted that Jakarta "should wait for further development in Beijing".[55]

It appears that President Suharto was eager to accelerate the normalization process. This was reflected in his congratulatory message to the Chinese President, Yang Shangkun, on China's National Day, 1 October 1989.[56] This was the first time that a top Indonesian leader had made this gesture. In October, the Indonesian Foreign Ministry announced that senior Chinese officials would visit Jakarta in either November or December 1989 to discuss the technical aspects of normalization with their Indonesian counterparts.[57] It was clear that Suharto was determined to get the ball rolling.

There were still many issues to be resolved. A. Dahana, an Indonesian sinologist, pointed out that the location and size of the Chinese Embassy in Jakarta would be delicate issues. If the PRC re-established its embassy in Jakarta's Chinatown, the Indonesian authorities would be suspicious. The problem of the stateless Chinese was another issue which needed to be resolved before normalization could occur.[58] Dahana argued that the Malaysian formula could be adopted; let older Chinese go on as before and grant Indonesian citizenship to the younger ones. However, Dahana did not discuss what action would be taken by those who disagreed with "early normalization".

These technical problems were indeed discussed during the Jakarta meeting between Xu Dunxin, head of the Chinese delegation and Assistant Foreign Minister of China, and John Louhanapessy, Director-General of Political Affairs in the Indonesian Ministry of Foreign Affairs, in early December 1989. The PRC agreed to accept a site for its embassy in an area where other embassies were located.[59] It was reported that there would be no more than 20 Chinese embassy staff during the initial period. The Chinese also agreed to allow Chinese citizens to return to China while those who wanted to stay would be given passports. The Chinese delegation wanted to verify the numbers of these Chinese and was unwilling to accept the figure of 320,000 given by the Indonesian Government.[60] The Chinese refused to discuss the problem of stateless Chinese, however, because they considered it Indonesia's internal problem.[61]

The Chinese agreed not to raise objections to the Taiwanese trade office in Jakarta as long as Indonesia did not raise its status to the diplomatic level. In fact, the Chinese delegates praised Indonesia's consistent policy of upholding the "One China" policy.[62]

The Chinese initially wanted Indonesia to use China's pre-coup name "Republik Rakyat Tiongkok". The Indonesians rejected this, however, and insisted on using "Republik Rakyat Cina". "Cina" was at one time considered derogatory by the Chinese, but, this time, the Chinese delegation bowed to Indonesian pressure.[63] Apparently, the PRC was anxious to speed up the normalization process. Beijing had felt isolated after the Tiananmen affair and wanted to cultivate friendships within ASEAN and especially with Indonesia.

The problem of debt to the PRC incurred by Indonesia during the Sukarno era was also discussed. *Kompas* estimated that the debt had amounted to US$15 million in 1965 but increased to US$46.5 million in 1977.[64] The World Bank's estimate at the end of 1988 was US$65.3 million.[65] No agreement was reached on the issue but it was decided that the matter would be settled at the next meeting in Beijing.

In February 1990, Ali Alatas told a parliamentary hearing that the talks on normalization of ties with China were almost completed, paving the way for the opening of the diplomatic missions.[66] He said that full normalization would take place in 1990. Although there were still Indonesian leaders who disagreed with "early normalization", there was little they could do as it was Suharto's decision. Consequently, in early August, a Chinese delegation led by Li Peng visited Jakarta and, on 8 August, the Foreign Ministers of the two countries signed a Memorandum of Understanding.[67] Suharto made a speech in which he said that both Jakarta and Beijing should forget the past and begin a new chapter in Indonesia-China relations. On 14 November, Suharto paid a state visit to Beijing to reaffirm the newly established ties.[68] In early June 1991, President Yang Shangkun visited Indonesia to promote economic and political ties.[69] Nevertheless, the regulation issued in 1985, which required Indonesians wanting to do business with China to get clearance from Bakin, was still enforced. It was only revoked in August 1991, one year after ties were restored.[70] In the last few years, Indonesia-China ties have improved further, as evidenced by the permission of Indonesian investment in mainland China, the presence of President Jiang Zeming at the APEC summit in Bogor, the visit of General Feisal Tanjung (Indonesian Commander-in-Chief of Armed Forces) to Beijing, and most recently, Alatas' visit to the PRC to discuss regional as well as bilateral issues. There is no doubt that the official relations have improved although there are still many challenges.

Issues Affecting Sino-Indonesian Relations

Despite improved relations, there are still issues which may affect this relationship. One of them is the question of ethnic Chinese. Many Indonesians still harbour suspicion towards Indonesian Chinese as they are felt to have links with the PRC. An example of this is the hiring of skilled labourers/professionals from the PRC by an Indonesian Chinese firm.

Eka Cipta Widjaya (Oey Ek Tjhong), a *totok* tycoon, needed more electricity for his Indah Kiat paper mill but was unable to get it from the government electric company. For this reason, he applied for permission to set up his own power stations and received the approval of the Ministry of Industry. Indah Kiat then negotiated with a PRC company which manufactured the power plant equipment. This Chinese Company agreed to sell the equipment to Indah Kiat on condition that the machinery be installed by PRC workers who would be involved in the establishment of the power stations. This was approved by the Indonesian Co-ordinating Body for Foreign Investment (BKPM) and the Ministry of Labour. More than 1,000 Chinese professionals/labourers from the PRC were "imported".

When this fact became known, Cabinet Minister Ginandjar Kartasasmita, who was not consulted on the project, protested the use of these foreign workers. He argued that the job could be done by Indonesian citizens and said that it was unpatriotic to use foreign workers when millions of Indonesians were unemployed. The media in Jakarta began to write about the situation and tension arose. In Riau, where one of the power stations was located, the Indonesian students demonstrated against Indah Kiat. The situation was also discussed in parliament. Although there were points for and against the project, the Government eventually backed down. The Chinese workers were forced to return to China in stages.[71] In fact, there are many foreign workers in Indonesia, and the Chinese are not the most numerous.[72] When Chinese workers were involved, however, it became an issue.

Ethnic Chinese investment in the PRC after normalization also generated debates in 1993 when local papers began to discuss the issues. Some felt that this was part of the global trend and the investment was for economic reasons rather than ethnic affiliation.[73] Others said that the investment was against Indonesian national interest when Indonesia still badly needed foreign investment.[74] There is still a lingering suspicion of Beijing. Jakarta fears that Indonesian capital may go to China to the detriment of the Indonesian economy where capital is badly needed. Not surprisingly, Indonesia has been monitoring investment by its nationals in the land of the dragon.[75]

Another example which involved ethnic Chinese was the labour unrest in Medan which developed into racial riots. In recent years, there has been increased political awareness among Indonesian workers who were demanding their rights, including better pay and better working conditions. Many employers refused to give in. Demonstrations, believed to have been organized by the independent trade union, Serikat Buruh Sejahtera Indonesia (SBSI), took place in many major cities. However, the most serious one was in Medan in April 1994. It was reported that the demonstrations were initially peaceful. The demonstrators demanded better pay for workers and also government recognition of the SBSI.[76] The peaceful demonstration later erupted into riots, resulting in three casualties, one of whom was ethnic Chinese.[77] Shops, houses and cars, many owned by ethnic Chinese, were destroyed.

Wu Jianmin, the spokesman of the PRC Foreign Ministry issued a statement expressing concern over the situation in Indonesia. Beijing hopes that the Indonesian Government settles the problem as "China is a friendly country with Indonesia".[78] Some Indonesian leaders, including a minister, considered this as an interference in Indonesian internal affairs.[79] Although the statement did not develop into conflict between Jakarta and Beijing owing to mutual restraint, it has given the impression that the PRC still wants to interfere in ethnic Chinese affairs.[80]

Situations involving ethnic Chinese in Indonesia may affect the relations between Indonesia and China if not handled with care. The PRC has shown its willingness to solve the problem of stateless Chinese and in general it has adopted a non-interventionist policy with regard to ethnic Chinese who are not its citizens. Clearly, future policy change will affect Sino-Indonesian relations.

In addition, there is still potential rivalry between China and Indonesia over regional leadership. Indonesia perceives China as a possible competitor in Southeast Asia. Both Indonesian military and civilian leaders consider Indonesia the natural leader in the region. For this reason, it is not surprising that as soon as the Kampuchean issue was under control, Indonesia began to pay attention to the South China Sea, particularly the Spratly Islands which have been claimed by the PRC as its sovereign territory. The Spratly Islands have also been claimed by four other Southeast Asian states: Vietnam, the Philippines, Malaysia and Brunei.[81]

Indonesia sees the Spratlys as a potentially explosive issue. Although Indonesia is not a claimant, armed conflict in the area would undoubtedly affect the stability of the region. Indonesia feels that it has a responsibility to involve itself in the management of this conflict. Since the late 1980s, Indonesia has sponsored four international workshops to discuss a peaceful settlement of this problem.

Initially, China refused to participate, but, after normalization of ties, Chinese delegates were sent to the conference. The Chinese appeared willing to exploit the Spratly Islands together with other claimants but refused to concede on the issue of sovereignty.[82] When the Foreign Ministers of ASEAN met in Manila in July 1992, Qian Qichen, Chinese Foreign Minister, suggested to the ASEAN participants that a "Sino-ASEAN forum" be set up to discuss the issue.[83] ASEAN's representatives were not interested in the proposal as shown in the declaration which had no mention about the proposal. They felt that there was no need to create a new forum just between China and ASEAN as there are enough forums to discuss the issue which has international implications.[84] The recent conflict (in March 1995) over Mischief Reef in the South China Sea between China and the Philippines has led to renewed suspicion among the ASEAN states concerning Beijing's promise to solve the dispute by peaceful means.[85]

Although Indonesia is not a party to conflict in the Spratly Islands, in recent months the question of the Natuna Islands has caused concern in Jakarta. The PRC has included Indonesia's Natuna gas field in "its maps of claims to a broad swath of South China Sea".[86] It was first seen by Indonesia in 1993,[87] but only in July 1994 did the Indonesian Government ask China for clarification. If the response of Indonesian Foreign Ministry was mild, the Indonesian military was not. Defence and Security Minister, Edi Sudrajat, was very critical of the PRC. He was quoted as saying that "the map, which showed that parts of Indonesian territorial waters around the Natunas — between Borneo and the Malaysian peninsula and near the multinationally disputed Spratly Islands — belonging to Chinese, was made 'without respect to international sea laws'".[88] However, a few days earlier, Alatas had announced that "Indonesia had no territorial problem with China near the Natuna Islands in the South China Sea" arguing that "the Chinese map was only an illustrative one and could not be seen as an effort to establish an actual position".[89] Nevertheless, the issue has not been completely solved.[90]

Another issue which may affect Indonesia-China relations is Jakarta's relations with Taiwan. Since Suharto came to power, Jakarta-Taipei relations have improved. Although Indonesia claims to pursue a "One-China" policy, it continues to maintain economic relations with Taiwan which often have political overtones. Bilateral trade and Taiwanese investments in Indonesia are quite significant. For instance, Indonesian exports to Taiwan amounted to US$561 million in 1991/1992 and Indonesian imports from Taiwan amounted to US$1.042 million. In the same year, Indonesian exports to the PRC were worth US$627 million and its imports from the PRC US$657 million.[91]

More significant is Taiwanese investment in Indonesia. In 1991, Taiwan invested more than US$1,057.5 million, but in 1992 and 1993 the amount was reduced to US$563.3 million and US$124.6 million respectively.[92] The drastic decline might be caused by the investment shift from Batam to mainland China. Nevertheless, the Taipei Government is committed to investing in ASEAN and has sent high level delegations to ASEAN countries. In February 1995, Lee Teng Hui, President of the ROC, led a delegation to pay a "private visit" to Thailand and Indonesia.[93] In Bali where Lee was "holidaying", he was received by Minister B.J. Habibie and Suharto, resulting in protests from the PRC.[94] Nevertheless, Indonesia insisted that this was a "private visit".

Conclusion

This chapter clearly shows that there was a division on Sino-Indonesian diplomatic relations. One group, represented by Foreign Minister Adam Malik, was pro-normalization, while the other group, represented by the military, was against it. Suharto sided with the military establishment. The relations improved only after Suharto changed his mind in the late 1980s as a result of the changing domestic and international situation, and Suharto's desire to play an active role in international affairs.

Although Sino-Indonesian relations have improved, there are still issues which may affect the relationship in the future: the question of ethnic Chinese, the possible conflict in the South China Seas over the Spratly Islands, the question of the Natuna territorial waters and Jakarta-Taipei relations. If China changes its policy towards the ethnic Chinese and becomes entangled in the affairs of the Indonesian Chinese again, it may affect the relationship of the two countries. Also, if China uses force in the Spratly Islands to settle the dispute over the islands' sovereignty, it may generate friction between Beijing and Jakarta. Last but not least, if Jakarta enhances its ties with Taipei and is perceived by Beijing to be pursuing a "Two-China" policy, it will definitely affect Beijing's attitude towards Jakarta.

NOTES

1. For a discussion on the Beijing-Jakarta Axis, see David Mozingo, *China's Policy Toward Indonesia 1949-1967* (Ithaca: Cornell University Press, 1981), pp. 205-230.
2. For a survey of the literature on the Coup, see Justus M. van der Kroef, "Interpretation of the 1965 Indonesian Coup", Vol. XLIII, No. 4, *Pacific Affairs* (Winter 1970-71), pp. 557-577.
3. US Central Intelligence Agency (CIA) *Indonesia — 1965: The Coup that Backfired* (Washington DC: Library of Congress, 1968), especially pp. 216-235; Justus M. van der Kroef, "Origins of the 1965 Coup in Indonesia: Probabilities and Alternatives", *Journal of Southeast Asian Studies*, Vol. 3, No. 2 (September 1972), pp. 277-298; also Arthur J. Dommen, "The Attempted Coup in Indonesia", *China Quarterly*, No. 25 (January-March 1966), pp. 144-170.
4. CIA, op. cit., p. 218.
5. For a summary of this view, see Peter van Ness, *Revolution and Chinese Foreign Policy: Peking's Support for Wars of National Liberation* (Berkeley: California University Press, 1970), pp. 101-110.
6. It is interesting to note that the Indonesian Government used the term *membekukan* (to freeze), rather than *memutuskan* (to sever), Indonesian-Chinese relations. The Indonesian argument goes like this: The ties were still there but were temporarily frozen (for 22 years!) This also meant that Indonesia still recognized the PRC as representing China. In practice, however, this was no different from suspension of relations.
7. *Yindunixiya Ribao*, 9 June 1969.
8. Leo Suryadinata, *Pribumi Indonesians, the Chinese Minority and China: A Study of Perceptions and Policies* (Kuala Lumpur and Singapore: Heinemann, 1986, 2nd edn.), pp. 185-186.
9. *Berita Buana*, 24 August 1971.
10. *Antara News Bulletin*, 16 August 1967, p. 23.
11. Cited in Harvey Stockwain, "Suharto Meets the Auditors", *Far Eastern Economic Review*, 19 March 1973, p. 11.
12. For the military perception of the "Overseas Chinese" in Indonesia, see Suryadinata (1986), op. cit., pp. 41-45.
13. For the Merdeka view on the PRC, see Soepeno Sumardjo, *Ancaman Dari Utara* (Jakarta: Karyaka, 1980).
14. Adam Malik, *Sepuluh Tahun Politik Luar Negeri Orde Baru* (Jakarta: Yayasan Idayu), p. 27.
15. *Straits Times*, 1 January 1977.
16. Ibid., 20 March 1978.
17. Suharto, *Otobiografi: Pikiran, Ucapan dan Tindakan Saya. (Seperti dipaparkan kepada G. Dwipayana dan Ramadhan K.H.)* (Jakarta: Citra Lamtoro Gung Persada, 1989), p. 333.
18. Ibid.
19. *Merdeka*, 18 August 1975; Also *Tempo*, 3 March 1989, p. 15.
20. *Angkatan Bersenjata*, 8 November 1984.
21. *Sinar Harapan*, 9 June 1984. See also Leo Suryadinata, *Military Ascendancy and Political Culture: A Study of Indonesia's Golkar* (Athens: Ohio University Press, 1992), pp. 127-128.
22. *Kompas*, 8 November 1984.
23. *Jakarta Post*, 17 July 1985.
24. See for instance, Djisman S. Simandjuntak, "Demythologising the China-Indonesia Trade", in *Indonesia Quarterly*, Vol. 13, No. 2 (1985), p. 146. However, Simandjuntak also argued that it is based on the following assumption: "Indirect trade may work well as long as it is in the interest of intermediaries".
25. This has been pointed out to me by a few Indonesian Chinese businessmen who have been involved in the Indonesian-Chinese trade.
26. *Straits Times*, 15 October 1988.
27. Ibid.
28. *Kompas*, 23 February 1988; *New Straits Times*, 24 February 1988.
29. Ibid.

30. The statement was made by Chinese Foreign Minister, Wu Xueqian, in his interview with *Shijie Zhishi*, a PRC foreign policy magazine. See Huang Shuhai, "Zhongguo ho Yinni liangguo fazhan qianjing", *Shijie Zhishi*, No. 11 (1985) pp. 2-3.
31. It is a generally held view that since Deng re-emerged, the PRC's support for ASEAN Communist parties has declined. For an academic treatment of the subject, see William R. Heaton, "China and Southeast Asian Communist Movements: The Decline of Dual Track Diplomacy", *Asian Survey*, Vol. 22, No. 8 (August 1982), especially pp. 779-800.
32. *Tempo*, 4 March 1989, p. 15.
33. On the personal and business relationship between Sudwikatmono and Liem Sioe Liong, see a detailed interview entitled "Kami besar bukan karena dekat dengan Pak Harto", in *Warta Ekonomi*, 21 February 1994, pp. 43-54.
34. In September 1986, the Vice-President of Indonesia attended the Non-Aligned Conference in Harare, Zimbabwe, but he failed to solicit support from the non-aligned states to make Indonesia the next chairman of the movement. Indonesia has continued to work towards this goal since then. In September 1989, President Suharto himself attended the Belgrade summit to campaign for support. *Straits Times*, 15 September 1989.
35. *Asia Yearbook 1986 (Far Eastern Economic Review)*, p. 159.
36. Justus M. van der Kroef pointed out that "the Cambodian question ... [is] more likely to determine the future pace of normalization", see his article, "Normalizing Relations with China — Indonesia's Policies and Perceptions", *Asian Survey*, Vol. 26, No. 8 (August 1986), p. 934. Hadi Soesastro agreed with Kroef's view. See "Indonesia-China Relations" in Joyce K. Kallgren et al. (eds.), *ASEAN and China: An Evolving Relationship* (Berkeley: Institute of East Asian Studies, University of California at Berkeley, 1988), p. 934. *Asahi Shibun* also considered the Cambodian issue one of the major factors for normalization. Cited in *Tempo*, 4 March 1989, p. 15.
37. Moerdiono was still co-ordinator of Sino-Indonesian trade in early 1991. See *Kompas*, 16 January 1991.
38. Some argue that Ali Alatas did all the spade work but made sure that Moerdiono got the credit — that way he would not undermine the normalization process. There are two problems with this argument. First, Moerdiono disagreed with normalization and hence was against Suharto's decision. Second, Moerdiono was supposed to do all the work by himself. In fact, Moerdiono was close to Suharto and was entrusted to do the job so that other military officers would not be able to sabotage it. Being a non-diplomat, Moerdiono certainly needed the expertise of Foreign Ministry personnel, including Alatas, to assist him in this matter. The fact remains, however, that it was Moerdiono who was in charge, not the Ministry of Foreign Affairs.
39. *Renmin ribao* (24 February 1989) reported the Indonesian decision to normalize relations with China very briefly. The Bandung principles were cited as the basis for normalization.
40. "Editorial", *Angkatan Bersenjata*, 25 February 1989; Also *Tempo*, 4 March 1989, p. 15.
41. *Japan Times*, 27 February 1989.
42. *Angkatan Bersenjata*, 28 February 1989.
43. *Kompas*, 25 February 1989.
44. *Angkatan Bersenjata*, 24 February 1989; *Berita Yudha*, 24 February 1989.
45. *Suara Karya*, 27 February 1989.
46. *Angkatan Bersenjata*, 28 February 1989.
47. Ibid.
48. *Merdeka*, 24 February 1989; *Jakarta Post*, 25 February 1989.
49. "Editorial", *Merdeka*, 25 February 1989.
50. *Suara Karya*, 2 March 1989.
51. *Angkatan Bersenjata*, 28 February 1989.
52. *Suara Karya*, 2 March 1989.
53. *Jakarta Post*, 27 June 1989.
54. *Jakarta Post*, 13 June 1989.
55. *Jakarta Post*, 16 October 1989.

56 *Straits Times*, 4 October 1989.
57 *Jakarta Post*, 6 October 1989.
58 *Kompas*, 31 July 1989.
59 *Kompas*, 5 December 1989.
60 She Wenxuo, "Yinni zhengzai yingjie Zhong Yin fujiao", *Lianhe Zaobao* (Singapore), 25 December 1989. This is the only detailed report on what was discussed at the December meeting of the Chinese and Indonesian delegations.
61 Ibid. However, after the normalization, China eventually agreed to issue passports to 240,000 stateless Chinese in Indonesia. *Straits Times*, 19 September 1992.
62 Ibid.
63 During a top level army seminar in Bandung in August 1966, the derogatory term "Cina" (old spelling Tjina) was adopted to replace the terms "Tionghoa" (Chinese) and "Tiongkok" (China) which had been used for years before the 1965 coup. One of the main reasons given by the army was "to remove a feeling of inferiority on the part of our people, while on the other hand removing the feeling of the superiority on the part of the group concerned within the state." The name of the PRC in Indonesian has also been changed to Republik Rakyat Cina. Beijing protested but Jakarta remained adamant. (See Charles Coppel and Leo Suryadinata, "The Use of the Terms 'Tjina' and 'Tionghoa' in Indonesia", in *Papers on Far Eastern History*, No. 2 (Australian National University, September 1970), pp. 97-118. In the 1989 discussion, the Chinese delegates eventually swallowed their pride and accepted the term "Cina" for "Tiongkok" indicating their eagerness to improve relations. It was reported that Xu Dunxin had told a Singaporean reporter that, "In the international world, we are called China, not Tiongkok. China accepts the translation term Republik Rakyat Cina [for the PRC]". (See She Wensuo, op. cit., *Lianhe Zaobao*, 25 December 1989.) It should be noted that in 1994, the PRC began to feel that Cina was improper for the name of the country and insisted on the English term "China". In the official documents, the PRC is now called "Republik Rakyat China" but most of the Indonesian newspapers and magazines continue to use "Cina" for both China and Chinese.
64 *Kompas*, 5 December 1989.
65 *Straits Times*, 7 December 1989.
66 Cited in *Straits Times*, 6 February 1990.
67 *Suara Pembaruan*, 8 August 1990.
68 *Tempo*, 24 November 1990, pp. 28-31; *Berita Yudha*, 19 November 1990.
69 *Renmin Ribao*, 6 and 7 June 1991.
70 *Suara Karya*, 8 August 1991.
71 For various discussions of the case, see "Pelajaran Mahal dari Serang", *Tempo*, 5 September 1992, p. 34; "Menguji Nasionalisme Konglomerat", *Forum Keadilan*, 1 October 1992, pp. 8-11; "Protes, Hanya Karena RRC", ibid., pp. 12-13 and "Kiat PT Indah Kiat Mengimpor TKA", ibid., pp. 15-17.
72 Up to mid-1992, there were 3,000 Americans and 1,500 Japanese working in Indonesia. (In 1991 there were 4,000 Americans and 2,500 Japanese.) Apart from them, there were also workers from Germany, England, South Korea and Malaysia. The total number of work permits issued by the Indonesian Government up to June 1992 was almost 20,000. See "Pelajaran yang Mahal dari Serang", *Tempo*, 5 September 1992, p. 34.
73 *Suara Pembaruan*, 7 April 1993; *Bisnis Indonesia*, 12 April 1993.
74 *Merdeka*, 2 April 1993; *Bisnis Indonesia*, 8 April 1993; "Analisis Kwik Kian Gie: Investasi pengusaha Indonesia di RRC", *Suara Pembaruan*, 16 April 1993.
75 *Kompas*, 6 April 1993; *Bisnis Indonesia*, 5 April 1993.
76 "Mencari Biang Teror dan Intimidasi", *Tempo*, 30 April 1994, p. 25.
77 For a brief discussion of the riot, see *Tempo*, 30 April 1994, pp. 21-32.
78 Amran Nasution, "Ini Medan, Bung", *Tempo*, 30 April 1994, p. 21.
79 *Straits Times*, 26 April 1994; *Lianhe Zaobao*, 27 April 1994.
80 However, Indonesian Foreign Minister Alatas was quoted as saying that he hoped Beijing did not doubt Indonesian ability to solve the Medan riot. He also noted that the PRC

Government may still have spiritual bonds with the ethnic Chinese community. See *Bisnis Indonesia*, 23 April 1994.
81 For a discussion of the dispute over the Spratly Islands, see *Indonesian Quarterly*, Vol. 18, No. 2 (1990), Special issue on "South China Sea: Views from ASEAN", especially articles by Hasyim Djalal, B.A. Hamzah and Lee Lai To.
82 On 28 March 1991, for instance, Chinese Foreign Minister Qian Qichen stated that "We are willing to talk to the countries concerned about joint exploration of the Nansha [i.e. Spratly] Islands, under (sic) the condition of Chinese sovereignty over the archipelago". Cited in Jin Dexiang, "China and Southeast Asia in a Changing Security Environment", in Ji Guoxing and Hadi Soesastro (eds.), *Sino-Indonesian Relations in the Post-Cold War Era* (Jakarta: Centre for Strategic and International Studies, 1992), p. 90 for the citation.
83 "Lain di meja lain di laut", *Tempo*, 1 August 1992, p. 77.
84 Ibid.
85 John McBeth, "Oil-Rich Diet", *Far Eastern Economic Review*, 27 April 1995, p. 28.
86 Ibid.
87 *Straits Times*, 30 June 1995, p. 19.
88 Ibid.
89 Simon Sinaga, "No problem with China over Natuna isles, says Alatas", *Straits Times*, 27 June 1995. In fact, Chen Jian, a Chinese Foreign Ministry spokesman earlier stated that there was no dispute between China and Indonesia over the possession of the gas-rich Natuna islands. However, Chen stated that China was willing to hold talks with Indonesia over the demarcation of the area. Ibid.
90 Alatas visited China to discuss a number of issues, one of which was "to clarify the inclusion of waters off Indonesia's Natuna islands on a Chinese map", *Straits Times*, 19 July 1995. It was reported that "China laid no ownership claim over the [Natuna] islands". Qian also said that China would base any solution of possible disputes on the 1982 Law of the Sea Convention. Alatas was quoted as saying "I see this explanation as quite satisfactory, because if China bases itself on the 1982 Law of the Sea Convention then we are in the same position". See Simon Sinaga, "Natunas 'belong to Indonesia'", *Straits Times*, 22 July 1995. However, *Far Eastern Economic Review* reported that "The Law of the Sea is a treaty on maritime boundaries; China hasn't ratified it". See John McBeth, "Oil-Rich Diet", *Far Eastern Economic Review*, 27 April 1995, p. 28.
91 **INDONESIAN TRADE WITH TAIWAN AND PRC: 1990-1993 (IN MILLION $)**

	Taiwan			Mainland China		
	1990/91	1991/92	1992/93	1992/93	1991/92	1992/93
Export to	411.6	561	779.1	614.9	627	788.9
Import from	1168	1042	1232	572	659	703

Source: Indonesian Trade Ministry, February 1994. Cited in "Diplomasi Liburan Presiden Taiwan", *Warta Ekonomi*, 21 February 1994, p. 10.
92 Ibid.
93 Ibid, see also an article in *Forbes Zhibenjia*, March 1994, pp. 21-25.
94 Qian Yongnian, Beijing Ambassador in Jakarta, was quoted as saying that Lee's visit to Indonesia "hurts the feeling of Beijing and harms friendly relations". Ibid.

8

Indonesia-Vietnam Relations and the Kampuchean Issue
The Security Factor

Introduction

Indonesia and Vietnam share a common historical experience in that these two Southeast Asian countries achieved their independence through revolution, and the leaders of each country have emphasized this point from time to time.[1] They have even argued that this common experience has formed the basis of Indonesia-Vietnam relations.[2] How true is this assertion? What is the nature of their relations? Has Communist ideology been a major factor in the relations between Communist Vietnam and anti-Communist Indonesia? What has really determined bilateral ties? What has been the role of Suharto in Indonesia's policy towards Vietnam? And last but not least, what are the prospects for the future?

Origins of Relations

Indonesia has had informal contacts with Vietnam since the 1940s. Diplomatic ties between Jakarta and Hanoi were only established after the Afro-Asian Conference in Bandung. Jakarta set up a Consulate-General in Hanoi in December 1955, three months after it had established a Consulate-General in Saigon.[3] This policy of equidistance to the two Vietnams was abandoned during the Sukarno period when revolutionary fervour was rising and Indonesia's foreign policy was moving towards the left.

In 1959, Ho Chi Minh was invited to visit Indonesia and was given an honorary degree by a regional Indonesian university. In the same year, Sukarno returned the visit. When the Vietnam war escalated, members of the Indonesian elite, many of whom had been involved in the anti-colonial movement, sympathized with the North Vietnamese. Many of them saw the South Vietnamese as American puppets. On 10 August 1964, Sukarno finally decided to upgrade diplomatic relations between Jakarta and Hanoi from consulate to ambassadorial level.[4] This led to the suspension of diplomatic ties between Jakarta and Saigon, and the Indonesian consulate in Saigon was closed.[5] Soon after, Indonesia decided to recognize the National Liberation Front of South Vietnam (NLFSV) and allowed the establishment of its representative office in Jakarta. Indonesian relations with Communist states, including North Vietnam, became much closer. Together with the PRC, they formed what was known as the Jakarta-Hanoi-Phnom Penh-Beijing-Pyongyang axis.[6] This was the so-called honeymoon period, not only between Indonesia and the PRC, but also between Indonesia and North Vietnam.

The fall of Sukarno after the 1965 coup and the rise of Suharto's anti-Communist Government abruptly ended the honeymoon. Indonesia's foreign policy was adjusted. Nevertheless, diplomatic ties between Jakarta and Hanoi were maintained during the Suharto era, while Jakarta's relations with Saigon were never re-established. This created an impression that Indonesia was still close to Hanoi, which was not entirely correct.

A Subtle Shift

In fact, there was a gradual and subtle shift in Indonesia's policy towards Hanoi. It should be noted that, after the 1965 coup, the PKI was dissolved and Marxism-Leninism was banned. Vietnam was critical of the new Indonesian authorities, and openly sided with the PKI.[7] It is not clear what happened to Jakarta-Hanoi relations after October 1967, following the suspension of relations between Jakarta and Beijing. There are two contradictory versions. Hardi, the Indonesian Ambassador to Hanoi from 1976 to 1979, maintained that diplomatic ties were severed prior to 1973. He did not explain whose initiative led to the break. Adam Malik and others argued that the ties were never severed.[8] Why was there this confusion?

It appears that after the Communist coup in 1965, Indonesia attached less significance to its foreign relations with Socialist/Communist states. However, there was no severance of ties between Jakarta and Hanoi. Even in the case of the PRC, the Indonesian Government referred to a "freezing of diplomatic ties" although, in reality, it was equivalent to the suspension of relations. Unlike Indonesia's relations with the PRC, relations with Hanoi never reached a critical point. The Indonesian Ambassador during that period was Soetrisno, an ex-senior journalist for the *Bintang Timur* who is believed to have been a Communist.⁹ Soetrisno was recalled but refused to return to Jakarta. Hanoi was critical of the new Indonesian authorities and relations between the two countries became estranged but were not "frozen".¹⁰ When Soetrisno later took refuge in the PRC and Eastern Europe, no one was sent to replace him in North Vietnam. Even so, a chargé d'affaires headed the Indonesian mission in Hanoi.

Indonesia-Vietnam relations may have been maintained for several reasons. First, North Vietnam did not play a significant role in the 1965 coup although it was then an ally of the PRC. There was also no influential "overseas Vietnamese community" comparable to that of the ethnic Chinese in Indonesia. Second, Adam Malik, with the endorsement of Suharto, wanted to project the image of a non-aligned foreign policy under the New Order. Third, Indonesian leaders held a certain admiration for the North Vietnamese struggle against the major Western powers.

Nevertheless, during the New Order period, Indonesia's attitude towards North Vietnam was divided. Nationalists, such as Adam Malik and Ruslan Abdulgani, were sympathetic to North Vietnam, which they perceived as a nationalist rather than a Communist nation, in its struggles against foreign domination, first from Imperial China, and later from France and the United States.¹¹ Some military leaders, including Ali Murtopo, were, however, suspicious of the Communist states, including North Vietnam, and were more cautious in dealing with the Vietnamese.

A subtle change of policy took place as early as 1968 when Suharto visited Sihanouk's Cambodia. At the end of his visit, a communiqué was issued in which Jakarta expressed its continuing support for Cambodia under Sihanouk. Although the communiqué mentioned the struggle of the Vietnamese people, Indonesia expressed the hope that a political rather than a military solution could be achieved.¹² This was quite different from Sukarno's policy which advocated military victory by the Viet Minh (the Vietcong), alias the National Liberation Front of South Vietnam (NLFSV) over the Saigon Government.

Indonesia under Suharto was very careful in dealing with the NLFSV, as shown at the Non-Aligned Movement (NAM) meeting in 1972. Indonesia and Malaysia walked out of the NAM Foreign Ministers meeting in Guyana because the NLFSV was admitted as a full member, rather than as an observer, to the meeting. An Indonesian Foreign Ministry document published in 1974 showed that Indonesia, represented by Malik, was sympathetic to the NLFSV but did not feel that it should be granted full member status in NAM which was reserved for sovereign states.¹³ At that time, the NLFSV was still struggling to overthrow the South Vietnamese Government. Perhaps Indonesia and Malaysia objected to the possibility that this would not only create a precedent but also encourage rebellion that would not be in their interests.

When Sihanouk was overthrown by Lon Nol who was supported by the

United States, the Suharto Government did not oppose the new regime. In 1970 it even sponsored the Jakarta conference aimed at finding a peaceful solution to the Indochinese problem.[14] North Vietnam, whose relationship with Indonesia was no longer cordial, and other socialist states were invited, but all turned down the invitation. The boycott indicated that Hanoi considered Indonesia's foreign policy hostile towards the socialist bloc.

Improvement of Ties

Jakarta-Hanoi relations continued to be cold but official contacts were maintained. Adam Malik was eager for a working relationship with the Vietnamese and Vietnam was responsive to Indonesian overtures. In 1973, Indonesia sent an ambassador to Hanoi without requesting that Vietnam sever its links with the PKI. In fact, as late as 1976, Hanoi still wanted to invite the PKI in exile to attend its Communist party congress. This will be discussed later.

It is important to note that Indonesia did not object to Vietnam conducting a dual track foreign policy consisting of state-to-state as well as party-to-party relations. Indonesia was anxious to maintain contact with Vietnam. Jakarta even sent civilian ambassadors to Hanoi instead of military officers as had been the practice immediately after the coup. The first such ambassador was Usep Ranuwidjaja of the Indonesian Nationalist Party or PNI, followed in 1976 by Hardi, who was also from the PNI.[15] According to Hardi, Suharto told him that "he [Suharto] was not ready to appoint a military or a career diplomat as ambassador in Hanoi. In fact, in order to have frank discussions with the Vietnamese Government, a nationalist was needed to head the Indonesian representative office in Hanoi".[16] Why was Jakarta eager to communicate with the Vietnamese? Perhaps it has something to do with Adam Malik's desire to project an image of a non-aligned post-coup Indonesia. Suharto and his generals might also have felt that it was important to cultivate a friendship with Vietnam because of its strategic position with respect to the PRC.

When Hardi became Ambassador, he wanted to persuade the Vietnamese not to recognize and assist the PKI which was illegal in Indonesia. He went to see Nguyen Co Thach, then the Deputy Foreign Minister of Vietnam.[17] A top party leader who happened to be with Thach in the office told Hardi that Vietnam would not abandon its support for the PKI. Hardi asked him whether this was Hanoi's official view on the matter but Nguyen Co Thach hurriedly explained that it was not, saying "It was the standpoint of the Communist Party of Vietnam".[18] This confirms that Vietnam was still pursuing a dual track policy similar to that of the PRC. In addition, Vietnam was supporting the Fretilin in East Timor and opposed Indonesia's annexation of the ex-Portuguese colony.[19]

Hardi also noted that the Vietnamese Government was very hostile towards Indonesian Embassy personnel in Hanoi. Despite this hostility, Jakarta never "froze" its relations with Hanoi nor did it condemn Vietnamese ties with the PKI. The explanation of this lies in the Indonesian military's perception of Vietnam — the military did not think that Vietnam would pose a security threat to Suharto's Indonesia.

Towards the end of 1976 when Vietnam was to hold a Communist party congress, Hardi heard that the PKI leaders in Beijing would be invited. He went to see Pham Hien, then Deputy Foreign Minister, to register his concern. He told Pham Hien that Indonesia would protest strongly if the PKI leaders were invited.[20] A few days later, the Vietnamese Foreign Ministry informed Hardi that Hanoi had decided not to invite the PKI leaders to the Vietnamese Party Congress.[21] Hardi, unaware of other developments in Vietnam, thought that the decision had resulted from his diplomatic offensive.[22] In fact, Hanoi had decided to distance itself from Beijing. It was during this congress that the Vietnamese purged all pro-Chinese elements from the Vietnamese Communist Party causing the relationship between Beijing and Hanoi to deteriorate.[23] The decision not to invite the PKI was therefore not a loss to Vietnam. In fact, it won a friend for Vietnam, for as the rift between Hanoi and Beijing widened, the Vietnamese attitude towards Indonesia improved greatly. Apparently, Vietnam wanted to gain Indonesia's support for its confrontation with the PRC.

Before the Vietnamese invasion of Cambodia, Pham Van Dong visited the ASEAN region to offer the member-states a treaty of friendship. He also promised that Vietnam would not interfere in their domestic affairs. Thus, even in the United Nations, the Vietnamese, who had been ardent supporters of Fretilin, abstained during the discussion on the East Timor issue in 1978.[24] It was clear that Vietnam was attempting to woo Indonesia prior to its dispute with the PRC over the Kampuchean issue.

In December 1978, Vietnam, at the invitation of Heng Samrin who was installed by the Vietnamese, invaded Cambodia which was then under the Khmer Rouge. The ASEAN states, including Indonesia, expressed their disapproval and urged Vietnam (without mentioning its name) to pull back and withdraw its troops.[25] In February 1979 when the PRC invaded Vietnam in order "to teach Vietnam a lesson", the ASEAN states again made a similar statement.[26]

The Indonesian press, especially the army dailies, *Angkatan Bersenjata* and *Berita Yudha,* were very restrained in their reporting of the Sino-Vietnamese war.[27] Only on 5 March 1979, did an editorial appear in *Angkatan Bersenjata* which discussed a meeting between Suharto and Hussein Onn, then Prime Minister of Malaysia, in Jakarta and mentioned the Sino-Vietnamese war. Interestingly, the army daily regretted the behaviour of the Vietnamese in Cambodia. It said that Pham Van Dong had visited the ASEAN states and promised not to assist rebels in these countries, stating that it would live in peaceful co-existence with its neighbours in accordance with the Afro-Asian principle. The daily noted that Dong had not kept his promise — Vietnam had helped Cambodian rebels take over Phnom Penh and establish a government.[28] The daily also said that China invaded Vietnam because the Pol Pot regime that it had once supported had collapsed and ethnic Chinese were being harassed by the Vietnamese. ASEAN, including Indonesia, was extremely concerned with the situation.

On 7 March 1979, Indonesia and Malaysia agreed to contact the parties involved to help solve the conflict. On the following day there was a report that Chinese troops would be withdrawn.[29] Again an *Angkatan Bersenjata* editorial commented that the announcement was encouraging. It stated that Vietnam had requested Mochtar Kusumaatmadja, Indonesia's new Foreign Minister, to use his good offices to help solve the border dispute between Hanoi and Beijing. There was also a report that Indonesia was prepared to host negotiations between Hanoi and Beijing.[30] The next day, however, Mochtar denied having made the offer. Both the Foreign Ministry and the army were careful in expressing their opinion on the Sino-Vietnamese war.

Although some of the military leaders were disappointed that the Vietnamese had broken their promise not to interfere in the internal affairs of other countries, they were alarmed by the Chinese willingness to use force to settle their differences with Vietnam. It was clear that soon after the Chinese invasion, Indonesia's attitude towards the Vietnamese changed. As noted earlier, despite their sympathy for the North Vietnamese, some military leaders had been suspicious of the Communist ideology before the war. After the war, it became clear that they looked at the region in strategic terms and were more concerned with the PRC's behaviour. They feared that the PRC might use military means to solve the conflict, reconfirming the idea that China posed a long-term threat.

Benny Murdani, then Chief of the Military Intelligence Body, was reported to have visited Hanoi at least twice. The first time was in May 1980 and the second in early 1981 when the UN was discussing the Kampuchean issue. Both trips were made for the purpose of sounding out Vietnam on the issue.[31] It was also reported that, on his second trip, he discussed the border dispute over the Natuna Islands with Vietnam. The Vietnamese apparently indicated that the planned continental shelf negotiations in Jakarta would depend in part on ASEAN's stand in the United Nations on the Kampuchean issue.[32] The result of the visit was not announced, but it was reported that Vietnam gave up its claim to the Natuna Islands.[33] A later report stated, however, that no headway had been made in boundary talks.[34] In 1982, Murdani made another trip to Hanoi but no information is available about what he did there.[35] It is very likely that Murdani was trying to promote closer co-operation with the Vietnamese.

Thus, it was strategic concerns — that is, the PRC's possible expansion southwards — that caused the Indonesian military to be more friendly with Vietnam after 1979. Consequently, Suharto and Hussein Onn decided to announce the Kuantan Principle in March 1980 — for the purpose of befriending Vietnam and preventing it from becoming part of the Soviet camp.

Two Positions

The Ministry of Foreign Affairs and the military differed in their views concerning Vietnam, especially regarding the Kampuchean issue. It appeared that the Foreign Ministry, then represented by Mochtar, was more in line with the common stand of the ASEAN states. It considered Vietnamese behaviour in Kampuchea aggressive and a violation of the sovereignty of the state.[36] This stand, of course, received the support of President Suharto. The military group, on the other hand was sympathetic to the Vietnamese venture. According to a reliable source, Indonesian military leaders, including Benny Murdani, felt that the Vietnamese had the right to unify the south and even the whole of French Indochina, just as Indonesia had the right to liberate West Irian (now Irian Jaya) and to "integrate" East Timor into Indonesian territory.[37] This view was not made public, however. Indonesian leaders had to be cautious in public, but it was apparent that Indonesia had a dual policy towards Vietnam.

It seems that the military view on Vietnam gradually prevailed over that of the Foreign Ministry. In 1984, for instance, the Indonesians stepped up their efforts to solve the Kampuchean issue by improving relations with the Vietnamese. It has been argued that Suharto wanted to be recognized as a regional leader from that time. It is not surprising, therefore, that Indonesia decided to sponsor the thirtieth anniversary of the Bandung Conference in Jakarta and offered to help solve the Kampuchean problem.

Closer Ties

In 1984, Indonesia, or at least the military, undertook a major initiative to win over the Vietnamese. In March, Benny Murdani visited Vietnam again[38] and, during the visit, publicly stated that Vietnam did not pose any threat to Southeast Asia. His statement created an uproar in the other ASEAN states, especially Thailand and Singapore which perceived Vietnam as an immediate threat. Murdani later clarified his statement, saying that it did not mean he was happy if "Vietnam remains in Kampuchea". But he did not revise his statement concerning the issue of threat. In fact, he noted that this was also the assessment of the military leaders in Jakarta. Murdani was quoted as having said that he had held this view before visiting Vietnam and reconfirmed it after the trip.[39] Following Murdani's visit, Hanoi announced that it planned to send a military attache to Jakarta.[40] Later in the year, Murdani gave an interview to Reuters in which he stated that "Vietnam and the rest of Southeast Asia should forge closer ties to face the potential threat from a strong China in the next century".[41] It is interesting to note that General Murdani, who is staunchly anti-Communist, was perceived to be Hanoi's "special friend". The *Far Eastern Economic Review* (*FEER*) reported that when he was moved from the post of Armed Forces Chief to Defence Minister in the 1988 cabinet reshuffle, the Vietnamese Embassy in Jakarta consulted "other embassies if Murdani's new post will mean the erosion of what Hanoi views as a special bilateral relationship with Indonesia".[42]

The Indonesian desire to develop better relations with Vietnam can also be observed in the visit of Thach to Jakarta in March 1984 and the holding of the first Indonesia-Vietnam seminar before this visit. The seminar was sponsored by the CSIS, but it was clear that Suharto and Hankam had given the go-ahead. The seminar was held in Hanoi and the Indonesian delegation included representatives from the CSIS and the Government, as well as the military. The Vietnamese delegation included high-ranking leaders such as Pham van Dong and Nguyen Co Thach. However, no concrete resolution was achieved at the seminar. Thach's visit to Jakarta was particularly significant because he was received by Suharto. Mochtar later disclosed that Suharto had suggested a possible modification of the ASEAN proposals for the settlement of the Kampuchean problem when he met Thach. According to Mochtar, Suharto suggested that Hanoi should participate in a proposed international peace-keeping force that would police the gradual withdrawal of Vietnamese troops. This was aimed at allaying Vietnamese fears that the proposals, contained in ASEAN appeals in September 1983 for Kampuchean independence, did not take into account Hanoi's security interests.[43] One source also revealed that Suharto suggested that Vietnam hold West Irian type elections in Kampuchea which would legitimize the Vietnamese presence there. Thach rejected this proposal out of hand.

Mochtar, who later noted that Thach had missed a golden opportunity, admitted that the proposals had not been endorsed by other ASEAN states. One source argued that Suharto might have felt that he could convince his ASEAN counterparts to go along with the proposals once the Vietnamese accepted the offer.[44] As they were not accepted by Thach, however, there was no need for discussion among the ASEAN members. Mochtar later announced that Indonesia was "calling off overtures on Cambodia".[45]

The overtures did not stop as evidenced by the second Indonesia-Vietnam seminar and the visit of Vietnamese Defence Minister, Van Tien Dung. The second seminar was held in February 1985 in Jakarta and it was attended by some high level Vietnamese.[46] The CSIS reported that there were no new developments in the discussion of international issues and the major stumbling block was still the question of the Khmer Rouge. Hanoi had refused to accept the Khmer Rouge as part of the government. The day after the meeting, a discussion was held between the CSIS and the Foreign Relations Committee (Komisi Satu) of the Indonesian parliament. Jusuf Wanandi, a top official in the CSIS, argued at the meeting that if the situation dragged on, Vietnam would encounter major economic setbacks. He said that "it was a challenge to Indonesia to find a way to solve the Kampuchean problem".[47] Apparently, Indonesia considered solving the Kampuchean problem to be one of its responsibilities as a regional power.

In April 1985, Van Tien Dung, the Vietnamese Defence Minister, visited Indonesia. Towards the end of the visit, Murdani announced that an agreement had been reached allowing Hanoi to send a military attache to Jakarta. A wire report stated that an agreement on military co-operation had also been signed by Jakarta and Hanoi which caused concern among Indonesia's ASEAN partners.[48] Mochtar, who was returning from the NAM conference in New Delhi, had to deny categorically that any agreement had been reached. Apparently, Mochtar and Murdani clashed on the issue. It appears that the military's move towards Vietnam continued.

Mochtar was under pressure to find another solution to the Kampuchean problem. Towards the end of his term, he proposed a "cocktail party" or "proximity talks" with Vietnam but the idea was later developed into the Jakarta Informal Meeting (JIM) that took place in 1988.[49] Mochtar went to Hanoi to persuade the Vietnamese to agree to a meeting and they eventually agreed to send representatives to Jakarta, mainly as a result of the changing international situation. Beijing and Moscow had been attempting to improve their relationship and the Vietnamese were under pressure to agree to concessions. For this reason, they reluctantly came to Jakarta. JIM I which was held in Bogor, a suburb of Jakarta, did not produce any significant results but it was a breakthrough in the sense that all the parties to the conflict were able to meet and talk for the first time. Again, the problem of the Khmer Rouge was a stumbling block in the solution of the Kampuchean problem. Phnom Penh and Hanoi insisted that the Khmer Rouge be excluded from future negotiations, while the other members of ASEAN wanted to involve the Khmer Rouge, at least for the time being.

The Kampuchean problem remained unsolved owing, in large part, to the Khmer Rouge issue. Some sources hold that Jakarta expected Beijing to pressure the Khmer Rouge and that the announcement of normalization of relations between Jakarta and Beijing in Tokyo in February 1989 was linked to the Kampuchean issue, among other things.[50] It is said that the Indonesians expected the Chinese to make concessions, but Jakarta has denied this.

JIM II, which was held a few days before the announcement of Sino-Indonesian normalization, was unsuccessful in that no agreement was reached by the warring factions. The Khmer Rouge was still a bone of contention and ASEAN insisted that any solution to the Kampuchean problem should involve the Khmer Rouge. Nevertheless, the effort to look for a solution to the Kampuchean problem continued. In July 1989, Indonesia and France co-sponsored the Paris International Conference on Cambodia (PICC). The opposing factions were in attendance, but no agreement was reached. Soon after the Paris Conference, Japan hosted a meeting of Hun Sen and Sihanouk in Tokyo, where the two leaders agreed to form a new coalition government to represent Cambodia in the United Nations. It would be known as the Supreme National Council and would consist of six members from the Hun Sen regime and six from the CGDK. This proposal was not accepted by the Khmer Rouge, which intensified its military operation against the Hun Sen regime. No clear winner emerged on the battle-field.

In February 1990, another informal meeting was held in Jakarta aimed at finding a solution to the Kampuchean problem. Prior to this, Sihanouk and Hun Sen had met in Bangkok and a partial agreement had been reached. When the informal meeting took place in Jakarta, however, Hun Sen, who had already met with the Vietnamese Foreign Minister, changed his mind.[51] He insisted that the solution must guarantee that there would be no possibility for the genocide regime, as he called the Khmer Rouge, to return to power. The CGDK accused the Vietnamese of maintaining a continued presence in Cambodia, but Vietnam claimed that its troops had been withdrawn in September 1989 as scheduled.[52] Thus, the talks failed again and Ali Alatas, the new Indonesian Foreign Minister, was extremely disappointed.[53]

Despite these failures, Indonesia continued to maintain a dual policy towards Vietnam. On one hand, Indonesia still honoured the ASEAN stand that the Khmer Rouge should be involved in any solution to the Kampuchean problem. On the other hand, Jakarta and Hanoi continued to enjoy close bilateral relations. In June 1990, a delegation of Vietnamese leaders led by General Vo Nguyen Giap was invited to Jakarta by Benny Murdani. Suharto met Giap in the presidential office at Bina Graha. Giap used this opportunity to convey his government's invitation to Suharto to visit Hanoi. Suharto accepted the invitation but the date of the visit was left open.[54] During the visit, Giap also expressed his gratitude to Indonesia and stressed the friendship between the two countries.

In July 1990, Washington announced a new policy towards Vietnam and stated that it would no longer support the Kampuchean coalition government in the United Nations. This was a result of the increasing Soviet-American accord on regional conflicts.[55] The American decision, which was made without prior consultations with its ASEAN partners, generated a sense of uneasiness among ASEAN members. When asked about the American move, Alatas was quoted as saying that ASEAN would adjust according to the developments but would still present a united stand.[56] Suharto, in his opening speech at the ASEAN ministerial conference in Jakarta, also said that ASEAN states should show their solidarity but at the same time adjust to the changing international situation.[57] In other words, Indonesia would attempt to persuade the other ASEAN states to be more flexible in solving the Kampuchean problem.

The United States and ASEAN eventually agreed to a Supreme National Council (SNC) to replace the CGDK in the United Nations, but the composition of the SNC became a problem at the last minute. A meeting to discuss it, held in Jakarta in September 1990, ended inconclusively and caused great disappointment in Indonesia.[58] Indonesia did not give up, however, and the matter was discussed again during Suharto's visit to Beijing and Hanoi in November 1990.

During his visit to Beijing, Suharto and his party discussed various issues, one of which was the Kampuchean problem. After meeting the Chinese leader, the Indonesian delegation talked with Sihanouk and leaders of the other warring parties (except Hun Sen) in Beijing. Both Indonesia and China wanted Sihanouk to head the SNC but Phnom Penh disagreed. When Suharto and his delegation visited Hanoi, the Kampuchean issue was also on the agenda. However, no concrete agreement was reached.

Although no significant result was achieved on the Kampuchean issue, the Indonesian delegation succeeded in gaining Vietnamese support on other issues. For example, Vietnam understood Indonesia's position on East Timor and "would help Indonesia explain the position to other countries".[59] Vietnam also agreed to support Indonesia as the host for the upcoming Non-Aligned Conference if Jakarta was nominated.[60] Hanoi further agreed that the dispute over the Natuna Islands should be settled as soon as possible in order to benefit both sides and a special meeting on the matter would be scheduled in Hanoi. In return, Vietnam would be given economic assistance by Indonesia as indicated in several treaties signed by the two countries.[61]

In fact, before Suharto landed at Hanoi, Vietnam had issued a permit allowing the establishment of the Indovina Bank. This was a joint venture between the Summa group of Indonesia and the Vietnamese Government.[62] It was also the first joint venture company allowed to be established in Vietnam. Soon after Suharto's visit, the Indonesian-Vietnamese Committee on Trade Promotion was established. However, it appears that many Indonesian businessmen were still reluctant to invest in Vietnam. Bureaucratic red tape and fear of "nationalization" were two major obstacles. In October 1991, Lee Van Triet, Minister of Trade and Tourism, visited Indonesia to improve economic co-operation.[63] During his visit, it was announced that PT Vietmindo, an Indonesian-Vietnamese joint venture company set up to explore coal mining, would begin operation in 1992.[64] It was also announced that the Prime Minister of Vietnam was scheduled to visit Indonesia soon.

The breakthrough in the Kampuchean problem only took place in October 1991 when a peace treaty was signed in Paris.[65] The process which eventually led to the signing of the treaty was complex. The decline of Communism in Eastern Europe and the Soviet Union was a major contributing factor to the final solution. The Soviet Union was no longer able to assist Vietnam. China, concerned with the survival of its Communist system, was also eager to improve its relations with Communist Vietnam. A secret Sino-Vietnamese summit held in Chengdu resulted in a thaw in relations between the two former enemies and this paved the way for the solution to the problem. The UN peace plan which aimed at a comprehensive settlement for Cambodia was eventually accepted by all parties concerned. A cease-fire was announced and Cambodia was immediately put under UN trusteeship in anticipation of a UN-sponsored general election. Peace — or hope for peace — had finally come.

The signing of the peace treaty in Paris, chaired by Indonesia and France, gave Indonesia a sense of participation in the process. Secretary of State James Baker and Assistant Secretary of State for East Asia and Pacific Affairs, Richard Solomon, in their respective speeches, thanked the five UN members and also the two sponsor nations of the Paris Conference for their efforts.[66]

Despite good Jakarta-Hanoi relations, as shown by the frequent visits of top level Vietnamese leaders to Jakarta, there are still many bilateral issues which have not been resolved, including the overlapping claims over some of the Natuna Islands and the issue of refugees. In the past, Hanoi appeared to insist on using the Vietnamese laws instead of international laws to solve the territorial dispute.[67] However, in April 1994, Le Duc Anh, President of Vietnam, led a high level delegation to visit Indonesia again. This time it was reported that Hanoi and Jakarta were ready to settle the territorial dispute based on international maritime laws.[68] There was also a report that Vietnam was prepared to accept more than 8,000 Vietnamese boat people who are now on Indonesian Galang islands.[69]

It appears that these were the concessions made by the Vietnamese to Indonesia in order to get Jakarta's support for Vietnam joining ASEAN. Perhaps Vietnam's eagerness to join ASEAN was so that it could strengthen its bargaining position *vis-à-vis* the PRC. However, some ASEAN states, including Indonesia, felt that the time was not yet ripe for ASEAN to accept Vietnam. According to the report, when Suharto was approached by his Vietnamese counterpart on that issue, Suharto noted that he was supportive of the Vietnamese intentions, but in his usual diplomatic language, Suharto was quoted as saying that "any final decision on increasing membership would have to be made collectively by ASEAN leaders".[70] Nonetheless, the preparation of Vietnam to join ASEAN was under way and in July 1995, during the ministerial summit in Brunei, Vietnam officially became the seventh member of ASEAN. Indonesian newspapers welcomed Vietnam and noted that with the inclusion of the new member, ASEAN will grow stronger as a regional organization.[71] The anti-Communist Indonesia no longer held Vietnamese Communist ideology to be objectionable. Djafar Assegaff, the Indonesian Ambassador to Vietnam, was quoted as saying that Communist ideology is no longer a problem as ASEAN states are now strong enough.[72] Many commentators also cited the economic benefit enjoyed by other ASEAN countries from Vietnam as the reason for welcoming Hanoi to join the club.[73]

Conclusion

Indonesian-Vietnamese relations under Suharto have been a function of Jakarta's policy towards both Beijing and ASEAN. It was a function of the former because Indonesia saw Vietnam as a buffer against China. This was based on strategic thinking rather than common revolutionary experience. In addition, after the 1982 general election, Indonesia aspired to be a regional leader and was eager to settle the Kampuchean problem under its leadership. Common historical experience became a factor only when it coincided with national interest as defined by the Indonesian power elite. Otherwise, it was conveniently overlooked.

Indonesia under Suharto was frustrated because Vietnam did not respond to its overtures which would have been quite beneficial to the Vietnamese. There was also a desire on the part of Indonesia to settle the boundary dispute with Vietnam through friendship and negotiations. Again, Jakarta made slow progress on this matter.

Jakarta's policy towards Hanoi was also a function of Indonesia's policy towards ASEAN. Suharto considered ASEAN important because it served certain useful purposes. First, it allowed Indonesia to play a leadership role, and second, it provided the region with political stability which was necessary for the ASEAN states to develop economically. Not surprisingly, then, Jakarta went along with the other ASEAN states to present a common stand on Kampuchea.

Even so, Indonesia's dual policy towards Vietnam continued. Despite many failures, Suharto was still interested in solving the Kampuchean problem under his leadership. The sudden collapse of Communism in the Soviet Union forced both China and Vietnam to come to terms, and the UN proposal for the solution of the Kampuchean issue was finally accepted in October 1991. It appears that Indonesia's efforts have borne fruit, but the success was mainly due to international rather than Indonesian efforts.

Jakarta-Hanoi relations continued to be warm after the end of the Cold War. However, Indonesia appears to be cautious in showing its support for Vietnam's policy towards the PRC.

NOTES

1 This is especially true with the Indonesian leaders. In the editorial of an Indonesian military newspaper, it was noted that the common struggle against the colonialists for independence was the reason for Indonesia to maintain diplomatic ties with Vietnam. "Kunjungan Presiden Soeharto Ke Vietnam" (*Berita Yudha*, 20 November 1990).
2 Although the leaders of the two countries emphasized their common experiences in the struggle for independence, it is worth noting that in the 1980s, the emphasis on common interests shifted somewhat: both sides, especially the Vietnamese, stressed their convergence of interest in facing China. For instance, Cao Xuan Pho, a Vietnamese historian stated that Vietnam and Indonesia "have both been victims of Chinese expansionism and hegemonism", in "Vietnam-Indonesia Concurrences: Past and Present", *Indonesian Quarterly*, Vol. XIII, No. 2 (1985), p. 217; Pham Binh, former Deputy Foreign Minister of Vietnam, citing Murdani's words, agreed that "Vietnam and the rest of Southeast Asia should forge closer ties to face the potential threat from a stronger China in the next century". In his "New Possibilities for a Peaceful Solution in Southeast Asia", *Indonesian Quarterly*, Vol. XIII, No. 2, p. 205.
3 *Dua Puluh Lima Tahun Departemen Luar Negeri 1945-1970* (Jakarta: Deparlu, 1971), p. 37.
4 See Cao Xuan Pho, op. cit., p. 221. Also Franklin B. Weinstein, *Indonesian Foreign Policy and the Dilemma of Dependence: From Sukarno to Suharto* (Ithaca: Cornell University Press, 1976), p. 131.
5 *Dua Puluh Lima Tahun Departemen Luar Negeri*, p. 40; also Weinstein, op. cit., p. 131.
6 See Sukarno's speech delivered on 17 August 1965, "Menemukan Kembali Revolusi Kita", cited in *Dua Puluh Lima Tahun Departemen Luar Negeri*, p. 294; For a discussion on this axis, see Peter Christian Hauswedell, "The Anti-Imperialist International United Front in Chinese and Indonesian Foreign Policy 1963-1965: A Study of Anti-Status Quo Politics", (Ph.D. thesis, Cornell University, 1976), especially pp. 242-292.
7 A Vietnamese writer claimed in 1985 that from the beginning Vietnam did not side with the PKI and therefore relations between Jakarta and Hanoi were fine. See Cao Xuan Pho, op. cit., p. 219. This contradicted reality. Hardi, the Indonesian Ambassador to Hanoi in 1976, noted chat when he assumed the ambassadorship, Hanoi still supported the PKI. See Hardi, *Api Nasionalisme: Cuplikan Pengalaman* (Jakarta: Gunung Agung, 1983), p. 205.
8 Hardi stated in his memoirs that, at one time there was a break in diplomatic relations between Hanoi and Jakarta. The ties were only resumed in 1973. See Hardi, op. cit., p. 203. No other writers have explicitly mentioned the severance of relations. Adam Malik, on the other hand, stated clearly in 1976 that Indonesia had always maintained diplomatic relations with North Vietnam. See *Sepuluh Tahun Politik Luar Negeri Orde Baru* (Jakarta: Yayasan Idayu, 1976), p. 12.
9 Information provided by a researcher in the Indonesian Foreign Ministry.
10 Dr Lie Tek Tjeng stated that it was impossible for Jakarta to have severed diplomatic ties with Hanoi. The absence of an Indonesian Ambassador did not indicate the suspension of diplomatic relations (Discussion, 1990). General Purbo S. Suwondo commenced that ties were not suspended but there was a downgrading of relations between Jakarta and Socialist/Communist states after the 1965 coup (Discussion, 1990).
11 Lie Tek Tjeng, "Vietnamese Nationalism: An Indonesian Perspective", *National Resilience*, No. 1 (March 1982) pp. 72-75.
12 For the text of the communiqué, see *Komunike Republik Indonesia dan Negara² Asia-Pasifik 1962-1969* (Jakarta: Departemen Luar Negeri R.I., no date), pp. 99-100.
13 Suli Suleiman, *Politik Luar Negeri Bebas Aktif Republik Indonesia* (Direktorate Research Departemen Luar Negeri, Penerbitan no. 008/1973), p. 20.
14 For a more complete discussion of the Jakarta Conference on Cambodia, see Lau Teik Soon, *Indonesia and Regional Security: The Jakarta Conference on Cambodia*, Occasional Papers, No. 14 (Singapore: Institute of Southeast Asian Studies, 1972).
15 Hardi, op. cit., pp. 205-206. It should be noted that Hardi's memoirs are informative although not always accurate on historical facts. The section on his service in Vietnam

has provided rare insights into Indonesian relations with Vietnam in the mid and late 1970s, which cannot be found elsewhere.
16 Hardi, op. cit., p. 199.
17 Ibid., pp. 205-207.
18 Ibid., p. 207.
19 Ibid., p. 211.
20 Ibid., p. 207.
21 Ibid.
22 Ibid.
23 On the Sino-Vietnamese split in 1976, see William Turley, "Vietnam Since Reunification", *Problems of Communism* (March-April 1977), p. 38. Also William Duiker, *The Communist Road to Power in Vietnam* (Boulder: Westview Press, 1982), p. 340. For the names of Vietnamese leaders who were purged because of their pro-Beijing attitude, see also Jaap van Ginnekan, *The Third Indochina War: The Conflicts between China, Vietnam and Cambodia* (n.p., 1983), p. 16.
24 Hardi, op. cit., p. 211.
25 Leo Suryadinata, "Indonesia in 1979: Controlled Discontent", *Southeast Asian Affairs 1980*, p. 135; Also *Angkatan Bersenjata*, 22 February 1979.
26 *Angkatan Bersenjata*, 22 February 1979.
27 This conclusion results from an examination of the two newspapers. However, other Indonesian newspapers appear to be critical of the PRC. *Merdeka*, for instance, was the strongest in its condemnation of Beijing.
28 "Editorial", *Angkatan Bersenjata*, 5 March 1979.
29 *Angkatan Bersenjata*, 8 March 1979.
30 Ibid., 9 March 1979.
31 Guy Sacerdoti, "The Troubleshooter's Trip", *Far Eastern Economic Review*, 25 September 1981, p. 12. It should be noted that the subsequent report in *Far Eastern Economic Review* by Susumu Awanohara only mentioned one trip made by Murdani in 1981. Murdani made another trip in 1982.
32 Ibid., p. 13.
33 *New Straits Times*, 13 August 1982; *Bangkok Post*, 13 August 1982.
34 *New Straits Times*, 26 November 1984; *Straits Times*, 26 November 1984.
35 Susumu Awanohara, "A Meeting of Minds", *Far Eastern Economic Review*, 9 February 1984, p. 19.
36 Initially, Mochtar was rather critical of the establishment of the Indochinese Federation. In 1984, however, he softened his stand. He only questioned the means used by the Vietnamese to realize their objectives. Mochtar was asked by a *Tempo* reporter: "Do you have any objections to the establishment of a kind of federation comprising Vietnam, Cambodia and Laos with Hanoi as a big brother?" Mochtar answered: "If this is done through aggression, the way it is done now, of course we have objections. But we never protested the posting of Vietnamese troops in Laos." *Tempo*, 24 March 1984, p. 19.
37 Discussion with an Indonesian scholar (1985). However, Dr Lie Tek Tjeng in his article also made this point but he was referring to Indonesian nationalists. See Lie, op. cit., p. 73.
38 *Straits Times*, 17 February 1984; *Straits Times*, 27 February 1984.
39 Susumu Awanohara, "Murdani's Modification", *Far Eastern Economic Review*, 8 March 1984, p. 36.
40 *Straits Times*, 23 February 1984.
41 Originally published in the *Jakarta Post*, 18-20 December 1984. Cited in Pham Binh, "New Possibilities for a Peaceful Solution in Southeast Asia", *Indonesian Quarterly*, Vol. 13, No. 2 (1985), p. 205.
42 *Far Eastern Economic Review*, 14 April 1988, p. 11.
43 *Nation Review*, 17 March 1984.
44 In Mochtar's interview with *Tempo*, he stated that "the offer contained risks for Indonesia. If they were accepted by Vietnam, we would have made serious efforts to convince our

colleagues in ASEAN". *Tempo*, 24 March 1984, p. 19.
45 *Straits Times*, 22 May 1984.
46 *Nawala CSIS*, Vol. 4, No. 5 (March 1985) pp. 3-4.
47 Ibid., p. 4.
48 *Far Eastern Economic Review,* 2 May 1985, p. 17.
49 Chang Pao-min, "Kampuchean Conflict: The Diplomatic Breakthrough", *Pacific Review*, Vol. 1, No. 4, pp. 429-437.
50 Asahi Shimbun considered the Cambodian issue as one of the major factors for normalization. Cited in *Tempo*, 4 March 1989, p. 15.
51 "Tajuk Rencana", *Kompas*, 3 March 1990.
52 It is interesting to note that Nguyen Co Thach "conceded in New York when he met the Secretary Baker a few weeks ago, several thousand military advisors do remain in Cambodia". See "Solomon Points to Issues Vietnam Must Deal with", *Official Text*, US Embassy in Singapore, 7 December 1990.
53 Alatas was quoted as saying that "God knows how hard that we have tried to pull them together and reduce their differences. Now it is the task of the Cambodian peoples themselves to show their eagerness and seriousness that they want to stop the killing and to end the tragedy in their country". *Kompas*, ibid.
54 *Kompas*, 5 July 1990.
55 See the article by Steven Erlanger which was first published in *New York Times*, reprinted in *Straits Times*, 23 July 1990.
56 "Alatas Doubts US Move Will Help to Bring Peace", *Straits Times*, 23 July 1990.
57 Suharto was cited as saying that "ASEAN should maintain a commensurate capacity for continuous dynamic adaptation while maintaining a unity stance and moves towards its common aims". *Straits Times*, 25 July 1990.
58 "Alatas Kecewa Pemimpin Kamboja Belum Menangani Isu Sebenarnya", *Kompas*, 5 September 1990.
59 Comparison of various reports published in Indonesian newspapers show that this point was only mentioned by *Kompas*, 21 November 1990.
60 *Kompas*, 21 November 1990.
61 Indonesia would provide Vietnam with the fertilizer and oil which it badly needed. See *Kompas*, 21 November 1990. Jakarta signed a series of agreements/treaties with Hanoi "ending Vietnamese 15-year isolation in the region". *Jakarta Post*, 22 November 1990.
62 The Indonesian investment in the bank was US$10 million. *Tempo*, 12 October 1991, p. 42.
63 Ibid.
64 The Indonesian investment in this company was US$27 million. Ibid.
65 For brief discussions on the Paris Peace Treaty, see *Straits Times*, 23 and 24 October 1991.
66 See "Solomon says Cambodian Peace Settlement Just First Step", *Official Text*, US Embassy in Singapore, 18 October 1991, p. 1 and "Baker Sees Prospect of 'New Era' in Southeast Asia" (Statement to conference on Cambodia), *Official Text*, 24 October 1991, p. 3.
67 *Lianhe Zaobao*, 28 April 1994.
68 Ibid.
69 Simon Sinaga, "Indonesia, Vietnam to step up efforts to resolve two issues", *Straits Times*, 28 April 1994.
70 Ibid.
71 *Republik*, 27 July 1995; *Kompas*, 30 July 1995; *Suara Pembaruan*, "Editorial", 1 August 1995.
72 *Republik*, 27 July 1995.
73 Ibid.

9

Indonesia-Superpower Relations
Economic and Non-Economic Factors

Introduction

This chapter focuses on Indonesia's relations with the two superpowers — the United States and the former Soviet Union — as well as the economic superpower, Japan.[1] It examines the importance of Indonesia's "economic dependence" on the United States and Japan during the early stage of the Suharto period and its impact on Jakarta's foreign policy behaviour. It also looks at the non-economic factors which affected Jakarta-Moscow relations before the disintegration of the Soviet Union in December 1991. In the last section of this chapter, Indonesian relations with major powers regarding regional order and security are also addressed.

Indonesia-US Relations: Convergence of Interests?

Indonesian-American relations were established during the revolutionary period when Indonesia was still fighting for its independence. Active support for Indonesia by the United States was only given after the Madiun Affair in 1948 when the Indonesian Government was under a Communist threat.

During the period of Constitutional Democracy, when the Islamic party, Masyumi, was in power, Indonesian-American relations could be described as close. An agreement on military alliance with the United States was made but it was short-lived. When Indonesian domestic politics moved towards the left and the nation's foreign policy became even more militant and nationalistic, Indonesian-American relations deteriorated. This was also partly due to such anti-Sukarno, anti-Communist rebel groups that gained the support of the United States in their efforts to topple the central Government. The rebellions were crushed, but, as a consequence, Indonesian-American relations suffered. Meanwhile, Sukarno moved further to the left and made a formal alliance with the PRC. The nation's relationship with the Soviet Union also became closer. The military group in Indonesia was basically anti-Communist, however, and quietly received support from the United States.

When the 1965 coup failed and the military emerged as the victor in Indonesia, Indonesian-American relations improved. The Indonesian economy before and soon after the coup was on the brink of collapse. Inflation was out of control, reaching 650 per cent annually. It was reported that, in 1966, inflation was as high as 900 per cent. The newly formed Government was aware that in order to maintain political stability, there had to be economic rehabilitation. It was also recognized that stabilizing the economy would be a way to legitimize the Suharto Government. Thus, the major task of the new government was to make Indonesia economically viable.

The Suharto Government abandoned Sukarno's policy of self-reliance and actively sought foreign investment and foreign aid. This New Order policy, which welcomed Western investment, made it possible for Western countries to play a major economic role in Indonesia again. In 1967, the Jakarta Government, in order to secure Western investment, especially American, not only issued investment regulations which gave many incentives to the West, but also signed an agreement with the United States to guarantee American investors. The signing of this agreement showed that the new Government was serious in its attempt to rehabilitate the Indonesian economy.[2]

The Indonesian Government was also very eager to borrow funds from the Western countries. Soon after Suharto came to power, he sent the technocrats in Bappenas, led by the Minister of Economics and Finance, Sultan Hamengku Buwono IX, to approach the West and Japan. Initially, the Indonesians succeeded in getting the Indonesian debt rescheduled for 30 years without interest, and later, in securing further aid.[3] Both the West and Japan realized that without assistance, Indonesia would not be able to survive. The Netherlands, Indonesia's former colonizer, was also active in organizing donor countries to help Indonesia.[4] In 1967, therefore, six donor countries met and formed the Inter-Governmental Group on Indonesia (IGGI). They were Australia, Germany, Japan, the Netherlands, the United Kingdom and the United States.[5] Of the six countries, the United States and Japan were the largest donors.[6] Up to 1973, one-third of IGGI aid came from the United States. In 1988, the amount of US aid declined drastically and was overtaken by Japan.[7]

Although the United States is still a major foreign investor in Indonesia, its position has been surpassed by Japan. From the time that the investment law was enacted in 1967 up to the end of 1988, investment in joint venture projects reached a total of US$21.2 billion. Japanese investment amounted to US$6.01 billion, while American investment was only US$ 1.91 billion.[8] Even the volume of Indonesia-US trade lagged behind that between Indonesia and Japan. In 1985, for instance, Indonesia's exports to Japan constituted 49.1 per cent of the nation's exports, while Indonesia's exports to the United States constituted only 22.7 per cent. Indonesia's imports from Japan made up 28.1 per cent of the country's total imports, while imports from the United States constituted only 14.4 per cent.[9]

Nevertheless, Indonesian-American relations were generally close but did not lead to an alliance. On the contrary, the Indonesians attempted to keep a certain distance. This was reflected in Jakarta's continued recognition of Beijing while, before 1972, Washington recognized Taipei as the legitimate government of China. Another example was Jakarta's diplomatic relations with Hanoi. In addition, Indonesia was not, and is not, interested in joining any military alliance with the superpowers and held the view that foreign military bases should be temporary in nature and should eventually be removed from Southeast Asia. Because of its anti-foreign bases attitude, which was a result of its nationalist history, Indonesia has never publicly supported the presence of American military bases in the Philippines. It has been argued, however, that the non-Communist Indonesian Government has in fact benefited indirectly from the presence of these bases. When, in 1986, the new Philippine Government urged the ASEAN states to share the burden of the bases and to express their support for these bases in the Philippines, Indonesia refused to make a commitment. Nevertheless, Indonesia is realistic enough to admit that it is impossible for Jakarta to chase a superpower away. In one of the interviews in 1993, Ali Alatas was quoted as saying that "America must stay because it will stay. It will stay because it's geographically part of the region".[10] However, he noted that "If there are any different views among the member states of ASEAN, it is in what form the US should stay".[11]

Most Indonesian leaders, both civilian and military, are very nationalistic. Adam Malik, for instance, noted that Indonesia did not share the view that if the United States withdrew from the region, there would be a power vacuum in Southeast Asia. He felt that its place could be taken by Southeast Asian states.[12] Although Malik did not mention the country or countries likely to play such a role, many observers feel that Indonesia would be the natural candidate.

The Indonesian military's view on the matter has been ambiguous. Military leaders, such as Ali Murtopo, advocated the concept of national and regional resilience. He argued that regional resilience was based on national resilience. This concept, in fact, is another way of saying that the superpowers, including the United States, should not interfere in regional affairs and that the Southeast Asian states can look after themselves as long as they have national resilience.

As early as 1971, Jakarta accepted the concept of a Zone of Peace, Freedom and Neutrality (ZOPFAN) and urged the superpowers to respect the freedom and neutrality of Southeast Asia. Indonesia later developed a related concept which was called the Nuclear Weapons Free Zone in Southeast Asia (SEANWFZ). This concept, officially proposed by Indonesia during the 1987 ASEAN summit, clearly had not been suggested by the United States as, if implemented immediately, it would have hurt the strategic interests of the United States in relation to the USSR. Jakarta was not concerned with this, however. The important thing was to enhance Indonesia's status and enable Jakarta to play a greater role in the region.

Another disagreement between Jakarta and Washington related to US policy towards the PRC. The Sino-Soviet split and the US decision to normalize relations with the PRC caused Washington to try to persuade Jakarta to do the same. The suggestion was rejected by Indonesia because it was perceived as being against its national interest. In fact, after 1978, the United States formed a "a strategic alliance" with the PRC against the Soviet Union. It supplied the PRC with sophisticated weapons and technology as part of China's military modernization programme. Indonesia was very critical of the US policy which caused friction between Jakarta and Washington. However, Jakarta was assured that the weapons supplied to the PRC were not really sophisticated and would not jeopardize the security of the ASEAN states.

Despite Indonesia's independent foreign policy, it is apparent that, economically, Indonesia has relied quite heavily on the United States. (Although it has not been as significant as Jakarta's reliance on Tokyo.) In terms of trade, Indonesian exports to the United States made up 20.2 per cent of its total exports in 1983, and 13.1 per cent in 1990 and 1992.[13] Its imports from the US made up 15.5 per cent of its total imports in 1983, but were reduced to 11.5 per cent in 1990 and then increased to 14 per cent in 1992.[14] US economic aid to Indonesia was also significant. In 1976 alone, aid amounted to about US$885 million.[15] Thus, Indonesia could not afford to be hostile towards the United States.

Occasionally, Jakarta has given in to American pressure. An example of this was with the issue of the political detainees. During the Carter Administration, the human rights issue was constantly stressed and economic assistance was often tied to a good human rights record.[16] Under American pressure, in 1978, the Indonesian Government finally released most of the political detainees who had been arrested soon after the 1965 coup. Another example was the protection of US intellectual property. Jakarta was forced to pass a copyright law banning pirated tapes. Despite this, American influence on Indonesia has been limited. Washington knows that it cannot push Jakarta too hard, as this will affect relations. The US has been careful in linking aid with the human rights issue. For instance, when the Dili shootings took place in November 1991, the United States was unhappy with the incident but was cautious in dealing with this issue.

However, the Netherlands and other EC countries withheld aid to pressure Indonesia to improve its human rights record. The Suharto Government responded to this external pressure by setting up a committee and investigating the shootings, which resulted in the removal of the military officers responsible for the incident. While the United States and Japan accepted Indonesia's explanation, the Netherlands was unhappy with the result of the investigation. Jakarta, furious with constant Dutch criticism, rejected Dutch aid and further demanded the dissolution of the IGGI which was chaired by the Netherlands.[17] It should be noted that before the Indonesian Government took action, it secured the continuous support of the United States and Japan who were its largest donors.[18]

Nevertheless, the 1991 killings in Dili posed a minor problem in Jakarta-Washington relations. While the Bush administration reaffirmed the "access policy" and acceptance of Indonesian sovereignty over East Timor, the Congress challenged this policy and eventually decided to penalize the Indonesian Government by terminating the US$2.3 million International Military Education and Training programme (IMET) for Indonesia in 1993. The State Department officials argued against the cut off, but in the end Congress got its way.[19] The Congress' sentiment was high. Many congressmen and senators wanted Indonesia to introduce the self-determination principle to the East Timorese, but the Clinton Administration did not alter the policy. Nevertheless, the human rights issue has become prominent again. Jakarta appears to be responsive to Washington. To pre-empt further criticism, Suharto decided to establish the Human Rights Commission in June 1993.[20] Jakarta had also accommodated American pressure by not only allowing Amos Wako, the UN Human Rights Representative, to visit Indonesia and talk to Xanana Gusmao, the captured Fretilin leader, but also permitting Stephen Kelly from the US Embassy in Jakarta and other foreign observers to attend the Xanana trial.[21] However, the East Timor issue has not been solved completely. It may affect Jakarta-Washington relations if violence recurs in the future.[22]

Since the end of the Cold War, Washington has given greater attention to the human rights issue and the Indonesian human rights record has been under scrutiny. In addition to Indonesian management of East Timor, the poor working conditions of Indonesian workers have also drawn American attention. Washington has threatened to terminate trade privileges if the Indonesian human rights record is not improved. It appears that the US under the Clinton administration is more serious in linking human rights to foreign policy. Indonesia was given the 15 February 1994 deadline to improve its human rights record if it wants to continue enjoying the low tariffs for its exports to the US under the Generalized System of Preferences (GSP).[23] Jakarta responded to the pressure by improving general work conditions, including the introduction of the minimum wage. Washington then postponed the deadline to give Jakarta more time to adjust.[24] Jakarta was displeased with American human rights policy. Ali Alatas stated publicly that Jakarta could not accept the link between the GSP and human and labour rights. He noted that "we will challenge it and we will not stay calm about it."[25] In 1995, the New York-based Human Rights Watch/Asia Group charged that Indonesia had not taken steps to guarantee internationally-recognized workers' rights, including freedom of association and military intervention in labour's disputes. Officials from the office of the US Trade Representatives visited Indonesia to find out the situation and "the findings would be used as a consideration in Indonesia continuing to receive the GSP".[26] It appears that Jakarta was co-operative. While accepting the US officials, Indonesian Manpower Minister, Abdul Latief, maintained that at least "there were 900 company-level unions which were not affiliated to the government-controlled SPSI Union.[27] He also noted that the military remained prohibited from involvement in labour disputes but it would intervene if the dispute spread beyond the factory premises, as occurred in April 1994 in the Medan riot. Latief also noted that there were differences between Washington and Jakarta on the issues and the Indonesian Government "had taken the position that it would live with any decision made on whether to grant GSP privileges".[28]

It should be noted that when Clinton attended the APEC Summit, the human rights issue was not discussed. Apparently, he did not want to "delve into issues which strayed from economic development".[29] However, immediately after the APEC Summit, Clinton engaged in extended talks discussing human rights issues and East Timor with Suharto. It was reported that the discussion, which was scheduled to last for 30 minutes, was extended to one and a half hours.[30] Apparently no agreement was reached on the issues. But Clinton "expressed his belief that it was through economic cooperation and the betterment of economic development that human rights could be forwarded".[31] Human rights will remain as an issue in the future Indonesia-US relations.

Indonesian-Soviet Relations: Reluctant Friendship

Indonesian-Soviet relations, like relations between Indonesia and the US, date back to the revolutionary period when Indonesia was still trying to defend its independence. The Soviets supported the Communist group in order to gain more influence in the newly independent Indonesia. However, during the Communist rebellions, known as the Madiun Affair, the pro-Soviet Communists were crushed. This marked the decline of Indonesian-Soviet relations for the next ten years. Relations improved again when there was a resurgence of Indonesian nationalism and the rebirth of the left-wing movement. This coincided with the campaign to liberate West Irian (Irian Jaya) for which the West refused to assist the Sukarno Government. Jakarta then turned to both the Soviets and the PRC for help. Soviet military assistance was most significant and this helped to bring the two countries closer.

Moscow's relations with the Indonesian Communist Party during the Sukarno era were not cordial. There were two groups within the PKI: a pro-Moscow group allegedly led by Njoto and the dominant Aidit group which was oriented towards Beijing. Nevertheless, there was no open split within the party. After the 1965 coup, because of the pro-Beijing elements in the party, Moscow was quite critical of PKI leadership. It accused the PKI of having abandoned Marxist-Leninist teachings and adopting Mao Zedong Thought.[32] It also criticized the PKI for not preventing extremist officers from staging a military coup leading to "a reign of terror against the Communist Party and other democratic organizations".[33] Moscow, in fact, noted that the army had been responsible for the coup and that the coup was not initiated by the PKI. Ironically, it also said that the PKI might have been able to "curb the extremist feelings of a group of officers",[34] indicating that the PKI had control or influence over the group.

After the 1965 coup, the Soviets "denounced the persecution of democrats and communists".[35] Moscow sheltered some PKI leaders and left-wing Indonesians. In spite of this, Jakarta-Moscow relations were not suspended, mainly due to the insignificant role played by the Soviets in the coup. Nevertheless, the immediate post-coup period saw a deterioration of Indonesian-Soviet relations. In 1968, Soviet leaders requested that the Indonesian Government spare the life of three PKI leaders involved in the coup, but the request was refused.[36] Despite Jakarta's anti-Communist attitude, the Soviets were still eager to improve relations with Indonesia. Jakarta also wanted to maintain relations with Moscow to gain certain economic benefits. Thus, in 1979, Adam Malik visited Moscow to request the rescheduling of Indonesia's debt repayment. An agreement was eventually signed, but trade and economic relations with Moscow did not improve significantly.

At the time when Jakarta began to demand more economic aid, Jakarta-Moscow relations appeared somewhat improved. The two sides signed an agreement on technical and economic co-operation in 1974. With this, Indonesia expected softer loan terms from the Soviets and hoped to project an image that Indonesia was still non-aligned. In 1975 it was announced that the Soviets would build two hydroelectric plants in Indonesia.[37] Nevertheless, economic co-operation was limited because the terms of the agreement were not really soft and the Soviets appeared to have limited resources for helping developing countries. The Indonesians found that they still had to rely heavily on the West and Japan for economic assistance and loans.

After 1969, when the Soviets attempted to form an alliance with some Asian and Southeast Asian states in an "Asian Collective Security System" with the aim of encircling the PRC, Indonesia was not interested in joining. Although Indonesia had always been critical of the PRC's behaviour, it did not want to get involved in a Sino-Soviet rivalry. Basically, it did not trust the Soviets. This can be seen in *Angkatan Bersenjata's* response to the Soviet proposal: "We in Indonesia believe that regional co-operation for prosperity is better than a defence system. We think that no Southeast Asian country is eager to join the Soviet defence system. The invitation is unwelcome".[38]

The military in Jakarta was also concerned with the Moscow-New Delhi alliance and its possible impact on the security of the Indian (Indonesian) Ocean.[39] The military noted, however, that as long as the US Seventh Fleet was present, there was no imminent danger. Moreover, the military noted that Moscow was far from Jakarta and, therefore, did not present an immediate threat to the security of Indonesia.[40]

Minor friction occurred in the early 1982 when Indonesia (following Malaysia) expelled two Russian spies from the country.[41] The affair did not jeopardize Indonesian-Soviet relations, however. In fact, in the 1980s the Soviets began to court Indonesia again. Many Soviet leaders visited Indonesia. In 1986, for instance, a Soviet delegation led by Salimov Akil Uturzanovich conveyed a message from the Soviet President, Andrei Gromyko, to Suharto, inviting him to visit the USSR.[42] Suharto accepted the invitation but did not visit the country until three years later. Apparently, Suharto did not think it necessary to be close to Moscow.

Nevertheless, the Soviets have some supporters within Indonesia. One of them is the *Merdeka* group. It is worth noting that Russian publications often described the Indonesian newspapers, *Merdeka* and the defunct *Sinar Harapan* as nationalistic.[43] It is not by coincidence that Gorbachev gave a special interview to *Merdeka* on his new policy.[44] In addition, many observers maintained that a Soviet bank gave financial assistance to the *Merdeka* group, but this was denied by *Merdeka*.[45] It is not known which particular generals were behind *Merdeka,* but it is generally believed that the newspaper had the support of a segment of the military elite in Indonesia.

Since the 1965 coup, no Indonesian leaders had visited Moscow, until September 1989 when President Suharto went there after attending the Non-Aligned Movement Conference in Belgrade.[46] The desire of Indonesia, and especially of President Suharto, to project a higher profile in world affairs and to become Chairman of the Non-Aligned Movement was the major motivation for his visit to Moscow.[47] During the visit, Suharto expressed his thanks for Soviet assistance to Indonesia during the West Irian campaign.[48] He also agreed to foster economic relations.[49] It was reported, however, that Suharto told Gorbachev that Indonesia would not change its stance on Communism but stated that his country bore no feelings of enmity towards Communist countries.[50]

It is worth noting that Suharto's visit to the Soviet Union began in the Republic of Uzbeck which is well known for its great Islamic heritage.[51] Only after visiting Tashkent and Samarkand, two Islamic holy places, did Suharto and his delegation proceed to Leningrad and Moscow. Suharto's visit to the Muslim republic and the Islamic holy places can be seen as a gesture aimed at Muslims both at home and abroad. It was also intended to gain the support of the Islamic countries in NAM.

The relations between Suharto's Indonesia and Gorbachev's Russia improved significantly. For one thing, Gorbachev's policy had downgraded the importance of ideology and military force in favour of pragmatism and diplomacy. This was shown by his new policy towards the West, China and Southeast Asia.[52] Courting Indonesia was part of this strategy to which Jakarta responded. When there was a coup in August 1991 aimed at overthrowing Gorbachev, Indonesia expressed its concern about the stability of the Union.[53] Suharto himself was quoted as saying that the solution should be in accordance with the "wish of the Soviet people", and it should not have a negative impact on the Soviet Union.[54] Apparently, Suharto was not eager to support the coup launched by Communist hardliners. When Gorbachev made his comeback, Suharto immediately congratulated the Soviet President indicating that he preferred Gorbachev to the coup leader.[55]

It is interesting to note that Jakarta did not insist that the Soviets suspend ties with the Communist parties in Southeast Asia as a condition for better relations. In the Indonesian perception, the links between the Communist parties of the USSR and the Southeast Asian states did not affect the political stability of the region or, more precisely, did not affect Indonesia's stability. Nevertheless, closer relations between the two countries were difficult to achieve owing partly to the fact that not much economic benefit could be derived by Indonesia and partly to their different ideologies. With the disappearance of the Soviet Union and the emergence of the Commonwealth of Independent States (CIS), the problem of ideology is no longer relevant. Economic and security issues have become the only significant factor in these relations. Nevertheless, at the moment the CIS is in chaos and does not pose a security threat. Economically the CIS is also on the brink of bankruptcy. Consequently, CIS-Indonesia relations have become insignificant.

Indonesia-Japan Relations: Economics or Politics?

Since the Sukarno years, relations between Indonesia and Japan have been close. In fact, Japanese relations with Indonesia began during the Japanese occupation of the Dutch East Indies. Many generals were trained by the Japanese, and after independence continued to maintain ties with Japan. When the 1958 regional rebellions in Sumatra and Sulawesi were crushed, some of the rebels took refuge in Japan. Gradually, the Sukarnoists gained influence in Japan, so that when Sukarno was ousted, the Sukarnoist group was active in Japan. Eventually, however, the New Order group became more influential.[56] Not only has there been a kind of Indonesian lobby in Tokyo, but there is also a Japanese lobby in Jakarta.[57]

Indonesian-Japanese relations are of an economic rather than political or security nature. Economic relations continued to develop especially after the fall of Sukarno, and Japan has been Indonesia's largest trading partner for many years since. Some sources have even said that Indonesia is now economically dependent on Japan, rather than the two nations being interdependent. In 1983, the value of Indonesian exports to Japan constituted 45.8 per cent of Indonesia's total exports while, in 1990, it was 42.5 per cent. In 1983, Indonesian imports from Japan made up 23.2 per cent of the nation's total imports. In 1990, it was 24.3 per cent.[58] Indonesian exports of crude oil to Japan are most significant. In 1983, 42.5 per cent of Indonesia's total exports of crude oil went to Japan. In 1990 the amount increased to 60 per cent.[59] One writer has noted that a suspension of Japan's importation of oil from Indonesia would "affect Indonesia's total exports, demonstrating the rapid growth of Japan's influence over Indonesia's economy".[60]

Japanese economic aid is also of considerable importance to Indonesia. Not surprisingly, in 1968 Suharto visited Japan in order to get more aid. At that time, Suharto was misinformed by his military advisers that Japan was ready to extend greater economic aid to Indonesia and, as a result, Suharto returned empty-handed.[61] After the visit, however, in order to assuage Indonesian resentment Japan did indeed announce that more aid would be given to Indonesia. A loan of US$200 million was eventually made to Indonesia in addition to the IGGI assistance. On 3 December 1973, Japan signed a 20-year agreement to purchase Liquefied Natural Gas (LNG) from Indonesia.[62]

Japan has now become the largest foreign investor in Indonesia (US$6.01 billion), surpassing Hong Kong and the United States. In January 1974, when Premier Kakuei Tanaka visited Indonesia, there were demonstrations against Japan by students in Jakarta. Although this was more a reflection of Indonesian internal conflict than anti-Japanese feelings,[63] the demonstrators were critical of Japan's dominant economic role. Following the demonstrations, the Japanese were asked to co-operate with indigenous businessmen rather than ethnic Chinese partners.[64]

Japan's importance to Indonesia's economic well-being and hence political stability can also be seen in the recent conflict between the Netherlands and Indonesia over human rights. As discussed earlier, before Jakarta took action against the Netherlands and its chairmanship of the IGGI, Jakarta made sure that it would receive continuous support from Japan and the United States. Japan and the United States supported Indonesia's move[65] and the IGGI was replaced by the Consultative Group on Indonesia (CGI). The Netherlands was excluded from the new organization. It is worth noting that at the CGI meeting in July 1992 the donor agencies and governments pledged $4.95 billion in new annual economic aid to Indonesia, which was higher than in 1991.[66] During the meeting, "US delegation raised the East Timor issue, and no government responded to the US initiatives".[67] Japan and other countries did not want to link economic aid to the Human Rights issue.

Indonesia, to an extent, depends on Japan as an economic source, but realizes the danger of depending on Japan completely as this might result in Indonesia compromising its independence. Therefore, Indonesia has attempted to diversify its trade and exports to other countries while maintaining good relations with Tokyo. Jakarta has also been concerned about Japan-China relations and their possible impact on Indonesia. In 1978, when the Sino-Japanese friendship treaty was signed and Tokyo recognized the PRC, there were two conflicting views in Indonesia. Foreign Minister Mochtar Kusumaatmadja, on one hand, maintained that "the treaty was a good development ... and would give a better opportunity for world peace".[68] He argued that the two countries needed each other for mutual benefit: Japan needed the Chinese market while China needed Japanese technology. Probably, Mochtar assumed that, if China developed economically, it would not be aggressive.

On the other hand, Sayidiman Suryohadiproyo, a military officer close to Lemhanas, held a different view. He was of the opinion that, if populous China and technologically advanced Japan co-operated closely, they could dominate and divide Southeast Asia, China would then be able to control mainland Southeast Asia while Japan would control maritime Southeast Asia.[69] He was implying that this would be against the interests of Indonesia. Some Indonesians have also worried that improved relations between China and Japan might increase Sino-Japanese trade at the expense of Indonesia. If Japan were to decide to import oil from China, which is nearer and has better grade oil than Indonesia, it would be at Indonesia's expense.[70]

Most of the oil imported by Japan comes from the Middle East through the Straits of Malacca. Japan regards the Straits as its life-line, so Indonesia's position on the Straits has always been of concern to the Japanese Government. When Indonesia suggested that oil tankers use the Straits of Makassar and Lombok instead of the Straits of Malacca, Japan responded positively.[71] Even so, Japan also conducted a survey on how to make the Straits of Malacca more secure and safe.

With the encouragement of the United States, Japan has increased its defence budget and the possible remilitarization of Japan has become a topic of debate in Southeast Asia. Indonesian leaders want Japan to continue to play an economic role in the region but are uneasy with Japan's security role. The memory of World War II is still fresh in the minds of many in Southeast Asia.[72] In 1989, however, when Benny Murdani was asked whether or not Indonesia feared

Japanese militarism and its possible expansion, he said that the situation was quite different from that during World War II because of the presence of the US Seventh Fleet, the Soviets, the PRC, Vietnam and ASEAN. It would not be easy for Japan to expand beyond its current boundaries.[73]

The Superpowers, China and Regional Order: An Indonesian Perspective

After analysing Indonesian bilateral relations with the US, USSR and Japan, Indonesia's perception of the superpowers' role must be considered, especially in light of the collapse of the USSR and the growing assertiveness of both the US and Japan. How does Indonesia visualize the role of the superpowers in regional order? Is the ASEAN Regional Forum (ARF) an answer to Indonesia's security problem?

It has been suggested that, in Indonesia, there are two different views on the issue. Civilian politicians, including those in the Foreign Ministry, are more ideological in the sense that they oppose military bases in Southeast Asia because, to them, foreign bases are a symbol of neo-colonialism. In addition, they believe that, if the superpowers should leave Southeast Asia, Southeast Asian countries would fill the vacuum left by their departure. Adam Malik was one of the advocates of this idea. Although he was aware that the Southeast Asian nations were not strong enough to force the superpowers to leave, he believed that foreign military bases ought to be temporary in nature.

Mochtar Kusumaatmadja pursued the idea of a Southeast Asia free from superpowers. He also realized that both the USSR and the US were present and that Indonesia did not have the power to expel them. He, therefore, hoped for a balance of power in the region. When asked whether or not he favoured the Soviet bases in Vietnam, he was once quoted as saying that " ... if the Americans have base facilities in the Philippines, there should be no objections to the Russians having them in Vietnam. It's no threat to us".[74] It was also Mochtar and his colleagues, however, who advocated the idea of a Nuclear Weapons Free Zone in Southeast Asia in the hope of reducing the role of the superpowers in the region (see Chapter 5).

Adam and Mochtar tried to emphasize the role of the Southeast Asian nations and did not discuss a major role for Indonesia in the region. Nevertheless, it seems clear that, without superpowers or external influence, Indonesia will naturally play a crucial role in regional order. It will emerge as a leader in the region. However, the Indonesian military has a different conception of regional security and regional order. They tend to include military and non-military factors in the concept of security.[75] Nevertheless, the strategic element is still crucial. The late Ali Murtopo, for instance, had a regional vision for the Asia-Pacific. He tolerated the temporary presence of the two superpowers in the region but advocated the formation of an Asia-Pacific Triangle to include Japan, Indonesia and Australia. When this was officially expressed, the Triangle became Japan, ASEAN and Australia.[76] The purpose of this Triangle was to "contain the competitive role of China". Murtopo believed that ASEAN and the PRC would view each other as rivals because they were "each fighting for the acquirement of capital and investment, the import of technology from Japan and also the export of primary goods to Japan. This should explain why ASEAN ought to prepare as soon as possible the infrastructure of this triangle".[77]

But, Japan and Australia were not responsive, and Australia, under Gough Whitlam, intended to establish a wider network of intra-Asian relations including the PRC. By 1974, Murtopo realized that his regional order would exclude the two superpowers and had become "an exclusive triangle association". He, therefore, revised it as a complementary group, arguing that "Our idea is not to confront the superpowers but to co-operate with them as long as they are able to adjust themselves to the condition and requirement of developing countries".[78] Nevertheless, his idea did not get off the ground and by 1982, Murtopo admitted that his vision had failed.[79] Nevertheless, it was clear that Indonesia's military, of which Murtopo was one of the most outspoken leaders, saw Indonesia as the leading actor in Southeast Asia which played a decisive role in regional order.

In fact, the vision of Ali Murtopo — and perhaps of his CSIS group as well — was one of the few Indonesian visions, if not the only one, that was clearly expressed. Although the PRC was considered the rival, its impact on regional order was limited. In 1987, Sayidiman, a leading military thinker, discussed the threat posed by the superpowers and other major powers to Indonesia. He was of the view that Southeast Asia in general, and Indonesia in particular, were not a high priority in the global competition between the two superpowers. Neither bloc wanted to see it controlled by one superpower, however. Therefore, Sayidiman argued, each attempted to subvert Indonesia.[80] Indonesia would be involved in the superpower struggle when there was a war between the US and the USSR, but such a scenario was unlikely because it would not be in the interest of the superpowers.

Sayidiman maintained that Japan and the PRC were unlikely to attack Indonesia because they would not be allowed to by the superpowers. He further noted that to stage a large scale war, the two countries would need a large and modern military, which required enormous resources. It was unlikely that they would be able to do it without sacrificing higher priorities.[81]

However, in a more recent article, Sayidiman has said that Japan is not a threat to Southeast Asia or to Indonesia, provided that there is a continuing US presence in Japan.[82] He believes that Japan "has no ambition to become a military power at all" because it has been able to benefit economically without being a military power. Arguing for improved relations between US and Japan, he further contends that Indonesia will benefit more from Japanese economic activities.

Nonetheless, Sayidiman argued that "[in] the economic field, Indonesia has to compete with China as China's domination in economy in this region will be even greater ... it is in our interest to have the US presence in the Western Pacific region to balance Chinese expansionism".[83] He went on to say that "the same also applies to Vietnam; the Soviet withdrawal from Cam Ranh Bay will create difficulties [for Southeast Asia to contain] China. Therefore, it is understandable if there are rumours saying that Vietnam is offering the naval base to the US in order to balance the construction of Chinese naval base in Hainan"(sic).[84]

It is clear that the Indonesian military has been concerned with the PRC. Both the US and Japan have been perceived as a possible force to counter the potential expansion of China. Sayidiman noted that "we do not at all expect that Japan will be on too good terms with China, much the same we do not want war between the two countries. What is needed is that there should be a limited tension between the two countries as it exists now"(sic).[85]

The Indonesian military tolerated, if it did not welcome, the US bases in the Philippines.[86] It also tolerated the use of facilities in Singapore by the US,[87] and did not want Japan to expand its role into the military field. During the Gulf War, Suharto reluctantly agreed that Japan could send its peace-keeping force to the Middle East provided that this was done under the command of a United Nations team.[88] In fact, Indonesia was sensitive to Japan's political aspirations. The military felt comfortable with a slightly more active role played by the Japanese as long as the as United States remained. However, many civilian politicians in Indonesia disagreed with the continued presence of the American bases in the Philippines. They were also critical of the use of Singapore military facilities by the US.

The differences in perception of American military power lie in the military's understanding of security issues. The Indonesian military has been aware of the function of the American military presence in the region. General Try Sutrisno, who was the Indonesian Armed Forces chief, stated in 1992 that a decrease in the military power of the US in the Asia-Pacific region would lead to "a condition in which major powers such as China, Japan and India merge and vie for influence in the region".[89] He noted that this could contribute to the arms race among these nations "which would then increase the risk of traditional conflict breaking out".[90] Perhaps this was why he tolerated a temporary American military presence but he did not openly ask the US to stay.

However, the end of the Cold War has not really changed Indonesian perception about the regional order. The recently formed ASEAN Regional

Forum is still acceptable as it is a forum rather than an alliance system. Also, although the PRC is a dialogue partner, the United States is a member of ARF. It seems that the security thinking of the leaders remains unchanged (see Chapter 5 for further discussion on ARF).

Conclusion

It is clear from the discussion above that economic factors have been most important in Indonesia's relations with the United States and Japan. Relations with these two countries have been close as a result of Indonesia's initial economic dependence on them. On the other hand, the lack of close relations between Jakarta and Moscow can partly be explained in terms of the absence of significant economic ties. It should be noted, however, that the different political ideologies of Jakarta and Moscow have contributed to the lukewarm relations between the two countries. The disintegration of the Soviet Union in December 1991 made the ideological issue irrelevant.

The above analysis also shows that Suharto and the military have been heavily involved in making Indonesia's policy towards the superpowers. On many occasions, Suharto himself went out of his way to obtain aid and loans for Indonesia. It must be pointed out, however, that Indonesia has not always gone along with the United States in its foreign policy. Suharto resisted American pressure when he thought that such pressure was against "Indonesian national interests".

Suharto and the military were instrumental in Indonesia's relations with the now defunct Soviet Union. An improvement in relations coincided with Sino-Soviet rapprochement and Suharto's desire for Indonesia to play a major role in the international arena.

Indonesia's perception of security issues in relation to the superpowers has been linked to ideology. During the Suharto era, the USSR was considered a threat to Indonesia. The Indonesian military group wanted the US to stay in the region in order to counterbalance the increased Soviet activities in the Asia-Pacific. With the collapse of the Soviet Union, the Russian factor has become less important.

It is worth noting that Indonesia is concerned with the military role of Japan. Its major concern is still with the role of the PRC however. The Indonesian military regards the PRC as the greatest challenge for the future and wants the US and Japan to balance China, both in the political and economic fields. However, in the case of the United States, Jakarta has tolerated its military presence as it has brought benefit to the balance of power in the region. It is possible to argue that this is perhaps a short-term strategy because, eventually,

Indonesia wants Southeast Asia to be free from a foreign military presence of any kind.

NOTES

1. Usually, a superpower is defined as a global actor which is able to influence world events through its extraordinary economic, political and military strength. In the past, only the US and USSR fitted into the category. After the collapse of the Soviet Union in 1991, there has only been one superpower — although, this superpower is also in decline. Nevertheless, since the discussion of this chapter goes back prior to 1991, i.e. it covers the period when the USSR was a superpower, the term is kept. Japan is discussed here together with the superpowers for two reasons: it is indeed an economic superpower and could overnight be transformed into a military superpower. It is also expedient to bring it together with the US and USSR.
2. Leo Suryadinata, "Indonesia Under the New Order: Problems of Growth, Equity and Stability", in Leo Suryadinata and Sharon Siddique (eds.), *Trends in Indonesia II* (Singapore: Singapore University Press, 1980), especially p. 9.
3. "Dari Mana Datangnya IGGI", *Tempo*, 4 April 1992, pp. 20-21; Muchtarudin Siregar, *Pinjaman Luar Negeri & Pembiayaan Pembangunan Di Indonesia* (Jakarta: Lembaga Penerbitan Fakultas Ekonomi Universitas Indonesia, 1991), pp. 75-91.
4. *Tempo*, 4 April 1992, p. 21. Due to the Indonesian support, the Netherlands became the chairman of the IGGI. However, the relationship between the countries soured because of the human rights issue. See the later section of this chapter, also Chapter 11 on the Timor issue.
5. Initially the members of the IGGI included only six countries, but by 1968, it had increased to eight countries: Australia, Belgium, Canada, France, Germany, Japan, Netherlands, UK, US and one institution, IDA (World Bank). By 1969, another institution, Asian Development, also joined. See G.A. Posthumous, *The Inter Governmental Group on Indonesia (IGGI)* (Rotterdam: Rotterdam University Press, 1971), pp. 51-52.
6. In 1967, the US aid through the IGGI was US$60.1 million while Japan's aid was $60 million. However, in 1968, US aid was US$163.9 million while Japan's aid was US$70. But after 1969, when the aid also included project aids, a significant sum was provided through IDA (World Bank). Posthumous, op. cit., pp. 51-52.
7. The amount of aid from US and Japan from 1984 to 1988 is as follows: 1984/1985: US$135 million, Japan US$321.3 million; 1985/1986: United States US$100 million, Japan US$303.3 million; 1986/1987: United States US$86 million, Japan US$473.5 million; 1987/1988: United States US$190 million, Japan US$606.8 million; 1988/1989: United States US$90.0 million, Japan US$1,400 million. See Sulaeman Krisnandhi, "Sekali Lagi, Bantuan IGGI", *Angkatan Bersenjata*, 29 June 1988. Also Gary Schuman and Clara Joewono, *Hubungan Indonesia-Amerika Serikat: Sebuah Laporan* (Jakarta: Centre for Strategic and International Studies, 1990), p. 33.
8. See *Indonesia: A Brief Guide for Foreign Investors. Policies and Incentives* (Jakarta: Investment Co-ordinating Board, BKPM and Business Advisory Indonesia, April 1989), p. 5. The amount of investment (up to December 1989) from ten countries was as follows: Japan US$6.01 billion, Hong Kong US$2.31 billion, US $1.91 billion, West Germany US$1.82 billion, Netherlands US$1.26 billion, Taiwan US$1.07 billion, Singapore, US$0.75 billion, United Kingdom US$0.53 billion, Australia US$0.46 billion and South Korea US$0.46 billion. The most recent study shows that in terms of cumulative approved foreign direct investment in Indonesia in the non-oil and non-financial sectors from 1967-1992, Japan is still far ahead of the US. The amount of the Japanese investment is US$13,068. million (20.74 per cent of the total foreign investment) while the US investment is US$2,716.4 million (4.31 per cent of the total foreign investment). See Thee Kian Wie and Mahmud Thoha, "Interactions of Japanese Aid and Private Investment in Indonesia's Manufacturing

Sector", (Research Report Submitted to the Ministry of Foreign Affairs of Japan, February 1993), p. 22 and Table 4.
9. Seiji Naya, "Economic Performance and Growth Factors of the ASEAN Countries", in Linda G. Martin (ed.), *The ASEAN Success Story: Social, Economic and Political Dimensions* (Honolulu: University of Hawaii Press, 1987), p. 63.
10. "Alatas on Security and Growth in Asia: Interview by Yang Razali Kassim", *Straits Times*, 11 January 1993.
11. Ibid. Later, Alatas stated that Southeast Asia should be free from foreign military bases but the reason was not because Indonesia is afraid of neo-colonialism but it was because such a presence is "not effective". Simon Sinaga, "Jakarta says it again: No US military bases for S-E Asia", *Straits Times*, 3 November 1994.
12. Adam Malik, *Sepuluh Tahun Politik Luar Negeri Orde Baru*, Jakarta: Yayasan Idayu, 1976, p. 14.
13. *Statistik Indonesia 1987* (Statistical Year Book of Indonesia) (Jakarta: Pusat Biro Statistik, 1988), p. 366; *Statistik Indonesia 1991* (Jakarta, 1992), p. 318; *Statistik Indonesia 1993*, (Jakarta, 1994), p. 362.
14. Ibid., *Statistik Indonesia 1991*, p. 341; *Statistik Indonesia 1993*, p. 385.
15. Ibid., p. 53.
16. It should be noted that Indonesia was not always happy with this link. When the amount of foreign aid was not crucial for Indonesia, for instance that offered by Netherlands in 1992, Indonesia rejected the Dutch assistance and even demanded the dissolution of the IGGI to remove the chairmanship of the Dutch in that organization. *Tempo*, 4 April 1992, pp. 14-17.
17. In fact, Holland-Indonesia relations only improved in 1995 with the official visit of Queen Beatrix to Indonesia. Although Indonesia continues to reject Dutch aid, economic relations between two countries improved significantly. Coinciding with the Queen's visit was the arrival of 61 top Dutch business and industry leaders led by Hans Wihers, the Dutch Economics Minister. (*Forum Keadilan*, 31 July 1995, pp. 21-22; also *Straits Times*, 22 August 1995.)
18. *Tempo*, 4 April 1992, p. 17; Also *Straits Times*, 27 March 1992, p. 20. For a more detailed discussion on the Dili affair, see Chapter 11.
19. For a discussion of the issue, see Larry Niksch, *Indonesian-US Relations and Impact of the East Timor Issue* (Washington DC: Congressional Research Service, Library of Congress, 15 December 1992), pp. 13-14.
20. "Sebuah Komisi yang Bisa Mandiri", *Tempo*, 19 June 1993, p. 34; Also Frank Ching, "New Human Rights Commission in Indonesia is a Step Forward", *Far Eastern Economic Review*, 10 June 1993, p. 30.
21. "Muslihat Xanana", *Editor*, 29 May 1993, p. 32. Other foreign observers include Alfredo (Italy), Alberto Siviliano (UN delegate) and Neil Mules (Australian Counseller).
22. It should be noted that although the US has recognized Indonesian sovereignty to East Timor, it continues to advocate self-determination (human rights) for the East Timorese.
23. Lee Kim Chew, "Why Clinton should renew trade privileges for Indonesia", *Straits Times*, 27 January 1994.
24. "Indonesia to keep US trade perks for 6 more months", *Straits Times*, 18 February 1994.
25. Ibid.
26. *Straits Times*, 18 June 1995.
27. Ibid.
28. Ibid.
29. "APEC meeting not the place to discuss human rights: Barry", *Jakarta Post*, 1 November 1995.
30. "Suharto, Clinton discuss rights issue", *Jakarta Post*, 17 November 1995.
31. Ibid.
32. V.I. Popov et al. (eds.), *A Study of Soviet Foreign Policy* (translated by David Skvirsky) (Moscow: Progress Publishers, 1975), p. 111.
33. Ibid., p. 112.

34 Ibid.
35 Ibid.
36 K.S. Nathan, *Detente and Soviet Policy in Southeast Asia* (Kuala Lumpur: Gateway Publishing House, 1984), p. 108.
37 Robert C. Horn, "The Soviet Union and Asian Security" in Sudershan Chawla and D.R. Sardesai (eds.), *Changing Patterns of Security and Stability in Asia* (New York: Praeger, 1980), p. 81.
38 *Angkatan Bersenjata's* editorial. Cited in Helmut G. Callis, "The Role of Indonesia in Asian Regionalism", Paper prepared for the 5th Annual Conference of ASPAC, 24-27 June 1970, p. 19.
39 Sajidiman Surjohadiprodjo, *Langkah-langkah Perdjoangan Kita* (Jakarta: Departemen Pertahanan Keamanan Pusat Sedjarah ABRI, 1971), p. 159.
40 It should be noted that in recent years, Jakarta began to be concerned with Indian naval activities. For instance, Indonesia was disturbed by the report that India was planning to build a major naval based on Great Nicobar Island. See *Far Eastern Economic Review*, 15 May 1986. The Indonesian military at one time protested against the "expansion" of the Indian navy, but the Indian authorities insisted that it carried out normal activities. See Mohamed Ayoob, *India and Southeast Asia: Indian Perceptions and Policies* (London and New York: Routledge, 1991), pp. 42-45.
41 For this episode, see H. Rosihan Anwar, *Indonesia 1966-1983: Dari Koresponden Kami di Jakarta* (Jakarta: Grafitipers, 1992), p. 239. It was reported that the Soviets "were obtaining sea charts, probably for their submarine operations". The persons involved were a Soviet Embassy official, the Jakarta manager of Aeroflot and an Indonesian naval officer. *Asia Year Book 1983 (Far Eastern Economic Review)*, p. 162.
42 *Jakarta Post*, 2 June 1986.
43 *Merdeka's* views have often been quoted by Moscow's and Hanoi's publications as representing Indonesia. See for instance, "Beijing Expansionist Plans in Southeast Asia", *International Affairs* (Moscow), No. 6 (1979), pp. 22-23; Hoang Nguyen, "When the Hoa Becomes Beijing's Political Cards against Vietnam", *The Hoa in Vietnam, Dossier II* (Hanoi, 1978), p. 16. It is also noticeable that in the last decade, the *Merdeka* Group published numerous articles attacking the PRC and the West. For instance, *Merdeka's* Editorial "Strategi Neo-Kolonial", 18 January 1980, and a book entitled *Ancaman Dari Utara* (Jakarta, 1980). The latest example was its editorial on 25 February 1989 in which it stated that the PRC could not be trusted as China has stabbed Indonesia in the back since the era of Kublai Khan. Note that *Sinar Harapan* was banned and *Suara Pembaruan* was permitted to publish in its place.
44 For the text of the interview, see Soviet News (USSR Embassy, Singapore), 30 July 1987, p. 3; Also "Answers by M.S. Gorbachev to the Questions of the Indonesian Newspapers Merdeka", in *Press Release* (USSR Embassy, Singapore), No. 37/87, pp. 1-5.
45 Rodney Tasker in his article entitled "Stopping Any Shade of Red" stated that 'Three years ago the paper [*Merdeka*] is understood to have received a US$3.5 million loan from the Soviets" (*Far Eastern Economic Review*, 24 August 1979, p. 24). Nurman Diah (son of B.M. Diah) denied this. He wrote that "*Merdeka* had no need of any loan, either from the West or from the Soviets". But Diah noted in the same letter that "The latest expansion of Merdeka was in 1971, when it modernized its plant with some modern presses. A foreign bank gave the loan, now repaid to the last cent". There was no mention of the bank's name. "Letters to the Editor: Asia and the Power of the Soviets", *Far Eastern Economic Review*, 19 October 1979, p. 8.
46 "Era Baru Itu Sudah Dimulai", *Tempo*, 16 September 1989, pp. 14-16.
47 Alatas insisted that the visit was primarily to discuss the promotion of economic contact. *Tempo*, 16 September 1989, p. 16. However, Juwono Sudarsono in his article in *Tempo* noted that "there is a strong belief that the visit may convince the leaders in Asia, Africa and Latin America, particularly the first and the second generation leaders who still possess the characteristics of 'revolutionaries' that Indonesia ... would not want to side with either

the US camp or the Soviet camp". See "Indonesia dan Uni Soviet", *Tempo*, 16 September 1989, p. 22. Apparently, it is related to Jakarta's desire to be accepted as the leader of the Non-Aligned Movement.
48 *Jakarta Post*, 9 September 1989.
49 The Soviet-Indonesian trade was small but was in Indonesia's favour. In 1986 Indonesian exports to the Soviets amounted to US$51.99 million, but Indonesian imports from the Soviets were only US$5.25 million. In 1987, Indonesian exports to the Soviets increased to US$82.40 million while Indonesian imports from the Soviets were US$15.46 million. Indonesia exports to the Soviets include rubber, pepper, coffee, palm oil, spices and cloths while imports included fertilizer, textile machinery etc. See "Editorial", *Angkatan Bersenjata*, 12 September 1989.
50 See Soedjati Djiwandono, "Indonesia's Response to Soviet Initiatives: An Update", Paper submitted to IV World Congress for Soviet and East European Studies, Harrogate, England, 21-16 July 1990, p. 18; See also *Jakarta Post*, 13 September 1989.
51 *Angkatan Bersenjata*, 12 September 1989, p. 1 and editorial.
52 Graeme Gill, "The Soviet Union and Southeast Asia: A New Beginning?", *Contemporary Southeast Asia*, Vol. 10, No. 1 (June 1988) pp. 69-81.
53 Tajuk Rencana, *Angkatan Bersenjata*, 22 August 1991.
54 *Kompas*, 22 August 1991.
55 *Kompas*, 23 August 1991.
56 For a discussion on Japan-Indonesia relations during the Sukarno era, see Masashi Nishihara, *The Japanese and Sukarno's Indonesia. Tokyo-Jakarta Relations, 1951-1966*, Monographs of the Center for Southeast Asian Studies, Kyoto University (Honolulu: The University Press of Hawaii, 1976). However, on the post-Sukarno era, there is no major study available in English, except an unpublished thesis, Michael Sean Malley, "A Political Biography of Major General Soedjono Hoemardani: 1918-1986" (M.A. thesis, Cornell University, 1990).
57 General Soedjono Hoemardani (Honorary Chairman of the CSIS) was identified as "Suharto personal representative to Japan". He continued to promote closer ties between Jakarta and Tokyo even after he was removed from his position as Presidential Personal Assistant. It was said that he was closely linked with Japanese major business firms. See Michael Sean Malley, M.A. thesis, especially pp. 62-114.
58 *Statistik Indonesia 1987* (Statistical Year Book of Indonesia) (Jakarta: Biro Pusat Statistik, 1988), p. 366; *Statistik Indonesia 1991* (Jakarta: Biro Pusat Statistik, 1992), pp. 318, 341.
59 *Statistik Indonesia 1987*, p. 389; *Statistik Indonesia 1991*, p. 321. According to Masashi Nishihara, between 1960 and 1970, at least 46 per cent of Indonesia's crude oil exports went to Japan. See Nishihara, op. cit., p. 18.
60 Nishihara, op. cit., p. 18.
61 Malley, "A Political Biography of Major General Soedjono Hoemardani 1918-1986", pp. 72-73.
62 Suli Suleiman, *Garis-Garis Besar Politik Luar Negeri Republik Indonesia* (Bagian I, Direktorat Research, Penerbitan no.003B/1974) (Jakarta: Departemen Luar Negeri, R.I., 1974), p. 21.
63 Leo Suryadinata, *Pribumi Indonesians, the Chinese Minority and China: A Study of Perceptions and Policies* (Kuala Lumpur: Heinemann, 1978), pp. 142-143; See also *Angkatan Bersenjata*, 15-17 January 1974; *Harian Kami*, 15-16 January 1974.
64 Suryadinata, *Pribumi Indonesians* ..., p. 143.
65 Japanese support appears to be greater than that of the US. It was reported that Japan was considering "Indonesia's call to dissolve a Dutch chaired group of international aid donors [IGGI]" and replace it with a separate forum grouped around the World Bank. *Straits Times*, 28 March 1992.
66 Niksch, "Indonesia-US Relations ...", p. 16; "Mengukur Pagu Pinjaman CGI", *Editor*, 29 May 1993, p. 67.
67 Niksch, "Indonesia-US Relations ...", p. 16.
68 *Kompas*, 19 August 1978.
69 Ibid.

70 I heard this argument at a discussion with a group of Indonesians at Cornell University, May 1989.
71 Suleiman, op. cit., p. 21.
72 See "Jepang: Bagaimana Kita Memandang", *Telstra* (Strategic Review), No. 6 (June 1990), p. 4. However, the article also argues that Japan today is not the pre-World War II Japan: it is now more peaceful.
73 See his talk at the MBA Lecture in Singapore, reported in the *Straits Times*, 21 July 1989. A similar view was also expressed by Major General Subijakto, Governor of Indonesian National Defence Institute, in his paper entitled "Indonesia's Perception of Southeast Asian Regional Security", Paper presented at Wilton Park Conference on Southeast Asia, 8 June 1989, Sussex, England. Mimeograph, p. 5. However, Subijakto noted that Southeast Asia (Indonesia included) should be more concerned with Japan's economic power and the possibility of "a neo-colonial relationship" in their economic relations with Japan. Ibid.
74 *Asiaweek*, 4 May 1986, p. 39.
75 It is interesting to note how the Indonesian military defines "security". "Security is generally equated with a nation's ability to defend its territory. But for Indonesia ... security involves much more than that. Other factors besides the military come into play. Issues such as their deteriorating terms of trade, decreasing access to the markets of the industrialised, increasing economic ... technological dependency on the major advanced countries, swelling debt burden, diminishing employment opportunity and so on, can have a detrimental effect on their political stability, thus jeopardising regional stability." See A. Hasnan Habib, "Indonesia, ASEAN: The Political and Security Environment in the Pacific", in *Indonesian Quarterly*, Vol. 16, No. 3 (1988), p. 292.
76 For a comprehensive discussion of this concept, see Michael Leifer, "Ali Moertopo: Regional Visionary and Regional Pragmatist", *Indonesian Quarterly*, Vol. 13, No. 4 (1985), pp. 524-530.
77 Ibid., p. 527.
78 Ibid., p. 528.
79 Leifer correctly argued that Japan was reluctant to join this association without participation of the US while Australia was interested in a broader co-operation in the region. Ibid., p. 259.
80 Sayidiman Suryohadiprojo, *Menghadapi Tantangan Masa Depan* (Jakarta: Gramedia, 1987), pp. 268-270.
81 Ibid., p. 271.
82 Sayidiman, "How Should the Southeast Asian Countries Regard Japan?" *Telstra*, Vol. 6 (May-June 1990), p. 11.
83 Ibid.
84 Ibid.
85 Ibid., p. 13.
86 Try Sutrisno made a statement that the American bases in the Philippines contributed to regional security. See *Kompas*, 21 November 1987.
87 Benny Murdani in his report to Indonesian parliament noted that the bases issue would become sensitive but he believed that "the ASEAN unity eventually will colour the policies of its members", *Straits Times*, 19 September 1989.
88 "Briefing", *Far Eastern Economic Review*, 14 March 1991, p. 14.
89 *Straits Times*, 6 October 1992.
90 Ibid.

10

Indonesia, the Middle East and Bosnia
Islam and Foreign Policy

Introduction
The influence of the military and President Suharto can also be seen in Indonesia's policy towards the Middle East and Bosnia. This chapter examines whether Islam is the major factor in determining Indonesia's relations with the Islamic and Muslim states,[1] with special reference to the Middle East and Bosnia. Six cases are briefly studied: Jakarta's policy towards the PLO, revolutionary Iran, the Organization of Islamic Conference (OIC), the Soviet occupation of Afghanistan, the Iraqi invasion of Kuwait and the religious conflict in Bosnia.

The Islamic Factor
As a country where Muslims make up the majority of the population, Indonesia is assumed to have close relations with the Islamic Middle East. When Indonesia-Middle East relations are examined, however, it turns out that they have been dictated by many considerations other than Islam. It is true that long before the transfer of political power in 1949, Indonesian officials had come into contact with many Middle-Eastern states. Owing partly to the activities of Indonesian students and partly to the efforts of Haji Agus Salim (a respected Indonesian Islamic figure who later became Foreign Minister), the Islamic states such as Egypt, Iraq and Syria supported the Indonesian nationalist struggle.[2] They were one of the earliest groups of countries which recognized Indonesian independence. However, Indonesia-Middle East relations did not expand rapidly.

During the Parliamentary Democracy period (1949-1956), when political parties were in power, Islamic parties such as Masyumi and NU were assumed to have introduced more Islamic foreign policy, but this was not the case. Even when Sukiman of Masyumi was Prime Minister, his foreign policy was very pro-American. This was during the Cold War period when Muslims sided with non-Communists in order to survive. In addition, the Islamic rebellions in Indonesia made identifying closely with Islam appear unpatriotic.[3] This may explain why Indonesia's foreign policy, even when an Islamic party was a major partner in the ruling coalition, was still non-Islamic.

From the beginning, Indonesia has adopted a policy of non-recognition towards Israel. Indonesian sympathy has been with the Arabs, who are Muslims. This policy has often been seen as reflecting Indonesia's close association with its Islamic brothers. However, if the situation is studied more closely, it can be seen that these relations were based on Third World nationalism rather than co-religious solidarity. For instance, Sukarno viewed Israel as an American imperialist ally and an enemy of the Third World. During the Asian Games, Sukarno even prohibited the Israeli delegation from entering Indonesia. Taiwan, an American ally, was not recognized by Indonesia either and was not allowed to participate in the games. Of course, Muslims were happy with these decisions, but co-religious solidarity was not their major reason.[4]

During the New Order era, Indonesia continued the same policy towards the Middle East, although the United States was no longer regarded as an enemy. However, Indonesian support for the Arabs was based on sober calculation of its national interests. Even the Director of Research in the Ministry of Foreign Affairs stated that Indonesian support for the Arab countries against Israel was based on the principle of justice *(dasar keadilan)*, which was also the principle of "our foreign policy"[5] "The factor of same religion is an additional one."[6] He also noted that Indonesia supported the Arab countries' use of oil as a foreign policy tool but hoped that the conflict would be solved within a short period of time. He argued that the use of oil as a weapon over the short term would harm the US, Europe and Japan, and would help the struggle of the Arabs. "However, if it is used for a long period of time, the developing countries will suffer, because economic relations with the developed countries are needed for the development of developing countries."[7]

The above quotation indicates two things: the support for the Arab cause was not due to co-religious feelings but based on the "principle of justice" which is non-religious; the Islamic factor was only secondary. Support for the Arab cause could, however, harm the Indonesian economy. Although the statement did not indicate clearly which one would prevail when the two were in conflict, it can be assumed that Indonesia's national interest would prevail.

On the Palestine Liberation Organization

A clearer statement was made by Suharto on 30 November 1987 when he renewed his pledge of Indonesian support for the Palestinians in their struggle to attain their inalienable rights. He stated that "as a nation, proud of its own legacy of struggle against colonial subjugation and for national independence, we in Indonesia have always considered the Palestinians a sacred cause, as our own struggle as part of the irreversible global movement against colonial rule and alien domination".[8] He also stated that the conflict in the Middle East could only be solved if the Palestinian people were given an independent state of their own and Israel withdrew unconditionally from all occupied Arab territories, including Jerusalem.[9] Islam was conspicuously absent from his statement.

Indeed, Islam has not been a major consideration in Suharto's foreign policy. The establishment of the Palestine Liberation Organization's (PLO) office can be used as an example. In 1974, Adam Malik indicated that he would not object to the opening of an office in Jakarta by the PLO although it had not officially requested such representation.[10] In the following year, Malik again stated that Indonesia basically agreed with the idea of a PLO mission if it were set up in accordance with "established norms".[11] However, Malik's plan was vetoed by the military and the question of the PLO office was pushed aside.[12] Apparently, the military was very concerned about terrorist activities conducted by the PLO and its possible impact on radical Muslims in Indonesia. In addition, the military was wary about the PLO's links with Communist countries which might also pose a security threat. Furthermore, there was an internal struggle within the PLO which could be brought to Indonesia.

When the PLO established a government in exile in 1987, Indonesia recognized it. It also announced that it would allow the PLO to establish an office in Jakarta. The timing of this statement coincided with Indonesia's desire to chair the conference of the Non-Aligned Movement. Indonesia apparently did not receive enough support from the member-countries because of its attitude towards the PLO,[13] that is, its earlier refusal to allow the PLO to open an office in Jakarta. The PLO was scheduled to open its mission in July 1989, but a delay occurred due to "technical" difficulties.

When Suharto attended the Non-Aligned Conference in Belgrade, Yugoslavia, in September 1989, Yasser Arafat brought up the problem of a Palestinian Embassy in Jakarta. It was then decided that a Palestinian Embassy would be set up soon.[14] Jakarta's handling of the PLO problem indicates Indonesia's concern with its security. The decision to let the PLO set up an office came only after Indonesia had decided that the PLO no longer posed a serious threat and that Indonesia wanted to gain the support of the Non-Aligned countries for its chairmanship. The co-religious factor did not come into the picture or, if it did, it was of secondary importance. The Non-Aligned Movement conference was eventually held in Jakarta between 1 and 6 September 1992. Shortly before the conference, the PLO Ambassador delivered his credentials to Suharto. Yasser Arafat also came to Jakarta to attend the conference.

When Arafat and Yitzhak Rabin of Israel conducted secret talks which resulted in the signing of the peace treaty in Washington DC on 13 September 1993, Suharto gave his support. Arafat was invited to visit Indonesia again. During the state banquet in honour of Arafat, Suharto was quoted to have said that Indonesia welcomed the peace initiative taken by Arafat.[15] *Tempo,* a leading news magazine in Jakarta, noted that Indonesia has consistently supported the struggle of Palestinians to gain independence from foreign occupation. "But until now there is no formal statement which indicates that Indonesia's support is linked to Islamic struggle."[16] Arafat himself also told *Tempo* during the interview that he did not intend to establish an Islamic state of Palestine, "but a democratic state, which can protect all religions, just like your Pancasila."[17]

As noted earlier, although Suharto gave his support to the PLO peace treaty with Israel, opinion within Indonesia is still divided. Some Muslims are in favour of establishing diplomatic ties with Israel since the PLO had done so, other are still reluctant — they want to wait till Israel returns all its occupied lands to the Arabs. Abdurrachman Wahid, the supreme leader of NU, is the strong advocate for the normalization. He even accepted the invitation of the Harry Truman Institute in Tel Aviv to attend a seminar and witnessed the signing of the peace treaty between Jordan and Israel.[18] However, he was criticized by the leaders of the Partai Persatuan Pembangunan (PPP) who suspected the sincerity of Israel. Aisyah Aminy, a member of parliament representing the PPP, argued that Israel "does not respect human rights" and to recognize Israel now would only strengthen the Israeli position.[19] However, the Indonesian Democratic Party (PDI) sided with Wahid on the issue. Perhaps Suharto is still testing the ground and thus has not yet moved to recognize Israel.

Following Arafat's visit on 15 October 1994, Rabin also came to Jakarta. The Indonesian press was caught by surprise. Apparently, the arrangements for the visit were made by Suharto's assistants without the knowledge of MFA and the press.[20] Some leaders used the opportunity to criticize Suharto. They maintained that since Israel had no diplomatic relations, Suharto should not have met Rabin.[21] However, State Secretary Moerdiono defended the visit, stating that Suharto received Rabin in his capacity as chairman of NAM, not as Indonesian President. It is clear that Suharto was trying to play a leadership role in world affairs. Islam is not the major consideration in his foreign policy.

On Iran and Libya

Indonesia's security concerns were also reflected in the nation's policy towards Iran. It had cordial relations with the Shah of Iran but when the Iranian

Revolution occurred and the Shah was overthrown by the Ayatollah Rohullah Khomeini, Indonesia's attitude was cautious. The Indonesian military strengthened security measures aimed at Iranians and watched the new Iranian Embassy closely. It was reported that some Muslim radicals in Indonesia wanted to maintain contact with the Iranians and literature on the Iranian revolution was being distributed in Indonesia. Indonesian authorities confiscated the publications and restricted Indonesians who wanted to study in Iran by requiring that they be cleared by the authorities before they were given permission. (However, many went there without official endorsement through Pakistan or other countries which were friendly to Iran.) The Minister of Religious Affairs, Munawir, called them "underground *santri*" (*santri gelap*).[22] The Government was concerned about these *santri* because information had been obtained that the masterminds of the Borobudur bombing incident in 1984 had hidden in Iran.[23]

Jakarta's relations with Libya have not been close either. The Indonesian army believes that Libya has supported the Islamic separatist movement in Aceh.[24] Once Indonesia was elected the Chairman of NAM, however, Indonesia and Libya established diplomatic relations at ambassadorial level on 17 October 1991. Alatas said that this would permit Libya to attend the next summit meeting of NAM in Jakarta.[25] Nevertheless, some army officials were unhappy despite the fact that Alatas had Suharto's blessings.

On the Afghan Interim Government

In the case of Indonesia's relations with Afghanistan, Indonesia has maintained diplomatic ties with the Moscow-backed Kabul regime, although it is sympathetic to the nationalist Mujahiddin. On 23 February 1989, the Mujahiddin group established an Afghan Interim Government in Pakistan and the Organization of Islamic Conference (OIC) recognized this government-in-exile. As individual countries, only Saudi Arabia, Sudan and Bahrain have recognized the Interim Government.[26] In April 1989, the Minister of Foreign Affairs of the Interim Government visited Malaysia and Indonesia with the purpose of gaining their recognition. As a result, Malaysia recognized the government, but Indonesia refused.[27]

When Ali Alatas was asked why Indonesia had refused to recognize the Interim Government of Afghanistan, his answer was that it was a government-in-exile. When asked why Jakarta recognized the PLO and the CGDK which were also governments-in-exile, Alatas answered that the PLO had been fighting for their rights more than 40 years while the Coalition Government of Democratic Kampuchea (CGDK) was recognized by the United Nations as the legitimate government of Cambodia.²⁸ The real reason for Indonesia's recognition of the PLO and the CGDK perhaps lies elsewhere. Unlike Malaysia which stresses Islamic solidarity because of domestic Islamic pressure, Indonesia does not attempt to project the Islamic factor in its foreign policy.

Perhaps Indonesia also did not want to jeopardize its relations with the Soviets by supporting the anti-Moscow government-in-exile. At that time Suharto was about to visit Moscow. His visit was first scheduled for June 1989, but was later postponed to September of that year. The second consideration may have been Indonesia's objection to supporting an Islamic group that planned to seize power and take over the government from outside as this might set a precedent for other Muslim countries or countries with a large Muslim population.

It is interesting to note that the pro-Moscow *Merdeka* group came out in support of Indonesia's decision. In an editorial, it argued that the establishment of the interim government-in-exile would only prolong the conflict in Afghanistan. Moreover, Indonesia subscribes to the principle of non-interference and therefore should not behave emotionally like other Islamic countries that seek religious solidarity.²⁹

On the Organization of Islamic Conference

Another example attesting to the non-Islamic nature of Indonesia's foreign policy and Suharto's role in the making of such policy is Indonesia's involvement in the Organization of Islamic Conference (OIC). The Organization was formed in 1970 at the Second Summit Meeting of the Foreign Ministers of 22 countries. All of them (except Indonesia) were considered Islamic states.³⁰

Between February and March 1972, there was a third meeting of foreign ministers of 33 countries. On this occasion they were to determine the character and direction of the OIC and consequently the OIC Charter was drafted. The Indonesian delegate was instructed by President Suharto to participate at the OIC to promote international co-operation between Indonesia and the Islamic states.³¹ This co-operation was to be based on the UN Charter rather than on Islamic principles; it would also correspond with Indonesia's 1945 Constitution.³²

The OIC Charter stated that its members were Islamic states, and as Indonesia was neither an Islamic nor a religious state, the Indonesian delegate refused to sign the Charter.³³ Nevertheless, the OIC permitted Indonesia to participate in its activities. As Michael Leifer has correctly pointed out, Indonesia has participated in the activities of the OIC, not as an Islamic state but as a state which honours the Principles of the Non-Aligned Movement and the Bandung Conference.³⁴ Indeed, Imron Rosyadi, an NU leader who was also on the Foreign Relations Committee of the DPR (Indonesian parliament), has stated that Indonesia's position in the OIC is unique. It has not only been accepted by the Islamic states but has served as a mediator in conflicts between OIC members.[35] It should be noted that Suharto attended the OIC summit in Senegal in December 1991 which could have been preparation for the future Non-Aligned Meeting in Indonesia the following year. Suharto wanted to project an image of leadership in the third world. In addition, it would have been part of Suharto's domestic politics to satisfy Muslims before the 1992 General Elections and the Presidential Election in 1993.

Indonesia's obsession with NAM can also be seen from Ali Alatas's speech at the OIC foreign ministers meeting in Karachi in April 1993. In that speech, Ali Alatas noted that both OIC and NAM would play more active role in the new world order. He intentionally identified NAM in his speech and de-emphasized the Islamic factor. When expressing his concern over the Israeli deportation of 400 Palestinians to no-man's land in southern Lebanon, he said that it "presented a violation of an international convention".[36] There was no mention of Islamic brotherhood in the statement. When expressing concern about the worsening relations between the Republic of Azerbaijan (an OIC member) and Armenia (a non-OIC member) over Nagorno-Karabakh, he was not defending Islamic Azerbaijan. He was quoted as saying that "the Indonesian delegation wants to see an end to the infringement initiated by an OIC member country [to a non-OIC member country]".[37]

On the Iraqi Invasion of Kuwait

Another example demonstrating the non-Islamic nature of Indonesia's foreign policy was Jakarta's reaction to the Iraqi invasion of Kuwait and the Gulf War which began on 16 January 1991. The Islamic factor was not taken into consideration at all. When Saddam Hussain invaded Kuwait in early August of 1990, it provoked a strong reaction from many countries, especially in the West. Indonesia's reaction was mild and there was no condemnation from Jakarta. A spokesman for the Ministry of Mines and Energy was even quoted as saying that Indonesia would continue to import oil from Iraq and that "Indonesia would not be influenced by any country ororganization".[38] Later Ginanjar, the Minister of Mines and Energy, stated that even if Indonesia stopped importing Iraqi oil, "there would be enough supplies in the international markets and its own stockpile for domestic demand"(sic).[39]

When the United Nations imposed a trade embargo on Iraq in order to force Saddam Hussain to withdraw from Kuwait, Indonesia announced that it would abide by the UN resolution.[40] Indonesia, however, did not openly condemn the Iraqi annexation of Kuwait. It held back from "outright condemnation of Iraq's action and offered to mediate in the far-off dispute".[41] Apparently, Indonesia was conscious of its non-aligned status and also of its domestic problems. Jakarta feared external intervention in Irian Jaya and East Timor.[42] To condemn Iraq outright might result in the alienation of Iraq's supporters in the Non-Aligned Movement. In addition, Indonesia wanted to convey the impression that it was playing a more independent role.

Indonesia's reluctance to condemn Iraq for its occupation of Kuwait might also have been due to the fact that Iraq had supported Indonesia in the UN debate on "integration of East Timor". On this occasion, however, the Indonesians, owing to international pressure, argued that Indonesia was a member of the United Nations and hence had to abide by its resolution.[43]

It is interesting to note, however, that when Saudi Arabia sent envoys to non-Arab Islamic countries to request volunteers, Indonesia refused. Alatas and the Indonesian Armed Forces stated that Indonesia did not have a tradition of sending volunteers overseas, except as part of a UN peace-keeping force.[44] Apparently, Indonesia did not wish to become involved in the politics of the Arab states due to domestic considerations. A poll conducted in *Tempo* indicated that the majority of the population did not wish to take sides.[45] Only a small number of Indonesian Muslims agreed to send volunteers, but this group was divided into pro-Iraq, pro-Saudi and pro-Kuwait sections. The majority were unwilling to send volunteers to the Gulf.[46]

It has also been suggested that Jakarta had a grudge against the Saudi Government because of the way the latter had handled the pilgrim disaster (known as the Mina Tragedy) in July 1990 when more than 700 Indonesian pilgrims died. Saudi Arabia had refused to give Indonesia necessary information concerning the tragedy.[47]

The cautious attitude of the Indonesian Government during the Gulf crisis can also be explained in terms of domestic politics. President Suharto, who had made known his intention to run for the Presidency in 1993, needed Muslim support. In fact, in December 1988, the Suharto Government had passed the Islamic Court Law which gave concessions to the Muslim community.[48] In March 1989, Suharto signed a new national education bill which made religious education (including Islam) a compulsory subject in Indonesian schools.[49] The most recent move was the formation of the Indonesian Muslim Intellectuals Association in December 1990, which was endorsed by the Government.[50] All of these are seen as concessions made by Suharto to the Muslim community. It is thus not surprising that when the Allied Forces attacked Kuwait, the Indonesian Government did not give it public support.

There were groups in Indonesia, however, that had pressured the Government to play a more active role after the Gulf War began in January. Some wanted the Government to take the side of Iraq, but Jakarta refused to comply. Alatas constantly argued that the war had been caused by the Iraqi invasion of Kuwait and it was not a war between Muslims and Non-Muslims. Indonesia's consistent position was that, while it could not condone Iraq's invasion and annexation of Kuwait, it deeply regretted the outbreak of hostilities. Some radical Muslim groups in Bandung and Jakarta demonstrated against the allies, but their members were arrested by the authorities.[51]

In November 1990, after the Iraqi invasion of Kuwait, the Government decided to try a Muslim radical named Husein Al Habsyi, who had been the mastermind behind the bombing of Borobudur and several buses and who had been captured a year earlier. He was found guilty and was sentenced to life imprisonment.[52] This was meant as a warning to Muslim radicals in Indonesia.

Opposition party leaders in parliament asked the Indonesian Government to take the initiative in seeking a political solution to the war. B.N. Marboen of the PDI commented that Indonesia was siding with the Allies because of its situation as beneficiary in the IGGI in which Japan and the United States were major donors.[53] However, Alatas categorically denied this accusation. He stressed that Indonesia was only observing the United Nations' decision. Marboen also noted that, in the past, Indonesia had been active in its foreign policy and had always taken the initiative, but on this occasion, it had become passive and reactionary. "We wait first and then speak out."[54]

Golkar MP Marzuki Darusman also criticized the Government for its delay in taking action. He stated that Singapore, Thailand and the Philippines had given medical aid to the victims of the Middle East war and argued that Indonesia could have sent its Red Cross to the Gulf to show its initiative.[55] He further noted that Jakarta had been eager to serve as Chairman of the Non-Aligned Movement but had not played a leadership role in searching for a peaceful solution to the Gulf crisis. This role had been taken by India, Yugoslavia and Jordan.

Ali Alatas replied that the Government had been trying to find an appropriate format to help solve the crisis, but had not been successful. He noted that the Gulf crisis was not a simple matter and Indonesia had to be cautious. "We cannot step into the Gulf crisis suddenly and offer our solution to the conflict. We would be kicked out." He added that "we do not want Algeria and Egypt to step into the Kampuchean issue suddenly either".[56]

On Bosnia

While Yugoslavia disintegrated and Christian Serbs began to purge the Muslim population in Bosnia — an area which was part of Yugoslavia — some Muslim countries, for instance Malaysia, suggested that the Non-Aligned Movement name Serbia as an aggressor.⁵⁷ However, Indonesia disagreed and the proposal was eventually excluded from the Jakarta Message — the document produced at the end of the NAM summit at Jakarta in September 1992. Apparently Indonesia did not wish to link NAM to the Islamic principle.

However, the "ethnic cleansing" in Bosnia continued and it drew the attention of the world, especially the Muslim countries. In April 1993, the Organization of Islamic Conference (OIC) held a meeting in Karachi to discuss the bloodshed in Bosnia. Indonesia expressed solidarity with other Muslim countries over the plight of Muslim Bosnians. Nevertheless, an Indonesian Foreign Ministry official noted that this did not necessarily mean sending troops.⁵⁸ Indeed, when the UN decided to send peace-keeping forces to six Muslim enclaves in Bosnia-Herzegovina, Wiryono Sastroandjojo, the political director of the Indonesian Foreign Ministry, stated that "traditionally Indonesia is always ready to take part in United Nations missions". But he noted that "Indonesia has not been asked to participate". He went on to say that "our priority is Cambodia" where two battalions of Indonesian troops were serving under UN auspices.⁵⁹ In September 1993, Jakarta was still studying a UN demand for Indonesia to send "standby forces" for UN peace-keeping efforts. Although Indonesia did not have any objections in principle, Susilo Sudarman, Co-ordinating Minister for Political and Security Affairs, noted that "the UN demand has to be approved by the President".⁶⁰

Indonesia's attitude towards Bosnia can be explained in terms of its reluctance in projecting an image that Indonesia is a Muslim state. It was also reluctant to get involved in a religious conflict which is out of its traditional areas. In September 1993, Ejup Ganic, Vice-President of Bosnia, flew in to Jakarta to request for help. He pleaded with Suharto that Indonesia use its influence as the Chairman of the Non-Aligned Movement to speed up the peace process in Bosnia.⁶¹ It was reported that Suharto received him, not in his capacity as a member of OIC, but as Chairman of NAM.

In January 1994, Alija Izetbegovic, the President of Bosnia-Herzegovina, led a ten-man delegation to visit Indonesia. He was received by Suharto. It was reported in the Army newspaper that while expressing his support for the Bosnian people, Suharto did not endorse the sending of Indonesian troops to Bosnia for peace-keeping purposes as they were trained for a different climate and situation.⁶² Nevertheless, Suharto instructed his Ambassador-at-Large for NAM Affairs to raise the issue with the movement's co-ordinating bureau at the UN whether the arms embargo against Bosnia should be lifted.⁶³ Suharto was also reported to have said that the international community should treat Bosnia fairly in its fight against much stronger enemies.⁶⁴

However, Jakarta apparently changed its stand on the UN peace-keeping forces. In February 1994, the Minister of Defence, Feisal Tanjung, stated that Indonesia had sent 25 soldiers to Bosnia to join the UN forces and in the near future approximately 200 more men would be sent there.⁶⁵ In fact, some Muslim organizations in Indonesia had proposed to send volunteers to Bosnia towards the end of 1992. However, the actual registration for volunteers took place later. Recently the Government's attitude towards Muslim volunteers has changed. In 1986, for instance, when 13 Indonesian Muslim volunteers wanted to leave for Afghanistan, they were arrested by the Government.⁶⁶ But this time, when the Islamic organizations registered Indonesians — mainly young men and university students — to be volunteers for Bosnia, the military did not take any action against them. However, the Minister of Defence went out of his way to discourage the volunteers. He was quoted as saying that "if volunteers are sent to Bosnia they will encounter difficulties because of weather conditions. It is also possible that they do not know who is Bosnian and who is Serb because both are white". He said that Indonesians should leave the matter to the Indonesian soldiers.⁶⁷

In July 1994, Indonesia sent a 200-strong medical detachment and a smaller team of civil police officers to Bosnia-Herzegovina as part of the UN peace-keeping force.⁶⁸ In October that year, Feisal Tanjung himself flew to Bosnia to observe the Indonesian military contingent. He was even quoted as saying that Indonesia was prepared to upgrade its participation by sending a "mechanized division" if requested by the UN.⁶⁹

In March 1995, Suharto himself made stopovers in Croatia and Bosnia-Herzegovina on his return journey from Copenhagen (Denmark), after attending the UN World Summit for Social Development. During the visit Suharto also suggested that the former Yugoslavia states form a federation to help resolve the conflict. "They could start such a process by recognizing each other and pledging to respect every minority group living in their states".⁷⁰ Suharto further suggested that Indonesia could act as "facilitator, not a mediator, for peace talks. The visit to the war-torn areas was highly publicized in Indonesia. Upon his return to Indonesia, a Muslim scholars' group visited Suharto and praised his courageous act of visiting Sarajevo.⁷¹

The change of the government attitude towards the peace-keeping force and Suharto's subsequent visit to Bosnia may be attributed to his personal decision rather than the military establishment in general. Suharto was projecting his high international profile and was responding to the domestic Islamic sentiments on the Muslim plight in Bosnia. However, the interesting point is that Suharto continued to stress that the support for Bosnia is given not in the context of OIC but under the auspices of NAM.⁷²

Conclusion

The above examples clearly show Indonesia's priority in its foreign policy as well as the limitation of its capability in influencing events beyond the Southeast Asian region. Yet, Indonesia still desires to be a leader of the Non-Aligned Movement. Indonesia has also attempted to conduct a foreign policy which is not based on Islam.

It should be noted that, as late as 1976, Indonesia's relations with the Middle East were not close at all. Adam Malik, who was then Foreign Minister, was asked to comment on whether he agreed with the description of Jakarta's policy towards the Middle East as a policy on pilgrimage affairs. Malik acknowledged that "Indonesia did not regard [those countries in] that region as important, except for pilgrimage every year. With the exploitation of oil, we then became aware of their importance".[73] Malik went on to say that "we want to approach them after they become rich. We have now corrected our past attitude".[74] Malik then noted that Indonesia was ready to assist Saudi Arabia and Oman by sending police instructors, agricultural experts and ice-makers.[75] It is also worth noting that, in the 1980s, many Indonesian workers, especially maids, were sent to the Middle East to work. The ties between Indonesia and the Middle East began to grow closer. However, they were not as close as many Muslims expected.

Suharto and the military have direct control over Indonesia's policy towards the Middle East, especially as it relates to Islam, because of the domestic repercussions. From the above analysis, it is clear that Indonesia's policy towards the Middle East has not been based on Islam but on Indonesian "national interest", as perceived by Suharto and other members of the military elite. The military's fear of Islamic fundamentalism in domestic politics has been the major reason for Indonesia's "non-Islamic" foreign policy. It is also important to note that Indonesia has never attempted to become a leader of the Islamic movement although it has the largest Muslim population in the world. On the contrary, Indonesia was interested in becoming the leader of the Non-Aligned Movement (NAM) which is not based on Islam.[76] Indonesia's changing policy towards the PLO and Bosnia also indicates that Suharto is the decision-maker. He overruled military objection and allowed the PLO to establish an Embassy in Jakarta. He also decided to play a more active role in the Bosnian affair.

Last but not least, it is worth noting that Indonesia is a multi-ethnic and multi-religious state. The nominal Muslims have formed the majority of the Indonesian elite, especially the military officers, during the Suharto era. They have been suspicious and critical of political Islam. They are nationalistic rather than Islamic. As long as this elite group is in power, Indonesia's foreign policy will remain "non-Islamic".

NOTES

1. John L. Esposito has divided states with a large Muslim population into three types: the Islamic State which is based on the supremacy of Islamic law (e.g. Saudi Arabia and Pakistan); the Muslim State which recognizes Islam as the state religion (e.g. Egypt and Malaysia); and the Secular State which "separates Islam from the state and hence restricts religion to private life" (e.g. Tunisia). See his *Islam and Politics* (Syracuse: Syracuse University Press, 1984), p. 94. However, a country that does not give special favour to one religion (i.e. Islam) can also be classified as a Secular State (e.g. Indonesia).
2. Muhammad Zain Hassan, "Hubungan Indonesia-Mesir dan Negara-Negara Liga Arab", in *Sekitar Perjanjian Persahabatan Indonesia-Mesir Tahun 1947* (Jakarta: Committee of the 32nd Anniversary of the Amity Agreement of Indonesia-Egypt, 1978), pp. 26-34, cited in Kirdi Dipoyudo, "Indonesia's Foreign Policy towards The Middle East and Africa", *Indonesian Quarterly*, Vol. 13, No. 4 (1985), p. 474; *Masalah Timur Tengah* (Jakarta: Departemen Luar Negeri, 1976), p. 126.
3. Leifer in fact argued that the Darul-Islam movement put the Islamic leaders in a difficult position. See his article, "The Islamic Factor in Indonesia's Foreign Policy: A Case of Functional Ambiguity", in Adeed Dawisha (ed.), *Islam in Foreign Policy* (New York: Cambridge, 1983), especially pp. 146 and 150.
4. Michael Leifer, *Indonesia's Foreign Policy* (London: Allen and Unwin, 1983), p. 138.
5. Suli Suleiman, *Garis-Garis Besar Politik Luar Negeri Republik Indonesia* (Bagian I, 1974), p. 24a.
6. Ibid.
7. Ibid.
8. *Indonesia News and Views* (Washington DC) Vol. 8, No. 3, pp. 4-5.
9. Ibid.
10. *Sinar Harapan*, 27 June 1974.
11. Franklin Weinstein, *Indonesian Foreign Policy and the Dilemma of Dependence* (Ithaca: Cornell University Press 1976), p. 126.
12. Gordon R. Hein, "Soeharto's Foreign Policy: Second-Generation Nationalism in Indonesia" (Ph.D. thesis, University of California at Berkeley, 1986), p. 243.
13. *Straits Times*, 9 September 1988.
14. *Straits Times*, 8 September 1989.
15. "Menyambut Arafat dengan Demo dan Qunut Nazilah", *Tempo*, 2 October 1993, p. 23.
16. Ibid.
17. Ibid. *Tempo* also noted that Palestine has a population of 5.5 million, of which 20 per cent are non-Muslim.
18. *Merdeka*, 7 November 1994; *Gatra*, 31 December 1994, p. 21.
19. *Merdeka*, 7 November 1994.
20. "Deplu tidak melempem", *Tempo*, 19 March 1994, p. 23.
21. "Pertemuan Soeharto-Rabin", *Telstra*, No. 25, November/December 1993, pp. 72-74.
22. *Tempo*, 7 September 1991, p. 25. Please note *"santri"* here is used to refer to religions school students.
23. Ibid.
24. *Far Eastern* Economic *Review*, 31 October 1991, p. 14.
25. Ibid.
26. *Angkatan Bersenjata*, 13 April 1989.
27. Ibid.
28. *Kompas*, 14 April 1989.
29. *Merdeka*, 14 April 1989.
30. Imron Rosyadi, *Organisasi Konperensi Islam dan Masalahnya* (Jakarta: Yayasan Idayu, 1981), p. 15.
31. This is included in the Presidential Instruction No. 2/1972 (Instruksi Presiden No. 2/1972). See Rosyadi, p. 15.
32. Ibid.
33. Ibid.

34 Leifer, *Indonesia's Foreign Policy*, p. 137.
35 Rosyadi, op. cit., p. 28.
36 *Jakarta Post*, 29 April 1993.
37 Ibid.
38 *Straits Times*, 10 August 1990.
39 Ibid.
40 *Editor*, 25 August 1990, p. 17.
41 Michael Vatikiotis, "Saddam or Satan", *Far Eastern Economic Review*, 20 September 1990, p. 20.
42 Ibid.
43 Ibid. However, it should be noted that Kuwait was initially against Indonesia on the integration of East Timor issue but later abstained during the voting in the UN. See *Tempo*, 29 October 1977, p. 8.
44 Ibid.
45 The *Tempo* survey shows that among the *ulamas*, 4.8 per cent were prepared to be volunteers for Iraq, 4.8 per cent for Saudi Arabia, 4.8 per cent for Kuwait, but 88.6 per cent refused to become volunteers. Among the Muslims, 10 per cent were for Iraq, 14.5 per cent were for Saudi and 6.1 per cent for Kuwait, but 69.4 per cent refused to become volunteers. See "Siapa Mewakili Semangat Islam", *Tempo*, 1 September 1990, pp. 31-32.
46 Ibid.
47 *Editor*, 25 August 1990, p. 17.
48 For a discussion on the bill, see *Tempo*, 24 June 1989, pp. 22-23.
49 *Undang-Undang Sistem Pendidikan Nasional* (Jakarta, PT Kreasi Jaya Utama, 1989), p. 23.
50 *Tempo*, 8 December 1990, pp. 26-27. *Kompas*, 10 December 1990.
51 *Tempo*, 26 January 1991, p. 15; 23 February 1991, p. 16.
52 Husein Al Habsyi was not acting alone. His associates (Abdul Kadir Ali Al-Habsyi and Achmad Muladawali) were captured earlier and sentenced to 20 years imprisonment. See *Tempo*, 17 November 1990, p. 26. See also *Utusan Malaysia*, 2 February 1991, p. 5.
53 *Tempo*, 9 February 1991, p. 22.
54 Ibid.
55 Ibid.
56 Ibid.
57 *Tempo*, 12 September 1992, p. 40
58 *Straits Times*, 10 June 1993.
59 Ibid. According to one source, Indonesian forces abroad involved in UN and peace-keeping are as follows: Cambodia (UNTAC): 1,180; Iraq/Kuwait (UNIKOM): 6 observers (in *The Military Balance 1992-1993*, p. 149.)
60 *Sunday Times*, 12 September 1993.
61 "Beri Kami Senjata", *Tempo*, 2 October 1993, p. 39.
62 "Tajuk Rencana", *Angkatan Bersenjata*, 27 January 1994.
63 Ibid., also *Straits Times*, 27 January 1994.
64 Ibid.
65 *Tempo*, 26 February 1994, p. 34.
66 *Tempo*, 26 February 1994, p. 35.
67 *Tempo*, 26 February 1994, p. 34.
68 *Tempo*, 11 June 1994, p. 43.
69 *Sunday Times*, 23 October 1994.
70 *Kompas*, 16 March 1995; Simon Sinaga, "Suharto outlines plan to end Balkans conflict", *Straits Times*, 16 March 1995.
71 *Kompas*, 20 March 1995.
72 See also *Straits Times*, 27 January 1994.
73 "Adam Malik Menjawab", *Tempo*, 7 February 1976, p. 6.
74 Ibid.
75 Ibid.
76 This point was made by a leading academic in Jakarta.

11

Indonesia, the Non-Aligned Movement and Apec
In Search of a Leadership Role

Introduction

This chapter examines Indonesia's role in the Non-Aligned Movement (NAM) and Asia-Pacific Economic Co-operation (APEC) Forum. In the first part, the following questions on NAM are asked: How important is NAM to Suharto's Indonesia? Why has Indonesia been interested in becoming the Chairman of the NAM conference? What has been done by Indonesian leaders to achieve this objective? Have they been successful? In the second part, another set of questions are posed: What has been the importance of APEC to Suharto's Indonesia? Why did Suharto change his mind on APEC? Was it for economic reasons or political reasons, or both? Is it the way for Suharto to project Indonesia's international leadership position?

The Non-Aligned Movement

Origins of NAM

Indonesia perceives itself as one of the founders of the Non-Aligned Movement, and it wants to be recognized as such. Not surprisingly, Indonesia has tried very hard in recent years to secure the chairmanship of the NAM conference.

In most Indonesian publications on the subject of Indonesian foreign policy, the Non-Aligned Movement has been considered to have originated at the 1955 Afro-Asian Conference, also known as the Bandung Conference. The Bandung Principles, or *Dasasila Bandung*, are believed to be the basis of the

NAM principles. In fact, the first conference of the Non-Aligned Movement was held in 1961 in Belgrade, Yugoslavia. Josip Broz Tito of Yugoslavia, Jawaharlal Nehru of India, and Abdul Nasser of Egypt are always linked with the Movement and the countries that they represented have, in turn, chaired the Movement. Indonesia was always left out.[1]

The first Conference of the Non-Aligned Movement was attended by 28 countries which had expressed concern over tensions in the international arena, especially relations between the two superpowers. The conference participants wished the superpowers to refrain from using military means to solve their differences and stated that they did not wish to be aligned with either superpower. The non-aligned countries would be willing to work with any country to achieve world peace. Although Indonesia was one of the participants in this conference, its role was not conspicuous.

The second NAM Conference was held in Cairo in 1964. At this conference, there was a conflict of interest between India and Indonesia. India was in favour of peaceful co-existence of countries with different political systems while Indonesia advocated confrontation between the New Emerging Forces (Nefos) and the Old Established Forces (Oldefos). The majority of the participants eventually accepted the concept of peaceful co-existence, but also used moderate terms in condemning colonialism.[2] During the conference, closer economic co-operation between the non-aligned countries was also proposed.

When the third Non-Aligned Movement Conference was held in 1970 at Lusaka, conflicts between the superpowers had lessened. However, regional and small wars were still prevalent. Suharto represented Indonesia at this conference. Indonesia's position under the New Order was very different from its position at the Cairo Conference. It advocated peace and development rather than confrontation, noting, however, that there was an increased danger of subversive activities in some of the non-aligned countries.

Two years later, a ministerial meeting of the NAM countries was held in Georgetown, Guyana. Indonesia walked out of the meeting as a result of a disagreement over the People's Liberation Front of South Vietnam (the Vietcong). At the NAM conference in Lusaka, the heads of state had decided to admit the Vietcong as an observer to the NAM conference. During the Georgetown Conference, this decision was altered and the Vietcong was made a full member of NAM. Indonesia and other Southeast Asian states had proposed a compromise. The Vietcong would be accepted as a full participant with full member's rights but it would remain an observer in terms of its status because the earlier decision should not be altered.

The chairman of the conference, the representative of Guyana, said that a majority wished to accept the Vietcong as a full member and pushed the decision through. Indonesia protested this decision and Malaysia and Laos followed suit.[3] The objection was understandable: to accept a rebel group as a member of the

Non-Aligned Movement would encourage rebellions and, in turn, would harm the stability of Indonesia and of Malaysia as well. Adam Malik made a statement after the walkout: "Indonesia will continue to work with and within the group to uphold the principles of non-alignment which we helped formulate ourselves. As had been said before, Indonesia has not opted for non-alignment, Indonesia was born a non-aligned country".[4] Suharto echoed Adam Malik's views, and stated that he was disappointed that the views of the Indonesian, Malaysian and Laotian delegates on Indochina had not been taken seriously.[5]

The NAM Conference held in Algeria in 1973 was dominated by countries which were critical of the United States. There were also a number of moderate countries which disagreed with the radicals. The concept of ZOPFAN (Zone of Peace, Freedom and Neutrality) was well received at the conference, but foreign investment was condemned by many countries. Indonesia was one of the countries that defended foreign investment, saying that it should be seen as a supplement to domestic capital and that it brought benefits to the country and the people concerned.

Growing Interest in NAM

At later NAM conferences, it appears that Indonesia kept a low profile. Only the Foreign Minister was sent to attend the summits until September 1986 when Indonesia's Vice-President, General Umar Wirahadikusumah, was sent to the meeting in Harare, Zimbabwe. One of his aims was to solicit support from the Non-Aligned states for making Indonesia the next Chairman of the movement. In Harare, however, Indonesia encountered strong opposition. Nicaragua also lobbied for the chairmanship and gained a measure of support from several countries, including India. Although the participants decided to delay the decision on the venue of the next conference, many observers realized that Indonesia was not popular with a number of African and Latin American states, partly as a result of its annexation of East Timor ten years earlier and its close ties to the United States.[6]

Although Umar returned home from Harare empty-handed, the Indonesian Government made another attempt when Prime Minister Rajiv Gandhi visited Jakarta soon after the Non-Aligned Conference. It was clear that Gandhi was reluctant to support Indonesia as he favoured a Latin American country as the host of the movement's next summit meeting.[7] When Gandhi was asked by the press whether he agreed with Indonesia being the next host, he simply replied that it was Latin America's turn. Apparently, to India, which had signed a friendship treaty with the USSR, Indonesia was not sufficiently non-aligned. It is also possible that India considered Indonesia a competitor in the Asian region for the leadership of NAM.

It is apparent that Indonesia was serious about becoming the Chairman of the NAM Conference. Even the leading member of the Karya faction (Golkar) in parliament, Marzuki Darusman, supported the idea. When asked about it by reporters, he stated that Indonesia should host the NAM Conference because it had received the support of the majority of the NAM members.[8] He believed that Indonesia was much more qualified than Nicaragua to be the host from a political or economic perspective. When asked what benefits Indonesia would gain by hosting the conference, he initially said that it was a matter of principle. Later he added that, if Indonesia succeeded in becoming the host, "the Indonesian image as a non-aligned nation will be enhanced".[9] It appears, however, that the response of technocrats and some military leaders was lukewarm.

Suharto was determined to vie for the chairmanship. When it was given to Yugoslavia as a compromise candidate, Suharto decided that he would personally attend the summit in Belgrade in September 1989. Nicaragua still wanted to host the next meeting but Indonesia refused to give in. At the Belgrade summit, Suharto commented that the international situation had changed and NAM should also adapt its roles and future actions accordingly. In his view, NAM "cannot avoid setting a realistic order of priorities as a flexible guide, rather than as a rigid prescription".[10] He argued that, if NAM did nothing, it faced the danger of being sidetracked. Later, Suharto was quoted as saying that Indonesia "would not allow the movement it helped found in 1961 to be turned by radicals into a satellite of the socialist bloc".[11] He said, "we have put forward our candidacy to host the next NAM summit. It is not for any particular ambition but to save NAM from being directed by radicals".[12]

Suharto perhaps felt that as Indonesia had hosted the Afro-Asian Conference but had subsequently failed to become a Chairman of NAM, it was time for Indonesia to take the lead and to be heard again in the international arena. Nevertheless, Indonesian domestic opinion was divided on the issue. Some complained that it would be a great financial burden for Indonesia to host such a conference.[13] Suharto was adamant.

To gain the support of the African nations, in October 1990, Suharto invited Nelson Mandela, the leader of the African National Congress (ANC) to visit Indonesia. During his visit, Mandela was awarded the Star of the Republic of Indonesia, the country's highest civilian award. In addition, Suharto donated US$10 million to the ANC for "its struggle to end racial segregation in South Africa".[14] Moerdiono, the Indonesian Secretary of State, announced that Indonesia would contribute an additional US$250,000 to help the ANC. This was the second of three yearly instalments pledged by Jakarta under the Non-Aligned programme to aid frontline African states in the struggle against apartheid.

Obviously, President Suharto wanted Indonesia to have a higher profile in international forums and NAM had been deemed as one channel through which it hoped to achieve this. Indonesia's dream was eventually fulfilled. This was partly due to international developments. Following the collapse of the Communist governments in Eastern Europe and the decline of Soviet Communism in August 1991, the Communist system began to be discredited and this affected the socialist-oriented states. The radicals within the NAM movement began to lose their influence. This paved the way for Indonesia to become the Chairman of NAM.

When the NAM Ministerial Meeting was held in September 1991 at Accra, Ghana, it became clear that firebrand members like Cuba and Ghana were no longer able to manipulate NAM. Even before the meeting, it was reported that Indonesia was the clear favourite for the next chairmanship. The Indian Ambassador to Indonesia revealed that his government would fully support Indonesia as the candidate while Nicaragua, Indonesia's competitor, offered to withdraw its candidature in return for a promise of support from President Suharto.[15] Apparently Nicaragua was not yet ready to host the meeting because it was still in the process of national reconciliation and its economy was in chaos.[16]

During the Ministerial Meeting at Accra, Indonesia was officially elected as the Chairman of NAM from 1992 to 1995.[17] During the meeting, a discussion was held on the relevance of NAM after the end of the Cold War, especially after the collapse of the Soviet bloc. Some wanted to change the organization's name and role, but others preferred to retain them. Indonesia belonged to the latter group. Although these countries claimed that the movement was still relevant, its focus appeared to have shifted from the Cold War to economic issues.

Indonesian insistence on chairing the NAM conference was linked to Indonesian leaders' perceptions of their nation's role in world affairs. This was clearly stated by Ali Alatas in a 1988 seminar at Gadjah Mada University. In the paper he presented, he disagreed with the opinion that NAM was no longer relevant.[18] He noted that NAM had been launched by Indonesia as evidenced in Indonesia's "independent and active" foreign policy, first proposed by Hatta in 1948. It aimed to promote "a new international order and international relations based on freedom, eternal peace, justice and common prosperity, through friendship and international co-operation without differentiating ideology, political system and economic system".[19]

Admitting that the recent developments made the situation more complex, he contended that NAM principles could still be used to solve these complex problems, especially the problems of the Third World, most notably socio-economic backwardness. After explaining the relevance of NAM, he discussed Indonesia's role in this movement. He argued that it was Indonesia's responsibility to work together with other NAM member-countries towards their common goals. He went on to say:

> In fact, political consolidation and economic progress that we have achieved through national development have enabled us to play not just a participatory role.
>
> As a founding member and the host of the Afro-Asian Conference and the founder of NAM; as a member of the Organization of Islamic Conference, OPEC, ASEAN, Group of 77, the Conference of Disarmament and other international organizations; as a major producer of raw materials, Indonesia has a remarkable position and potential among the Third World states.
>
> Therefore if we play a pioneering role, as evidenced in our decolonization process and North-South negotiations, the world will also accept this role as natural. This is also expected by us.[20]

He then concluded by saying that "this is time for Indonesia to play a more active and assertive role and this coincides fully with our national interests".[21]

In fact, using various *Garis-Garis Besar Haluan Negara* (General Guidelines of State Direction), which are issued by the Indonesian People's Consultative Assembly, it is possible to see the changing perceptions of Indonesia's role in international affairs. In 1973, Indonesia's foreign policy centred on ASEAN.[22] In 1978, ASEAN was still the centre of Indonesia's foreign policy.[23] In 1983, however, the centre began to shift to other areas. It was more concerned with "the Indonesian role in participating in world order". Indonesia's role was "to help solve world problems which threaten peace and are in conflict with feelings of justice and humanitarianism".[24] In that year, ASEAN was mentioned only after discussing those international (rather than regional) roles. By 1988, the perception of Indonesia's foreign policy role became even clearer. It was to help solve world problems based on the spirit of the Bandung Principles *(Dasasila Bandung)*.[25] Indonesia also stated that it would make use of various forums (UN, ASEAN, NAM and OIC). The place of ASEAN in Indonesia's foreign policy appeared to be much lower than before, as Indonesia now saw itself playing a larger role in world affairs. It is clear that Indonesia considers itself a leading Third World country. It wants to be recognized as a leader. The contest for the chairmanship of NAM was one means to achieve this goal.

The NAM conference was finally held in Jakarta between 1 and 6 September 1992. Invitations were sent to 104 member states, but only 60 heads of state attended the meeting. This number is comparable to attendance in Belgrade in 1989.[26] Many radical leaders such as Muammar Qadhafi of Libya and Fidel Castro of Cuba were absent. Husni Mubarak of Egypt, who suggested that NAM be merged with the Group of 77, did not attend either.[27]

From the start, Suharto wanted to focus the movement on economic issues. He was quoted as saying that "the movement can play a constructive role in the North-South dialogue. It must not be haunted by a confrontational atmosphere but with a spirit to build a more advanced, prosperous and equitable world for all nations and individuals".[28] Ali Alatas noted that Indonesia wanted an action programme for economic co-operation among the Non-Aligned countries.[29] However, during the meeting, there were countries that wanted to focus their discussions on political issues. The Vice-President of Iraq, for instance, wanted the meeting to condemn the American blockade of southern Iraq. Some Islamic and Muslim states, including Malaysia, were eager to condemn Serbia's (formerly Yugoslavia) treatment of Bosnian Muslims. Other countries deplored Western economic protectionism and American domination of the United Nations. A major disagreement on the Bosnian question went on until the last minutes of the meeting. While NAM members in general agreed to make a statement condemning the massacre of Bosnian Muslims in the former Yugoslavia, Iran and Malaysia wanted NAM to name Serbia as the aggressor.[30] There was no agreement on this issue which resulted in the postponement of the closing session. Nevertheless, Indonesia appeared to be able to mediate between the conflicting parties and focused on economic issues.

When the Jakarta Message was issued at the end of the meeting, there was a collective view that "economic co-operation and development must be their top priority if the grouping is to play a major role in shaping the new world order."[31] The declaration was also accompanied by some "action-oriented" measures to boost such co-operation.

If the NAM summit was a victory for Suharto, his address to the General Assembly of the UN soon after the NAM summit was a greater victory. Representing the view of the Non-Aligned nations, Suharto delivered a speech at the UN, calling for the restructuring of the UN Security Council.[32] He argued that the composition of the Security Council was outdated because it was based on the situation after the Second World War. Today, there are major countries which should be included in the interest of making the world organization more representative. He then suggested that Japan, Germany, Indonesia, India and two other countries (one from Africa and the other from Latin America) be admitted to the UN Security Council as permanent members.[33] In fact, the issue of the UN Security Council had been discussed during the summit. However, Suharto made use of this opportunity to benefit Indonesia. He wanted Indonesia to be recognized as a leader of the international community.

As a matter of fact, in 1960, President Sukarno had delivered a similar speech to the UN General Assembly. He was also representing the Non-Aligned countries (Afro-Asian nations) when he made his well-known speech entitled "Build the World Anew".[34] He criticized the UN as being outdated and argued:

> The organization and membership of the Security Council, that most important body, reflects the economic, military and power map of the world of 1945, when the organization was born of a vast inspiration and vision. That is also true of most other agencies. They do not reflect the rise of the socialist countries, nor the rocketing of Asian-African independence.[35]

Sukarno further noted that "it is essential that the distribution of seats in the Security Council and the other bodies and agencies should be revised".[36] Unlike Suharto, Sukarno did not mention that Indonesia should be a member.

Nevertheless, Sukarno was conscious of Indonesia's position in the international community. In the same speech, he noted the significance of Pancasila, the Indonesian state ideology. He said that "in speaking to you of Pantja Sila, I am expressing the essence of two thousand years of our civilization".[37] He told the UN Assembly that the UN Charter was inadequate and that Pancasila should be incorporated into the Charter in order to make the charter "more whole-heartedly acceptable to all members, both the old and the new".[38]

Sukarno noted that, at the root of tension, was Imperialism and Colonialism. He urged the UN to support the struggle for freedom and independence all over the world. He also urged the US and USSR to resume contacts in order to maintain world peace. Sukarno made his speech at the height of the Cold War. Not surprisingly, he suggested that the headquarters of the UN be moved from New York to either Asia, Africa, or Geneva.[39]

Because of differences in personality and different international conditions, Sukarno, who spoke during the Cold War, used revolutionary language while Suharto, who spoke after the end of the Cold War, used more docile words. Nevertheless, both were concerned with Indonesia's role in the international community. Not surprisingly, some Indonesian observers saw similarities between Sukarno's vision and that of Suharto. Both wanted to make Indonesia an internationally recognized leader.

It appears that Suharto has taken Indonesia's leadership in NAM seriously. Two examples illustrate this. First, on his way back to Jakarta from the UN, he made a stop-over in Tokyo to talk to Japanese leaders on the South-North dialogue. He made it clear that he was discussing the economic matter as the leader of NAM. Second, he made it known that he wanted to be invited to address the Group of Seven (G-7) in Tokyo as the NAM leader. Again, he intended to talk about South-North dialogue.[40] When G-7 rejected his request, he flew in to Tokyo before the G-7 summit to meet Japanese Prime Minister Miyazawa to deliver the message for the conference participants. He also had lunch and discussions with Bill Clinton separately on a similar topic.[41] He wanted to show that Indonesia was playing the role of a Third World leader.

Asia-pacific economic co-operation

Apart from the Non-Aligned Movement, Suharto has also used the Asia-Pacific Economic Co-operation (APEC) to project the Indonesian leadership position. However, initially Indonesia, if not Suharto himself, had some reservations about

APEC. Jakarta was afraid that it might come into conflict with ASEAN — which was then the corner stone of Indonesia's foreign policy.[42] Indonesia or, more appropriately, Suharto began to change his view after the end of the Cold War.

In fact, the change of Indonesia's attitude towards APEC is linked to Indonesia's perceived role in world affairs rather than Indonesian economic needs. It is a well-known fact that Indonesian economic development was behind many ASEAN states and hence was most protective in its trade policy. When the ASEAN Free Trade Area was first proposed, Indonesia had strong reservations as Jakarta feared that free trade would give the other ASEAN states access to the huge Indonesian market, while Jakarta was unable to reap profit from this arrangement because of the low level of Indonesian industrialization. Understandably Jakarta resisted the proposal until the 1992 ASEAN Summit in Singapore. Only then, as a compromise, Jakarta accepted the concept of ASEAN Free Trade Area, later known as AFTA, but the timetable was shortened from 20 years to 15 years. This change of attitude also took place in the last minutes — people were taken by surprise when Suharto agreed to AFTA.

Indonesia's attitude towards APEC began to change in 1993 when President Suharto accepted the invitation of President Bill Clinton to attend the Seattle Summit. The summit proposed that APEC would work towards liberalization of the Asia-Pacific region. First established in November 1989 by Australia under the prime ministership of Bob Hawke, APEC's original members comprised six ASEAN states, Australia, Canada, Japan, South Korea, New Zealand and the United States.[43] It was later joined by China, Hong Kong, Taiwan, Papua New Guinea, Chile and Mexico. The establishment of APEC was in anticipation of the possible failure of the Uruguay Round. If the Uruguay Round failed, APEC could be used as an effective measure to protect the trading interest of the Asia-Pacific countries.

However, Malaysia suddenly disagreed with APEC. Prime Minister Mahathir suggested the creation of East Asia Economic Grouping (EAEG), which was not well received by President Suharto (see Chapter 5 on the section of Indonesia-Malaysia relations). Mahathir was of the view that with the entry of economically powerful countries such as the United States into APEC, weak Asian countries might be victimized. When the APEC Summit was held in Seattle, Mahathir refused to attend and instead, sent his Minister of Trade and Industry, Rafidah Aziz, on his behalf. However, Mahathir attended the Bogor Summit in November 1994, although again he noted his reservations about the agreed timetable.[44]

The success of the Seattle Summit in November 1993 led to the subsequent success of the Uruguay Round in December 1993. Indonesia, which was initially skeptical of APEC, changed its view. After the Seattle Summit, Indonesia was the chairman of the Summit in 1995. Beyond the expectation of many observers,

Indonesia which was initially reluctant to open up its domestic market has now emerged as the advocate of the free trade concept. It is interesting to pose the question why Jakarta suddenly accepted the Eminent Persons Group (EPG) of APEC which suggested free trade for the Asia-Pacific countries in the year 2020.

According to Professor Suhadi Mangkusuwondo, the Indonesian member of EPG, Indonesia's change of heart on APEC was due to a number of factors, one of them was the fear of-being left behind by Thailand, Vietnam and India in getting foreign investment if there is no trade liberalization.[45] Vietnam, Thailand and India have opened up their domestic markets to foreign investors, resulting in the phenomenal increase in foreign investment. In the post-Cold War period when foreign investment is an important means to promote economic development, it is understandable that Indonesia finally agreed to trade liberalization.

Nevertheless, the economic factor alone does not explain the sudden change of the Indonesian Government attitude towards free trade. An equally possible explanation was President Suharto's eagerness to be recognized as a leader who is able to contribute to world affairs. After Indonesia was elected to be the Chairman of NAM in 1992 and began to play the role of a leader of the Third World seriously (see above), Suharto also felt that the chairmanship of the APEC Summit would bring him prestige and recognition as one of the international leaders. Suharto knew very well that the world focus would be on Indonesia again when the APEC Summit was held in Bogor.

The challenge to Suharto to make the summit a success was a tremendous one. Initially he wanted to ensure that all members would attend the summit. Mahathir, who was absent in Seattle, agreed to attend the meeting personally, although he was still in opposition to the free trade timetable for APEC. The PRC had also opposed the free trade timetable, but later changed its view, although with reservations about the 2020 deadline.[46] The Trade Ministers Conference prior to the APEC Summit encountered some obstacles, and there was still doubt that there would be an agreement on the timetable for free trade when it ended.

However, the Indonesian leaders succeeded in making all participants agree on the timetable. Acknowledging different stages of economic development in the Asia-Pacific, the Indonesian proposal suggested that there would be a two-tiered time table: developed countries will be required to introduce free trade by the year 2010, while developing countries will also do so by the year 2020. With regard to the NICs, there was no timetable but each is expected to introduce free trade between 2010 and 2020. On 15 November 1994, the Indonesian proposal, later known as the Bogor Declaration, was eventually accepted.[47]

Indonesian success in holding the APEC Summit and the promulgation of the Bogor Declaration brought prestige to Jakarta, especially Suharto. He was credited by Bill Clinton as an Asian leader who "is trying to spearhead ... and tear down ... trade barriers. It is a very significant thing".[48]

It should be noted that China's high level participation in the Bogor Summit was partly due to Indonesian handling of the Taiwan issue. Jakarta continued to use the Seattle formula that Taiwan's delegation be led by the Minister of Trade (not President Lee Teng Hui), following the One-China policy. Indonesia also allowed Malaysia to record its reservation on the timetable as the annex of the Declaration, in return for the Malaysian support of the free trade principle.

The holding of the APEC Summit cost Indonesia Rp. 250 billion.[49] An indigenous businessman, Pontjo Sutowo (son of Ibnu Sutowo), was given the responsibility of arranging the accommodation of APEC participants.[50] It was reported that he was not after the profit but many believe that some indigenous businessmen made money out of this international event.

c onclusion

Indonesia has always perceived itself as a founding member of NAM. Nevertheless, it was not accorded proper recognition. With Indonesia's rising aspiration to play a prominent role in international affairs, Suharto's Indonesia has seen the chairmanship of the NAM conference as a symbol of such recognition. Not surprisingly, Suharto had been very active in gaining international support and finally succeeded in winning the NAM chairmanship for his country.

NAM in the 1990s differs from the NAM of the past as a result of the end of the Cold War and the collapse of the Soviet Union as a Communist power. Many members of NAM have questioned the relevance of NAM in the post-Cold War world. Indonesia and others have insisted that it is still relevant by encouraging a new interpretation of the movement. The focus is now on economic issues rather than on political/ideological ones. NAM has, therefore, become the association of developing countries that desires to carry on a dialogue with industrialized nations. Indonesia wants to lead the member states in a new direction but it is debatable whether it has succeeded in this. However, for Indonesia, form is often as important as substance. The fact that Indonesia has become the Chairman of the movement and has succeeded in hosting the Conference means that half the battle has been won. The speech that Suharto made to the UN General Assembly on restructuring the UN Security Council has been considered by some observers as another victory for Indonesia, although the impact of the speech is still far from clear.

It should be noted that Indonesia gained confidence after becoming NAM Chairman. Not only has Suharto gone overseas to participate in international forums, but he has also received foreign leaders who seek Indonesia's good offices or support. He repeatedly noted that he received these leaders in his capacity as NAM Chairman, not as Indonesian President. Indirectly he has put Indonesia on the map of world affairs, making Indonesia one of the leaders in the international community. When the successor-country, Nicaragua, wanted more time to decide whether it wished to pursue the position, Suharto expressed Indonesia's willingness to continue leading NAM "for up to a year beyond its current three-year term if the 110-member body has difficulty finding a new chairman".[51] However, there was no need for Indonesia to extend its service as Colombia offered to take over the chairmanship in place of Nicaragua.

Apart from NAM, some analysts may maintain that Indonesia's success in holding the APEC Summit in November 1994 has brought prestige to Indonesia in general and Suharto in particular.[52] Others may argue that again, this is more in form rather than in substance as the Bogor Declaration is only a statement of intent rather than a binding document.

NOTeS

1 In his interview with a Singapore journalist (Yang Razali Kassim) in 1987, Mochtar Kusumaatmadja was quoted as saying that "It is time for Indonesia to be chairman of NAM and we'd very much like to be the next one ... Because we are the only founding member who has not been host of the movement". *Straits Times,* 17 August 1987.
2 Suli Suleiman, *Garis-Garis Besar Politik Luar Negeri Republik Indonesia* (Bagian I, Direktorat Research-Penerbitan No.003B/1974; Bagian II, No.004/1973) (Jakarta: Departemen Luar Negeri RI, 1974), p. 19.
3 Ibid., p. 20. Adam Malik, in one of his interviews also commented on the incident. He said to *Tempo* that in the 1970s, the Communist countries penetrated the Non-Aligned Movement. He specifically mentioned North Korea and Cuba, arguing that the Non-Aligned Movement had abandoned its original principles. He argued that this was the reason he walked out of the Ministerial meeting at Georgetown. *Tempo,* 7 February 1976, p. 6.
4 Ibid., p. 21.
5 Ibid.
6 *Straits Times,* 9 September 1988. For a discussion of the issue, see Yang Razali Kassim, "Issues which Kept Indonesia from Non-Aligned Leadership", *Straits Times,* 13 September 1988. It is interesting to note that in September 1985 during the NAM Foreign Ministers' Conference, some ex-Portuguese colonies were hostile towards Indonesia. Angola even attempted to insert a mention of East Timor into the conference's draft declaration and it was only deleted with the help of India and Singapore. See *Asia Year Book 1986* (*Far Eastern Economic Review*), p. 159.
7 Leo Suryadinata, "Suharto's Indonesia: Two Decades On", in *Southeast Asian Affairs 1987,* pp. 131-135.
8 *Angkatan Bersenjata,* 15 June 1988.
9 Ibid.
10 *Straits Times,* 7 September 1989.
11 *Straits Times,* 15 September 1989.
12 Ibid.
13 Discussions with observers in Jakarta, 1988. The state budget allocated Rp 85 billion (about US$40 million) for the conference. The rest would be provided by the Government from

other sources. However, the economic factor later turned out to be another reason for Indonesia to host the NAM meeting. Various groups close to the Government would benefit from involvement in the conference. For instance, Indocitra, a firm which was affiliated with the Suharto family, obtained a special permit to import 112 luxury cars (Mercedes Benz 300 Sel) and 207 minibuses (VW Caravelle GL). These cars would be loaned to the conference committee for the use of the delegation but after the conference, they would be sold freely. It was reported that all the luxury cars had been sold in advance at Rp 500 million each (about US$270,000). *Tempo*, 5 September 1992, p. 32.

14   *Sunday Times*, 21 October 1990.
15   *Straits Times*, 26 August 1991.
16   *Tempo*, 14 September 1991, p. 78.
17   *Straits Times*, 11 September 1991.
18   Ali Alatas, "Politik Luar Negeri Bebas-Aktif clan Peranannya Di Masa Mendatang", Universitas Gadjah Mada, Yogyakarta, 2 September 1988 (mimeograph).
19   Ibid., pp. 7-8.
20   Ibid., p. 15.
21   Ibid.
22   Arnicun Aziz (ed.), *Empat GBHN: 1973, 1978, 1983, 1988* (Jakarta: Bumi Aksara, 1990), p. 269.
23   Ibid., p. 224.
24   Ibid., pp. 166-167.
25   Ibid., pp. 96-97.
26   *Tempo*, 5 September 1992, p. 22. By the end of the summit, NAM had 108 members.
27   Ibid., p. 23. The Group of 77 is an association of 77 less developed countries.
28   *Straits Times*, 16 August 1992.
29   *Tempo*, 5 September 1992, p. 23.
30   "Dari Bosnia ke Hak Asasi", *Tempo*, 12 September 1992, p. 40. For the full text of the Jakarta Message", see Bantarto Bandoro (ed.), *Non-Aligned Movement: Its Future and Action Programme* (Jakarta: CSIS, 1992), pp. 108-114.
31   *Straits Times*, 7 September 1992.
32   For the contents of the speech, see *Suara Pembaruan*, 28 September 1992; *Kompas*, 30 September 1992.
33   Ibid.
34   For the text of the speech, see George Modelski (ed.), *The New Emerging Forces: Documents on the Ideology of Indonesian Foreign Policy*, (Documents and Data Paper No. 2) (Department of International Relations, Australian National University, 1963), pp. 1-31.
35   Ibid., p. 28. In 1960 the PRC was not yet admitted to the UN and China's UN Security Council Seat was still occupied by Taiwan.
36   Ibid.
37   Ibid., p. 19.
38   Ibid., p. 27.
39   Ibid., p. 27.
40   *Jakarta Post*, 10 April and 23 April 1993; *Sunday Times*, 25 April 1993.
41   "Pesan Buat Pembawa Mandat", *Tempo*, 10 July 1993, p. 46.
42   For instance, Suhadi Mangkusuwondo, a leading Indonesian economist, noted in his paper presented in Tokyo on 23 March 1990 at the International Development Center of Japan that there is a problem in institutionalizing APEC: "One of the difficulties comes from ASEAN's concern that it may undermine ASEAN's own co-operation." He further noted that "the member states of ASEAN, or at least Indonesia, have always viewed ASEAN co-operation as the most important part of their foreign policies." See the Indonesian version of the above paper entitled "Kerjasama Ekonomi Pasifik dan Indonesia", published in *Analisis CSIS* (July-August 1990), pp. 335-343, quotations are from p. 340 (the English translation is my own.) Later, Hadi Soesastro also stated that "ASEAN's (read: Indonesian) fears of dilution in a wider regional organization and the concern of being dominated and

overshadowed by the much larger economies have led to insistence on the informal arrangements and on institutionalization of APEC". "ASEAN and the New Pacific Economic Community (APEC, EAEC, NAFTA)", Paper presented at ASEAN-ISIS Colloquium on New Directions for ASEAN, 12-14 September 1994, Singapore, p. 10.

43 For a brief discussion of APEC, see William Bodde Jr., *View from the 19th Floor: Reflections of the First APEC Executive Director* (Singapore: ISEAS, 1994), Appendix 1, "What is APEC?", pp. 65-68.
44 Tan Kim Song, "Malaysia is the odd one out", *Straits Times*, 16 November 1994.
45 Suhadi Mangkusuwondo, "Why is Indonesia Pushing for APEC Liberalisation", Trends No. 50, *Business Times Weekend Edition*, 19-30 October 1994.
46 John McBeth and V.G. Kulkarni, "APEC, Charting the Future", *Far Eastern Economic Review*, 24 November 1994, p. 15.
47 Ibid., also Lee Kim Chew, op. cit., *Straits Times*, 16 November 1994.
48 See Paul Jacob, "Free Trade moves 'Remarkable'", *Straits Times*, 15 November 1994.
49 "Dari Bogor Menembus Ekonomi Global", *Gatra*, 19 November 1994, p. 30.
50 "Pontjo di tengah Pertemuan Besar", *Gatra*, 19 November 1994, p. 43.
51 Paul Jacob, "Indonesia willing to chair Non-Aligned body one more year", *Straits Times*, 31 March 1994.
52 An American commentator wrote: "President Suharto of Indonesia, the host of this year's summit, has provided most of the leadership in galvanizing the consensus that could emerge at the resort city of Bogor". C. Fred Bergsten, originally published in *Washington Post*, reprinted in *Straits Times*, 15 November 1995.

CONCLUSION

To Lead and Not to Be Led

In analysing the foreign policy of a country, one has to identify the major elements of the foreign policy, for instance, the goals of foreign policy as defined by the power elite, the means to achieve this policy and the effectiveness of the policy. The aims of foreign policy usually include preserving national security, including the survival of the government or political system; maintaining territorial integrity; and promoting the welfare of the population. In addition to these, there are other goals which differ from country to country, depending on its size and capability and the role perception of its power elite. For instance, Indonesia under Sukarno was eager to project its image as that of a major nation, not only in the Southeast Asian region, but beyond. During the New Order period, however, it appears that Indonesia's economic development became the major concern of the Government. This, however, did not mean that the New Order Government had abandoned its desire to become a regional leader and beyond.

As shown in this study, Indonesia's foreign policy goals have been influenced by historical experience and the political culture of the elite. Since Indonesia obtained its political independence, partly through armed struggle and partly through diplomatic negotiation, the experience of the independence movement appears to have left an imprint on Indonesia's foreign policy behaviour. Nationalism has been strong among Indonesia's political leaders. This was reflected in Indonesia's persistence in rejecting foreign military bases in Southeast Asia, especially in Indonesia. The second factor which has a bearing on Indonesia's foreign policy goals has been its leaders' perception of their role in world affairs. They consider Indonesia a major power or possibly even a global actor, the desire to be the Chairman of NAM and to hold the APEC Summit are two recent examples.

For global actors, the means for achieving a foreign policy goal are many, because they usually have tremendous resources which they can mobilize. They have both the economic and military capability to influence the course of world events. However, Indonesia's resources are limited. It is true that Indonesia is rich in natural resources and has a large population, and thus has the potential to become a major power, but not a global power like the United States. At one time, Indonesia had an ambition to become the vanguard of the so-called New Emerging Forces (Nefos). However, its limited capabilities could not sustain this aspiration. Even as a regional power, Indonesia's achievements have been limited. An example of this is the Indonesian effort to solve the Kampuchean problem.

Indonesia is still a potential medium power. Its aspirations to become a regional leader and to play an active role in regional and world affairs have been constrained by its limited capability. These aspirations were present throughout the pre-Suharto period as well as during the Suharto era. Because of different domestic and international situations, these aspirations have been manifested in different forms. During the Sukarno era, owing to the presence of various power centres and Sukarno's left-wing ideology, Indonesia gradually moved to the left and became an advocate of Nefos. The legitimacy of the Government did not lie in economic development but in revolutionary ideology. Indeed, Sukarno was able to make use of such ideology to divert attention from the domestic problems to external issues. Therefore, during the Sukarno era, Indonesia's foreign policy took on a high profile. Its militancy was expressed in the campaign to liberate West Irian, which has since been recognized by the international community as part of Indonesian territory, and *konfrontasi*, the goal of which was not entirely clear. However, domestic economic problems were neglected.

During the Suharto era, domestic economic development has been the basis for the regime's legitimacy. Foreign policy has been utilized to improve economic conditions in the country. Moreover, due to a different type of ideology, which is anti-Communist, Indonesian foreign policy has leaned towards the West and towards regional co-operation. ASEAN has become the cornerstone, or at least one of the pillars, of Indonesia's foreign policy.

Nonetheless, for at least a decade, Indonesia had been bogged down by domestic problems and the East Timor issue. Only after the 1982 general election did the Indonesian leadership, especially Suharto, feel comfortable with the domestic situation. Indonesia once again looked to the external world and adopted a higher profile in its foreign policy as manifested in the nation's eagerness to host the Afro-Asian Conference anniversary and the Jakarta Informal Meeting aimed at resolving the Kampuchean issue and also to vie for the chairmanship of the NAM. Indonesia has been able to attain some of the goals that it has set for itself.

During the Suharto era, differences between the Ministry of Foreign Affairs and the military became very pronounced. Adam Malik and, to a lesser extent, Mochtar Kusumaatmadja, attempted to resist the military's "intrusion" into the foreign policy domain. Thus, there were conflicts over foreign policy decisions. The Kampuchean issue is a good example. The military did not want to be bound by ASEAN on the Kampuchean issue. It wanted to lead ASEAN in order to achieve a quicker settlement of the Kampuchean issue. As a result of this, there was a dual policy towards Kampuchea . While the Foreign Ministry continued to promote ASEAN solidarity with respect to Kampuchea, the military attempted to make a deal with Vietnam. It appears that it was Suharto who tried to keep the balance.

The conflict between the Foreign Ministry and the Military has also been reflected in the issue of diplomatic normalization with the PRC. The Foreign Ministry was eager to improve relations while the military was against it. The normalization was finally achieved after Suharto decided to end the animosity between Jakarta and Beijing. Apparently, President Suharto was increasingly concerned with Indonesia's role in both regional and world affairs. He appeared to be more anxious than ever to propel Indonesia, under his leadership, into the international limelight. Many observers have noted that Suharto wants to be remembered as a leader of international standing.

Indeed, during both the Sukarno and Suharto eras the importance of the Presidents' individual personalities was clear. Each era was characterized by its leader's imprint on foreign policy. During the New Order period, for instance, Suharto's views seemed to be decisive. One example, which has just been mentioned, is the decision to normalize Indonesia-China relations, in which Suharto's role was very clear. In the contest for the chairmanship of the NAM, Suharto's mark was noticeable, as it was in Indonesia's relations with the Middle East, especially on the issue of Islam. The most recent example is the Dili tragedy and Suharto's initiative in responding to international pressure by removing some of his local commanders. The Indonesian decision to send a peace-keeping force to Bosnia was also closely linked with Suharto's ideas of having a higher international profile and responding to domestic pressure.

It is clear, therefore, in the last 15 years or so, that the leader rather than the institution largely determined Indonesia's foreign policy. The military is by no means unimportant. In the earlier period, on a number of issues which are often related to security, the military tended to have the upper hand. However, the role of the military has weakened considerably as Suharto has become more confident. This pattern of decision-making has been particularly obvious during the later part of the Suharto era. It has been argued that the pattern in the post-Suharto era will be different. Other political institutions will have a greater say in foreign policy-making. However, this will really depend on who Suharto's successor is and whether the political system in Indonesia changes. If his successor is a strong leader and the political system remains unchanged, it is likely that a similar pattern of decision-making will prevail. Nevertheless, it is unlikely that the successor will be as powerful as Suharto.

It has been argued that Sukarno's foreign policy was more militant and aggressive than that of the New Order period. During the Sukarno era, despite its sound and fury, Indonesia did not annex any territory beyond what was known as the Dutch East Indies. It is ironic then that, during the Suharto era, Portuguese East Timor, which was not a part of the Dutch East Indies, was integrated into Indonesia.

This leads to the question of Indonesia's foreign policy in the future and whether past action can be used as an indicator of what will occur. Western scholars were very critical of Sukarno and considered his foreign policy aggressive and expansionist. The most outspoken of these was Bernard Gordon.[1] As for the Suharto era, no major Western scholar has subscribed to this expansionist view. In fact, the most popular view among Western writers/scholars is of Indonesia under Suharto as a benign and non-expansionist nation. This group is represented by Guy Pauker[2] who has argued that the present Indonesian leaders, (i.e. the New Order leaders) are not aggressive and are primarily concerned with economic development. The annexation of East Timor occurred, in fact, more for security reasons and is not likely to be repeated. Hamish McDonald has argued that the West Irian and East Timor issues were isolated cases.[3] Indonesians are basically *status quo*-minded, and there is, therefore, no need to worry about the future.

The future behaviour of Indonesia's leaders is less clear. It seems that Indonesia's aspiration to lead in the region and beyond remain constant. However, whether or not Indonesia would pursue an aggressive policy is a matter of debate. Two factors are important: the kind of leadership that will emerge after Suharto steps down; and the economic condition of the country in the post-Suharto era. These factors will determine the future direction of Indonesia's foreign policy. If a prediction must be made, it seems likely that the younger generation of the Indonesian elite will be concerned with economic development which requires political stability. What economic conditions will be like after Suharto is unclear. However, it is possible, although unlikely, that new Indonesian leadership after Suharto would become more nationalistic and less accommodating. If that happens, Indonesian-ASEAN relations will be adversely affected.

Apart from these issues, a number of other problems may arise. Indonesia's perceptions of threat and the *Wawasan Nusantara* concept may produce conflicts with its neighbours. Indonesia's desire to play a larger role in the region may also cause friction with other ASEAN states, if a compromise is not reached. As long as Indonesia's leadership is aware of the existence of the different national interests in the region and is prepared to give and take, however, no major problems are likely to arise in Indonesia's relations with its ASEAN neighbours.

NOTES

1   Bernard Gordon, *Dimensions of Conflict in Southeast Asia* (New Jersey: Prentice Hall, 1966).
2   Guy J. Pauker, "Indonesia in the Pacific Community", Paper presented at the Seminar on The Pacific Community: Toward a Role for Latin America, The Institute for International Studies, University of Chile, 18-23 October 1979.
3   McDonald wrote: "Australian concerns about Indonesian 'expansionism' or 'aggression' should be put to a rest. Indonesia will be inward-looking for the economic reason ... and all the signs point to the West Irian and Timor seizures being isolated cases." Hamish McDonald, *Suharto's Indonesia*, p. 257.

Postscript

Indonesia's Foreign Policy from the Fall of Suharto to Joko Widodo
Still Aspiring to International Leadership?

One of the objectives of Suharto's foreign policy was to make Indonesia the leader of the Southeast Asian region and beyond. Although Indonesia's leadership position was more in form than in substance, there was no doubt that Suharto's Indonesia had played a leading role, at least in Southeast Asia, if not in Asia-Africa.

However, with the 1997 Asian economic crisis and the fall of Suharto in May 1998, Indonesia's leadership position in Southeast Asia has also declined. In addition, the President is no longer the sole foreign policy maker. The role of parliament becomes important. This postscript examines Indonesia's foreign policy from the final years of the Suharto period until the early years of Joko "Jokowi" Widodo's second-term presidency. The discussion in this postscript will follow the general structure of the book, i.e., it begins with Indonesia and ASEAN, followed by Jakarta's relations with the six other ASEAN states, especially with Malaysia and Singapore. Its relations with other medium powers and superpowers such as Australia, Japan, the People's Republic of China (PRC) and the United States are also examined. The last section deals with the Middle East, in which Islam in Indonesia's foreign policy is addressed. This order is mainly followed in accordance with the geographical proximity to Indonesia, which simultaneously reflects Indonesian geopolitical concerns.

Foreign Policy Decision-Making in Post-Suharto Indonesia

Let us look briefly at foreign policy decision-makers in Indonesia. During the New Order period (March 1966 to May 1998), foreign policy was initially in the hands of the military and President Suharto, and over time came to be concentrated in the hands of the president. The parliament was more a rubber stamp than the real decision-maker. Suharto often used his presidential power to decide on foreign policy issues, and his appointed ambassadors did not have to be endorsed by the parliament. However, during the post-Suharto period, especially after the fall of President Habibie, the presidential power was curtailed and ambassadors have to be endorsed by the parliament.[1] This implies that the parliament began to play a role in foreign policy-making. The parliament could also refuse to rectify a treaty signed with a foreign country by the president. This context should be borne in mind when discussing post-Suharto Indonesia's foreign policy.

Another point to be remembered is the foreign policy elite.[2] Despite their different backgrounds and different group interests, it appears that they have been brought up in the same environment with a similar mindset. They continue to perceive Indonesia as a major country in the region and have the perception of the country's leadership entitlement in the region and beyond. Besides this, the principle of "independent and active foreign policy" continues to be held as the principle of Indonesia's policy with some different nuances, depending on the background of the president.

The international situation after the fall of Suharto has changed. There is the rise of China and the relative decline of the United States. The dramatic rise of China as an economic and political power, if not a military power, is particularly significant. This has been a factor in post-Suharto's foreign policy which was absent during the Suharto era.

In the domestic scene, the rise of Islam, including both conservative and radical Islam, is also important to bear in mind. Indonesia's domestic politics during the Yudhoyono years had been increasingly Islamized; this has manifested more clearly during the Jokowi presidency. Notably, Islam has become a more important factor in Indonesia's foreign policy although national interests, including territorial integrity and national security, remain paramount.

Indonesia and ASEAN/ASEAN States

In 1997, one year before Suharto's fall, Indonesia's relations with the other ASEAN countries were influenced by two problems: the haze issue and the monetary crisis.

Let us look at the haze issue. This issue was partially caused by dry season and El Niño and partially by the burning of forests to clear the land by individuals or plantation companies in Indonesia. Forest fires began to spread in July 1997 and the haze started to engulf the skies of the Philippines, Thailand and Australia. But the most seriously affected were Indonesia's closest neighbours Malaysia (particularly Sarawak) and Singapore. Over the next few weeks, the haze worsened and was beyond control, which affected the health of people in these areas. By mid-September 1997, President Suharto was forced to extend his apologies to Indonesia's neighbours.

Despite this, the haze situation saw no signs of letting up and Indonesia appeared to be hapless in the face of the forest fires. People of the neighbouring states began to deplore Indonesia. Malaysian Prime Minister Mahathir Mohamad eventually sent a letter to President Suharto, asking him to put down the fire. Suharto was forced to make a second round of apologies[3] but nothing much was done as the forest fires were out of control. Neighbouring countries, together with the United States, assisted Indonesia to put down the fires. The effort eventually succeeded when the rainy season arrived. Nevertheless, the danger of forest fires and haze remains. This issue has continued to affect intra-ASEAN relations until today.

If the haze issue had a negative impact on intra-ASEAN member relations, the monetary crisis seemed to have a mixed impact. The crisis, which started in Thailand, and then spread to Indonesia, led to looser relations between some ASEAN countries. The worst hit by the monetary crisis was Thailand and Indonesia. Between July and October 1997, the Thai baht and Indonesian rupiah declined by 50 per cent. Singapore had helped Thailand and Indonesia to sustain the values of the baht and rupiah, but to no avail. Both Thailand and Indonesia eventually asked for assistance from the International Monetary Fund (IMF). Both Singapore and Malaysia also offered S$5 billion and S$1 billion loan respectively to Indonesia, although Malaysia itself also suffered from the crisis.

When the crisis persisted, the governments of Malaysia, Thailand and Indonesia attempted to conduct trades in their own currencies. Mahathir even visited Jakarta to discuss the economic situation and promised not to repatriate Indonesian workers who were already in Malaysia in order to reduce the burden on Jakarta. However, due to the continuous influx of illegal Indonesian workers, Malaysia later deported 30,000 illegal migrant workers in January and April 1998 and another 200,000 were planned to be deported in August of the same year.[4] Jakarta-Kuala Lumpur relations became tense over this issue.

In fact, Indonesia-Malaysia relations were not always this tense. In 1996, Jakarta and Kuala Lumpur reached an agreement to solve the dispute over Sipadan and Ligitan peacefully. Prior to October 1996, Jakarta insisted that the dispute should be resolved internally, i.e., through the ASEAN High Court. However, after meeting Mahathir in Kuala Lumpur on 7 October 1996, Suharto suddenly changed his attitude, agreeing to bring the dispute to the International Court of Justice.[5]

It is not clear why Suharto changed his mind over the two disputed islands. Probably Suharto required Mahathir's support in matters relating to the Indonesian national car and Indonesian negotiation with the World Trade Organization (WTO) for giving big tax breaks to this project;[6] in addition, Suharto wanted to show the world that he was the one who made the decision, not the military, which always stood firm in any territorial dispute.[7] The Sipadan and Ligitan were eventually awarded to Malaysia, but the issue of the nearby Ambalat Sea block is still contested between the two countries and remains unresolved.[8]

In early 1997 prior to the monetary crisis, ASEAN was busy preparing the entry of new members: Cambodia, Myanmar and Laos. It was estimated that in July 1997 during the ASEAN Foreign Ministers Meeting, the three states would be announced as the new members of ASEAN. In fact, the United States opposed Myanmar's membership of ASEAN due to the frequent violation of human rights by the State Law and Order Restoration Council (SLORC), the military regime in power at that time. However, ASEAN members, especially Indonesia, ignored the US objection.

At the end of February 1997, Suharto visited Myanmar to meet the head of the military regime, General Than Shwe, who had visited Jakarta in December 1996 to attend the Informal ASEAN Summit where the seven members of ASEAN decided to accept the three countries as new members.

In July 1997, both Laos and Myanmar became official members of ASEAN, but the membership of Cambodia was postponed. This was due to the coup in Phnom Penh during which Prince Ranariddh, the Cambodian Prime Minister, was removed by Hun Sen.[9] Indonesia's foreign minister Ali Alatas led a delegation to Cambodia in order to offer Jakarta's good offices. They met both Hun Sen and Norodom Sihanouk, father of Ranariddh, to solve the issue. On 23 July 1997, Ranariddh flew to Jakarta. Nevertheless, the ASEAN efforts which were led by Indonesia failed to resolve the leadership split. As a result, Cambodia only became an ASEAN member in April 1999, after the fall of Suharto.

The fall of Suharto also marked the end of Indonesia's leadership in ASEAN. B.J. Habibie (21 May 1998–20 October 1999) who succeeded Suharto was busy with domestic politics but planned to visit Malaysia. However, he eventually cancelled the trip as his friend Deputy Prime Minister Anwar Ibrahim was disposed by Mahathir Mohamad. Nevertheless, Habibie attended the APEC and ASEAN summits in Hanoi in December 1998 to show Indonesia's support.[10] However, Habibie was critical of Singapore. On 4 August 1998, the *Asian Wall Street Journal* quoted him as saying that Singapore was just "a little red dot", did not help Indonesia and was "not a friend".[11]

When Abdurrahman Wahid, popularly known as Gus Dur (20 October 1999–23 July 2001), replaced Habibie to serve as the fourth president of

Indonesia, Gus Dur travelled frequently in order to gain support and economic assistance for Indonesia. Nevertheless, he was unable to gain any leadership recognition within ASEAN. As the old saying goes, a weak and poor country cannot lead. After he was forced to step down and replaced by Megawati Sukarnoputri (23 July 2001–20 October 2004), Jakarta attempted to revive Indonesian leadership in ASEAN by proposing the ASEAN Security Community concept through her foreign minister Hassan Wirajuda.

Indonesia under Megawati appeared to be eager in promoting ASEAN and keen to play a leading role again. The Ninth ASEAN Summit in Bali (7–8 October 2003) was a modest success, marking the beginning of the creation of the ASEAN Economic Community (AEC). Jakarta also introduced the ASEAN Security Community concept to make ASEAN a zone of peace and prosperity. It proposed the use of legal mechanisms instead of force to resolve bilateral disputes and sought to develop a "habit of trust". Indonesia first mooted the concept in June 2003 during the ASEAN Foreign Ministers Meeting in Phnom Penh. As a Jakarta analyst puts it, "this new initiative signals Indonesia's return to normalcy. Once again, Indonesia is making a bid to affirm its position and role as a key member of ASEAN."[12]

Indonesia attempted to regain the leadership in ASEAN during the Susilo Bambang Yudhoyono (SBY) presidency (20 October 2004–20 October 2014). The test case of Indonesia's relations with ASEAN under President Yudhoyono can be seen during the tsunami disaster in late December 2004. The earthquake and resultant killer waves hit Thailand and Indonesia, of which Aceh and North Sumatra were the worst hit. Singapore under Prime Minister Lee Hsien Loong immediately sent aid to Indonesia and proposed an ASEAN Summit in Jakarta to deal with the tsunami disaster. Jakarta responded favourably and on 6 January 2005 a summit was held.

Apart from ASEAN leaders, major countries also sent high-ranking officers to the summit and pledged to give aid to rebuild the affected areas. It was reported that some Indonesian leaders who were Islamic in their orientation, were suspicious of the presence of foreign troops, especially the Americans, but their attitude towards the Singapore troops was ambiguous. Nevertheless, President Yudhoyono noted that Indonesians should be thankful to the foreign aid and that the foreign troops were on a humanitarian mission.[13] Many observed that the tsunami disaster offered an opportunity to strengthen Indonesia-ASEAN relations, but not really its leadership position.

The haze issue also offered an opportunity for Indonesia to lead ASEAN. But in 2006 when the ASEAN Agreement on Transboundary Haze Pollution was proposed, Indonesia suddenly set up a special committee which rejected the proposal as it was reluctant to give up control over its sovereignty.[14] In 2013 when the haze recurred seriously affecting its neighbours, especially Singapore and Malaysia, Yudhoyono had no choice but to apologize to

Malaysia and Singapore.¹⁵ However, the haze problem has not been resolved and it recurred during the Jokowi presidency.

Yudhoyono's Indonesia was also unsuccessful in mediating the dispute between ASEAN members, namely Thailand and Cambodia over the ownership of Preah Vihear Temple on the borders in 2011. Indonesia as ASEAN chairman then was supposed to lead mediation efforts but failed as both Bangkok and Phnom Penh did not stop fighting. The dispute was eventually resolved only in 2013 through the International Court of Justice which awarded the ownership of the temple to Cambodia.¹⁶

President Yudhoyono continued to pay attention to ASEAN and beyond. His foreign minister Marty Natalegawa was active in leading the ASEAN countries on the South China Sea issue. In 2012, no ASEAN Communique was issued after the summit due to the objection of Cambodia which had been close to Beijing. This is the first time that ASEAN failed to issue a joint communique, and Yudhoyono was very concerned. In order to secure a common communique, Natalegawa flew from one capital city to another capital of the ASEAN countries in order to resolve the issue. He was eventually successful in producing a watered-down joint communique.¹⁷

Jakarta's relations with Singapore under Yudhoyono were cordial. He wanted to deepen cooperation between the two countries. In April 2007 Singapore and Indonesia signed an extradition treaty as well as a defence cooperation agreement as a package, but both had not been ratified by the Indonesian parliament.¹⁸ Apparently the Indonesian parliament did not share Yudhoyono's perceptions and refused to endorse the package. Despite the absence of a formal treaty, security cooperation on combating terrorism has increased.

ASEAN had been a corner stone of Indonesian foreign policy up to Yudhoyono's presidency. However, it is not the case with Jokowi who assumed power in October 2014 as he is more concerned with the domestic economy and infrastructure projects of the country. Nevertheless, his foreign minister Retno Marsudi, just like other Indonesian foreign ministers, has been concerned with Indonesia's position in ASEAN. This can be seen in Indonesia's role in formulating the concept of Indo-Pacific region in which Jakarta wanted to project its leadership position.¹⁹

During his visit to Asia in November 2017, President Donald Trump started to use the term "Indo-Pacific" to replace "Asia-Pacific", marking the new strategy of the United States and its ally to "contain rising China". The term Indo-Pacific was first used by Japanese Prime Minister Shinzo Abe in 2007, which later (in April 2017) became the "Free and Open Indo-Pacific" (FOIP). In fact, Abe in January 2017 proposed the "Indo-Pacific Strategic Proposal" to Indonesian President Jokowi but this was not well received as Jokowi wanted to remain neutral in the struggle between the two major powers.²⁰

In May 2013, before Trump started using the term Indo-Pacific, former Indonesian foreign minister Marty Natalegawa proposed the "Indo-Pacific Wide Friendship and Cooperation Treaty" to the East Asia Summit (EAS) countries based on the 2011 EAS Declaration. However, no country expressed any interest as the proposal was unrealistic. In January 2018, current foreign minister Retno Marsudi eventually proposed Indonesian "Indo-Pacific (Cooperation) Concept" which differs from FOIP in its contents. It includes all countries in EAS (including China) in the concept. It is also proposed to comprise mechanisms within the existing EAS structure, not a new organization. The proposal was quite similar to that of Natalegawa, except it was not a treaty.[21]

Indonesia wanted to make this an ASEAN-led concept and tabled it for discussion in the 2018 ASEAN Summit. After long negotiations among the ASEAN states, ASEAN eventually came out with the "ASEAN Outlook on the Indo-Pacific Concept". This concept was a further improvement from the Indonesian proposal, but Indonesia was not mentioned anywhere. It should also be pointed out that the ASEAN Outlook on the Indo-Pacific Concept is merely an outline or a guideline for further discussion, it is not yet operational.

In his second term in office, Joko Widodo appears to have a slight change in his policy in ASEAN regarding Myanmar. Regarding the Rohingya issue, his foreign minister Retno earlier adopted a low profile and private diplomacy towards Myanmar, but Jakarta appears to have changed its strategy towards the coup that ousted Aung San Suu Kyi on 1 February 2021. After Malaysian Prime Minister Muhyiddin Yassin flew to Jakarta to meet Jokowi on 5 February, Retno started her "shuttle diplomacy"[22] reminiscent of Marty Natalegawa when he was dealing with the joint communique on the South China Sea issue in 2012.

Retno flew to Brunei, the current chairman of ASEAN, to discuss the situation in Myanmar. She then went to Singapore to meet her counterpart Vivian Balakrishnan to discuss the ASEAN strategy; she even flew to Bangkok on 24 February to meet the Thai foreign minister Dom Pramudwinai, and together with him, she met Myanmar's newly appointed representative Wunna Maung Lwin to discuss the situation in Myanmar. Earlier it was reported that she planned to fly to Myanmar to meet Wunna but cancelled her trip after protesters gathered in front of the Indonesian embassy in Yangon accusing Jakarta of backing the junta.[23] Reuters had reported that Jakarta agreed with the junta that there should be a new election one year later.

Retno insisted that Indonesia was misunderstood. On 2 March a virtual unofficial meeting of ASEAN foreign ministers was held which among others discussed the Myanmar crisis. At the end of the meeting, Retno warned that the ASEAN Charter has to be respected. Otherwise, it would undermine the centrality of ASEAN. She also noted that there is non-interference policy in ASEAN. Nevertheless, each member has to uphold and implement democratic principles, human rights, good governance and constitutional government.[24] She noted that the parties concerned should resolve their difference peacefully. It seems that Jakarta would like to look for a practical solution to make the junta keep the promise of holding a fair election. This differs from the Western approach which wanted the junta to return the power to Aung San Suu Kyi.

When the military began to kill demonstrators, Indonesia, like Singapore and other countries, asked the junta to stop the violence and respect popular will.[25] But there was no sign of softening on the part of the junta. On 19 March, Joko Widodo called ASEAN chairman Brunei to call for a high-level meeting to discuss the Myanmar crisis. However, it had not materialized yet. The Indonesian efforts have not borne fruit.

Indonesia, East Timor and Australia

The East Timor issue has domestic and foreign dimensions. East Timor was annexed by Indonesia in 1976 and was not recognized by the United Nations as part of the Republic of Indonesia. Since the 1990s, sectarian conflict in East Timor escalated, demonstrations against the central government also increased, indicating that East Timorese rebelled against the Indonesian rule.

After the fall of Suharto, the conflict in East Timor further intensified. President Habibie decided to hold a memorandum for the independence of East Timor. This sudden decision stunned the Indonesian military. Not surprisingly, the military supported the militia and began to terrorize the East Timorese voters. However, the result of the 1999 referendum was overwhelmingly for independence. It was also at that time atrocities in East Timor occurred. The UN was asked to intervene in East Timor, and Australia sent the peacekeeping force to the troubled province under the umbrella of the United Nations. By doing this, the Mutual Defence Treaty between Jakarta and Canberra which was signed during Keating prime-ministership was in fact revoked. The relations between Indonesia and Australia were at its lowest.

The Bali bombings in October 2003 and the bombings of the Australian embassy in Jakarta in September 2004 gave rise to an opportunity for the improvement of relations between Jakarta and Canberra. However, due to mutual suspicion, the relationship did not really improve. Only after the election of Yudhoyono as president, and Prime Minister John Howard attended the swearing-in ceremony, did Canberra appear to move closer to Jakarta.

Canberra proposed a new security treaty between the two countries but the response of Jakarta was lukewarm. When the tsunami disaster took place on Boxing Day of 2004, the Australian Government responded positively and even pledged A$1 billion (about US$760 million) aid to Indonesia. The assistance to Indonesia, according to Howard, "would be distributed over a five-year period, and would include an economic reconstruction and development program."[26]

The normal relations became tense again over the refugees from Papua who sought political asylum in Australia in 2006.[27] However, the issue which impacted the further improvement of the relationship was a leak in 2013 (when Tony Abbott was the Prime Minister) on the electronic surveillance of Yudhoyono's inner circle, including his wife, that was conducted in 2009.[28] The relations were further complicated by the so-called asylum and people-smuggling issues in 2014. It was reported that the Australian government pushed back the refugee boats (mainly from the Middle East and South Asia) to the Indonesian waters.[29] It took quite a while for the two countries to repair the damage.

Since the rise of China in the twenty-first century, Australia had been more concerned with security matters, especially on the issue of the South China Sea. Canberra as the ally of the United States had been eager to have joint cooperation with Indonesia in the South China Sea but Jakarta was not interested in such a proposal as it did not want to choose sides in the conflict between the two super powers.

When Jokowi assumed the presidency, Canberra attempted to improve bilateral relations. Australian Prime Minister Malcolm Turnbull, who just came into office in September 2015, visited Jakarta in November 2015. This was a gesture at mending ties, but Jokowi only returned the visit in February 2017. Before Jokowi's return visit, there was a dispute over military cooperation.

About a month before Jokowi's Australian visit, General Gatot Nurmantyo, the Indonesian military chief, suspended Indonesian-Australian military cooperation in January 2017 when offensive materials about Indonesia were found at a military training centre in Perth. Despite Gatot accepting an apology from Australia's army chief, bilateral military ties were not fully restored until after Jokowi's visit.

On the eve of the visit, Jokowi was interviewed by the Australians. Jokowi was reported as saying that he was open to the possibility of joint Indonesian-Australian patrols in the South China Sea, provided such an arrangement would not further inflame tensions.[30] However, throughout the visit, he did not talk about regional security issue but only on trade and investment matters.

It is quite noticeable that there exists a perception gap between Jakarta and Canberra. On the one hand, Canberra's primary concern relates to strategic-security, especially with regard to the South China Sea, not least because of its paramount importance to Australian shipping and trade. On the other hand, Jakarta is far more concerned with economic benefits, derived in considerable part from foreign trade and investment.

Their joint press conference is indicative of the different interests of the two countries. While Turnbull noted that "President Widodo and I agreed to fully restore cooperation in defence, training activities and [military] exchange",[31] Jokowi spoke instead about a free trade deal to be signed by

Indonesia and Australia later in the year. He was likely referring to the Comprehensive Economic Partnership Agreement. The agreement was initiated a decade ago and was only revived in 2016 under the Jokowi presidency. Further underscoring the economic imperative, Jokowi articulated: "I have discussed several key issues with Prime Minister Turnbull. Most importantly is to remove both the tariff and non-tariff obstacles in trade for Indonesian products such as paper and palm oil."[32]

Indonesia and Japan

The relations between Indonesia and Japan during the Suharto era were close, as Japan was the largest trade partner of Indonesia surpassing Hong Kong and the United States. It therefore can be argued that the relationship between the two countries was more economic than political. This economic relationship between Jakarta and Tokyo remained cordial after the fall of Suharto. However, when Shinzo Abe became the Prime Minister of Japan, he wanted to enhance not only economic relations but also political and security issues, coinciding with China's increasing assertiveness in the Asia-Pacific region. Abe made his two-day maiden visit to Indonesia on 15 January 2017. He was warmly welcomed by Jokowi, who had already met Abe four times since Jokowi become president in 2014.[33]

At first glance, Abe's Indonesia visit had a clear economic purpose as he brought with him a delegation of around thirty prominent Japanese businessmen. Japan was a leading foreign investor in Indonesia, with investments reaching US$4.5 billion in the first nine months of 2016. Bilateral trade also increased, reaching US$24 billion in the first ten months of 2016. According to Coordinating Maritime Affairs Minister Luhut Pandjaitan, who held Japan up as an "ideal model for infrastructural development", Jokowi and Abe were expected to discuss four major strategic projects, namely the Patimban port, the Jakarta-Surabaya rail project, the East Natuna oil and gas block, and chemical and fertilizer projects.

On closer inspection, however, Abe's Indonesia visit was more strategic than economic. While Abe was mainly concerned with security matters, Jokowi was primarily concerned with economic benefits. With the exception of the project details regarding the Patimban port, which is located near Bekasi in West Java where quite a number of Japanese companies are located, remarks made by both Abe and Jokowi at the joint press conference after the closed-door meeting in Bogor Palace were rather anodyne, with both leaders merely stressing continued bilateral economic cooperation.

But what was telling from the press conference was Abe saying that Japan attaches huge importance to maintaining and promoting a rules-based order in the South China Sea by resolving disputes peacefully in accordance with international law. In this regard, Abe pledged for Japan to cooperate with Indonesia on maritime security, not least in and around the Natunas where Chinese incursions have taken place in the waters within Indonesia's exclusive economic zone (EEZ). In reality, however, this proposition was likely to face a push-back and be rejected altogether as the Jokowi administration, not least the navy, would be reluctant to draw a foreign country into jointly patrolling Indonesian waters.

Cooperating with Japan on maritime security in the South China Sea could also generate consternation among the Chinese political leadership in Beijing. This is something Indonesia prefers to avoid, given the enhanced bilateral economic engagement in Sino-Indonesian relations. Perhaps less controversial could be for Abe's Japan, as encouraged by Jokowi's Indonesia, to enhance its maritime cooperation with member countries of the Indian Ocean Rim Association (IORA), chaired currently by Indonesia.[34]

Curiously, no mention was made of Abe's "Indo-Pacific Strategy proposal" at the press conference, though the proposal was reported to have been discussed in the closed-door meeting. Abe's proposal seeks to promote "cooperation among Japan, ASEAN countries, the United States, Australia and India". His proposal was similar to Chinese President Xi Jinping's One Belt-One Road (OBOR) maritime initiative, with the *Jakarta Post* calling it, rather aptly, the "Japanese vision of OBOR".[35]

One plausible reason for not mentioning this proposal publicly was that Abe might have sensed, as was echoed by several Indonesian scholars, that Jokowi would not be keen to partake in such an initiative, as he was primarily interested in domestic economic development. Moreover, Jokowi did not want to be seen as taking sides between Japan and China on similar, but competing, maritime initiatives.

It appears that the Indonesian newspapers were not very enthusiastic about Abe's visit as most of the projects involving Japan were more pledges than actual concrete outcomes. Local Chinese papers, chiefly the pro-Beijing *Yinhua Ribao*, saw Abe's visit as obstructing Sino-Indonesian relations. It listed those Japanese investments in Indonesia which brought much benefit to Japan at Indonesia's expense. The editorial in *Jakarta Post*, entitled "PM Abe's Visit", described the visit as disappointing and unsatisfactory. The editorial called on Japan to open its markets for Indonesian agricultural and fishery products, and cheap and quality workers. The editorial also attributed the sluggishness in Japan's relations with Indonesia as "Indonesia tilting towards China, which Japan fiercely competes".[36]

But the editorial also proceeded to say that "Indonesia knows however, it needs Japan not only economically but also in regional security terms. With Indonesia to a certain extent showing hostility to rising China, Japan is among the few countries that can play a deterrent role vis-à-vis the world second's largest economy." As such, Japan could present Indonesia with a useful hedge of not being over-reliant on China. Japan could also use this opportunity to further engage with Indonesia.

On the whole, it appeared that Jokowi's Indonesia wanted to focus more on economic matters, and thus expected Abe's Japan to do more in helping Indonesia in economic terms. In contrast, Abe's Japan was more concerned with security issues and less on economic benefits. It is perhaps understandable that both Jakarta and Tokyo may not be completely satisfied with the outcomes of Abe's maiden visit to Jokowi's Indonesia. Japan's relations with Indonesia, despite carrying immense potential with the establishment of a Strategic Partnership in 2006, remain underdeveloped.

Indonesia and the People's Republic of China

Towards the end of Suharto's rule, Indonesia was also active in improving Jakarta-Beijing relations. During the Asia-Europe summit on 1–2 March 1997 in Bangkok, Suharto met Li Peng, Premier of the PRC, for 40 minutes. It was reported that during the meeting, Jakarta reaffirmed the One China Policy while Beijing reaffirmed China's stand on the Convention on the Law of the Sea (UNCLOS) and its commitment to the maintenance of regional political stability.

Despite Beijing's promise of maintaining peace and stability, Indonesia still conducted military exercise around the Natuna islands. There was no dispute between China and Indonesia over the Natuna islands but Jakarta was still not sure about the historical claim which was used by Beijing on the South China Sea issue. The military exercise was meant to show to the Chinese that the Natuna islands and the Natuna's EEZ belong to Indonesia and that Jakarta would not accept China's authority if it extended beyond the Spratly Islands.[37]

Nevertheless, Jakarta-Taipei relations were close. One third of Taiwan's investment in Southeast Asia was in Indonesia.[38] In September 1998, Taiwan foreign minister John Chang quietly visited Jakarta and met Suharto.[39] Towards the end of December 1997, Taiwan Prime Minister Vincent Siew also quietly met Suharto and discussed economic issues.[40] Beijing issued strong protest but Jakarta did not respond. Nevertheless, this did not seriously affect Jakarta-Beijing diplomatic relations. In fact, before Suharto stepped down, despite anti-ethnic Chinese movements in Indonesia, Jakarta-Beijing relations improved. China even promised to assist Indonesia economically so that Suharto would be able to overcome economic difficulty.

During May 1998 there were anti-ethnic Chinese movements in Indonesia that resulted in the killings and systematic raping of ethnic Chinese women. However, Beijing did not stage any protest. Only in July, Beijing began to express "concern" over the organized attacks on the ethnic Chinese. Then the new president of Indonesia was B.J. Habibie, a president who was well known for his unsympathetic attitude towards Chinese Indonesians prior to assuming presidency.[41]

During the short period of Habibie's presidency, Indonesia was too weak to conduct active foreign policy. Habibie was mainly concerned with his survival. It was during his presidency that he allowed East Timor to have a referendum which resulted in the departure of East Timor from the Republic of Indonesia.

It was only during the Gus Dur presidency that Indonesia began to improve relations with the PRC. In December 1999, Gus Dur, accompanied by Foreign Minister Alwi Shihab and Coordinating Minister of Economic Affairs Drs Kwik Kian Gie, visited Beijing and secured Chinese support to help Indonesia. But the Gus Dur presidency was too short to produce any results. Friendly relations between Jakarta and Beijing only took place during the Megawati presidency. Zhu Rongji, Prime Minister of the PRC, visited Indonesia on 7–11 November 2001 and was warmly received by Megawati. They mainly discussed bilateral economic cooperation, including the reopening of the Bank of China, which was closed down during the New Order period.[42]

Megawati's husband Taufik Kiemas, established good relations with Chinese leaders and led a delegation to Beijing to promote better bilateral ties. It was also reported that Taufik intended to sell Indonesian gas/oil to China, which needed them badly. On the other hand, China promised to help build bridges and railways in Indonesia. On 19 September 2002, PRC Defence Minister Chi Haotian visited President Megawati and her Defence Minister Matori Abdul Djalil to discuss the possibility of military cooperation. It was reported that Chi Haotian offered to sell arms to Indonesia.[43] In fact, the exchange visit of high-ranking military personnel took place earlier. On 15 May 2000, Deputy Chief of General Staff of PLA Let-Gen Qian Shugen visited Indonesian Defence Minister.[44]

The good relationship resulted in a rumour that the Megawati government was friendly with Beijing at the expense of the United States, while the new government of Yudhoyono was rumoured to be closer to the United States than to Beijing. This was perhaps due to the historical image of the Indonesian armed forces, especially the Army, which was often critical of the PRC and considered China as a potential security threat. However, it appeared that Beijing was eager to improve relations with Jakarta. Even before Yudhoyono was officially sworn in as president, the PRC sent a high-level trade delegation to meet Yudhoyono at his residence in Bogor, to discuss future cooperation.[45]

During the tsunami disaster in December 2004, Beijing rushed to provide humanitarian aid to Banda Aceh, sending the medical team to save the survivors and pledged to donate US$63 million in aid.[46] The Chinese leader also expressed China's desire to attend the ASEAN Summit in Jakarta held on 6 January 2005 to discuss and coordinate the assistance programme on this catastrophe, showing its sympathy to the Indonesians.

Yudhoyono appeared responsive to the Chinese overture. In April 2005, Yudhoyono signed the Strategic Partnership with President Hu Jintao, demonstrating the close cooperation between the two countries.[47] In October 2013, towards the end of his second term, Yudhoyono and President Xi Jinping signed another Comprehensive Strategic Partnership, raising the level of their cooperation.[48] In the MOU of the comprehensive partnership, Beijing and Jakarta stated that "the two leaders agreed that it is the common responsibility of the countries in the region to maintain peace and stability in the South China Sea".[49]

It was not clear if it was Yudhoyono's intention to exclude other extraregional powers from getting into the South China Sea matters. It seemed that it was unlikely as Yudhoyono had allowed joint exercise between the Indonesian navy and the American naval unit earlier (see the next section on Indonesia and the United States). This clause is also in contradiction with the statement in the 2010 Comprehensive Partnership between Jakarta and Washington. However, the fact is that the exclusion of non-regional power was reflected in the Jakarta-Beijing MOU which showed that Yudhoyono was accommodative towards Beijing. In fact, it was during the Yudhoyono presidency that trade between the two countries increased, and the Surabaya-Madura bridge project, which was started during Megawati's time and built by the PRC, was eventually completed in 2009 during the Yudhoyono presidency.[50] This is perhaps the first infrastructure project of Beijing in Indonesia.

It is also worth noting that during the Yudhoyono presidency, incursions of the Chinese fishing vessels were quietly handled and there was no report of Chinese fishing vessels encroaching into Indonesian waters or its EEZ.

Joko Widodo replaced Yudhoyono in October 2014 as the president of Indonesia, and his policy towards the PRC in general has been similar with that of his predecessor. But unlike Yudhoyono, Jokowi is an "economy-oriented" president as he is most concerned with the economic growth and development of the country. It was not surprising that when the Asian Infrastructure and Investment Bank (AIIB) was formed in China, Jokowi, who had just assumed office, immediately visited Beijing to join the AIIB. Jokowi also met Xi Jinping to ask for an increase in Chinese tourists. In addition, Jokowi welcomed PRC's investment in Indonesia. He even granted the project of Jakarta-Bandung High-Speed Railways to Beijing at the expense of the Japanese companies.[51]

When China proposed the Belt and Road Initiative (BRI), Jokowi also had his own Tol Laut (Maritime Axis). But these two concepts do not really match.⁵² Jokowi's opponents accused him of being too friendly with the PRC and criticized him of selling out to Beijing. However, on the Natunas issue, it appears that Jokowi has been more nationalistic than Yudhoyono as China has become more assertive during Jokowi's time compared to during the SBY presidency.

In his cabinet, Jokowi appointed Susi Pudjiastuti as Maritime Affairs and Fishery Minister who introduced a tough policy towards illegal, unreported and unregulated (IUU) fishing. She was the one who started to detain foreign fishing vessels who encroached into the Indonesian EEZ and sank some of the captured vessels. It was also during Susi's term that Jakarta and Beijing confronted each other over the illegal fishing issues in the Natuna waters.⁵³

In order to appeal to Indonesian nationalism, Jokowi even boarded a warship to the Natunas and held a limited cabinet meeting on the warship. Beijing was reported to have sent a special envoy to settle the issue, and Jokowi appeared to be accommodative.⁵⁴ Nevertheless, after three and half years, the incursion of Chinese fishing vessels recurred. However, this time both sides appeared to have confrontation for a few days but eventually returned to normal when the Chinese coast guards and fishing vessels left the contested waters.⁵⁵ Jokowi again visited the Natunas before the Chinese vessels left the disputed areas. This issue has not been resolved and will be an issue which directly impacts Jakarta-Beijing relations in the near future.

Despite the bumpy relations over the Natuna Seas, Beijing and Jakarta relations appeared to be quite cordial, especially during the COVID-19 pandemic. Beijing invited Defence Minister Prabowo Subianto to improve relations.

Prabowo did not achieve much from his trip except that the vaccine for COVID-19 was brought back by the military flight to Jakarta.⁵⁶ It appears that Beijing vaccine diplomacy has been quite successful in Indonesia. Jakarta has received Sinovac vaccine which started the first round of vaccination. Beijing also promised to help Indonesia to become the production centre of the joint Indonesia-China COVID-19 vaccine in Southeast Asia.⁵⁷ According to the plan, Indonesia would use 30 per cent of the vaccine from China and the rest would come from the West (especially the United States). In practice, Indonesia may rely more on Beijing as the Western vaccines are not forthcoming as they have problem in meeting demands.

Jakarta's acceptance of Beijing's offer to help salvage an Indonesian sunken submarine in the northern part of the Bali Sea in May 2021 also showed the closer cooperation between Indonesia and China.⁵⁸ The fact that China's navy ships entered Indonesia's waters to assist Indonesia has been interpreted as closer military cooperation between the two countries, although it seems that it is more a "humanitarian" rather than a "security cooperation".

Indonesia and the United States

Towards the end of the Suharto rule, Jakarta-Washington relations did not improve. Two events influenced these relations: one was the bloody attacks on the PDI-P headquarters by the paramilitary group on 27 July 1996, and the other was riots in East Timor in 1997.

The United States originally wanted to sell nine F-16 fighter jets to Indonesia in 1996 but because of the 27 July affair, Clinton decided to postpone the sale until early 1997. In fact, the United States was eager to sell the fighter jets for more than a year but was forced to do this to show its unhappiness.[59] In August 1997 a Trade Union leader Muchtar Pakpahan was arrested, which resulted in the protest of the US Congress. Twenty-nine Congressmen petitioned the government to review the Generalized System of Preference given to Indonesia because of the Indonesian violation of basic labour rights.

In June 1997, there was an accident in East Timor. Guerillas ambushed sixteen policemen and one soldier in Baucau, 16 miles from Dili. This took place five days after the general election in East Timor where seventeen people died.[60] The US Congress criticized Indonesian government's action, rather than the guerillas', of not honouring basic human rights. During the same month, Suharto who was "tired" of being reminded of violating human rights by the United States announced that Jakarta decided not to buy the fighters F-16 from the United States. In his letter to Clinton, he stated that his decision was due to "wholly unjustified criticism by the US Congress".[61]

However, the fall of Suharto did not result in the improvement of Indonesia-US relations. During the Habibie presidency the East Timor issue remained a thorn, especially with regard to Indonesian army's violation of human rights in the ex-Portuguese colony. The military atrocities committed after the referendum in East Timor caused the United States to take action against Jakarta—the US Congress imposed an arms embargo on Indonesia.[62]

When Gus Dur became president the relationship did not improve much either. Gus Dur did not have a clear idea of Indonesia's foreign policy. On the one hand, he cultivated good relations with US high officials but on the other hand, he proposed the concept of "Strategic Alliance" between Indonesia, India and China.[63] Although the concept was only a rhetoric, it caused concern among countries in the West, especially the United States. It was interpreted as anti-West (or anti-American).[64] The development of events in September and October 2000, for instance, did not help to improve Indonesia-US relations either. On 6 September 2000, Indonesian militias burned down the office of UN High Commission on Refugees (UNHCR) in Atambua (West Timor) and slayed three UNHCR members, leading to the withdrawal of 400 UN workers. Bill Clinton, and later the Security Council, called on Indonesia to disarm the militias and "bring those responsible to justice".[65] Foreign Secretary William Cohen also visited Indonesia to apply extra pressure on Jakarta, which made the government unhappy.

In October 2000, there were also a number of events which caused tension, if not friction, between Jakarta and Washington. These included the harassment of American citizens by Indonesian radical Muslim, the arrest of an American air force retiree in Papua, the visit of US embassy personnel to Poso after the riots and the subsequent Indonesian rejection of American aid offer for Poso refugees, and the closure of American embassy for a few days due to possible "terrorist attack".[66] Some radicals in the parliament pressured Gus Dur to expel the American ambassador in Indonesia but it was rejected.

In fact, Indonesia's foreign policy had been constrained by domestic politics, as shown in Indonesian attitude towards terrorism. Nevertheless, under international pressure, the Megawati government had been able to show to the United States that she worked hard in combating terrorism.

As a matter of fact, Megawati took initiatives to improve relations with the United States. Soon after the 11 September 2001 attacks on New York, Megawati who had just assumed the presidency, decided to visit Washington, siding with the United States in the war against terror. She also supported the United States in its decision to invade Afghanistan that supported Al-Qaeda. However, when she returned to Jakarta, she faced the opposition of Muslim groups who were sympathetic to Afghanistan. As a result, she had to modify her stand.[67]

Megawati's foreign policy can be explained in terms of the influence of the coalition of government. Megawati could not stand alone and she needed to cooperate with both the Islamists and the military. She had to give concessions to both and make adjustments in order to survive. She was more interested in maintaining the status quo rather than changing the foreign policy, signifying the position of a weak government. However, like her predecessor, she played an "active and non-aligned policy" between the United States and the East, occasionally tilted towards Russia and the PRC when there was a rise of opposition against the Bush administration. Of course, this was not a response to an international situation but, more importantly, to domestic demands.

The Megawati administration was critical of the US-led invasion of Iraq, partially due to the fact that the invasion was without the support of the UN, and also due to the sentiments of the Muslim population in Indonesia, including her deputy and cabinet members, who were critical of Bush's policy towards the Islamic world. Megawati herself was against radical Islam and terrorism. However, her deputy, Hamzah Haz, was defending radical Islam and labelled President George W. Bush "king of terrorism" when the United States invaded Iraq.[68] Nevertheless, under international pressure, Hamzah

Haz had to sing a different tune and stated that the United States was an Indonesian friend.[69] Despite being criticized by radical Muslims, on 22 October 2003, Megawati welcomed George W. Bush in Bali, reiterating Indonesia's commitment to combat terrorism. George W. Bush probably discovered that it was better to have a Megawati government than others who might not cooperate with him at all.

Before Bush's Bali visit, Megawati and her senior officials visited the United States on 19–26 September, soliciting goodwill and support for her government. She was invited to make a speech at the UN general assembly at which she addressed the issue of international terrorism. She condemned all forms of terrorism, including terrorist acts in the name of Islam but appealed to major powers to introduce a just and fair policy towards the Middle East. Megawati was especially happy on this occasion because her father, the first president of Indonesia, had also been invited to address the assembly in 1960.

To maintain some sort of balance in Indonesia's foreign policy, Megawati visited Russia in late April 2003. In fact, the visit coincided with the US-led war against Iraq despite the opposition of three other major powers (including Russia) in the UN. Jakarta's view on the matter coincided with Russia, and this easily brought the two countries together. Megawati's visit to Russia was part of her East European trip starting on 17 April for ten days. It was also linked to Indonesia's effort to look for new weapon supplies, as there was an embargo on arms sales to Indonesia by the United States due to the alleged human rights abuse ten years ago.[70] Indeed, Megawati was able to conclude a number of purchases with Russia, including the Sukhoi aircraft, which later became a topic of debate in the parliament. Towards the end of the visit, Megawati stated in Moscow that Jakarta and Moscow would cooperate in the "project of joint production in the military industry".[71]

Unlike Megawati who was not educated in the United States, the new president, Susilo Bambang Yudhoyono, received military training and a Master's degree from the United States.[72] He was familiar with the US system and was perceived as being sympathetic to America. His stand on terrorism was also welcome in Washington.

It seems that the opportunity for better Indonesia-US relations came when the tsunami disaster took place in December 2004 when the US military offered assistance to rescue the survivors in Aceh. President Yudhoyono permitted international aircraft, "including US helicopters from a battle fleet carrier", to land at the military airport there.[73] It was reported that, "in normal times, Indonesia's worst nightmare was having American marines arrive on the Banda Aceh tarmac... Yet here we are in the middle of this operation and we have marines here. It's a sign of progress."[74]

Jakarta-Washington relations improved further under President Yudhoyono. Indonesia-US trade continued to grow during the SBY period, and security cooperation also continued. Some even argued that Indonesia's relations with the United States under SBY was warm. This was mutual as Yudhoyono got his training in the United States, and Barack Obama, the 44th President of the United States, spent his childhood in Indonesia. Unlike his relationship with the PRC, Yudhoyono appeared to be proactive in improving Jakarta-Washington relations. In November 2008, he proposed the Strategic Partnership between Indonesia and the United States to President Obama, and in 2010 this partnership was enhanced to the "Comprehensive Partnership" during Obama's visit to Indonesia.

In the joint communique of this Comprehensive Partnership, it was stated that "President Yudhoyono welcomes the US leadership role in promoting multilateral diplomacy, promoting peace ... and expanding engagement in Southeast Asia."[75] It also stated:

> They agreed to energetically harness the new Partnership so that it will contribute to the continued progress and prosperity of both countries, while also serving as an important pillar for growing US-ASEAN cooperation, and for advancing regional peace and prosperity.[76]

Apparently, Yudhoyono's Indonesia welcome the presence of the United States in Southeast Asia and did not have the intention to exclude this superpower from the region. This joint declaration was not in harmony with the Comprehensive Strategic Partnership that he signed with President Xi Jinping (see the section on Indonesia and the People's Republic of China).

This incompatibility may be explained in terms of Yudhoyono's foreign policy approach to have "a million friends and zero enemies". Yudhoyono, known as the "foreign policy president", wanted to be recognized not only in the region but also beyond. He actively participated in the G-20 meetings and mingled with world leaders.[77] His role was recognized by Obama as reflected in the joint declaration between the United States and Indonesia:

> The two leaders also committed to work together to strengthen the G-20 as the premier forum for the world economy, and to work towards progress of the Doha Round. President Obama welcomed Indonesia's co-chairmanship of the G20's anti-corruption working group.[78]

Yudhoyono's presence was noticed by many countries, including the United States, China and Europe. Many observers considered Yudhoyono as successful in raising Indonesia's reputation and some even argued that due to his success Indonesia has become "a rising power" again. Not many people agree with the assessment as this was "not supported by the reality of a country that has limited economic and political influence".[79]

When Jokowi assumed the presidency in October 2014, it appears that he paid more attention to the PRC than to the United States as he was looking for investments and funding for infrastructure projects. He went to Beijing to attend the Asia-Pacific Economic Cooperation (APEC) conference in November 2014, several weeks after assuming the presidency, and met President Xi Jinping. He went again in early 2015 and issued a joined statement with Xi Jinping reiterating Jakarta and Beijing's continuing strong partnership.[80] In late October 2015, Jokowi visited the United States at the invitation of President Obama, where a similar statement expressing strong partnership between the two major democratic countries was made.[81] It is obvious that Indonesia would like to keep good relations with the superpowers without choosing sides.

However, some observers maintained that Jakarta's ties with Washington was actually closer than with Beijing. This is reflected in their comprehensive cooperation in various fields, especially in defence and security matters. While with the PRC, the cooperation in security and defence tended to be more symbolic than substantial.[82]

Jakarta relations with Washington received a test when Donald Trump became the president of the United States. His anti-Muslim and pro-Israel rhetoric and policies made Indonesian government cautious in dealing with his administration. Reversing Obama's "Pivot to Asia" policy, Trump introduced "America First", as if the United States wanted to leave Asia. However, he still sent his senior envoys to visit Indonesia. US Vice-President Michael Pence and Defence Secretary Jim Mattis (who was later dismissed by Trump) did visit Indonesia. As Indonesia's exports to the United States exceeded US exports to Indonesia, Jakarta has become a problem in the eyes of Trump.[83] Nevertheless, it appears that no real action against Indonesia was taken on this matter.

Jokowi did not accept the Indo-Pacific concept of the United States but put forward Indonesia's own via his foreign minister. Nevertheless, Indonesia's security cooperation continued with the United States, including the training of the Special Forces Command (KOPASSUS) which was stopped for a while.[84] If Jokowi met Xi Jinping at least five times, he only met Trump during the G-20 meeting once, and the second one which was scheduled in early 2020 was cancelled during the Trump impeachment process in the Congress.[85]

Jokowi's Indonesia appeared to play a balancing game in the relationship with major powers. Minister for Defence Prabowo was invited by Trump to visit the United States in mid-October 2020, aiming at promoting closer relations with the two countries, especially in the military modernization and security matters.[86] In late October, Trump's Secretary of State Mike Pompeo visited Jakarta, attempting to draw Indonesia closer to the United States in its opposition to China. Pompeo even visited Ansor, the Nahdlatul Ulama (NU) youth organization, to spread the American view on the oppression of the Muslims in Xinjiang, China. But the NU leadership was not responding to Pompeo's appeal.[87]

When Joe Biden succeeded Trump as president and returned to more normal diplomacy, Indonesia's response was not especially enthusiastic. Jakarta wanted to know what sort of policy Biden is likely to adopt towards Indonesia. Nonetheless, the so-called equal distance diplomacy would be adopted by Jokowi towards the Biden administration as Jakarta still practises "active and independence" foreign policy.

However, recent developments showed that security cooperation between Jakarta and Washington has increased. This is a clear indication that in security matters, Jakarta tended to lean more towards Washington. Between 1 and 14 August 2021, the United States and Indonesia conducted the Garuda Shield military training exercise, the largest joint exercise with a foreign country in the Indonesian military history. About 4,500 military personnel from both sides participated in this exercise involving the air force and other forces.[88] Even though Indonesia is very concerned with China's assertiveness in the South China Sea and its frequent encroachments to the Indonesian Natuna EEZ, Jakarta did not agree with Washington's "contain China" policy.

Indonesia, the Middle East and Islam

As discussed in the 1996 edition of the book, since the end of the 1980s, especially at the beginning of the 1990s, the position of Islam, particularly that of "Cultural Islam", had become more prominent in Suharto's Indonesia. Although Indonesia's foreign policy during the Suharto era was not based on Islam, it was obvious that Indonesia had moved closer towards Muslim and Islamic countries. Suharto's attitude towards the Organization of Islamic Conference, (OIC) had also changed.[89]

Before 1990, Suharto deliberately did not attend the OIC summits. However, due to domestic political change in Indonesia and Suharto's need for support from the Islamic groups, a pro-Islam domestic policy was introduced.[90] This was reflected in foreign policy as well. In December 1991, Suharto led a delegation to attend the OIC Summit in Senegal. In June 1997, Suharto also led a delegation to attend the Developing 8 (D-8) Summit in Turkey. D-8 is an organization of eight countries with large Muslim populations—Turkey, Indonesia, Iran, Malaysia, Nigeria, Bangladesh, Pakistan and Egypt.[91]

In December 1997, Suharto had planned to attend the OIC Summit which was held in Iran. However, it was reported that Suharto did not go because he fell sick. Some observers in Jakarta were of the view that Suharto was very reluctant to attend this summit as Iran was seen to be anti-West (especially anti-US). He was worried that the Summit would be used by the anti-American group to attack the United States. This would not be favourable for Jakarta as it was hit by the economic crisis and badly needed the IMF assistance.

However, in May 1998 towards the end of his rule, Suharto led a delegation to Cairo to attend the OIC Summit, hoping to show the world that Indonesia was still "stable" and under control. He also wanted to use the opportunity to show the domestic Muslim groups that he was also a leader of the Islamic world. But his attempt appeared to be futile as he was forced to step down soon after his return from the summit.

Although it was clear that between 1990 and 1998, Suharto had the intention of showing that Indonesia was a member of a big Islamic family, it did not shift the basis of Indonesian foreign policy to Islam. In other words, Islam was not the prime factor in Indonesia's foreign policy, especially towards the Middle East, but it was a major consideration when dealing with foreign relations.

The relations between Islam and Indonesia's foreign policy in the post-Suharto period appeared to remain similar. The basis of Indonesia's foreign policy is still non-Islamic but Islamic factors have become more important than in the Suharto era, at least in symbolism. When Habibie was the president his "power-base" was the Islamic Intellectual Association of Indonesia (ICMI), but his term was too short to make a change. When Gus Dur, a respected liberal clergy, was the president, he visited many Middle Eastern countries but he was not eager to make a foreign policy based on Islam. His presidency was also too short to deal with the OIC Summit.

During the Megawati presidency, with Hamzah Haz of the Islamic United Development Party (Partai Persatuan Pembangunan, or PPP), as the vice-president, the Islamic factor appeared to be more obvious but the foreign policy remained non-Islamic. Indonesia disagreed with America's invasion of Iraq and continued to be critical of Israel. Although agreeing with anti-terrorism, Jakarta was very careful in handling Muslim terrorists. Megawati resisted American pressure to ban Jemaah Islamiah (JI). This is due to the resurgence of Islam within Indonesia itself. Megawati also criticized the United States when it attacked Afghanistan without mentioning the name of the country, stating that it was unacceptable for a government that "attacks people or another country for whatever reason".[92]

In fact, the Islamic issue began to receive attention during the Yudhoyono presidency. Following his attendance at the OIC Summit in 2008, Yudhoyono went on to participate at the 2013 Summit which can be viewed as attempts to bolster Indonesia's Islamic credentials. At the summit, he urged the members of OIC to improve their economic cooperation.

Jokowi continued the tradition of attending OIC summits. On 6 December 2017, Trump had announced the recognition of Jerusalem as the capital of Israel and decided to move the US embassy to this new capital.[93] This move was condemned by the Arab world and Muslim countries. On 11 December Jokowi led a delegation to the OIC extraordinary meeting in Turkey, demonstrating Indonesian solidarity with the Muslim/Islamic states in opposing such a move. Jokowi also made a proposal at the summit, suggesting East Jerusalem as the capital of the Palestinian state.[94] In May/June 2019, Jokowi sent his foreign minister to attend the OIC Summit at Mecca to show Indonesia's support. The OIC, in turn, congratulated Jokowi for winning the election and serving as the president of Indonesia for the second term.

In fact, the Palestine issue has gradually become the Indonesian focus after the fall of Suharto. In 2005, Yudhoyono reinvented New Asian African Strategic Partnership (NAASP) based on the spirit of Bandung of 1955.[95] A hundred and six countries from these two continents attended the meeting in Jakarta. It was said that Palestinians were the only participants in the 1955 conference which had not achieved independence. In 2008, Yudhoyono's government hosted the NAASP Ministerial Conference on "Capacity Building for Palestine" where 218 participants from 56 countries attended.[96]

The NAASP was supposed to be held in April 2009 but failed due to unforeseen circumstances. It was only convened in April 2015 when Jokowi became president. Jokowi wanted to return to the original Asian-African (AA) Conference, but the Palestinian agenda could not be pushed aside, especially when the position of Islam domestically became more important. During the sixtieth anniversary of the AA Conference, Jokowi continued to commit Jakarta's support for the Palestinian state.[97] As noted earlier, he opposed the recognition of Jerusalem as the capital of Israel in 2017 and was also critical of the Trump Peace Plan of January 2020 which favoured Israel. It appears that it is increasingly difficult for the Jokowi government not to be drawn into the Middle East politics.

Most Indonesian foreign policy scholars admitted that Indonesia's foreign policy has not been based on co-religionist solidarity. Although Islam is important, its role in Indonesia's foreign policy is still limited.[98]

It is worth noting that King Salman of Saudi Arabia led a 1,500 strong delegation to Indonesia in March 2017, making contributions to Indonesian tourism. Salman also announced Saudi's new investment in Indonesia. Jokowi was eager to maintain good relations with the king for at least three reasons: first, Indonesia, being the biggest source of haj pilgrimage, needs to get more haj quota from Saudi; second, Indonesia needed Saudi's cooperation as more than 1 million Indonesian maids were in Saudi as domestic helpers; and third, Indonesia needed more investments from Saudi to diversify investment sources.[99] In fact, it was reported that Jokowi also approached Saudi's Prince Mohammed bin Salman to invest in Indonesian projects.[100]

Conclusion

It is clear that Indonesia's foreign policy during the Suharto era was made by President Suharto and implemented by his foreign ministers. It was an authoritarian state with strong central government. However, after the fall of Suharto, with the democratization of the political system, foreign policy decision-making is no longer in the hands of the president alone. Parliaments and other institutions became important decision-makers, although the role of the president in the Indonesian presidential system is still crucial.

Indonesia under Suharto had attempted to become a regional power to lead Southeast Asian states and beyond. As the largest country and also the richest in terms of natural resources, Suharto's Indonesia was held in deference by the ASEAN states. However, due to its limited capabilities, its lack of military strength, advanced technology and economic strength, the political influence of Jakarta was in fact quite limited. During the economic crisis, Suharto was forced to step down. He was succeeded by B.J. Habibie who was largely preoccupied with domestic issues, who in turn was followed by weak presidencies of Gus Dur and Megawati.

Only after the ex-general Susilo Bambang Yudhoyono assumed presidency did he manage to stabilize the situation and attained economic growth. However, initially Yudhoyono focused more on domestic issues. He only had a chance to pay more attention to foreign policy in his second term, He even became known as the "Foreign Policy President". Nevertheless, he was constrained by the harsh Indonesian reality: limited resources, weak military, and the absence of political influence.

Although active in the international scene, he was only perceived as a regional leader with certain credentials. His regional influence was far behind Suharto. This may be due to the changing international situation of a rising China, a relative decline of American power and also the growth in power of many Southeast Asian states. The Indonesian position as a leading state in Southeast Asia appeared to further decline as Jokowi has focused more on economic infrastructure of Indonesia than its role in regional affairs and beyond.

It is worth noting that my 1996 book is entitled *Indonesia's Foreign Policy under Suharto: Aspiring to International Leadership*, while this postscript is entitled "Indonesia's Foreign Policy from the Fall of Suharto to Joko Widodo: Still Aspiring to International Leadership?". Indonesian foreign policy elite under the Jokowi presidency continues to have aspirations to international leadership, but under the present condition, it is unlikely that Indonesia can assume even a regional leadership.

As to the "independent and active" principle, Indonesia's presidents after Suharto continued to proclaim this as the foundation of their foreign policy. However, unlike during the Suharto era, with the rising China and relative decline of the American power, Indonesia appears to have adjusted its policy vis-à-vis the PRC. Jakarta is no longer hostile towards Beijing. On the economic front, Indonesia tended to be closer to China. This was also the case with combating the COVID-19 pandemic cooperation. Nevertheless, Indonesia remains friendly, if not close, to the United States, especially on security matters. The South China Sea issue, which remains unresolved, may push Indonesia and other ASEAN claimant states further into the camp of the United States. However, at the moment, Indonesia continues to stay as a non-aligned nation between the two major powers.

NOTES

1. In 2002 after the amendment of the 1945 Constitution, the Committee 1 in parliament which was in charge of foreign relations rejected seven ambassadorial candidates proposed by the Foreign Minister/President. See also "DPR Mulai Uji Kelayakan Calon Duta", *Tribunenews.com*, 17 September 2013 (accessed 24 September 2014).
2. Indonesia's foreign policy elite during the post-Suharto period include the president, those in the Ministry of Foreign Affairs, cabinet ministers, military leaders, political party leaders and directors of key research institutions on social sciences.
3. *Derwin Pereira Media Journal*, "Suharto Apologises for the Worsening Haze Condition", 17 September 1997, http://derwinpereiramedia.com/derwin-pereira-suharto-apologises-for-the-worsening-haze-condition/ (accessed 18 March 2020).
4. "Malaysia and Singapore", *Migration News,* vol. 5, no. 6 (June 1998), (https://migration.ucdavis.edu/mn/more.php?id=1561 (accessed 26 March 2020).
5. O.C. Kaligis & Associates, *Sengketa Sipadan-Ligitan: Mengapa Kita Kalah* (Jakarta: O.C. Kaligis Associates, 2003), p. 3. On 17 December 2002, the International Court of Justice eventually announced that both Sipadan and Ligitan belong to Malaysia. See ibid., p. 4 The book asserted that Malaysia won the case based on the argument of "effective occupation" of the two islands.
6. It was reported in mid-1996 that Suharto's national car project, led by his youngest son Tommy, enjoyed big tax breaks which were opposed by many WTO member countries, including the United States. See Eduardo Lachicha, "U.S. Criticizes Indonesia for National Car Program", *Wall Street Journal*, 8 May 1996, https://www.wsj.com/articles/SB831500697247740000 (accessed 31 March 2020). Some argued that Suharto needed Mahathir's support as Malaysia also has a national car.
7. The above arguments were obtained from my discussion with some Indonesian observers in Jakarta.
8. Yanyan Mochammad Yani and Ian Montratama, *Quo Vadis: Politik Luar Negeri Indonesia* (PT Elex Media Komputindo, Kelompok Gramedia, 2017), pp. 123–26.
9. CNN.com, "ASEAN Halts Cambodia Mediation", 19 July 1997, http://edition.cnn.com/WORLD/9707/19/cambodia/ (accessed 26 March 2020).
10. Leo Suryadinata, "A Year of Upheaval and Uncertainty: The Fall of Soeharto and Rise of Habibie", *Southeast Asian Affairs 1999* (Singapore: Institute of Southeast Asian Studies, 1999), pp. 111–27.
11. PM Goh Chok Tong responded in the National Day speech that "Singapore pledged a S$12 million humanitarian aid package to Indonesia to aid their recovery efforts after the 1997 financial crisis and May 1998 riots". According to the *Business Times*, "at the time, it was the largest aid amount Singapore had ever extended to any country", http://www.businessinsider.sg/former-indonesian-president-habibie-once-called-singapore-a-little-red-dot-heres-what-actually-happened/ (accessed 11 October 2019).

12 Dewi Fortuna Anwar, "Reflections on ASEAN Security Community", *Tempo,* 13 October 2003.
13 Leo Suryadinata, "Indonesia: The Year of a Democratic Election", *Southeast Asian Affairs 2005* (Singapore: Institute of Southeast Asian Studies, 2005), p. 145.
14 Helena Varkkey, "Indonesian Perspectives on Managing the ASEAN Haze", *Jurnal Sarjana* 24, no. 1 (2009), https://www.researchgate.net/publication/256982049_Indonesian_perspectives_on_managing_the_ASEAN_haze (accessed 18 March 2020).
15 *BBC News*, "Indonesia President Susilo Bambang Yudhoyono Apologises for Haze", 25 June 2013, https://www.bbc.com/news/world-asia-23026599 (accessed 18 March 2020).
16 *Al Jazeera*, "UN Rules for Cambodia in Thai Border Row", 11 November 2013, https://www.aljazeera.com/news/asia-pacific/2013/11/un-rule-thai-cambodian-border-row-201311116485209849.html (accessed 18 March 2020).
17 B. Saragigh, "RI: A Regional Trouble Shooter Struggling with Its Missions", *Jakarta Post*, 16 October 2014. In this common communique, it reiterated ASEAN adherence to the 2002 DOC of the parties in the South China Sea and to the 1982 United Nations Convention on the Law of the Sea.
18 https://www.channelnewsasia.com/news/singapore/singapore-refutes-reports-of-non-cooperation-with-indonesia-s-ex-8707760 (accessed 18 March 2020).
19 Leo Suryadinata, "Indonesia and Its Stance on the 'Indo-Pacific'", *ISEAS Perspective*, no. 2018/66, 23 October 2018.
20 Ibid.
21 Ibid.
22 *Jakarta Post*, "Indonesia 'Shuttles' to Brunei for Myanmar Coup Response", 17 February 2021 (accessed 10 March 2021).
23 *Yahoo.com*, "Indonesian Foreign Minister to Visit Myanmar as Pressure Mounts on Generals", 23 February 2021 (accessed 11 March 2021).
24 *Jakarta Post*, "Indonesia Pressures Myanmar Junta to Respect Popular Will, Open Dialogue", 2 March 2021 (accessed 10 March 2021)
25 Ibid.
26 *Jakarta Post*, "Donors Pledge Long-Term Aid", 7 January 2005.
27 *New York Times*, "Tense Ties on Refugees for Canberra and Jakarta", 3 April 2006, https://www.nytimes.com/2006/04/03/world/asia/tense-ties-on-refugees-for-canberra-and-jakarta.html (accessed 6 June 2020).
28 On the event, see Dave McRae, "A Fair Dinkum Partnership? Indonesia-Australia ies during the Yudhoyono Era", in *Aspirations with Limitations: Indonesia's Foreign Affairs under Susilo Bambang Yudhoyono*, edited by Ulla Fiona, Siwage Dharma Negara and Deasy Simandjuntak (Singapore: ISEAS – Yusof Ishak Institute, 2018), pp. 220–23.
29 Antje Missbach, "Asylum Seekers' and Refugees' Decision-Making in Transit in Indonesia", *Bijdragen tot de taal-, land- en volkenkunde* 175, no. 4 (2019): 419–45, https://doi.org/10.1163/22134379-17504006 (accessed 6 June 2020)
30 Leo Suryadinata and Mustafa Izzuddin, "Mismatch of Expectations in Jokowi's Maiden Visit to Australia", *The Diplomat*, 3 March 2017.
31 Ibid.
32 Ibid.
33 This section on Japan has been derived from my joint article with Mustafa Izzuddin, "Divergence of Interests in Abe's Maiden Visit to Indonesia", *Straits Times*, 28 January 2017, https://www.straitstimes.com/opinion/divergence-of-interests-in-abes-maiden-visit-to-indonesia (accessed 18 March 2020)
34 Ibid.
35 Ibid. It should be noted that initially, One Belt One Road (Strategy) was abbreviated as OBOR and Indonesia continued to use the term for quite a while. The term was later changed to Belt and Road Initiative (BRI).
36 See *Jakarta Post*, "PM Abe's Visit", 17 January 2017, https://www.thejakartapost.com/news/2017/01/17/pm-abe-s-visit.html (accessed 18 March 2020).

37. *Asia Year Book 1997*, p. 138.
38. *Foreign Broadcast Monitor*, 23 January 1998, p. 6.
39. *Asia Year Book 1997*, p. 138.
40. *Foreign Broadcast Monitor*, 23 January 1998, p. 6.
41. In March 1998, Habibie as Vice-President of Indonesia said in an interview with a Japanese newspaper that "it is absurd that the ethnic Chinese, who make up 3 per cent of the population, are controlling 90 per cent of the economy. I would like to give opportunities to *pribumi*, who make up the majority of the population and build them up." See Leo Suryadinata, "How Will Habibie Handle the Ethnic Chinese Issue?", *Straits Times*, 15 June 1998, p. 32.
42. *Liputan 6*, "Zurongjhi [*sic*] Bertemu Megawati Membicarakan Bank of China", 8 November 2001, http://www.liputan6.com/fullnews/23309.html (accessed 25 November 2004).
43. *Liputan 6*, "Cina Menawarkan Senjata Kepada Indonesia", 20 September 2002, https://www.liputan6.com/news/read/41762/cina-menawarkan-senjata-kepada-indonesia (accessed 25 November 2004).
44. Departemen Pertahanan RI, "Menhan RI Terima Dubes Republik Rakyat Cina", http://www.dephan.go.id/modules.php?name=News&file=print&sid=733 (25 November 2004).
45. Derwin Pereira, "Reality Bites for Yudhoyono", *Straits Times*, 25 December 2004.
46. Leo Suryadinata, *The Growing "Strategic Partnership" between Indonesia and China Faces Difficult Challenges*, Trends in Southeast Asia, no. 15/2017 (Singapore: ISEAS – Yusof Ishak Institute, 2017), p. 2.
47. Embassy of the People's Republic of China in Australia, "China, Indonesia Forge Strategic Partnership", 27 April 2005, http://au.china-embassy.org/eng/xw/t193421.htm (accessed 7 March 2020).
48. *Antara News*, "Indonesia, China Forge Comprehensive Strategic Partnership in Various Field", 7 October 2003, https://en.antaranews.com/news/91035/indonesia-china-forge-comprehensive-strategic-partnership-in-various-field (accessed 7 March 2020).
49. Suryadinata, *The Growing "Strategic Partnership" between Indonesia and China Faces Difficult Challenges*, p. 3.
50. Ibid., p. 4.
51. For a brief analysis of this project, see Siwage Dharma Negara and Leo Suryadinata, "Jakarta Bandung High Speed Rail Project: Many Challenges", *ISEAS Perspective*, no. 2018/2, 4 January 2018.
52. Jokowi's Tol Laut concept is meant to improve the infrastructure of specific areas in Indonesia to enhance connectivity within the country while China's BRI aims at meeting the need and development of China. Beijing and Jakarta have different perceptions of BRI projects. Until today, there is as yet no concrete BRI project agreed to between the two countries. See Siwage Dharma Negara and Leo Suryadinata, *Indonesia and China's Belt and Road Initiatives: Perspectives, Issues and Prospects*, Trends in Southeast Asia, no. 11/2018 (Singapore: ISEAS – Yusof Ishak Institute, 2018), pp. 12–19.
53. Leo Suryadinata, "Did the Natuna Incident Shake Indonesia-China Relations", *ISEAS Perspective*, no. 2016/19, 26 April 2016.
54. Ibid.
55. Leo Suryadinata, "Recent Chinese Moves in the Natunas Riles Indonesia", *ISEAS Perspective*, no. 2020/10, 19 February 2020.
56. *Jakarta Post*, "Prabowo Talks Joint COVID-19 Mitigation Plan with Chinese Defense Minister", 9 September 2020 (accessed 1 November 2020).
57. *ThinkChina*, "Winning Indonesia over: US and China Seek Indonesia's Support in Southeast Asia", 26 January 2021 (accessed 27 January 2021).
58. *Liputan 6*, "Angkatan Laut China Bakal Ikut Bantu Proses Pengangkatan KRI Nanggala-402", 5 May 2021, https://www.liputan6.com/global/read/4549736/angkatan-laut-china-bakal-ikut-bantu-proses-pengangkatan-kri-nanggala-402 (accessed 11 August 2021).

59. *Straits Times*, 8 September 1996, p. 16.
60. *Asia Year Book 1998*, pp. 128–29.
61. Ibid., p. 129.
62. Derwin Pereira, "Reality Bites for Yudhoyono", *Straits Times*, 25 December 2004.
63. Simela Victor Muhamad, "Hubungan Indonesia-Amerika Serikat Pada Masa Setahun Pemerintahan Abdurrahman Wahid", in *Analisis Kebijakan Luar Negeri Pemerintah Abdurrahman Wahid (1999–2000)* (Jakarta: Pusat Pengkajian dan Pelayanan Informasi, DPR-RI, 2001), pp. 293–95.
64. Ibid.
65. "The Aftermath of Atambua–Wimar Witoelar", http://www.perspective.net/articles/view.asp?id=63 (accessed 25 November 2004).
66. Simela Victor Muhamad, "Hubungan Indonesia-Amerika Serikat Pada Masa Setahun Pemerintahan Abdurrahman Wahid", pp. 267–316.
67. For an analysis of Megawati and political Islam in Indonesia, see Azyumardi Azra, "The Megawati Presidency: Challenge of Political Islam", in *Governance in Indonesia: Challenges Facing Megawati Presidency*, edited by Hadi Soesastro, Anthony L. Smith and Han Mui Ling (Singapore: Institute of Southeast Asian Studies, 2003), pp. 44–69; on Afghanistan, see p. 52.
68. Leo Suryadinata, "Indonesia: Continuing Challenges and Fragile Stability", *Southeast Asian Affairs 2004* (Singapore: Institute of Southeast Asian Studies, 2004), p. 101.
69. Ibid.
70. Bantarto Bandoro, "Significance of Mega's East European Trip", *Jakarta Post*, 2 May 2003.
71. "Indonesia-Rusia Sepakati Kerja Sama Militer" [Indonesia and Russia agree to have military co-operation], *Kompas*, 22 April 2003.
72. Leo Suryadinata, "Susilo Bambang Yudhoyono: A Retired General Turned Politician", in *Regional Outlook: Southeast Asia 2005–2006* (Singapore: Institute of Southeast Asian Studies, 2005), p. 23.
73. Jane Perlez, "In Crisis, Jakarta Was Slow to Respond", *New York Times*, 4 January 2005.
74. Ibid.
75. The White House, "Joint Declaration on the Comprehensive Partnership between the United States of America and the Republic of Indonesia", 9 November 2010, https://obamawhitehouse.archives.gov/the-press-office/2010/11/09/joint-declaration-comprehensive-partnership-between-united-states-americ (accessed 7 March 2020).
76. Ibid.
77. Evi Fitriani, "Yudhoyono's Foreign Policy: Is Indonesia a Rising Power?", in *The Yudhoyono Presidency: Indonesia's Decade of Stability and Stagnation*, edited by Edward Aspinall, Marcus Mietzner, and Dirk Tomsa (Singapore: Institute of Southeast Asian Studies, 2015), p. 80.
78. "Joint Declaration on the Comprehensive Partnership between the United States of America and the Republic of Indonesia".
79. Fitriani, "Yudhoyono's Foreign Policy", p. 76.
80. Rendi A. Witular and Hasyim Widhiarto, "Jokowi on World Stage, First Stop Beijing", *Jakarta Post*, 9 November 2014, https://www.thejakartapost.com/news/2014/11/09/jokowi-world-stage-first-stop-beijing.html (accessed 11 March 2020).
81. "Joint Declaration on the Comprehensive Partnership between the United States of America and the Republic of Indonesia".
82. Donald Weatherbee, *Understanding Jokowi's Foreign Policy*, Trends in Southeast Asia, no. 12/2016 (Singapore: ISEAS – Yusof Ishak Institute, 2016), p. 49.
83. Leo Suryadinata and Mustafa Izzuddin, "US-Indonesia: Growing Distance", *Straits Times*, 23 November 2016.

84 John McBeth, "Indonesia Treads Tight Line between China and US", *Asia Times*, 26 February 2020, https://asiatimes.com/2020/02/indonesia-treads-tight-line-between-china-and-us/ (accessed 25 April 2020).
85 Ibid.
86 U.S. Department of Defense, Release, "Joint Statement Regarding Secretary of Defense Dr. Mark T. Esper's Meeting with Indonesian Minister of Defense Prabowo Subianto" (accessed 1 November 2020).
87 *ThinkChina*, "Winning Indonesia over".
88 Resty Woro Yuniar, "US and Indonesia Stage Joint Military Drill as Washington Steps up Engagement with Southeast Asia", *South China Morning Post,* 3 August 2021. https://www.scmp.com/week-asia/politics/article/3143709/us-indonesia-stage-joint-military-drill-washington-stepsS; *Daily Motion*, "Potret Latihan Tempur TNI AD-Militer AS Terbesar dalam Sejarah!", https://www.dailymotion.com/video/x836e28 (accessed 11 August 2021).
89 See pp. 163-64, this volume. Since 2011, the Organization of Islamic Conference has been renamed as Organization of Islamic Cooperation, still abbreviated as OIC.
90 Leo Suryadinata, *Golkar dan Budaya Politik* (Jakarta: LP3ES, 1994), pp. 148–49.
91 M. Handam Basyar, "Islam dan Politik Luar Negeri Indonesia Masa Orde Baru", *Studia Politika* 2 (LIPI journal, n.d.), pp. 114–15.
92 Azyumardi Azra, *Indonesia, Islam and Democracy: Dynamics in a Global Context* (Jakarta: Solstice, 2006), pp. 64–65.
93 *New York Times*, "Trump Recognizes Jerusalem as Israel's Capital and Orders U.S. Embassy to Move", 6 December 2017, https://www.nytimes.com/2017/12/06/world/middleeast/trump-jerusalem-israel-capital.html (accessed 11 March 2020).
94 Cabinet Secretary of the Republic of Indonesia, "President Jokowi Issues Statement with Six Proposals at OIC Extraordinary Summit", 13 December 2017, https://setkab.go.id/en/president-jokowi-issues-statement-with-six-proposals-at-oic-extraordinary-summit/ (accessed 16 May 2020).
95 Museum Konperensi Asia-Afrika, "Asian-African Summit 2005 and the Anniversary of the Golden Jubilee of the Asian-African Conference", 22–24 April 2005, asianafricanmuseum.org/en/konferensi-tingkat-tinggi-asia-afrika-2005-dan-peringatan-50-tahun-konferensi-asia-afrika/ (accessed 15 May 2020).
96 See Ministry of Foreign Affairs of the Republic of Indonesia, "New Asia-Africa Strategic Partnership (NAASP)", 8 April 2019, https://kemlu.go.id/portal/id/read/165/halaman_list_lainnya/kemitraan-strategis-baru-asia-afrika-naasp (accessed 15 May 2020).
97 Ministry of Foreign Affairs of the Republic of Indonesia, "Palestine Issue", 26 March 2019, https://kemlu.go.id/portal/id/read/23/halaman_list_lainnya/isu-palestina (accessed 16 May 2020).
98 The first scholar who brought up this issue was Michael Leifer. I also agreed with his view. Former student of Leifer, Rizal Sukma, in his book and recent article also put forward a quite similar view. See "Domestic Politics and International Posture: Constraints and Possibilities", in *Indonesia Rising: The Repositioning of Asia's Third Giant*, edited by Anthony Reid (Singapore: Institute of Southeast Asian Studies, 2012), pp. 65–67.
99 Liao Jianyu 廖建裕, "The significance of Saudi's King visit to Indonesia" ("沙特国王出访印尼的意义"), *Lianhe Zaobao* 《联合早报》, 18 March 2017.
100 Viriya Singgih and Arys Aditya, "Jokowi Courts Softbank, Saudi Prince in Pursuit of Investment", *Bloomberg.com*, 23 July 2019, https://www.bloomberg.com/news/articles/2019-07-23/jokowi-courts-softbank-saudi-prince-in-pursuit-of-investment (accessed 12 March 2020).

SELECT BIBLIOGRAPHY

Books/Monographs

Abdulgani, H. Roeslan. *Asia Tenggara di Tengah Raksasa Dunia* (Jakarta: Lembaga Studi Pembangunan, 1978).

Abdulgani, H. Roeslan. *Indonesia Menatap Masa Depan* (*Kumpulan Karangan*) (Jakarta: Pustaka Merdeka, 1986).

Agung, Anak Agung Gde. *Twenty Years Indonesian Foreign Policy 1945-1965* (The Hague: Mouton, 1973).

Ali, Fachry. *Refleksi Paham "Kekuasaan Jawa" dalam Indonesia Modern* (Jakarta: Gramedia, 1986).

Ali Sastroamidjojo. *Milestones on My Journey: The Memoirs of Ali Sastroamidjojo, Indonesian Patriot and Political Leader* (translated by Christine Whittington-Lelo, edited by C.L.M. Penders). (Brisbane: Queensland University Press, 1979).

Alias Mohamed. *Malaysia's Islamic Opposition: Past, Present and Future* (Kuala Lumpur: Gateway Publishing House, 1991).

Anand, R.P. & Purification V. Quisumbing (eds.). *ASEAN: Identity, Development and Culture* (Quezon City: U.P. Law Center & East West Center, 1981).

Anshari, H. Endang Saifuddin. *Piagam Jakarta 22 Juni 1945* (Bandung: Pustaka Perpustakaan Salman ITB, 1981).

Antolik, Michael. *ASEAN and the Diplomacy of Accommodation* (New York: M.E. Sharpe, 1990).

Anwar, Dewi Fortuna. *Indonesia and the Security of Southeast Asia* (Jakarta: Centre for Strategic and International Studies, 1992).

Association of Southeast Asian Nations [ASEAN]. (Jakarta: Department of Information, Republic of Indonesia [Special Issue 039/1969].

Ayoob, Mohamed. *India and Southeast Asia: Indian Perceptions and Policies* (London & New York: Routledge, 1991).

Aziz, Arnicun (ed.). *Empat GBHN: 1973, 1978, 1983, 1984* (Jakarta: Bumi Aksara, 1990).

Bandoro, Bantarto (ed.). *Non-Aligned Movement: Its Future and Action Programme* (Jakarta: CSIS, 1992).

Bartholomew, James. *The Richest Man in the World: The Sultan of Brunei* (London: Penguin Books, 1990).

Bone, Robert C. *The Dynamics of the Western New Guinea (Irian Barat) Problem* (Ithaca: Cornell Modern Indonesia Project, Interim Report Series, 1958).

Broinowski, Alison (ed.). *Understanding ASEAN* (London: Macmillan, 1982).

Broinowski, Alison (ed.). *ASEAN into the 1990s* (London: Macmillan, 1990).

Budiman, Arief (ed.). *Politik Luar Negeri Indonesia Dewasa Ini* (Jakarta: Jajasan Indonesia, 1972).

Buszynski, Leszek. *Soviet Foreign Policy and Southeast Asia* (London & Sydney: Croom Helm, 1986).

Che Man W.K. *Muslim Separatism: The Mora of Southern Philippines and the Malays of Southern Thailand* (Kuala Lumpur: Oxford University Press, 1990).

Crouch, Harold. *The Army and Politics in Indonesia* (Ithaca: Cornell University Press, 1978).

Dawisha, Adeed (ed.). *Islam in Foreign Policy*. (New York: Cambridge University Press, 1983).

Djalal, Hasjim. *Perjuangan Indonesia di Bidang Hukum Laut* (Jakarta: Badan Pembinaan Hukum Nasional Departemen Kehakiman, diedarkan oleh Penerbit Binacipta, Oktober 1979).

Djamily, Mizwar. *Mengenal Kabinet RI Selama 40 Tahun Indonesia Merdeka* (Jakarta: PT Kreasi Jaya Utama, 1986).

Djonovich, Dusan J. (ed.). *United Nations Resolutions: Series II*, Vols. IX, X and XI (New York: Oceana Publications, 1990).

Dua Puluh Lima Tahun Departemen Luar Negeri 1945-1970 (Jakarta: Departemen Luar Negeri, 1971).

Duiker, William. *The Communist Road to Power in Vietnam* (Boulder: Westview Press, 1982).

Encyclopaedia Britannica, 15th edn. (1974).

Feith, Herbert & Lance Castles (eds.). *Indonesian Political Thinking 1945-1965* (Ithaca: Cornell University, 1970).

Feith, Herbert. *The Decline of Constitutional Democracy* (Ithaca: Cornell University Press, 1962).

Geertz, Clifford. *The Religion of Java* (New York: Free Press, 1959).

Gordon, Bernard. *Dimensions of Conflict in Southeast Asia* (New Jersey: Prentice-Hall, 1966).

Gowing, Peter. *Muslim Filipinos — Heritage and Horizon* (Quezon City: New Day Publishers, 1979).

Hardi. *Api Nasionalisme: Cuplikan Pengalaman* (Jakarta: Gunung Agung, 1983).

Harris, Stephen V. & Colin Brown. *Indonesia, Papua New Guinea and Australia: The Irian Jaya Problem of 1984*, Australia-Asia Papers No. 29 (Nathan: Centre for the study of Australia-Asian Relations, Griffith University, February 1985).

Harsono, Ganis. *Recollections of an Indonesian Diplomat in the Sukarno Era* (edited by C.L.M. Penders & B.B. Hering) (Brisbane: University of Queensland Press, 1977).

Hatta, Mohammad. *Mendajung Antara Dua Karang* (Keterangan Pemerintah Diutjapkan oleh Drs Mohammad Hatta dimuka Sidang B.P. K.N.P. di Djokja pada tahun 1948) (Jakarta: Kementerian Penerangan R.I., 1951).

Hatta, Mohammad. *Dasar Politik Luar Negeri Republik Indonesia* (Jakarta: Tintamas, 1953).

Hatta, Mohammad. *Kumpulan Pidato Dari tahun 1942 s.d. 1949* (edited by I. Wangsa Widjaja & Meutia F. Swasono) (Jakarta: Yayasan Idayu, 1981).

Hiorth, Finngeir. *East Timor: Past and Present* (Townsville, Queensland: James Cook University, 1985).

Hoadley, J. Stephen. *The Future of Portuguese Timor: Dilemmas and Opportunities*, Occasional Paper No. 27 (Singapore: Institute of Southeast Asian Studies, 1975).

Holt, Claire et al. *Culture and Politics in Indonesia* (Ithaca: Cornell University Press, 1972).

Hong Yuanyuan (Ang Jan Goan). *Hong Yuanyuan Zizhuan (Autobiography of Ang Jan Goan*, translated by Liang Ying Ming) (Beijing: Zhongguo Huaqiao Chubanshe, 1989).

Indonesia: A Brief Guide for Foreign Investors: Policies and Incentives (Jakarta: Investment

Coordinating Board (BKPM) and Business Advisory Indonesia (BAI), April 1989).

International Institute of Strategic Studies (IISS). *The Military Balance 1989-1990* (London: Brassey's, 1989).

International Institute of Strategic Studies (IISS). *The Military Balance 1992-1993* (London: Brassey's, 1992).

Japan-Indonesia Relations: Past, Present, Future. (Jakarta: Centre for Strategic and International Studies, 1979).

Jenkins, David. *Suharto and His Generals: Indonesian Military Politics 1975-1983*, Monograph Series, Cornell Modern Indonesia Project (Ithaca: Cornell University Press, 1984).

Ji Guoxing & Soesastro Hadi (eds.). *Sino-Indonesian Relations in the Post-Cold War* (Jakarta: Centre for Strategic and International Studies, 1992).

Jones, Howard P. *Indonesia: The Possible Dream* (Singapore: Gunung Agung (S), 1980).

Kahin, George Mc. *Nationalism and Revolution in Indonesia* (Ithaca: Cornell University Press, 1962).

Kallgren, Joyce C. et al. (eds.). *ASEAN and China: An Evolving Relationship* (Institute of East Asian Studies, University of California, Berkeley, 1988).

Kartodirdjo, Sartono, A. Sudewo & Suhardjo Hatmosuprobo. *Perkembangan Peradaban Priyayi* (Yogyakarta: Gadjah Mada University Press, 1987).

Kartodirdjo, Sartono. *Modern Indonesia: Tradition & Transformation: A Socio-Historical Perspective* (Yogyakarta: Gadjah Mada University Press, 1984).

Kelompok Kerdja Staf Angkatan Bersendjata (ed.). *Sedjarah Singkat Perdjuangan Bersendjata Bangsa Indonesia* (Jakarta: n.p., 1964).

Koentjaraningrat. *Introduction to the Peoples and Cultures of Indonesia and Malaysia* (California: Cummings, 1975).

Koentjaraningrat. *Javanese Culture* (Kuala Lumpur: Oxford University Press, 1985).

Komunike Republik Indonesia dan Negara-Negara Asia Pasifik 1962-1969 (Jakarta: Departemen Luar Negeri R.I., n.d).

Kondisi Ketahanan Nasional (Yang dipersyaratkan sebagai prakondisi dalam Rangka mengamankan dan menyukseskan tahap tinggal landasan) (Jakarta: Lembaga Pertahanan Nasional (Lemhanas), 1989).

Kusumaatmadja, Mochtar. *Politik Luar Negeri Indonesia dan Pelaksanaannya Dewasa Ini*, Kumpulan Karangan dan Pidato (Bandung: Penerbit Alumni, 1983).

Kusumaatmadja, Mochtar. *Hukum Laut Internasional*, 3rd edn. (Bandung: Binacipta-Badan Pembinaan Hukum Nasional Departemen Kehakiman 1986).

Kusumohamidjojo. *Asia Tenggara Dalam Perspektif Netralitas dan Netralisme* (Jakarta: Gramedia, 1985).

Lau Teik Soon & Bilveer Singh (eds.). *The Soviet Union in the Asia Pacific Region* (Singapore: Heinemann Asia, 1989).

Lau Teik Soon. *Indonesia & Regional Security: The Jakarta Conference on Cambodia*, Occasional Papers Series No. 14 (Singapore: Institute of Southeast Asian Studies, 1972).

Lee Khoon Choy. *Indonesia between Myth and Reality* (Singapore: Federal Publications, 1977).

Lee Khoon Choy. *An Ambassador's Journey* (Singapore: Times Books International, 1983).

Leifer, Michael. *Malacca, Singapore and Indonesia,* Vol. II (International Straits of the World), Alphen van den Rijn (Netherlands: Sijthoff and Noordhoff, 1978).

Leifer, Michael. *Indonesia's Foreign Policy* (London: Allen & Unwin, 1983).

Leirissa, R.Z. *Terwujudnya Suatu Gagasan: Sejarah Masyarakat Indonesia 1900-1950* (Jakarta: Akademika Pressindo, 1985).

Lie Tek Tjeng. *R.R.T. dan Singapura: Suatu Pandangan.* (Seri No. IX/4) (Jakarta: Lembaga Research Kebudayaan Nasional-LIPI, 1970).

Lie Tek Tjeng. *Studi Wilayah Pada Umumnya Asia Tenggara Pada Khususnya,* Jilid 1 (Bandung: Alumni, 1981).

Mackie, J.A.C. *Konfrontasi: The Indonesia-Malaya Dispute 1963-1966* (Kuala Lumpur: Oxford University Press, 1974).

Macridis, Roy C. *Foreign Policy in World Politics: States and Regions,* 7th edn. (New Jersey, Englewood Cliffs: Prentice-Hall International, 1989).

Malik, Adam. *Sepuluh Tahun Politik Luar Negeri Orde Baru* (Jakarta: Yayasan Idayu, 1976).

Malik, Adam. *In the Service of the Republic* (Jakarta: Gunung Agung, 1980).

Martin, Linda G. (ed.). *The ASEAN Success Story: Social, Economic and Political Dimensions* (Honolulu: University of Hawaii Press, 1987).

Masalah Timur Tengah. Dokumentasi Masalah Luar Negeri, Penerbitan No. 01/Dok/1976 (Jakarta: Badan Penelitian dan Pengembangan Masalah Luar Negeri, Departemen Luar Negeri, Republik Indonesia, 1976).

Masalah Timur Tengah. Latar Belakang Masalah Luar Negeri, Penerbitan No. 01N/LB/1976 (Jakarta: Badan Penelitian dan Pengembangan Masalah Luar Negeri, Departemen Luar Negeri, Republik Indonesia, 1976).

May, Brian. *The Indonesian Tragedy* (Singapore: Graham Brash, 1978).

McDonald, Hamish. *Suharto's Indonesia* (Victoria: Fontana/Collins, 1980).

McVey, Ruth (ed.). Indonesia (New Haven: Yale University Press, 1963).

Modelski, George (ed.). *The New Emerging Forces: Documents on the Ideology of Indonesian Foreign Policy,* Document and Data Paper No. 2 (Canberra: Department of International Relations, Australian National University, 1963).

Mozingo, David. *China's Policy Towards Indonesia 1949-1967* (Ithaca: Cornell University Press, 1981).

Mukmin, Hidayat. *TNI Dalam Politik Luar Negeri: Studi Kasus Penyelesaian Konfrontasi Indonesia-Malaysia* (Jakarta: Pustaka Sinar Harapan, 1991).

Nathan, K.S. *Detente and Soviet Policy in Southeast Asia* (Kuala Lumpur: Gateway Publishing House, 1984).

Niksch, Larry. *Indonesian-U.S. Relations and Impact of the East Timor Issue. CRS Report for Congress* (Washington DC: The Library of Congress, 15 December 1992).

Nishihara, Masashi. *The Japanese and Sukarno's Indonesia. Tokyo-Jakarta Relations, 1951-1966.* Monographs of the Center for Southeast Asian Studies, Kyoto University (Honolulu: University of Hawaii Press, 1976).

Osborne, Robin. *Indonesia's Secret War. The Guerilla Struggle in Irian Jaya* (Sydney: Allen & Unwin, 1985).

Otobiografi Soeharto, see Soeharto.

Ovsyany, I.D. et al. *A Study of Soviet Foreign Policy* (Moscow: Progress Publishers, 1975).

Park, Jae Kyu & Melvin Gurtov (eds.). *Southeast Asia in Transition: Regional and International Politics*. IFE Research Series, No. 10 (Seoul: Institute for Far Eastern Studies, Kyung Nam University, 1977).

Perjalanan, Tantangan dan Kemungkinan: Rangkuman Sarasehan Menyongsong Lima Windu Kemerdekaan Indonesia (Jakarta: n.p., 1987).

Philippines, Department of Public Information, Bureau of National and Foreign Information. *Manado Talks*. President Marcos of the Philippines at Manado, North Sulawesi, 29-30 May 1974 (Manila, 1974).

Posthumus, G.A. *The Inter Governmental Group on Indonesia* (Rotterdam: Rotterdam University Press, 1971).

Pour, Julius. *Benny Moerdani: Profile of a Soldier Statesman* (translated by Tim Scott) (Jajasan Kejuangan Panglima Besar Sudirman, 1993).

Reid, Anthony. *The Indonesian National Revolution 1945-1950*. Studies in Contemporary Southeast Asia (Victoria: Longman Australia, 1974).

Ricklefs, M.C. *A Short History of Modern Indonesia* (London: Macmillan, 1981).

Robison, Richard. *Indonesia: The Rise of Capital* (Sydney: Allen & Unwin, 1986).

Roem, Mohamad. *Diplomasi: Ujung Tombak Perjuangan R.I* (Jakarta: Gramedia, 1989).

Rosyadi, H. Imron. *Organisasi Konperensi Islam dan Masalahnya* (Jakarta: Yayasan Idayu, 1981).

Sabir, H.M. *Politik Bebas Aktif: Tantangan dan Kesempatan* (Jakarta: Haji Masagung, 1987).

Saravanamuttu, J. *The Dilemma of Independence: Two Decades of Malaysia's Foreign Policy, 1957-1977* (Penang: Penerbit Universiti Sains Malaysia, 1983).

Scalapino, Robert A. et al. (eds.). *Asia and the Major Powers: Domestic Politics and Foreign Policy*. Research Papers and Policy Studies 28 (Berkeley: Institute of East Asian Studies, University of California, 1988).

Scalapino, Robert A., Seizaburo Sato, Jusuf Wanandi & Sung-joo Han (eds.). *Asia and the Major Powers: Domestic Politics and Foreign Policy*. Research Papers and Policy Studies 28 (Institute of East Asian Studies, University of California Berkeley, 1988).

Schuman, Gary & Clara Juwono. *Hubungan Indonesia-Amerika Serikat: Sebuah Laporan* (Jakarta: Centre for Strategic and International Studies, 1990).

Sekar Semerbak: Kenangan Untuk Ali Moertopo (Jakarta: Centre for Strategic and International Studies, 1985).

Singh, Bilveer. *Soviet Relations with ASEAN 1967-88* (Singapore: Singapore University Press, 1989).

Soedjono Hoemardani, Perintis CSIS: 1918-1986 (Jakarta: Centre for Strategic and International Studies, 1987).

Soeharto. *Pikiran, Ucapan dan Tindakan Saya: Otobiografi*. Seperti dipaparkan kepada G. Dwipayana dan Ramadhan K.H. (Jakarta: Citra Lamtoro Gung Persada, 1989).

Soeharto (ed.). *Butir-Butir Budaya Jawa*. Hanggayuh Kasampurnaning Hurip Berbudi Bawaleksana Ngudi Sejatining Becik (Jakarta: Yayasan Purna Bhakti Pertiwi, 1990).

Soesastro, Hadi & A.R. Sutopo (eds.). *Strategi dan Hubungan Internasional: Indonesia di Kawasan Asia-Pasifik* (Jakarta: Centre for Strategic and International Studies, 1981).

Statistik Indonesia 1987 (Statistical Year Book of Indonesia) (Jakarta: Pusat Biro Statistik, 1988).

Statistik Indonesia 1990 (Statistical Year Book of Indonesia) (Jakarta: Pusat Biro Statistik, 1991).

Steinberg, David Joel et al. *In Search of Southeast Asia: A Modern History* (Kuala Lumpur & Singapore: Oxford University Press, 1975).

Sugomo, Yoga. *Memori Jenderal Yoga* (Seperti diceritakan kepada penulis B. Wiwoho dan Banjar Chaeruddin) (Jakarta: Bina Rena Pariwara, 1990).

Sukarno, *Lahirnja Pantja Sila* (Departemen Penerangan RI, Penerbitan Chusus 153, n.d.).

Suleiman, Suli. *Politik Luar Negeri Bebas Aktif Republik Indonesia*. Direktorat Research — Penerbitan No. 008/1973 (Departemen Luar Negeri Republik Indonesia, 1973).

Suleiman, Suli. *Garis-Garis Besar Politik Luar Negeri Republik Indonesia* (Bagian I, Direktorat Research-Penerbitan No. 003B/1974; Bagian II, Direktorat Research Penerbitan No. 004/1974).

Sumardjo, Soepeno. *Ancaman Dari Utara* (Jakarta: Karyaka, 1980).

Suraputra, D. Sidik. *Revolusi Indonesia dan Hukum Internasional* (Jakarta: Penerbit Universitas Indonesia, 1991).

Suryadinata, Leo. *Pribumi Indonesians, the Chinese Minority and China: A Study of Perceptions and Policies* (Kuala Lumpur & Singapore: Heinemann, 1978, 1st edn.; 1992, 3rd edn.).

Suryadinata, Leo. *China and the ASEAN States: The Ethnic Chinese Dimension* (Singapore: Singapore University Press, 1985).

Suryadinata, Leo. *Military Ascendancy and Political Culture: A Study of Indonesia's Golkar* (Athens: Ohio University Press, 1989).

Suryadinata, Leo. *Golkar dan Militer. Studi tentang Budaya Politik* (Jakarta: LP3ES, 1992).

Surjohadiprodjo, Sajidiman. *Langkah-langkah Perdjoangan Kita* (Jakarta: Departemen Pertahanan Keamanan Pusat Sedjarah ABRI, 1971).

Suryohadiprodjo, Sayidiman. *Menghadapi Tantangan Masa Depan* (Jakarta: Gramedia, 1987).

Swift, Ann. *The Road to Madiun*: *The Indonesian Communist Uprising of 1948*, Cornell Modern Indonesia Project, Monograph Series (Ithaca: Cornell University Press, 1989).

Taylor, John G. *Indonesia's Forgotten War: The Hidden History of East Timor* (London & New Jersey: Zed, 1992).

Tilman, Robert. *Southeast Asia and the Enemy Beyond: ASEAN Perception of External Threats* (Boulder: Westview Press, 1987).

Van Ginnekan, Jaap. The *Third Indochina War: The Conflicts Between China, Vietnam and Cambodia* (Amsterdam: Personally published, 1983). (The original book was in Dutch, published by Sjaloom/Odijk, 1980.)

Van Ness, Peter. *Revolution and Chinese Foreign Policy: Peking's Support for Wars of National Liberation* (Berkeley, California: California University Press, 1970).

Wanandi, Jusuf. *Security Dimensions of the Asia-Pacific Region in the 1980s* (Jakarta: CSIS, 1979).

Weinstein, Franklin. *Indonesian Foreign Policy and the Dilemma of Dependence: From Sukarno to Soeharto* (Ithaca: Cornell University Press, 1976).

Yamin, Muh (ed.). *Naskah Persiapan Undang-Undang Dasar 1945*, Vol. 1 (Jakarta: Jajasan Prapantja, 1959).

Zaini, Haji Ahmad (ed.). *Partai Rakyat Brunei, The People's Party of Brunei: Selected Documents* (Kuala Lumpur: Insan, 1987).

Articles and Papers

"Alatas on Security and Growth in Asia", (Interview by Yang Razali Kassim) *Straits Times*, 11 January 1993, p. 13.

Alatas, Ali. "Politik Luar Negeri Bebas Aktif dan Peranannya Di Masa Mendatang", Yogyakarta, 2 September 1988 (mimeograph).

Anderson, Benedict. "The Idea of Power in Javanese Culture", in Claire Holt (ed.), *Culture and Politics in Indonesia* (Ithaca: Cornell University Press, 1972), pp. 1-69.

Cao Xuan Pho. "Vietnam-Indonesia Concurrences: Past and Present", *Indonesian Quarterly* Vol. XIII, No. 2 (1985), pp. 214-221.

Chan Heng Chee. "Singapore: Domestic Structure and Foreign Policy", in Robert A. Scalapino et al. (eds.), *Asia and the Major Powers: Domestic Politics and Foreign Policy* (Institute of East Asian Studies, University of California Berkeley, 1988), pp. 280-305.

Chang Pao-min. "Kampuchean Conflict: The Diplomatic Breakthrough", *Pacific Review*, Vol. 1, No. 4, pp. 429-437.

Charles Morrison. "Progress and Prospects in Foreign Policy and Cooperation Among the ASEAN Countries", in R.P. Anand & Purification V. Quisumbing (eds.), *ASEAN: Identity, Development and Culture* (Quezon City: UP Law Center & East West Center, 1981).

Darusman, Marzuki. "Persepsi Lingkungan Strategi Indonesia di Tengah-Tengah Perubahan Internasional", *Telstra*, No. 10 (Jan-Feb 1990), pp. 14-19.

Dipoyudo, Kirdi. "Indonesia's Foreign Policy towards the Middle East and Africa", *Indonesian Quarterly*, Vol. 13, No. 4 (October 1985), pp. 474-485.

Djiwandono, J. Soedjati. "The Kampuchean Conflict and the Future of ASEAN", *Indonesian Quarterly*, Vol. 13, No. 4 (October 1985), pp. 435-440.

Djiwandono, J. Soedjati. "The Role of Major Powers and the Role of Indonesia as a Middle Power in Southwest Pacific", in *The Role of Middle Powers in the Pacific* (Jakarta: CSIS, 1985), pp. 5-21.

Djiwandono, J. Soedjati. "Forty Years Indonesian Foreign Policy: Change and Continuity", *Indonesian Quarterly*, Vol. 13, No. 4 (October 1985), pp. 441-451.

Djiwandono, J. Soedjati. "Indonesia's Response to Soviet Initiatives: An Update", Paper submitted to IX World Congress for Soviet and East European Studies, Harrogate, England, 21-26 July 1990.

Draguhn, Werner. "The Indochina Conflict and the Positions of the Countries Involved", *Contemporary Southeast Asia*, Vol. 5, No. 1 (June 1983), pp. 95-116.

Hatta, Mohammad. "One Indonesian View of the Malaysian Issue", *Asian Survey*, Vol. 5, No. 3 (1965), pp. 139-143.

Horn, Robert C. "The Soviet Union and Asian Security", in Sudershan Chawla & D.R. Sardesai (eds.), *Changing Patterns of Security and Stability in Asia* (New York: Praeger, 1980), pp. 63-98.

Jin Dexiang. "China and Southeast Asia in a Changing Security Environment", in Ji Guoxing & Hadi Soesastro (eds.), *Sino-Indonesian Relations in the Post-Cold War Era* (Jakarta: Centre for Strategic and International Studies, 1992), pp. 80-91.

Leifer, Michael. "Ali Moertopo: Regional Visionary and Regional Pragmatist", *Indonesian Quarterly*, Vol. XIII, No. 4 (1985), pp. 524-530.

Leo Suryadinata. "Indonesia-China Relations: A Recent Break Through", *Asian Survey*, Vol. 30, No. 7 (July 1990), pp. 682-696.

Lie Tek Tjeng. "Vietnamese Nationalism: An Indonesian Perspective", *National Resilience* (Jakarta), No. 1 (March 1982), pp. 72-75.

Lubis, T. Mulya. "Human Rights Standard Setting in Asia: Problems and Prospects", *Indonesian Quarterly*, Vol. XXI, No. 1 (1993), pp. 25-37.

McMichael, Heath. "Indonesian Foreign Policy: Towards a More Assertive Style", Research Paper No. 40 (Centre for the Study of Australian-Asian Relations, Brisbane: Griffith University, February 1987).

Mozingo, David. "China's Policy Towards Indonesia", in Tang Tsou (ed.), *China in Crisis*, Vol. 2 (Chicago: University of Chicago Press, 1968).

Seiji Naya. "Economic Performance and Growth Factors of the ASEAN Countries", in Linda G. Martin (ed.), *The ASEAN Success Story: Social Economic and Political Dimensions* (Honolulu: University of Hawaii Press, 1987), pp. 47-87.

Soemitro. "Memulihkan Postur Politik Luar Negeri", *Kompas*, 11 March 1989.

Sukma, Rizal. "Jakarta-Beijing Relations and Security Challenges in Southeast Asia". *Indonesian Quarterly*, Vol. XVIII, No. 4 (1990), pp. 280-286.

Suryadinata, Leo. "Indonesia: A Year of Continuing Challenge", *Southeast Asian Affairs 1979* (Singapore: ISEAS, 1979.)

Sutopo, A.R. "US and Soviet Military Presence in Southeast Asia: An Overview", *Indonesian Quarterly*, Vol. XVIII, No. 4 (1990) pp. 287-299.

Tan Kong Yam. "Whither ASEAN?", *ASEAN-ISIS Monitor*, No. 2 (January 1992), pp. 6-10

Villegas, Bernardo. "The Challenge to ASEAN Economic Co-operation", *Contemporary Southeast Asia*, Vol. 9, No. 2 (September 1987), pp. 120-128.

Wanandi, Jusuf. "The Correlation Between Domestic Politics and Foreign Policy in Indonesia", in Robert A. Scalapino et al. (eds.), *Asia and the Major Powers: Domestic Politics and Foreign Policy* (Institute of East Asian Studies, University of California at Berkeley, 1985), pp. 181-199.

Wanandi, Jusuf. "Indonesia-Malaysia Bi-Lateral Relations", *Indonesian Quarterly*, Vol. 16, No. 4 (1988), pp. 454-463.

Wanandi, Jusuf. "Human Rights and Democracy in the ASEAN Nations: The Next 25 Years", *Indonesian Quarterly*, Vol. XXI, No. 1 (1993), pp. 14-24.

Wawancara Khusus Dengan Menlu Ali Alatas. *Telstra* (Telaah Strategis), No. 10 (Jan-Feb 1991), pp. 4-13.

Newspapers and Periodicals

Angkatan Bersenjata (daily, Jakarta)

Asia Yearbook (annually, Hong Kong)

Asia Week (weekly, Hong Kong)

Bangkok Post (daily, Bangkok)

Beijing Review (weekly, Beijing)

Berita Yudha (daily, Jakarta)

Editor (weekly, Jakarta)

Far Eastern Economic Review (weekly, Hong Kong)

Forum Keadilan (bi-weekly, Jakarta)

Gatra (weekly, Jakarta)

Indonesian Observers (daily, Jakarta)

Jakarta Post (daily, Jakarta)

Kompas (daily, Jakarta)

Merdeka (daily, Jakarta)

New Nation (daily, Bangkok)

New Straits Times (daily, Kuala Lumpur)

Pelita (daily, Jakarta)

Prisma (monthly, Jakarta)

Renmin Ribao (daily, Beijing)

Republic (daily, Jakarta)

Shijie Zhishih (monthly, Beijing)

Sinar Harapan (daily, Jakarta)

Straits Times (daily, Singapore)

Suara Pembaruan (daily, Jakarta)

Suara Karya (daily, Jakarta)

Tempo (weekly, Jakarta)

Utusan Malaysia (daily, Kuala Lumpur)

Unpublished Theses

Hein, Gordon Robert. "Soeharto's Foreign Policy: Second-Generation Nationalism in Indonesia" (Ph.D. thesis, University of California at Berkeley, 1986).

Malley, Michael Sean. "A Political Biography of Major General Soedjono Hoemardani: 1918-1986" (M.A. thesis, Cornell University, 1990).

Wong Hup Wah, Andrew. "Singapore-Indonesia Relations, 1973-1984" (B.A. Honours thesis, National University of Singapore, 1985).

APPENDIX I

Indonesian Foreign Policy Elite

* PM = Prime Minister
* FM = Foreign Minister

Information:

Name, position held, date, profession/training, party-affiliation, religion.

I. Pre-Suharto Era

Ahmad Soebardjo (FM, 19 August - 14 November 1945, 27 April 1951 - 3 April 1952; 3 April 1952 - 30 July 1953, lawyer, later joined Masyumi, Muslim)

Wilopo (PM/FM, 3 April 1952 - 30 July 1953, lawyer, Nationalist, Muslim)

Sutan Sjahrir (PM/FM, 12 March - 2 October 1946, intellectual, Socialist)

H. Agus Salim (FM, 3 July - 11 November 1947; 11 November 1947 - 29 January 1948, 29 January - 4 August 1949; 4 August 1949 - 20 December 1949, journalist, politician, Muslim)

Sukiman Wirjosandjojo (PM, 27 April 1951 - 3 April 1952, physician, Masyumi, Muslim)

Amir Sjarifuddin (PM, 3 July-November 1947; 11 November 1947 - 29 January 1948, lawyer, Socialist/Communist)

A.A. Maramis (FM, 19 December 1948 - 13 July 1949, lawyer, Christian)

Moh. Hatta (PM 19 December 1948 - 13 July 1949, economist, socialist-inclined, only during the New Order period, he became more Islamic, but then he was out of power)

Sjafruddin Prawiranegara (PM, 4 August 1949 - 20 December 1949, lawyer, Masyumi, Muslim)

Moh. Roem (FM, 6 September 1950 - 27 April 1951, lawyer, Masyumi, Muslim)

Ali Sastroamidjojo (PM, 30 July 1953 - 12 Aug.1955; 24 March 1956-14 March 1957, lawyer, nationalist [PNI])

Burhanuddin Harapan (PM, 12 August 1955 - 3 March 1956, lawyer, Masyumi, Muslim)

Sunarjo (FM, 30 July 1953 - 12 August 1955, lawyer, nationalist [PNI])

Ide Anak Agung Gde Agung (FM, 12 August 1955 - 3 March 1956, lawyer, democrat, Hindu-Bali)

Djuanda (PM, 9 April 1957 - 10 July 1959, engineer, Muslim)

D.N. Aidit (Chairman of the PKI, politician, Communist)

Roeslan Abdulgani (FM, 24 March 1956 - 28 January 1957, politician, nationalist [PNI], Muslim)

Sukarno (President, architect, pre-War PNI, Muslim)

Subandrio (FM, July 1959-1960, 1960-1966, physician, nationalist [PNI], Muslim)

II. Suharto Era

Adam Malik (FM, 1966-1978; journalist, Murba [populist])

Suharto (President, 1966-date, military, Muslim)

Mochtar Kusumaatmadja (FM, 1978-1983, university law professor, Muslim)

Ali (Alex) Alatas (FM, 1983 to date, career diplomat, Muslim)

B.J. Habibie (technocrat, Muslim)

Ali Murtopo (military, Muslim)

Sudjono Humardani (military, Muslim)

Sumitro (military, Muslim)

Benny Murdani (military, Catholic)

Try Soetrisno (military, Muslim)

Moerdiono (Sekneg, military, Muslim)

Sudharmono (Sekneg, Vice-President, military, Muslim)

Yoga Sugama (military, Muslim)

Soebijakto (military, Muslim)

Sajidiman (military, socialist, Muslim)

Jusuf Wanandi (CSIS leader, lawyer, Catholic)

Sources: *Mengenal Kabinet RI Selama 40 Tahun Indonesia Merdeka* (Jakarta: Kreasi Jaya Utama, 1986); *Dua Puluh Lima Tahun Departemen Luar Negeri 1945-1970* (Jakarta: Deplu, 1971). Also *Apa dan Siapa 1985-1986* (Jakarta: Grafitipers, 1986); Others.

APPENDIX II

Indonesian Diplomatic Representatives Abroad (as of June 1996)

Information: Country and Ambassador

Afghanistan – *Alwi Anas

Algeria (plus Guinea & Mali) – Lulahi Grahana Sidharta

Argentina (plus Paraguay & Uruguay) – *Drs Aswin Darwis

Australia – Wirjono Sastrohandojo

Austria – Prof. Dr Sumaryo Suryokusumo

Bangladesh – Dr Hadi Wayarabi Alhadar

Belgium (plus Luxemburg) – Dr H. Sababa Karta Sasmita

Brazil – Adian Silalahi

Brunei Darussalam – Koesnadi Poedji Winarto

Bulgaria – Samsu Bahri Siregar SH

Cambodia – Taufik Rachman Soedarbo

Canada – Benjamin Parwoto

Chile – Noor Handono

China, People's Republic – Juwana

Colombia – Samsi Abdullah

Czech Republic – Leonard Tobing

Denmark (plus Lithuania) – Drs Andjar Soedjito Mangkoewijoto

Egypt (plus Sudan, Somalia & Djibouti) – Dr Boer Mauna

Ethopia – Rochsyad Dahlan

Finland (plus Estonia) – Petronella Margaretha Luhulima SH

France – Prof. Dr Satrio Budhihardjo Joewono

Germany – Hartono Martodiredjo

Greece – Irawan Abidin

Hungary – Drs R.M. Soelaeman Pringgodigdo

India – Vice-Admiral Gatot Suwandi[†]

Iran – Drs Soekadari A. Honggowongso
Iraq – Drs Umar Hussein
Italy (plus Malta) – Witjasana Sugarda
Japan – Wisber Luis
Jordan – Eddy Sumantri
Kenya (plus Seychelles & Uganda) – Drs Mohammad Seng Paselleri
Korea, North (not available)
Korea, South – Drs M. Singgih Hadipranowo
Kuwait (plus Bahrain and Qatar) – Drs D. Soesjono
Laos – Herry Haryono
Lebanon – Drs H. Dalindra Aman
Madagascar – Slamet Suyata Sastramihardja
Malaysia – Maj.-Gen. (retired) Yacob Dasto[†]
Morocco – Iskandardinata
Mexico (plus Cuba & Panama) – Ir Usman Hasan
Myanmar (plus Nepal) – Maj.-Gen. (police, retired) A. Poerwanto Lenggono[†]
Nambia – Soegio Sosro Soemarto MA (Minister)
Netherlands – Drs J.B. Soedarmanto Kadarisman
New Zealand – Dahlia Joemolang
Nigeria (plus Ghana, Liberia, Cameroon & Burkina Faso) – Drs Johannes Sutantio
Norway – Amiruddin Noor
Papua New Guinea (plus Solomon) – Maj.-Gen. (retired) Abinowo Mukmin[†]
Pakistan – Drs Dodi Sutanto
Philippines – Abu Hartono
Poland – Noeraina Labde Hamimyar
Romania (plus Moldavia) – **Ir Mario Viegas Carrascalao
Russia (plus Mongolia) – Ir Rachmat Witoelar
Saudi Arabia (plus Sultanate of Oman) – Prof. Ismail Suny
Senegal (plus Gambia, Gabon, Ivory Coast and Zaire) – Trenggono
Singapore – Lt.-Gen. (retired) Herman Mantiri[†]
Spain – Air Marshal (retired) Siboen Dipoat Modjo[†]
Sri Lanka (plus Maldives) – Yunizar Yacab
South Africa – Rachadi
Surinam – Suwardi Wosono
Sweden (plus Latvia) – Drs Haringun Hardjotanojo

Switzerland – Vice Admiral (retired) Mahmud Subarkah†

Syria (plus Cyprus & Lebanon) – Drs Baginda Djamaris Buyung Sulaiman

Tanzania (plus Burundi, Comores, Mauritius, Rwanda & Zambia) – Drs Rizal Charis

Thailand – Lt.-Gen. (retired) Isbandi Gondo†

Tunisia (plus Palestine) – Ambiar Tamala

Turkey – Maj.-Gen. (retired) Soelarso H Soebroto†

Ukraine (plus Georgia and Armenia) – Roni H. Jurniadi

United Arab Emirates – Drs Husny Sunkar

United Kingdom (plus Ireland) – Junus Effendy Habibie

USA in New York (plus Bahamas, Nicaragua, Guatemala & Jamaica) – Nugroho Wisnumurti SH, LLM

USA in Washington DC (plus Grenada) – Dr Arifin Siregar

Uzbekistan (plus Kirgyzstan & Tajikistan) – Drs Hassan Abdul Djalil

Yemen – Ibnu Ash Jamil Siregar SH

Yugoslavia – Slamet Budiadi

Vatican – R. Soenaryono

Venezuela (plus Trinidad, Tobago & Equador) – Amin Rianom

Zimbabwe (plus Mozambique & Swaziland) – Drs Sutedja Kartawidjaya

---

*Drs = Doctoradus, an Indonesian degree which is equivalent to BA Honours
**Ir °= Insinyur, an Indonesian degree for engineer

† military officer. It is interesting to note that in 1996 there are only nine retired military officers appointed as Ambassadors (India, Malaysia, Myanmar, Papua New Guinea, Singapore, Thailand, Spain, Switzerland and Turkey).

Source: *Buku Susunan Kabinet Pembangunan VI RI Beserta Daftar Nama dan Alamat Pejabat-Pejabat Negara (Pemerintah) Republik Indonesia 1995/1996,* 3rd edn. (Jakarta: CV Berkat Usaha & BP Dharma Bhakti, 1995), pp. 499-528. Please note that this source is incomplete and has many errors. Some of the errors have been corrected when known. The countries which have not been listed include: Azerbaijan, Bolivia, Costa Rica, Croatia, Equador, Iceland, Libya, Micronesia, Peru, Slovakia and Slovenia. *See Kabinet Pembangunan VI Beserta Pejabat Negara RI 1994* (Jakarta: Badan Penerbit Alda, March 1994), pp. 731-767; *Angkatan Bersenjata*, 5 June 1996.

APPENDIX III

Abbreviations

ABRI – Angkatan Bersenjata Republik Indonesia (Indonesian Armed Forces)

AFTA – ASEAN Free Trade Area

ANC – African National Congress

APEC – Asia Pacific Economic Cooperation

Apoedeti – Associacao Popular Democratica Timorense (Popular Democratic Association of Timor)

ARF – ASEAN Regional Forum

ASA – Association of Southeast Asia

ASEAN – Association of Southeast Asian Nations

BAIS – Badan Intelijen Strategis (Strategic Intelligence Body)

Bakin – Badan Koordinasi Intelijen Negara (State Intelligence Co-ordinating Body)

Bappenas – Badan Perencanaan Pembangunan Nasional (National Development Planning Board)

BKPM – Badan Koordinasi Penanaman Modal (Indonesia Co-ordinating Body for Foreign Investment)

BPI – Badan Pusat Intelijen (Central Intelligence Board)

CGI – Consultative Group on Indonesia

Conefo – Conference of New Emerging Forces

CSIS – Centre for Strategic and International Studies

Deplu – Departemen Luar Negeri (Ministry of Foreign Affairs)

DPR – Dewan Perwakilan Rakyat (People's Representative Council or House of Representatives, Indonesian Parliament)

EAEC – East Asia Economic Caucus

EAEG – East Asia Economic Grouping

FEER – Far Eastern Economic Review

Fretilin – Frente Revolucionana de Timor Leste Independente (Revolutionary Front for Independent Timor)

GBHN – Garis-Garis Besar Haluan Negara (Broad Outlines of National Policy)

Golkar – Golongan Karya (Functional Groups)

Hankam – Departemen Pertahanan Keamanan (Ministry of Defence and Security)

IGGI – Inter-Governmental Group on Indonesia

IMF – International Monetary Fund

JIM – Jakarta Informal Meeting

Kadin – Kamar Dagang dan Industri (Chamber of Commerce and Industry)

Lemhanas – Lembaga Pertahanan Nasional (Institute of National Defence)

Maphilindo – Malaya-Philippines-Indonesia

MPR – Majelis Permusyawaratan Rakyat (People's Consultative Council, Indonesian Congress)

MFA – Ministry of Foreign Affairs. See Deplu

MNLF – Moro National Liberation Front

NAM – Non-Aligned Movement

Nefos – New Emerging Forces

NWFZ – Nuclear Weapons Free Zone

NU – Nahdlatul Ulama (Muslim Scholars Association)

OIC – Organization of Islamic Conference; (since 2011) Organization of Islamic Cooperation

Oldefos – Old Established Forces

PLO – Palestine Liberation Organization

PKI – Partai Komunis Indonesia (Indonesian Communist Party)

PNG – Papua New Guinea

PNI – Partai Nasional Indonesia (Indonesian National/Nationalist Party)

PRC – People's Republic of China

PRRI – Pemerintah Revolusioner Republic Indonesia (Revolutionary Government of the Republic of Indonesia)

ROC – Republic of China

RRC – Republik Rakyat Cina (China) (People's Republic of China)

SEANWFZ – Southeast Asia Nuclear Weapons Free Zone

SEATO – Southeast Asian Treaty Organization

Sekneg – (Sekretaris Negara/Sekretariat Negara) State Secretary/State Secretariat

Sesneg – (Sekretaris Negara) State Secretary

Setneg – (Sekretaris Negara/Sekretariat Negara) State Secretary/State Secretariat

UDT – Uniao Democratica Timorense (Timor Democratic Union).

ZOPFAN – Zone of Peace, Freedom and Neutrality

INDEX

Abdul Rahman, Tunku, 67
Abdurrahman Wahid. *See* Gus Dur
Afghanistan, 162
Afro-Asian Conference, 172
  first, 8
  thirtieth anniversary, 51
Aidit, D.N., 8, 25
Alatas, Ali (Alex), 17, 38, 52, 57, 61, 63, 65, 71, 90, 95, 97, 100, 113, 116, 120, 121, 131, 137, 140, 142, 162, 164, 166, 176, 177, 178
Amir Sjarifuddin, 24, 25
Anand Panyarachun, 83
Aquino, Corazon, 80, 81
Arafat, Yasser, 160, 161
Asia-Pacific Economic Co-operation (APEC), 73, 74, 179-182
  Bogor Declaration, 181
  Eminent Persons Group (EPG), 181
  Summit, 143
    Bogor, 181, 182
    Seattle, 180
Association of Southeast Asia (ASA), 67
Association of Southeast Asian Nations (ASEAN), 35, 56, 57, 66-69, 70, 73, 74, 116, 126, 128, 129, 130, 131, 132, 133, 177, 184, 180
  Bangkok Declaration, 35
  Communist parties, 107, 108
  Free Trade Area (AFTA), 83, 180
  Manila Declaration, 71
  Regional Forum (ARF), 84, 90, 152
  relations with Indonesia, 191-197
  summit, 52, 70, 80, 141
  Vietnam membership, 133
Australia, 2, 58, 63
  relations with Indonesia, 91-96

Bandung Conference
  thirtieth anniversary, 109
Bandung Principles, 27, 110, 172, 177
Bangkok Agreement, 43
Batam, 76
Bosnia, 166-168, 178, 188

Brunei
  relations with Indonesia, 83-84
Cambodia, 124
  Vietnamese invasion, 126
  See also Kampuchea
Chatichai Choonhavan, 83
China, People's Republic of (PRC), 3, 11, 12, 30, 31, 35, 36, 44, 70, 126, 127, 141, 144, 148, 150, 151, 152, 181, 182
  diplomatic ties, 104
  Four Modernizations Programme, 104
  in the United Nations, 103
  relations with Indonesia, 101-117
    direct trade, 106-108
    issues, 114-117
    normalization, 108-110, 113
  relations with Vietnam, 133
    Sino-Vietnamese war, 104, 126
Chuan Leekpai, 83
Clinton, 143
Commonwealth of Independent States (CIS), 3, 146
Communism, 67
Conference of New Emerging Forces (CONEFO), 8, 30, 101
Consultative Group on Indonesia (CGI), 58, 147, 148
COVID-19, 204

Darusman, Marzuki, 175
Deng Xiaoping, 104, 108
Diah, B.M., 56
Dibb, Paul, 94
  Report, 94
Dong, Pham Van, 126
Dutch East Indies, 6

East Asian Economic Caucus (EAEC), 73, 74
East Asian Economic Grouping (EAEG), 73, 180
East Timor, 2, 6, 10, 35, 43, 53-62, 92, 93, 95, 96, 126, 132, 142, 154, 171, 188, 189
  annexation, 7

Dili tragedy, 58, 60-62, 141, 142
invasion, 43, 44
relations with Indonesia, 197-199
Evans, Gareth, 95

Fiji, 98
Fraser, Malcolm, 92
Free Papuan Movement (OPM), 10
Fretilin (Revolutionary Front for an Independent East Timor), 10, 54, 55, 56, 58, 61, 64, 92, 93

Gadjah Mada, 6, 7
Gandhi, Rajiv, 174
Ganie, Ejup, 167
Giap, General Vo Nguyen, 131
Goh Chok Tong, 76
Gorbachev, 145, 146
Great Indonesia concept, 6
Gus Dur, 193-194, 202, 205, 211

Habibie, B.J., 41, 42, 191, 193
Hardi, 125, 126
Hatta, Mohammad, 6, 23, 24, 25, 27, 28
capture, 25
Hawke, Bob, 180
haze issue, 191-192, 194
Ho Chi Minh, 122
Holland. *See* Netherlands
Hun Sen, 131
Hussein Onn, 70

India, 155, 173
Indonesia
and the ASEAN Regional Forum, 84-85
Archipelago Concept, 12, 13
Archipelago Outlook, 13
Bakin, 39
Bappenas, 41-42
capabilities, 9-10
Centre for Strategic and International Studies (CSIS), 40, 41, 45, 129, 130
Chinese, ethnic, 11, 30, 108, 114, 115
investment in China, 115
Committee One, 41

Communist rebellions, 12, 25
Continental Shelf Law, 13
coup, 102-103
debt, foreign, 9, 139, 144
economic aid, 60, 61, 64, 139, 144, 148, 153
Japanese, 147
US, 141
education, 9
election, general
1982, 50
election, presidential
1983, 50
1993, 61
external threat perception, 11
Federal Republic, 26
foreign military bases, policy on, 140
Foreign Ministers, 17
foreign policy determinants, 1, 5-18
Islamic factor, 15, 158-168
Generalized System of Preferences (GSP) benefits, 142, 143
GDP, 9
Hankam (Ministry of Defence and Security), 39, 45
Lemhanas, 39
human rights issue, 141, 142, 143
Human Rights Commission, 142
independence, 23
inflation, 31, 139
investment, foreign, 139, 147, 153
American, 139
Japanese, 139
Taiwanese, 117
Islamic factor, 15, 158-168
Jakarta Charter, 15
Kadin (Chamber of Commerce and Industry), 106, 108
Masyumi (Modern Islamic Party), 26, 27, 28
Merdeka group, 145, 155
military
Fifth Force, 102
rebellion, 28
rise of, 34-47
strength, 10
Ministry of Foreign Affairs (MFA), 38, 45
Nahdatul Ulama (NU), 26, 28
New Order, 34-47
nuclear energy, 10, 19

oil, 9, 10, 19
Palestine Liberation Organization, policy towards, 159-161
Pancasila ideology, 15, 179
Partai Komunis Indonesia (PKI), 26, 27, 28, 29, 30, 38, 102, 103, 105, 107, 125, 126, 144
Partai Sosialis Indonesia (PSI), 26, 28
periods
   Guided Democracy, 8, 29-31
   Parliamentary Democracy, 26-28
   Revolutionary, 22-26
PNI, 26, 27, 28
political culture, 14-17
population, 9
Prime Ministers, 17
purchase of German battleships, 42
racial riots, 115
relations with Afghanistan, 162-163, 168
relations with Australia, 91-96
relations with Brunei, 83-84
relations with China, 101-117
   China policy, 43
   direct trade, 106-108
   issues, 114-117
   normalization, 44, 52, 108-110, 113
relations with Iran, 161-162
relations with Japan, 146-149
relations with Libya, 162
relations with Malaysia, 69-74
relations with Middle East, 158-159
relations with Netherlands, 154
relations with Papua New Guinea, 91-98
   Status of Forces Agreement (SOFA), 98
relations with the Philippines, 78-82
relations with Singapore, 74-78
   military co-operation, 77
relations with Soviet Union, 143-146
relations with Taiwan, 103, 117
relations with Thailand, 82-83
relations with the United States, 138-143
relations with Vietnam, 122-134
   Indonesia-Vietnam seminar, 129, 130
   Vietnamese refugees, 133
Round Table Conference Agreement of 1949, 26
rupiah devaluation, 9
Setneg, 39, 40, 45
Territorial Sea Concept, 13

Territorial Waters Law, 13
territory, 10
trade, 140, 141
   with Japan, 147
   with Soviet Union, 156
United Struggle, 24
withdrawal from United Nations, 8
Inter-Governmental Group on Indonesia (IGGI), 139, 142, 153
Iran
   relations with Indonesia, 161-162
Iraq
   invasion of Kuwait, 164-166
Irian Jaya, 2, 7, 27, 29, 91, 143
   referendum, 43
Israel, 159, 161
Izetbegovic, Alija, 167

Jakarta Informal Meeting (JIM), 52, 109, 130
Japan, 3, 23, 42, 139, 142, 150, 151
   relations with Indonesia, 146-149, 199-201
Javanese, 14, 15, 16
Jenkins, David
   Affair, 93
Joko Widodo (Jokowi), 190-191, 198-201, 203-204, 208-213

Kampuchea, 52
   issue, 109, 126-133, 187
   See also Cambodia
Keating, Paul, 96
Khmer Rouge, 130, 131
Konfrontasi, 30, 35, 43, 69, 74
Kuantan Principle, 52, 63, 70, 83, 128
Kuwait, 171
   Iraqi invasion, 164-166

Laos, 173
Latief, Abdul, 143
Lee Kuan Yew, 51, 75, 76, 77, 89
Lee Ting Hui, 117
Linggajati Treaty, 24
Lombok Straits
   closure, 46

Madiun Affair, 138, 143
Mahathir, 51, 73, 74, 87, 180, 181
Majapahit Empire, 6, 7
Malaya, 6, 67
Malaysia, 162, 163, 173, 182
 ASEAN formation, 68
 foreign policy, 16
 formation, 8
 Konfrontasi, 30
 politics, 20
 relations with Indonesia, 69-74
  illegal Indonesian immigrants, 71, 72
 relations with Philippines, 78, 79, 80
 relations with Singapore, 77
Malik, Adam, 17, 19, 38, 42, 43, 44, 45, 53, 55, 56, 103, 105, 125, 140, 144, 149, 160, 169, 174, 183
Mandela, Nelson, 175
Mantiri, Lt.-Gen. Herman, 96, 100
Maphilindo, 67, 69, 78
Marcos, 78, 79, 89
Mar'ie Muhammad, 42
Mbak Tutut, 61, 62
Medan riot, 143
Megawati Sukarnoputri, 194, 202, 206-207, 211
Middle East, 3
 relations with Indonesia, 158-159, 210-212
Mochtar Kusumaatmadja, 12, 13, 17, 38, 63, 81, 89, 94, 97, 98, 106, 127, 129, 130, 136, 148, 149
Moerdiono, 110, 119
Moluccans, 26
Moro National Liberation Front (MNLF), 78, 79, 81
Mubarak, Husni, 177
Murdani, General Benny, 39, 40, 46, 94, 95, 97, 98, 127, 128, 129, 130, 148, 157
Murtopo, Ali, 19, 40, 53, 54, 55, 140, 150
 group, 43

Namaliu, 97
Nasution, General A.H., 28, 31
 Middle Way doctrine, 34
Natuna Islands, 116, 121, 127, 132, 133
Netherlands, 24, 25, 26, 28, 29, 31, 139, 141, 142, 147
 relations with Indonesia, 154
New Emerging Forces (Nefos), 29

Nicaragua, 176
Non-Aligned Movement (NAM), 51, 59, 109, 124, 145, 146, 160, 162, 164, 167, 172-179
 Jakarta Message, 178
Nuclear Weapons Free Zone (NWFZ), 70, 71, 141

Old Established Forces (Oldefos), 29
Organization of Islamic Conference, 163-164, 167

Papua New Guinea
 relations with Indonesia, 97-98
  Status of Forces Agreement (SOFA), 98
Paris International Conference on Cambodia (PICC), 131
Philippines
 ASEAN formation, 68
 foreign military bases, 140
 relations with
  Indonesia, 78-82
  Malaysia, 78, 79, 80
Pope
 visit to Indonesia, 59
Portugal, 54, 55, 59, 62, 92
 Flower Revolution, 54

Rabin, Yitzhak, 161
Ramos, Fidel, 81, 82
Razak, Tun, 70
Renville Treaty, 24
Riau, 76

Sastroamidjojo, Ali, 8, 27, 28
Saudi Arabia, 165
Sayidiman. *See* Suryohadiproyo, Sayidiman
Sihanouk, 124, 131, 132
Sijori, 76
Singapore
 ASEAN formation, 68
 diplomatic ties with China, 104
 East Timor issue, 56, 57
 military facilities to United States, 77, 151
 relations with Indonesia, 74-78
  military co-operation, 77

Index

relations with Malaysia, 77
  visit of Israeli President, 51
Siti Hardiyanti Hastuti Rukmana, 61, 62
Sjahrir, 23, 24
Soetrisno, 123, 124
Southeast Asian Treaty Organization (SEATO), 67
Soviet Union, 24, 29, 109
  Asian Collective Security System, 144
  relations with Indonesia, 143-146
Spratly Islands, 116
Sriwijaya, 6
Straits of Malacca, 70
Sudwikatmono, 109
Suharto, 7, 13, 16, 17, 35, 40, 44, 45, 66, 73, 74, 75, 77, 78, 79, 80, 81, 84, 102, 104, 105, 106, 109, 110, 112, 113, 114, 119, 124, 129, 131, 132, 133, 137, 145, 146, 151, 159, 160, 161, 164, 165, 167, 168, 174, 175, 177, 178, 180, 181, 188
  as a Javanese ruler, 36-37
  foreign policy, higher profile, 50-53
  leadership in NAM, 179
  mediator between Singapore and Malaysia, 51
  on United Nations, 178
  visit to
    Japan, 42, 147
    Soviet Union, 145, 146, 163
Sukarno, 6, 7, 8, 17, 19, 23, 24, 28, 29, 30, 31, 43, 53, 69, 101, 102, 122, 123, 139, 159, 187, 188
  capture, 25
  Manifesto Politik, 29
  Naskom concept, 31
  on United Nations, 178, 179
  Pancasila
    ideology, 15
    speech, 6
Sukiman, 17, 27
Sumitro, General, 8
Sunda Straits
  closure, 46
Suryohadiproyo, Sayidiman, 148, 150, 151
Susilo Bambang Yudhoyono, 194, 207-208, 213

Taiwan, 159, 182
  relations with Indonesia, 103, 117
    investment in Indonesia, 117
Tan Malaka, 23, 24, 25

Tanjung, Feisal, 167, 168
Thach, Nguyen Co, 125, 129, 137
Thailand, 70
  ASEAN formation, 68
  relations with Indonesia, 82-83
Timor Gap Agreement, 95
Timorese Democratic Union (UDT), 54, 55, 56, 64
Timorese Popular Democratic Party (Apodeti), 54, 56
Timorese Social Democratic Association (ASDT), 53
tsunami, 194, 202-203, 207
Try Sutrisno, General, 81, 151, 157

Umar Wirahadikusumah, General, 174
United Nations, 28, 30, 55, 57, 164, 167, 178
  in Cambodia, 133
United States, 3, 25, 27, 28, 29, 30, 67, 73, 132, 150, 151, 152
  relations with China
    normalization, 141
  relations with Indonesia, 138-143, 206-210
  Vietnam policy, 131
Uruguay Round, 180

Vietnam, 3, 36, 52, 70, 82, 104, 109
  joining ASEAN, 133
  National Liberation Front of South Vietnam (NLFSV), 124, 173
  relations with Indonesia, 122-134
    Indonesia-Vietnam seminar, 129, 130
  Sino-Vietnamese war, 104, 126

Wahid, Abdurrachman, 161
West Irian. *See* Irian Jaya
Whitlam, Gough, 54, 92, 99
Wingti, Paias, 97
Wu Xueqian, 107

Yamin, Mohammad, 6
Yoga Sugomo, 78, 79, 80

Zone of Peace, Freedom and Neutrality (ZOPFAN), 35, 70, 140, 174